The euro and Britain

Implications of moving into the EMU

Editor

Ali M. El-Agraa

An imprint of PEARSON EDUCATION

London New York Toronto Sydney
Tokyo Singapore Hong Kong Cape Town New Delhi Madrid
Paris Amsterdam Munich Milan Stockholm

PEARSON EDUCATION LIMITED

Head Office:
Edinburgh Gate, Harlow CM20 2JE
Tel: +44 (0)1279 623623 Fax: +44 (0)1279 431059

London Office:
128 Long Acre, London WC2E 9AN
Tel: +44 (0)20 7447 2000 Fax: +44 (0)20 7240 5771
Website: www.financialminds.com

First published in Great Britain in 2002

The right of Ali M. El-Agraa to be identified as Author of this Work has been asserted by him in accordance with the Copyright, Designs and Patents Act 1988.

ISBN: 0 273 65699 6

British Library Cataloguing in Publication Data
A CIP catalogue record for this book can be obtained from the British Library.

This publication is designed to provide accurate and authoritative information in regard to the subject matter covered. It is sold with the understanding that neither the authors nor the publisher is engaged in rendering legal, investing, or any other professional service. If legal advice or other expert assistance is required, the service of a competent professional person should be sought.

The Publishers and contributors make no representation, express or implied, with regard to the accuracy of the information contained in this book and cannot accept any responsibility or liability for any errors or omissions that it may contain.

10 9 8 7 6 5 4 3 2 1

Typeset by Northern Phototypesetting Co. Ltd, Bolton
Printed and bound in Great Britain by Biddles Ltd, Guildford & King's Lynn

The Publishers' policy is to use paper manufactured from sustainable forests.

About the editor

 Ali M. El-Agraa is Professor of International Economics, International Economic Integration and EU Studies in Fukuoka University in Japan. He was previously Lecturer in Economics, then Senior Lecturer at the then School of Economics and Business Studies in the University of Leeds, UK. He was also Head of the Office of the University of Leeds Adviser to Overseas Students during 1979–82. Before that he was Assistant Lecturer, then Lecturer in Economics in Khartoum University in Sudan. He was also Visiting Professor of International Economics and Middle Eastern Studies with the International University of Japan, Visiting Professor of Economics with Vanderbilt University in the USA and Visiting Distinguished Professor of International Economic Integration, Fudan University in Shanghai. He has been granted a Lifetime Visiting Professorship at Wuhan University in China and is entered in several *Who's Whos*, including *Who's Who in European Integration Studies*. He is now Senior Technical Advisor for the United Nations' Economic Commission for Africa in Addis Ababa, Ethiopia. He has published numerous academic articles and about 20 books including *The European Union: Economics and Policies*, the 6th edition of *The Economics of the European Community*, first published in 1980.

Contents

The contributors

Brian Ardy is Research Fellow at the European Institute, South Bank University, currently working on an ESRC 'One Europe or several?' project on economic and monetary union. He is also Visiting Lecturer in Economics at the University of Reading. In addition to EMU, his research and publications cover the EU budget, EU enlargement and the EU and Russia. This academic work has been augmented by practical experience working on projects funded by the EU, the Westminster Foundation for Democracy and the Department for International Development in Bulgaria, Croatia, Hungary, Latvia, Lithuania and Poland.

Philip Arestis is Professor of Economics and Director of Research (South Bank Business School) at South Bank University, London. He has also taught at the universities of Surrey and Cambridge (Department of Extra-Mural Studies), Greenwich University (where he was Head of Economics Division) and the University of East London (where he was Head of Department of Economics and subsequently Research Professor). He has been academic consultant for publishers and institutions, including the Central Bank of Cyprus and the Centre of Economic Research, Athens, Greece. He is currently Senior Research Fellow at the Levy Institute, New York City, USA. He has been a member of the Council of the Royal Economic Society (RES) and is now the Secretary of the RES Standing Conference of Heads of Department in Economics (CHUDE). He is currently the Vice-Chair of the ESRC-funded Macroeconomics, Money and Finance Research Group. He has published as sole author or editor, as well as co-author and co-editor, a number of books, ranging from *Introducing Macroeconomic Modelling: An Econometric Study of the United Kingdom* (Macmillan, 1982) to *Money, Pricing Distribution and Economic Integration* (Macmillan, 1997). He has contributed in the form of invited chapters to numerous books and produced research reports for research institutes. He has published widely in academic journals including *American Journal of Economics and Sociology*, *Cambridge Journal of Economics*, *Economic Journal*, *Journal of Macroeconomics* and *Mathematical Modelling*. He has been editor and joint editor, and has served on the editorial board, of a number of journals, including the *Economic Journal*.

Iain Begg is Professor of International Economics at South Bank University, London, UK and is the joint editor of the *Journal of Common Market Studies*, the leading academic periodical dealing with European integration. He served during 1994–97 as the Programme Director of a major research project on the Single European Market, funded by the UK Economic and Social Research Council. He has directed several studies for different directorates of the EU Commission and for the European Parliament, the most recent of which was on the future of the 'own resources' of the EU general budget. He is currently leading research projects looking at how economies deal with economic problems under EMU and at the reform of social protection.

Andrew Brown is currently Lecturer at the University of Leeds and was previously Research Associate at the University of East London. He has a BA in Economics and Philosophy and an MA in Economics from the University of Leeds and will shortly complete his PhD on 'Economic and theoretical perspectives on economic growth and crises'. He has published in the areas of critical realism and methodology and on the political economy of the single European currency.

Forrest Capie is Professor of Economic History at the City University Business School, London. After a doctorate at the London School of Economics in the 1970s and a teaching fellowship there, he taught at the University of Warwick and the University of Leeds. He was a British Academy Overseas Fellow at the National

Bureau, New York, and a Visiting Professor at the University of Aix-Marseille. He has written widely on money, banking and trade and commercial policy. He was Head of the Department of Banking and Finance at City University from 1989 to 1992. He was Editor of the *Economic History Review* from 1993 to 1999. He is a member of the Council of the Economic History Society and a member of the Council of the recently established New Europe.

Gerhard Fenz was Assistant Professor at the Research Institute for European Affairs in the Jean Monnet Centre of Excellence at the Wirtschaftsuniversität Wien (Vienna University of Economics and Business Administration), Vienna, Austria, when he authored his joint contribution with Professor Fink. He has since moved to the Economic Analysis Division at the Oesterreichische National Bank.

Gerhard Fink is Director of the Research Institute for European Affairs and Professor in the Jean Monnet Centre of Excellence at Wirtschaftsuniversität Wien (Vienna University of Economics and Business Administration), Vienna, Austria.

Nigel Grimwade is Head of the Economics and Finance Division at South Bank University in London. His main research has been on the subject of international trade, particularly in regard to the European Union. The second edition of his textbook on international trade has recently been published by Routledge. He is the joint author with Iain Begg of *Paying for Europe*.

Sara Horrell is a Senior Lecturer in the Faculty of Economics at the University of Cambridge, UK, and Fellow of New Hall, Cambridge. Her previous research included work on European stock exchanges and the effects of the Single European Market on employment and British economic history. She is currently working on a project for the UK Department of International Development.

Iris Biefang-Frisancho Mariscal is Senior Lecturer in the Department of Economics at the University of East London. Her research interests are in applied econometrics and macroeconomics, particularly in money demand, wage and unemployment determination and EMU developments. She has contributed to books and published in various journals, including *Applied Economics*, *Economics Letters*, *Empirica* and *Scottish Journal of Political Economy*.

David G. Mayes is Advisor to the Board at the Bank of Finland, Professor of Economics at South Bank University in London and Adjunct Professor in the Centre for Research on Europe at the University of Canterbury in New Zealand. Previously he was the Chief Economist at the Reserve Bank of New Zealand and co-ordinator of the ESRC Single European Market research initiative and a member of the European Commission's Maas Group on the introduction of the single European currency. He has published widely on European integration and monetary union and financial integration in particular.

Malcolm Sawyer is Professor of Economics, University of Leeds, and Head of Economics Division; he was formerly Professor of Economics at the University of York. He is Managing Editor of *International Review of Applied Economics* and Managing Co-editor of *International Papers in Political Economy*. He is the Editor of the series *New Directions in Modern Economics* published by Edward Elgar and elected member of the Council of the Royal Economic Society. He is the author of 10 books, the two most recent being (with P. Arestis and A. Brown) *The Euro: Evolution and Prospects* (Edward Elgar, forthcoming) and (with K. O'Donnell) *A Future for Public Ownership* (Lawrence & Wishart, 1999). He has edited 15 books including *The UK Economy* (Oxford University Press, forthcoming) and *The Legacy of Michal Kalecki* vols 1 and 2 (Edward Elgar, 1999). He has published nearly 100 articles and chapters, and recent articles include 'Kalecki on money and finance' (*The European Journal of the History of*

Economic Thought, 8, 4, Winter 2001), 'Kalecki on imperfect competition, inflation and money' (*Cambridge Journal of Economics*, 25, 2, pp. 245–61) and (with P. Arestis and K. McCauley) 'An alternative stability pact for the European Union' (*Cambridge Journal of Economics*, 25, 1, pp. 113–30). His current research interests include the economics of the European single currency, conceptualizing the nature of barriers to full employment and the analysis of endogenous money.

Matti Virén is Professor of Economics at the University of Turku in Finland and Adviser in the Research Department of the Bank of Finland. He has an extensive range of publications, particularly relating to empirical aspects of European integration. His main areas of current work are econometrics, forecasting methods, monetary theory and saving and asset choice. He was a member of the Commission set up by the Prime Minister to advise on Finland's entry into the euro area.

Geoffrey E. Wood is currently Professor of Economics at City University, London. He has also taught at the University of Warwick, and has been with the research staff of both the Bank of England and the Federal Reserve Bank of St Louis. He is the co-author or co-editor of 10 books, which deal with finance of international trade, monetary policy and bank regulation, among other subjects. His professional papers include studies of exchange rate behaviour, interest rate determination, monetary unions, tariff policy and bank regulation. He has also acted as an adviser to the New Zealand Treasury. He is a Managing Trustee of the Institute of Economic Affairs and of the Wincott Foundation.

Preface and acknowledgements

British Prime Minister Tony Blair was certain to stay at the helm after the 7 June 2001 general election since he was expected to lead his Labour Party to a second victory, if not by a landslide of equal magnitude to that of 1997, at least by a wide margin and, indeed, that is precisely what he managed to accomplish. He has avowed that he will take a decision on whether or not Britain should adopt the euro within the first half of his second term as Prime Minister, i.e. within the first two years in office. Also, that if his decision, based on the five tests announced by Gordon Brown, Chancellor of the Exchequer, in October 1997, is positive, he will ask the British people, through a referendum, to vote for his recommendation for euro adoption and hence for the UK to become a full member of the Economic and Monetary Union (EMU) of the European Union (EU).

Before the general election, however, the then leader of the opposition and Conservative Party, William Hague, had declared that the replacing of sterling by the euro would transform Britain into an alien country and declared that the general election would be the last chance for the UK to survive as a sovereign nation. He stuck to his guns, thinking that the election campaign would provide a bloody battleground for the euro. But it did not since Tony Blair kept reminding the electorate that they will have their say when voting in the referendum, at a time when the opinion polls were increasingly clearly indicating that the adequate provision of public and social services was uppermost in the minds of the voters. Indeed, the battle was so one-sided that William Hague had to vacate the leadership of his party in the swiftest of fashions.

When the Labour Party promised in its manifesto for the 1983 general election to take Britain out of the European Communities (EC) if returned to power, I decided that the issue of whether or not membership of the EC had been disastrous should be debated in an informed manner and edited the book *Britain Within the European Community: The Way Forward* for that purpose. Since I deem the euro debate to be far reaching and hence much more serious relative to the question of withdrawal, I felt it essential that a book on the issue should be edited and timely published, and invited recognized authorities on the subject to contribute to it; hence this current venture.

The book is in three main parts. Part I provides a general background, with Chapter 1 explaining in detail the need for this book and why it is not necessary to write a new edition of the 1983 book. However, due to the fact that there are still those who continue to claim that EU membership has been disastrous for the UK, the chapter also tackles pertinent aspects of the costs and benefits for the UK from EU membership and Chapter 12 supplements this by examining in detail how British trade with the EU and inward foreign direct investment have fared; thus the two chapters together go a long way towards updating the main part of that book. Chapter 12 is not placed after Chapter 1 because it deals mainly with the consequences of euro adoption or otherwise. Chapter 2 provides a general perspective on the EU, paying special attention to its historical development, since those not conversant with the subject should be aware of why the EU needs EMU and the euro, and those in the know need to be reminded, otherwise the discussion would be vacuous. This section is therefore essential for a *proper* understanding of EMU, the euro and the British attitude towards it; the impatient reader can skip it, of course, but it would be at a cost.

Part II, comprising five chapters, concentrates on EMU, the euro and the European Central Bank (ECB), which issues and controls it (Chapter 3), with specific chapters being devoted to the global historical experience with EMUs (Chapter 4), the policy co-ordination and economic adjustment in EMU (Chapter 5) and the development and progress of the euro since its official introduction on 1 January 1999 (Chapters 6 and 7).

Part III, containing six chapters, is devoted to built-in problems concerning the system of operating EMU and the euro within the specific context of the UK, with Chapter 8 setting the scene by discussing pertinent issues relating to the 'optimum currency area' criteria and Britain's reluctance regarding euro adoption and Chapter 9 raising important macroeconomic considerations that need tackling if Britain is to apply for membership of the eurozone. Chapter 10 tackles the UK banking and other financial services since this is the sector that most analysts expect euro adoption would have a great impact on. There is also a chapter on the EU general budget (Chapter 11) since a number of chapters deal with various aspects of it; the chapter clearly demonstrates, as did the MacDougall *Report of the Study Group on the Role of Public Finance in European Integration* (published by the European Commission in 1977), that it should play an essential role in a successful EMU. I should draw attention to the fact that Chapters 8 and 9 could also fit in nicely in Part II, since large sections of them belong there. Chapter 12 deals with the scantly studied consequences for UK trade from British adoption or otherwise of the euro. Chapter 13 tackles the most important question regarding whether Britain would adopt the euro and is therefore in the nature of a concluding chapter.

This book would not have been possible in its present form without the contributions by my distinguished collaborators. A mere glance at the positions held by those in the list of contributors and their input to the subject would immediately reveal their standing in this area, and those who are specialists in the field would, I am sure, find their own preferences greatly overlapping with those in my list. Because of this and the number involved, I shall abstain from the usual courtesy of mentioning them individually, but I take this opportunity to thank them all for their excellent contributions and perseverance with my editorial demands.

Finally, I should add that the book has, on the whole, been written in a fairly non-technical manner so that it can be read by the intelligent layperson. This is deliberate since, given the importance of the subject, the aim is to reach the widest possible audience. Moreover, and naturally, if and when the time comes for a referendum on the euro, it would be that kind of reader who will be looking for such a book.

Ali M. El-Agraa
Fukuoka, Japan

Britain and the
European Union

Britain within the European Union

Ali M. El-Agraa

The background

As Britain's general election for 1983 was looming on the horizon, the Labour Party promised in its manifesto that, if returned to power, denying the Thatcherite Conservatives a second term, one of its three priorities would be UK withdrawal from the European Communities (EC). This was because the Party was adamant that the UK was suffering from its membership of the EC, hence 'British withdrawal from the Community is the right policy for Britain' and would be 'completed well within the lifetime of the Parliament'. Given my field of specialization, I felt it an obligation on my part that an enlightened discussion of the costs and benefits of UK membership of the EC should take place before the election and invited recognized British authorities on the subject to contribute to the book *Britain Within the European Community: The Way Forward* (El-Agraa 1983). I invited only British citizens because I felt that, given the sensitive nature of the exercise, all of us concerned should be not just academically qualified, but also personally involved.

In reality, however, the subject was never mentioned by any of the major parties during the election. The obvious explanation for this was the parties' realization that none of them could have gained an edge by raising the issue, hence a tacit agreement between them that silence was the best available option. This obvious rationale could have been arrived at more concretely, one step at a time. First, as Hugo Young argues in his excellent 1998 book, the Labour Party had until then a consistent record of vehement anti-EC utterances when in opposition, equally matched by pro-EC policy inclinations when in power. Second, it was Mr Michael Foot, then leader of the Labour Party, who personally demanded that withdrawal should be written in the manifesto due to his unwavering belief that the 'British parliamentary system has been made farcical and unworkable by the superimposition of the EEC apparatus . . . It is as if we had set fire to the place as Hitler did with the Reichstag' (quoted in Young 1998, p. 292). Third, it became patently clear during the election campaign that Mr Foot was leading his party to slaughter. Fourth, Labour had no solid evidence to substantiate its claim that UK membership of the EC was disastrous, hence silence was golden. Fifth, the other main parties did not have in their possession evidence which they could convincingly sell to the voting public of net benefit for the UK from EC membership, hence silence was equally golden for them.

> **The Labour Party had a consistent record of vehement anti-EC utterances when in opposition**

Nevertheless, it did not really matter what the truth was, since I still felt that discussion was warranted, especially when the book's emphasis was on the 'way forward'. Consequently, I organized a conference on the subject depicted by the title of the book, held at the University of Leeds, with the main speakers being the contributors to the book and the discussants equally qualified persons. I followed this with my paper in *Applied Economics* on 'Has membership of the European Community been a disaster for Britain?' (El-Agraa 1984), with the purpose of attracting wider academic debate.

My answer to the question raised in that paper, after considering the balance of all aspects involved, was in the negative, and here a restatement on why is in order. That conclusion was reached by examining the basic economic indicators. Table 1.1 provides the rate of growth of real income between 1955 and 1981 (the latest year for which data were available; Greece was excluded because it joined in 1981) for the then EC of nine, but Luxembourg was included with Belgium. The table shows that during 1955–73 (the period prior to the

Table 1.1 | Growth of real income

	1955–73 (1)	1973–81 (2)	Change (2)–(1)
Belgium	4.2	0.7	–3.5
Denmark	4.8	0.4	–4.4
France	5.4	1.9	–3.5
West Germany	5.1	1.7	–3.4
Ireland	4.2	1.6	–2.6
Italy	5.2	1.6	–3.6
Netherlands	4.7	1.1	–3.6
United Kingdom	3.0	0.2	–2.8
EC9	4.6	1.3	–3.3

Source: *Cambridge Economic Policy Review*, 7, 2, 1981

UK's joining the EC) and 1973–81, Britain experienced the slowest rate of growth of real income when compared with either the individual EC members or the average for the entire nine members. However, of particular significance was the fact that Britain and Ireland were the only two countries within the EC to have had a below average rate of fall between the two periods.

Table 1.2 contains information on the rates of inflation between 1960 and 1979; no data could be obtained for the desired periods as given in Table 1.1. The data clearly reveal that there was an increase in inflation rates in all the specified members of the OECD. Indeed, rising inflation rates were a worldwide phenomenon (World Bank 1981, pp. 134–35). However, the rate of change in the UK's inflation between 1960–70 and 1970–79 was below that of only Greece and Italy and also was more than four times that of West Germany and more than twice that of the USA.

Information on monetary expansion (both M_1 and 'real') during the period 1976–80 is given in Figure 1.1. The chart clearly portrays the severe nature of the restrictive monetary policy being pursued by Britain at the time. Indeed, monetary control was shown to have been more stringent than that of any of its eight EC partners (see Figure 1.1b). This information was confirmed by the high British interest rates and their high rate of increase (see Figure 1.2).

Table 1.2 | Average annual rate of inflation (%)

	1960–70 (1)	1970–79 (2)	Change (2)–(1)
Belgium[a]	3.6	8.1	+4.5
Denmark	5.5	9.8	+4.3
France	4.2	9.6	+5.4
West Germany	3.2	5.3	+2.1
Greece	3.2	14.1	+10.9
Ireland	5.2	14.6	+9.4
Italy	4.4	15.6	+11.2
Luxembourg[a]	3.6	8.1	+4.5
Netherlands	5.4	8.3	+2.9
United Kingdom	4.1	13.9	+9.8
Portugal	3.0	16.1	+13.1
Spain	8.2	15.9	+7.7
Canada	3.1	9.1	+6.0
Japan	4.9	8.2	+3.3
USA	2.8	6.9	+4.1

Note: [a] Belgium and Luxembourg are counted together
Source: World Bank (1981)

Table 1.3 provides data on recorded unemployment as a percentage of labour force for the EC Nine for 1973, 1979 and 1981 with then projections for 1985. The picture that clearly emerged was that the UK's performance in 1973 and 1979 coincided with the average for the EC as a whole. However, that average had gone completely out of line by 1981 and was then expected to deteriorate further by 1985. The table also shows that higher unemployment was a general phenomenon; indeed, it was a global one. However, Britain seemed to be significantly worse off in this respect than any of its EC partners.

Table 1.4 gives the growth rates of output, employment and productivity in the EC as a whole for the periods 1955–65, 1965–73 and 1973–81. The table also provides the equivalent rates for manufacturing and market services. Although this table does not relate specifically to individual nations, it provides a general perspective since it clearly shows that output, employment and productivity all declined between the two latter periods for the whole economy as well as for the two singled out sectors.

Figure 1.1a Monetary expansion in EC countries (M_1) (change against previous year)

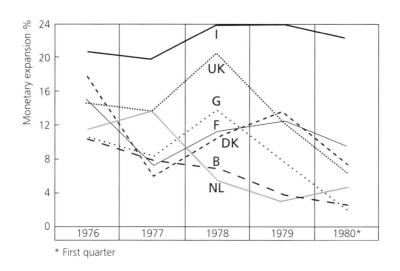

* First quarter

Figure 1.1b Real monetary expansion in EC countries (change against previous year)

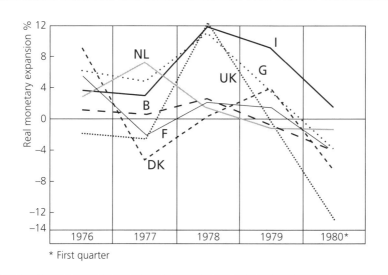

* First quarter

Source: *International Financial Statistics* (August 1980) pp. 44–45

Figure 1.2a | Monetary market rates in EC countries (three months)

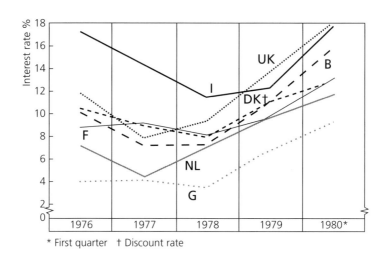

* First quarter   † Discount rate

Figure 1.2b | Real interest rates in EC countries (three-month money market rates minus rate of consumer price increase, year over year)

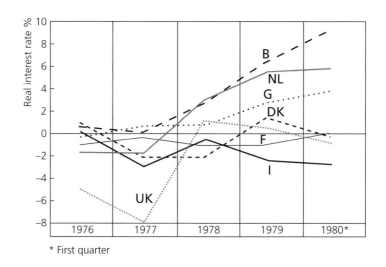

* First quarter

Source: *International Financial Statistics* (August 1980) p. 45; *Weltwirtschaft*, 1 (1980) Table 5

Table 1.5 provides the growth rates for government and private expenditures between 1973 and 1981. While for the whole EC, government expenditure on goods and services, on transfers and on privately financed expenditure all increased respectively by 2.5, 4.7 and 0.3, the equivalent rates for Britain were respectively 0.6, 4.9 and –1.4. This showed that Britain was completely out of line in both government expenditure on goods and services and privately financed expenditure.

Table 1.6 gives comparative information on Britain and the EC as a whole in terms of net balances as a percentage of total income; growth rates of exports of manufactures; changes in the ratio of manufactured imports to real income and changes in real income; and the ratio of manufactured exports to manufactured imports. A glance at the two 1965–73 and 1973–81 columns and a comparison with the figures for the EC as a whole (given in brackets) clearly shows that Britain became better off as a result of North Sea oil (an unfavourable balance turned favourable); Britain's current balance swung from a deficit to a surplus; and Britain was faring relatively worse in terms of manufactures and exports of manufactures.

The information in Table 1.6 is supplemented by that given in Tables 1.7–1.9 to show that UK trade with the EC increased by about a third since joining the EC; that UK exports of manufactures to the EC had a constant trend; and that since 1980 the trade balance became positive with both the EC and the rest of the world.

Table 1.3 | Recorded unemployment in the EC (% of labour force)

	1973	1979	1981	1985
Belgium	3	8	11	14 (0.62)
Denmark	1	5	9	12 (0.32)
France	2	6	8	12 (2.29)
West Germany	1	3	5	7 (1.78)
Ireland	6	8	11	15 (0.18)
Italy	5	7	8	12 (2.88)
Netherlands	2	4	8	12 (0.64)
United Kingdom	2	5	10	16 (4.09)
EC9	2	5	8	12

Note: Figures in brackets are in millions
Source: *Cambridge Economic Policy Review*, 7, 2, 1981

Table 1.4 Growth in output, employment and productivity in the EC (growth rates % per annum)

	1955–65 (1)	1965–73 (2)	1973–81 (3)	Change (4)
Whole economy				
Output	4.7	4.6	1.7	–2.9
Employment	0.6	0.2	–0.2	–0.4
Output per head	4.1	4.4	1.8	–2.6
Manufacturing				
Output	6.0	5.5	0.6	–4.9
Employment	1.0	0.0	–1.8	–1.8
Output per head	4.9	5.6	2.5	–3.1
Market services				
Output	4.7	4.8	2.6	–2.2
Employment	1.5	1.3	1.1	0.2
Output per head	3.2	3.5	1.5	–2.0

Source: *Cambridge Economic Policy Review*, 7, 2, 1981

Table 1.5 Growth of government and private expenditure (growth rate % per annum)

	Government expenditure on goods and services	Government expenditure on transfers	Privately financed expenditure
Belgium	3.9	4.8	0.2
Denmark	3.6	6.0	–2.3
France	3.3	5.5	0.5
West Germany	2.9	4.5	1.3
Ireland	4.0	4.7	2.0
Italy	3.2	3.1	0.8
Netherlands	2.3	5.9	0.1
United Kingdom	0.6	4.9	–1.4
EC9	2.5	4.7	0.3

Source: *Cambridge Economic Policy Review*, 7, 2, 1981

Table 1.6 | Changes in the balance of payments of the UK relative to EC countries, 1965–73

Changes in net balances as % of total income	1965–73	1973–81
Food and raw materials	+1.4 (+1.1)	+2.9 (+1.4)
Fuels	0.5 (–0.4)	+2.7 (–2.9)
Manufactures	3.8 (–0.4)	–1.1 (+0.5)
Services and transfers	1.3 (–0.5)	–1.4 (–0.4)
Current balance	1.6 (–0.2)	+3.1 (–1.4)
Growth rates (% per annum)		
Exports of manufactures	4.9 (7.5)	1.6 (4.3)
Ratios of manufactured imports to income	8.5 (4.5)	2.7 (3.3)
Total real income	2.9 (4.4)	0.2 (1.3)
	1965	*1973*
Ratio of manufactured exports to manufactured imports (%)	190 (144)	116 (128)

Note: Figures in brackets relate to the EC average
Source: *Cambridge Economic Policy Review*, 7, 2, 1981

Finally, Table 1.10 provides data on changes in government deficits and net external borrowing for the EC between 1973 and 1981. The table shows that over this period Britain was the only member of the EC to reduce its government deficit with the consequence of reduced borrowing or increased lending – i.e. the increased savings shown in column 1 and the falling government deficit shown in column 2 led to reduced government borrowing or increased lending.

Thus the economic facts clearly show that the UK was experiencing a slow and declining rate of growth of real income, but this was a deep-seated problem, with voluminous literature being advanced in its support – see, *inter alia*, Kaldor (1966) and Brown (1977, 1979). In spite of this, the rate of decline slowed down since the UK joined the EC. Hence, I concluded that if any inference could have been made on this count alone, it must have pointed to a favourable effect on Britain from EC membership. Of course, I added that this was only one of the possible interpretations but the fact remained that it was plausible.

The inference was reinforced when two other UK factors were taken into consideration: the stringent monetary control policies and the reductions in government deficits. Moreover, the stringent monetary control policies and the reductions in the government budgetary deficits at the time coincided, with a lag, with exceptionally high levels of and rates of increase in unemployment as well as lower productivity rates. Hence, irrespective of any positions taken by trade unions regarding wage bargaining at the time, it seemed that less stringent policies would have slackened the rate of fall of growth of real income further. I added that it was, of course, possible to argue that these policies could have led to a slower rate of inflation even though inflation was still very high; thus both 'Keynesians' and 'monetarists' had their joy and there was no need for dogmatic views on either side.

When added to this interpretation the evidence against trends for 1960–80 that UK trade with the EC was increasing and running at a surplus since 1980, at a time of severe world recession triggered by the upheavals of the 1970s (the Nixon shock, oil shock, etc.), it became even more apparent that UK membership of the EC was proving beneficial for Britain. Without that extra share in trade there would

Table 1.7 | UK visible trade with the EC, 1970–88

	UK exports to EC10		UK imports from EC10		Balance with EC10	Balance all areas
	Million pounds	% of total exports	Million pounds	% of total imports	Million pounds	Million pounds
1970	2416	29.7	2325	28.4	+91	−34
1971	2536	28.1	2720	30.7	−184	+190
1972	2849	30.2	3441	33.8	−592	−748
1973	3851	32.3	5178	35.7	−1327	−2586
1974	5546	33.8	7680	35.3	−2134	−5351
1975	6227	32.2	8734	38.5	−2507	−3333
1976	8936	35.5	11194	38.4	−2258	−3929
1977	11674	36.8	13606	40.0	−1932	−2284
1978	13348	38.1	15863	43.3	−2515	−1542
1979	17306	42.6	19935	45.2	−2629	−3458
1980	20422	43.1	19713	42.7	+709	+1178

Source: Mayes (1983)

Table 1.8 | Imports from EC countries (% share of total imports of importing country)

	Bel.[a]	Den.	Fr.	W.G.	Gr.	Ire.	It.	Neth.	UK	Port.	Sp.	Can.	Jap.	USA
1957	43.5	31.2	21.4	23.5	40.8	—	21.4	41.1	12.1	37.1	21.3	4.2	—	11.7
1958	46.6	35.6	21.9	25.8	42.7	—	21.4	41.9	14.2	39.2	23.8	4.7	4.9	12.8
1959	47.1	36.7	26.8	29.0	37.9	—	26.7	44.4	14.0	39.0	22.3	5.3	5.0	15.6
1960	47.9	38.5	29.4	29.9	33.6	—	27.7	45.8	14.6	38.2	25.2	5.3	4.7	15.0
1961	50.6	39.4	31.5	31.3	38.1	—	29.5	49.2	15.4	38.1	26.1	5.5	5.4	15.2
1962	51.0	37.8	33.6	32.5	43.4	—	31.2	50.2	15.8	36.6	29.7	5.5	6.1	15.0
1963	52.5	35.9	35.8	33.4	39.8	15.4	33.0	51.6	16.0	34.7	33.6	5.2	5.9	14.8
1964	53.3	35.4	37.4	34.9	42.3	15.6	32.7	52.0	16.6	33.1	35.9	5.4	5.6	15.2
1974	66.1	45.5	47.6	48.1	43.3	68.3	42.4	57.4	30.0	43.5	35.8	9.6	6.4	19.0
1975	67.2	45.8	48.8	49.5	42.5	69.2	43.0	56.9	32.4	40.2	33.6	9.8	5.8	17.3
1976	67.5	47.2	50.0	48.2	39.7	69.4	43.6	55.2	32.2	41.7	33.1	8.5	5.6	14.8
1977	67.7	47.7	49.4	49.0	42.5	68.2	43.1	54.8	38.5	43.6	34.2	—	5.9	15.2
1978	69.1	49.7	51.5	50.1	43.8	70.2	44.7	57.4	38.0	45.8	34.7	9.3	7.6	17.0
1979	64.5	50.4	52.5	50.2	43.6	71.9	44.9	56.8	41.1	40.8	36.0	8.9	6.8	16.4
1980	63.1	49.2	46.3	47.8	39.7	74.5	44.3	53.7	38.7	42.1	31.0	8.1	5.6	15.3

Note: [a] Data include Luxembourg's; — means not available

Source: Various issues of Eurostat's *Basic Statistics of the European Communities*

Table 1.9 | Exports from EC countries (% share of total exports of exporting country)

	Bel.[a]	Den.	Fr.	W.G.	Gr.	Ire.	It.	Neth.	UK	Port.	Sp.	Can.	Jap.	USA
1957	46.1	31.2	25.1	29.2	52.5	—	24.0	41.6	14.6	22.2	29.8	8.3	—	15.3
1958	45.1	31.2	22.2	27.3	47.9	—	23.6	41.6	13.9	24.6	28.2	8.6	4.3	13.6
1959	46.3	31.7	27.2	27.8	44.1	—	27.2	44.3	14.8	22.8	27.8	6.2	3.9	13.6
1960	50.5	29.5	29.8	29.5	33.0	—	29.6	45.9	15.3	21.8	38.5	8.3	4.3	16.8
1961	53.2	29.1	33.5	31.7	30.5	—	31.3	47.6	17.4	21.8	37.7	8.4	5.0	17.0
1962	56.8	28.4	36.8	34.0	35.7	—	34.8	49.2	19.3	23.2	38.0	7.3	5.6	16.8
1963	60.8	28.8	38.2	37.3	32.8	7.5	35.5	53.3	21.1	21.8	37.9	7.0	6.1	17.0
1964	62.6	28.1	38.8	36.5	37.5	11.5	38.0	55.7	20.6	20.7	38.9	6.8	5.5	17.2
1974	66.9	43.1	53.2	53.2	50.1	74.1	45.4	70.8	33.4	48.2	47.4	12.6	10.7	21.9
1975	70.6	45.0	49.2	43.6	49.7	79.4	45.1	71.1	32.3	50.3	44.7	12.5	10.2	21.3
1976	73.7	45.7	50.6	45.7	50.0	75.8	47.8	72.1	35.6	51.5	46.4	11.9	10.8	22.1
1977	71.2	42.3	50.4	44.9	47.7	76.5	46.5	70.4	36.6	51.8	46.3	—	10.9	22.0
1978	71.6	47.9	52.5	45.8	50.8	77.7	48.0	70.9	37.8	55.5	46.3	9.3	11.3	22.3
1979	73.3	49.6	53.8	49.5	49.1	77.9	51.0	73.2	42.4	56.4	48.0	10.8	12.3	23.4
1980	71.8	50.5	51.9	49.1	47.6	74.9	49.0	72.2	42.7	57.8	50.1	12.9	12.8	25.2

Note: [a] Data include Luxembourg's; — means not available

Source: Various issues of Eurostat's *Basic Statistics of the European Communities*

have resulted an appropriate fall in UK output and employment, since the extra exports could not have been sold to the rest of the world, i.e. outside the EC, particularly when the UK's overall share in world markets had been declining. Of course, some authorities then argued that our trends were questionable and that the actual performance of the UK would have been better in the absence of EC

UK membership of the EC was proving beneficial for Britain

membership. However, although their criticism seemed perfectly reasonable, it was not backed by any results obtained by them either by applying their own data to our model or by using alternative *anti mondes* or both. Since these were vital considerations, it is worthwhile expanding on one of them.

In that paper (El-Agraa 1984, but also see Chapter 12 for detailed information), I also mentioned that one should draw attention to an

Table 1.10 | Changes in government deficits and net external borrowing, 1973–81[a] (changes in net borrowing as % of total income)

	Deterioration in personal and business financial balances	Increase in government deficit	Increase in net external borrowing
Belgium	2.9	6.6	9.5
Denmark	−10.1	11.3	1.2
France	−1.7	2.8	1.1
West Germany	−1.6	5.0	3.4
Ireland	3.6	6.3	9.6
Italy	0.3	0.0	0.3
Netherlands	1.0	5.5	6.5
United Kingdom	−2.0	−1.0	−3.0
EC9 average	−1.3	2.7	1.4

Note: [a] Positive figures indicate increased borrowing or reduced lending. A minus sign indicates a fall in borrowing or a rise in lending

Source: *Cambridge Economic Policy Review*, 7, 2, 1981

analysis by commodity categories conducted for Britain in terms of: (i) imports coming from the EC Six; (ii) exports to the Six; and (iii) exports in total Six imports. Figures 1.3–1.5 clearly demonstrate how well the UK fared relative to the trend (the straight lines). The figures also reveal two important points. First, 'crude materials' performed consistently close to the trend, which was what one would have expected, given that this commodity category had not been subject to tariff imposition prior to the establishment of the EC. Second, Figure 1.3 reveals the vital information that increased British exports to the Six were not due to the Six growing faster than the UK. These results were later corroborated by Winters (1984).

The renewal

Since the vastly transformed Labour Party assumed power in 1997 and leader Tony Blair declared that he will ask the British people, through a referendum, to adopt the euro after the conditions set by Chancellor Gordon Brown are met, a repeat of the 1983 situation seemed to be in the offing for the general election, this time orchestrated by the Conservative Party. This is not a surprising claim since some influential voices were suggesting, and continue to suggest, that membership of the EU has been disastrous for the UK and/or recommending British withdrawal from the EU. Indeed, at their spring conference, held in Harrogate on 4 March 2001, the then leader of the Conservative Party William Hague clearly showed that his long-standing opposition to Britain's adopting the euro has hardened into 'an assault on all things European'. He took his loyal supporters, and, through them the whole of Britain, on a 'journey to a foreign land'. The tour took UK citizens to a Britain in which pence were melted down to be replaced by euros, where a Labour chancellor followed instructions on tax and spending from Brussels and British soldiers marched under German and French command. He claimed that it is only his party that would 'defend our right to live under our own laws'; hence the 'general election would be Britain's last chance to survive as an independent nation'. One may argue that such political rhetoric does not amount to advocating withdrawal from the EU, but as Philip Stephens clearly argues ('Time to be bold on Europe', *Financial Times*, 9 March 2000), the only logical conclusion of Hague's diagnosis is precisely that. This is because, since Hague is demanding a renegotiation of the Nice Treaty on enlargement, is asking for a recasting better to serve narrow UK interests of the common agricultural/fisheries policies (CAP and CFP)

Figure 1.3 Percentage of UK imports coming from EC6

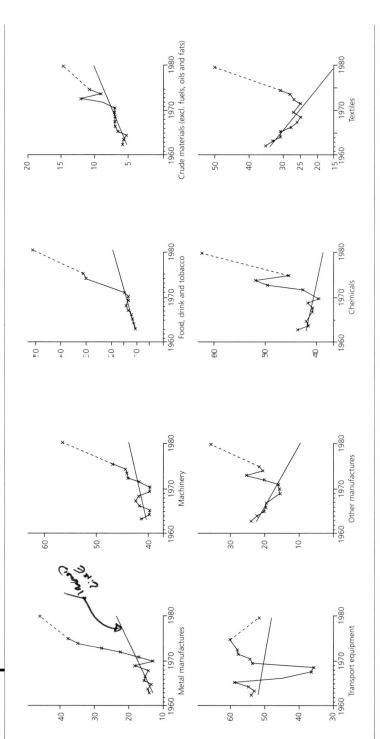

Figure 1.4 Percentage of UK exports to EC6

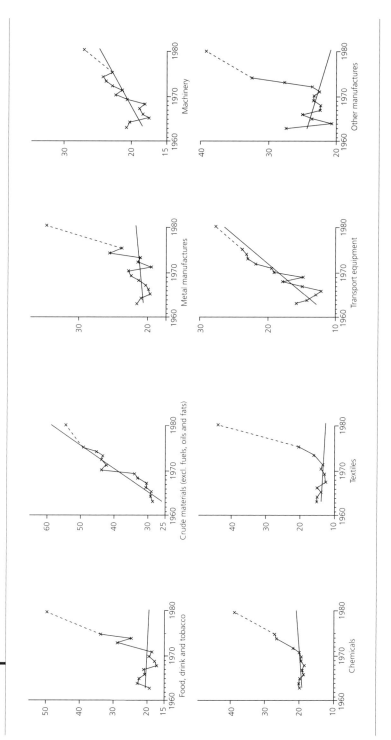

Figure 1.5 Percentage of UK exports in total EC6 imports

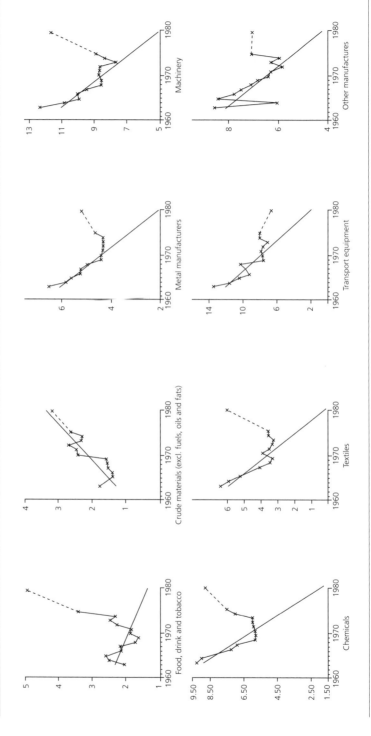

and is insisting on the Westminster parliament's reclaiming the right simply to ignore those rulings of the EU Court of Justice that it may find inconvenient, he is in effect demanding that Britain must be allowed to set its own rules for participation in the EU. One does not have to read the following chapter to recognize that such a proposition is not only 'absurd – certain to be dismissed by the other 14 members' of the EU, to use Stephens' own words, but, importantly, cannot be realized while Britain remains a member of the club.

It may therefore seem vital that a new edition of the 1983 book should be prepared and published in timely fashion during the run up to the referendum on euro adoption. However, this would not be necessary since all the pertinent elements in the calculation of the costs and benefits discussed in that book, and mentioned earlier, have either not changed at all, have developed along the lines then analyzed (for example, Tables 2.2–2.5 update the data on unemployment, growth of GDP and intra-EU trade) and appear in the various chapters in this book,

> # Hague is in effect demanding that Britain must be allowed to set its own rules for participation in the EU

especially in Chapter 2, or have been reformed in ways favourable to the UK. For example, the two items that were prominent on the cost side for the UK were the CAP and the net contribution to the EU general budget. These are, of course, not unrelated. First, since at the time about three-quarters of EC budgetary expenditures fell on the CAP and of this the UK, given its small farming sector (only about 2.5 per cent of the UK working population was engaged in agriculture), received an insignificant amount of CAP subsidies. Second, the EC budgetary revenues came from basically two sources: tariffs on industrial imports and agricultural levies; and up to 1 percentage point of VAT. Hence, the UK, being less than self-sufficient in most agricultural products, importing the difference from outside the EC, contributed the levy proceeds to the EC coffers as an EC 'own resource' (see El-Agraa 2000, Ch. 16).

Regarding the net budgetary contribution, in June 1984 the EC reached agreement on the 'Fontainebleau settlement' which guaranteed the UK a refund of one billion ECUs in 1984 and 66 per cent of the difference between its VAT contribution and EC budgetary expenditures in the UK for subsequent years, and this was reaffirmed in 1997, subject to minor adjustments to avoid windfall benefits due to changes in own resources and future enlargement (see *Agenda 2000*,

Commission of the European Union 1997) and in the Berlin summit of 24–25 March 1999 (for more on this, see Chapter 11). This affirmation has been achieved despite rightful claims by other EU member states that the UK's fortunes have changed dramatically since the settlement was reached in 1984 (at the time, the UK was third from bottom of the league of EC per capita GDP).

As to the CAP, the number of changes that have been introduced that are favourable to Britain are too many to mention here (see El-Agraa 2000, Ch. 11 for a detailed specification). However, the most salient are in order. On 31 March 1984 the member nations agreed on a package which for the first time reduced the EC common farm prices (by 0.5 per cent) and decided to rely on a system of quotas to restrict milk production and to extend the quota system, which had already been applied to sugar beet, to a number of products, including cereals and oil seeds. In February 1988, the EC decided that the annual growth rate of the European Agricultural Guidance and Guarantee Fund (EAGGF) should not exceed 70–80 per cent of the annual growth rate of EC GDP. More importantly, in June 1992 the MacSharry reform package was adopted which not only applied price cuts to practically all the major agricultural products, but also generalized a system of 'set-aside payments' to encourage farmers to abstain from the production of certain crops. These measures were further reinforced in May 1999. In our present context, it does not really matter who or what was the driving force behind these changes (see El-Agraa 2000, Ch. 11 for the role played by the USA during the Uruguay round of GATT negotiations); what is vital is that, relative to the pre-1983 level, they have reduced the CAP burden on the UK.

> The MacSharry reform package generalized a system of 'set-aside payments' to encourage farmers to abstain from the production of certain crops

Thus, on these two counts alone, there has been an increase on the benefit side as well as a reduction on the cost side for the UK. Moreover, there have been no other new policy areas which have added to UK costs. Hence, given that our argument for net UK benefits from EC membership for the period up to 1983 is reinforced when brought up to date and that an alternative approach given in Chapter 12 supports this conclusion, a new edition of the 1983 book is not warranted. However, with Blair avowing to take a decision on UK adoption of the euro during the first half second government, i.e. during the first two years of office, a book on the costs/benefits of EMU and the euro and the British debate regarding euro adoption is certainly needed; hence the idea behind this book.

About this book

The book is in three parts. Part I comprises this and the following chapter. As we have seen, this chapter provides a general background by explaining in detail the need for this book, why it is not necessary to have a new edition of the 1983 book and why Britain continues to reap net economic benefits from its membership of the EU. Chapter 2 provides a general perspective on the EU, paying special attention to its historical development. Although Chapter 2 may seem unwarranted, it actually constitutes an essential part of the book, since those not conversant with the subject should be aware of why the EU needs EMU and the euro, and those in the know need to be reminded, otherwise the discussion would be vacuous. Thus the two chapters together not only set the scene, but are also essential for a proper understanding of EMU, the euro and the British attitude to it and to the EU in general.

Part II consists of five chapters. Chapter 3 is about the EMU, its costs and benefits and the road taken by the EU to achieve it and the euro. Chapter 4 takes this further by questioning the practicality of the 'optimum currency area' concept, which lies at the very heart of the economic discussion on EMUs, and provides a longer historical perspective by examining how earlier attempts have fared and the necessary conditions for their survival. Chapter 5 reviews the series of mechanisms set up by the EU to co-ordinate fiscal, structural and monetary policies in order to accomplish the objectives of the EMU for the 12 member nations concerned and provides an empirical assessment of how they are faring in practice. Chapters 6 and 7 are devoted to the evolution of the euro since its official introduction on 1 January 1999. Since that time, and much to the surprise of those who predicted a strong euro, the trend has generally been one of decline relative to the US dollar. These chapters offer a comprehensive coverage of the possible explanations for this trend.

Part III contains six chapters, devoted to matters mainly relating to the UK, but also to the euro institutions. Chapter 8 examines the position of the UK in relation to the euro, but naturally also overlaps in areas covered in the first two parts. However, the overlaps are minimal and they help drive the pertinent points home. Chapter 9 concentrates on macro-economic issues fundamental to the operations of the euro system itself and shows how they make it difficult for the UK, or for that matter any other member nation, to participate in the absence of much-needed changes in the system. Chapter 10 examines the competitiveness of the UK financial services industry with especial emphasis on its position within the EU and assesses how the advent of the euro might alter the picture. Since several chapters, especially 3, 4, 9 and 10, clearly indicate that a 'common fiscal stance' would sooner or later prove necessary for operating a successful EMU, a point much emphasized in the *MacDougall Report* more than two decades ago (see Commission of the European Communities 1979), Chapter 11 on the EU general budget is vital since it demonstrates the limitations of the EU fiscal stance in this respect and at the same time corroborates what was stated earlier. Chapter 12 points to four major concerns regarding UK adoption of the euro: the exchange rate for the pound at entry may be misaligned; the fixing of the exchange rate with respect to some trading partners but not others may affect the composition of trade through a change in the volatility of relative prices; some of the remaining gains expected from the completion of the single European market may be realized in terms of reduced costs; and, importantly, whether there will be dynamic benefits from both increased pressures of competition and lower interest rates. The chapter addresses these concerns by taking a backward look at the attempts that have been made in the past and showing how they might be extrapolated to the present; thus the chapter makes a contribution in this important yet scantily researched area and in the process supplements the arguments advanced in this chapter.

There is no consensus among the contributors to this book regarding whether EMU and the euro as tailored by the EU are desirable or not, but that does not really matter in the case of the final chapter since it examines how Britain would fare if it decided to adopt the euro. In this respect, the UK must satisfy not only the Maastricht criteria on inflation, long-term interest rates, government budgetary deficits, public borrowing and exchange rate stability, but also the five extra constraints (tests) added by Chancellor Gordon Brown in October 1997 (see UK Treasury 1997). The first is about business cycles and economic structures being compatible so that 'we and others could live comfortably with euro interest rates on a permanent basis'. The second relates to whether there would be enough flexibility to deal with any problems. The third concerns whether joining EMU 'would create better conditions for companies making long-term decisions to invest in the UK'. The fourth is about the impact of membership 'on the competitive position of the UK's financial services industry, particularly the City's wholesale markets'. The final constraint sums up the other four since it is about whether joining the EMU would 'promote higher growth, stability and a lasting increase in jobs'. I should add, however, that several chapters, especially Chapters 8 and 9, also contain pertinent information and analysis in this area.

Finally, I should add that the book has been written in a fairly non-technical manner so that it can be read, on the whole, by the intelligent layperson. This is deliberate since if the time comes for a referendum on the euro, it is that kind of reader who is going to bother to cast a vote!

References

Brown, Arthur J. (1977) 'What is wrong with the British economy?', *University of Leeds Review*, 20.

Brown, Arthur J. (1979) 'Inflation and the British sickness?', *Economic Journal*, 89.

Commission of the European Communities (1977) *Report of Committee of Inquiry on Public Finance in the Community* (The MacDougall Report). Brussels.

Commission of the European Union (1997) *Agenda 2000: For A Stronger and Wider Union*. Brussels.

El-Agraa, Ali M. (1984) 'Has membership of the European Community been a disaster for Britain?', *Applied Economics*, 16, 2, pp. 299–315.

El-Agraa, Ali M. (2000) *The European Union: Economics and Policies*. London: Pearson Education, Prentice Hall and Financial Times.

El-Agraa, Ali M. (ed.) (1983) *Britain within the European Community: The Way Forward*. London: Macmillan; New York: Crane Russack.

Kaldor, Nicolas (1966) *Causes of the Slow Rate of Economic Growth of the United Kingdom*. Cambridge: Cambridge University Press.

Mayes, David G. (1983) 'EC trade effects and factor mobility' in El-Agraa (ed.) 1983.

UK Treasury (1997) *UK Membership of the Single Currency: An Assessment of the Five Economic Tests*. ***www.hm-treasury.gov.uk***

Winters, L. Alan (1984) 'British imports of manufactures and the Common Market', *Oxford Economic Papers*, 36.

World Bank (1981) *World Development Report*. Oxford: Oxford University Press.

Young, Hugo (1998) *This Blessed Plot: Britain and Europe from Churchill to Blair*. London: Macmillan.

2

A bird's-eye view of the European Union

Ali M. El-Agraa

To appreciate why most EU nations have always wanted both EMU and the single currency, one needs to appreciate the history of European unity. This is because in a world presently dominated by purely economic considerations, the driving force behind European integration is often forgotten. Therefore, this chapter begins with a brief history of European unity (those interested in a comprehensive picture are advised to consult Lipgens 1982) and adopts a historical perspective throughout so that the reader can make sense of the ongoing debate on this issue. It then goes on briefly to consider the EU's

> To appreciate why most EU nations have always wanted both EMU and the single currency, one needs to appreciate the history of European unity

aims and the progress it has achieved to date (a detailed account can be found in El-Agraa 2000). The chapter does not provide a specific section on EU institutions simply because doing so would be a distraction, but the main institutions are tackled as part of the historical development. The chapter concludes with an assessment of the success (or otherwise) of the EU.

An overview

The European Union (EU) is the most significant and influential of international economic integration schemes (see El-Agraa 2000 and 'A short history of European unity' below).[1] Three reasons account for the significance. First, the EU comprises some of the most advanced nations of Europe, each with its own unique and complicated economic and political system: Austria, Belgium, Denmark, Finland, France, Germany, Greece, Ireland, Italy, Luxembourg, the Netherlands, Portugal, Spain, Sweden and the UK. Second, from a voluntary viewpoint, it is the oldest such scheme. Third, and most importantly, it is the only scheme seeking the most involved and demanding type of international integration (see Chapter 3, 'What is EMU?'). The influence is simply due to the relative global weight of the EU: the data in Table 2.1 clearly show that both present EU population (94 per cent) and GNP (88 per cent) are similar to those of the North American Free Trade Agreement (NAFTA, which comprises Canada, Mexico and the USA), the only comparable trading bloc. Adding the potential members would make it difficult to find any differences between the two groups in this particular respect.

The EU was founded by Belgium, France, West Germany, Italy, Luxembourg and the Netherlands, usually referred to as the Original Six (simply the Six hereafter), by two treaties, signed in Rome on the same day in 1957. The first created the *European Economic Community* (EEC), the second the *European Atomic Energy Community* (Euratom). However, the Six had then been members of the *European Coal and Steel Community* (ECSC) which was established by the Treaty of Paris in 1951. Thus the Six belonged to three communities, but in 1965 it was deemed sensible to merge the three entities into one and call it the *European Communities* (EC). Denmark, Ireland and the UK joined in 1972. Greece acceded as a full member in 1981, having been an associate member for a long time before then. Portugal and Spain were admitted in 1986 after a lengthy period of negotiations. Austria, Finland and Sweden joined in 1995.

At present, the EU recognizes 13 candidates for membership. Six began full accession negotiations in 1998 and if all goes well they are expected to join in 2004: Cyprus, the Czech Republic, Estonia,

Table 2.1 | Population, GNP, per capita GNP and life expectancy, 1999

Country	Population (millions)	GNP US$bn	Per capita GNP (at normal conversion) US$	Per capita GNP (at PPP[a]) US$	Life expectancy at birth (years)[b] M[c]	Life expectancy at birth (years)[b] F[d]
EU (15)	**375.0**	**8,212.6**				
Austria	8.1	210.0	25,970	23,808	75	81
Belgium	10.2	250.6	24,510	24,200	75	81
Denmark	5.3	170.3	32,030	24,280	73	78
Finland	5.1	122.9	23,780	21,209	74	81
France	58.8	1,427.2	23,480	21,897	75	82
Germany	82.1	2,079.2	25,350	22,404	74	80
Greece	10.6	124.0	11,770	14,595	75	81
Ireland	3.7	71.4	19,160	19,180	73	79
Italy	57.6	1,136.0	19,710	20,751	75	82
Luxembourg	0.4	19.3	44,640	38,247	77	81
Netherlands	15.7	384.3	24,320	23,052	75	81
Portugal	9.9	105.9	10,600	15,147	71	79
Spain	39.4	551.6	14,000	16,730	75	82
Sweden	8.9	221.8	25,040	20,824	77	82
United Kingdom	59.2	1,338.1	22,640	20,883	75	80
EFTA	**11.67**	**427.6**				
Iceland	0.27	8.1	29,280	26,283	79	79
Norway	4.4	146.4	32,880	26,522	76	81
Switzerland	7.0	273.1	38,850	27,486	76	82
CEECs[e]	**170.01**	**556.0**				
Bulgaria	8.1	11.3	1,380	4,914	67	75
Cyprus	0.73	9.1	11,960	18,395	78	78
Czech Republic	10.3	52.0	5,040	12,289	71	78
Estonia	1.5	5.0	3,480	7,826	64	75
Hungary	10.2	46.8	4,650	10,479	66	75
Latvia	2.5	6.0	2,470	5,938	64	76
Lithuania	3.7	9.7	2,620	6,093	67	77
Malta	0.38	3.5	9,210	15,066	77	77
Poland	38.7	153.1	3,960	7,894	69	77
Romania	22.5	34.2	1,520	5,647	66	73
Slovak Republic	5.4	19.4	3,590	9,811	69	77
Slovenia	2.0	19.6	9,890	15,062	71	79
Turkey	64.0	186.3	2,900	6,126	67	72
NAFTA	**401.0**	**9,371.2**				
Canada	31.0	591.4	19,320	23,725	76	82
Mexico	97.0	428.8	4,400	7,719	69	75
United States	273.0	8,351.0	30,600	30,600	74	80
Other						
Japan	127.0	4,078.9	32,230	24,041	77	84
Russian Federation	147.0	332.5	2,270	6,339	61	73

Notes: [a] Purchasing power parity; [b] data are for 1998; [c] for males; [d] for females; [e] = Central and Eastern European Countries

Source: World Bank (2001)

Hungary, Poland and Slovenia. Also, the Helsinki EU summit of December 1999 ruled that six more could commence full negotiations from February 2000, each at its own pace: Bulgaria, Latvia, Lithuania, Malta, Romania and Slovakia. Moreover, after 36 years of temporizing, it was also agreed at the same summit that Turkey is a recognized candidate, but negotiations are unlikely to start for a long time since the EU wants to see big improvements in Turkey's political and human rights behaviour, including the rights of Kurds and other minorities and the constitutional role of the army in political life, which might require changes in its constitution. The EU also wants the country to resolve territorial squabbles with Greece in the Aegean Sea and to help end the division of Cyprus, where a Turkish-backed regime has occupied the north of the island since 1974. However, one should hasten to add that these conditions are not new since they are consistent with those in *Agenda 2000*, the EU's official document on enlargement (see Commission of the European Union 1997).

Norway successfully negotiated EC membership and was set to join at the time of the first enlargement in 1973, but its citizens decided (by 53 per cent) against ratification of the agreement, and repeated the same act when it was set to join at the same time of the last enlargement in 1995, but its citizens again opted against ratification (by 52.2 per cent). However, Norway, together with Iceland and Liechtenstein, i.e. the European Free Trade Association (EFTA) minus Switzerland (which is odd, given that it still has an application for EU membership on the table; the rejection, by 76.7 per cent, on 11 March 2001 by Swiss voters of their government's call for starting membership negotiations does not mean withdrawal of the application), is locked in together with the EU in the *European Economic Area*, which provides both sides with full access to each other's markets for most manufactured products, but without the non-EU nations' being able to influence EU policy decisions.

> **If all goes according to plan, the EU is set to comprise the whole of Europe**

Thus, if all goes according to plan, the EU is set to comprise the whole of Europe, and, as Table 2.1 shows, the inclusion of the immediate potential members alone will make the EU a formidable economic association.

A short history of European unity

Philosophical underpinnings

Most, if not all, actual steps taken to achieve economic and political unity in Europe originated after 1945. However, the idea of European unity is deeply rooted in European thinking. History shows that there have been a number of proposals and arrangements designed to create it: in the 14th century, the idea of a united Christendom inspired Pierre Dubois to propose a *European Confederation* to be ruled by a *European Council* of wise, expert and faithful men; in the 17th century, Sully proposed to keep peace in Europe by means of a *European Army*; in 1693, William Penn, the English Quaker, proposed the creation of a *European Diet, Parliament* or *State* in his *Essay Towards the Present and Future Peace of Europe*; in the 19th century, Proudhon was strongly in favour of the formation of a *European Federation* and predicted that the 20th century would witness an era of federations, forecasting disaster in the absence of such a development; and immediately after World War I, politicians began to give serious consideration to the concept of European unity for example – in 1923 Count Coudenhove Kalergi, the Austrian founder-leader of the *Pan-European Movement*, called for the formation of a *United States of Europe*, his reason being the successful assertion of Swiss unity in 1848, the forging of the German Empire in 1871 and, most significantly, the independence of the United States in 1776. On 5 September 1929, in a renowned speech, delivered to the *League of Nations Assembly* in Geneva, the French Foreign Minister, Aristide Briand, with the backing of his German counterpart, Gustav Stresmann, proposed the creation of a *European Union* within the framework of the League of Nations and reiterated this later, when Prime Minister, by declaring that part of his political manifesto was the building of a *United States of Europe*.

The main reason for the pursuit of European unity was the achievement of lasting peace in Europe; it was realized that there was no other means of putting an end to the continent's woeful history of conflict, bloodshed, suffering and destruction. However, economic reasons were also a contributing factor. These were influenced by the tradition of free trade and Adam Smith's argument that 'the division of labour is limited by the extent of the market', which the German philosopher Friedrich Naumann utilized to propose in 1915 that European nation states were no longer large enough to compete on their own in world markets, therefore they had to unite in order to survive.

Despite the fact that there was no shortage of plans for creating a united Europe, it was not until 1945 that a combination of new forces and an intensification of old ones prompted action. First, Europe had been at the centre of yet another devastating war, caused by the ambitions of nation states. Those who sought and still seek a united Europe have always had at the forefront of their minds the desire to prevent any further outbreak of war in Europe. It was felt that if the nations of Europe could be brought closer together, such war would become unthinkable. Second, World War II left Europe economically exhausted and this led to the view that if Europe were to recover, it would require a concerted effort on the part of the European states. Third, World War II also soon revealed that for a long time Western Europe would have to face not only a powerful and politically alien USSR, but also a group of European nations firmly fixed within the Eastern European bloc. It was felt that an exhausted and divided Europe (since the war embraced co-belligerents) presented both a power vacuum and a temptation to the USSR to fill it. Fourth, the ending of the war soon revealed that the wartime allies were in fact divided, with the two major powers (the USA and USSR) confronting each other in a bid for world supremacy. Hence, it should come as no surprise to learn that members of the *European Movement*, who wanted to get away from intergovernmental co-operation by creating institutions leading to a *Federal Europe*, felt the need for a third world force: 'the voice of Europe'. This force would *represent the Western European viewpoint and could also act as a bridge between the Eastern and Western extremities.*

Concrete unity efforts

The first concrete move for regional integration in Europe was made in 1947 with the establishment of the *Economic Commission for Europe* (ECE), which was set up in Geneva as a regional organization of the United Nations (UN). Its objective was to initiate and participate in concerted measures aimed at securing the economic restructuring of the *whole* of Europe. A year later, the *Brussels Treaty Organization* (BTO) was founded by the UK, France, Belgium, the Netherlands and Luxembourg. It was designed to create a system of mutual assistance in times of attack on Europe. The BTO took an Atlantic form in 1949 when the five nations, together with the USA and Canada as well as Denmark, Norway, Portugal, Iceland and Italy (significantly, since it had been an Axis power), founded the *North Atlantic Treaty Organization* (NATO). The aim of NATO was, and continues to be, to provide military defence against attack on any of its members. Greece and Turkey joined NATO in 1952, West Germany became a member in 1955 and Spain was added in 1982, after the disappearance of General Franco from the political scene. After the collapse of communism in Eastern Europe, not only were the Czech Republic, Hungary and Poland added in 1997 to give NATO 19 members, but, vitally, NATO and Russia signed the *Act on Mutual Relations, Co-operation and Security*.

Also, in 1948 the *Organization for European Economic Co-operation* (OEEC) was formed and was followed a year later by the *Council for Europe*. These marked the beginning of the division of Western Europe into two camps, with, on the one hand, the UK and some of the countries that later formed the EFTA and, on the other, the Six who subsequently established the European Economic Community (EEC). The main reason for this division was that the UK was less committed to Europe as the main policy area than the Six, since, until the second half of the 1950s, the UK was still a world power which had been on the victorious side and a major participant in some of the fateful geo-political decision making at the time and it still had the Empire to dispose of.

The idea of a politically united Europe was not a concept that thrilled British hearts

Therefore, British policy was bound to incorporate this wider dimension: relations with Europe had to compete with Empire (later, Commonwealth) ties and with the *special relationship* with the USA. In addition, the idea of a politically united Europe[2] was strongly held by the other countries, particularly by France and the BENELUX[3] countries, but, despite the encouraging noises made by Winston Churchill, then British Prime Minister, both during World War II and after, this was not a concept that thrilled British hearts.

The different thinking between the UK and the Six about the political nature of European institutions was revealed in the discussions leading up to the establishment of the OEEC and the Council for Europe. World War II had left Europe devastated. The year 1947 was particularly bleak: bad harvests in the previous summer led to rising food prices; the severe winter of 1946–47 led to a fuel crisis; and the continental countries were producing very little, and what was produced tending to be retained rather than exported, while imports were booming, and hence foreign exchange reserves were running out. It was at this point that the USA entered on the scene to present the *Marshall Plan*. General George Marshall proposed that the USA make aid available to help the European economy find its feet and that European governments should get together to decide how much assistance was needed. In short, the USA did not feel it appropriate that it should unilaterally decide on the programme necessary to achieve this result. Although it seemed possible that this aid programme could be elaborated within the ECE framework, the USSR felt otherwise. Soviet reluctance was no doubt due to the fear that if its satellites participated, this would open the door to Western influence. Therefore, a conference was convened without the USSR and a *Committee for European Economic Co-operation* (CEEC) was established.

The attitude of the USA was that the CEEC should not merely provide it with a list of needs. The USA perceived that the aid it was to give should be linked with progress towards European unification. This is an extremely important point since it shows that right from the very beginning *the European Movement* enjoyed the encouragement and support of the USA. Of course, the driving force behind US insistence on European unity was its desire to establish a solid defence against any Western advance by the USSR, i.e. the USA did not insist on unity for unity's sake. It also asked that its multinational companies should have free access to European markets. The CEEC led in turn to the creation of an aid agency: the OEEC. Here, the conflict between the UK and the Six, especially France, came to a head over the issue of *supra-nationalism*. France in particular (and here it was supported by the USA) wanted to introduce a supra-national element into the new organization. But what is supra-nationalism? It can mean a situation in which international administrative institutions exercise power over, for example, the economies of the member states; or ministerial bodies, when taking decisions (to be implemented by international organizations) work on a majority voting system rather than insisting on unanimity.

The French view was not shared by the British since they favoured a body which was to be under the control of a ministerial council in which decisions should be taken on a unanimity basis. The French, by the same token, preferred an arrangement in which an international secretariat would be presided over by a secretary-general who would be empowered to take policy initiatives on major issues. Significantly, the organization which emerged was substantially in line with the British wish for a unanimity rule. This was undoubtedly a reflection of the UK's relatively powerful position in the world at the time.

In the light of subsequent events, it is also interesting to note that the USA encouraged the European nations to consider the creation of a customs union. Although this was of considerable interest to some continental countries, it did not appeal to the UK. In the end the OEEC convention merely recorded the intention to continue the study of this proposal. For a variety of reasons, one of which was the opposition of the UK, the matter was not pursued further.

The creation of the Council for Europe also highlighted the fundamental differences in approach between the countries which later founded the EC, on the one hand, and the British and Scandinavians, on the other. The establishment of the Council for Europe was preceded by the *Congress of Europe* at The Hague in May 1948. This was a grand rally of 'Europeans' which was attended by leading European statesmen, including Winston Churchill. The Congress adopted a resolution which called for the giving up of some national sovereignty before the accomplishment of economic and political union in Europe. Subsequently, a proposal was put forward, with the support of the Belgian and French governments, calling for the creation of a *European Parliamentary Assembly*, in which resolutions would be passed by majority vote. A *Committee of Ministers* was to prepare and implement these resolutions.

Needless to add, the UK was opposed to this form of supra-nationalism and in the end the British view largely prevailed. The Committee of Ministers, which was the executive organ of the Council for Europe, alone had power of decision and generally these were taken on the unanimity principle. The *Consultative Assembly* which came into existence was a forum,[4] not a European legislative body. In short, the British and Scandinavian *Functionalists*, those who believed that European unity, insofar as it was to be achieved, was to be attained by *intergovernmental co-operation*, triumphed over the *Federalists*, those who sought unity by the radical method of creating European institutions to which national govern-

The West German economic miracle was about to unfold

ments would surrender some of their sovereignty. The final disillusionment of the federalists was almost certainly marked by the resignation of Paul-Henri Spaak, a devoted European federalist, from the presidency of the Consultative Assembly in 1951.

The next step in the economic and political unification of Western Europe was made without the British and Scandinavians. It took the creation in 1951 of the *European Coal and Steel Community* (ECSC) by the Six and marked the parting of ways in post-war Western Europe.

The immediate factor in these developments was the revival of the West German economy. The passage of time, the efforts of the German people and the aid made available by the USA through the Marshall Plan all contributed to this recovery. Indeed, the West German *economic miracle* was about to unfold.

It was recognized that the German economy would have to be allowed to regain its position in the world and that the Allied control of coal and steel under the *International Ruhr Authority* could not last indefinitely. The fundamental question was how the German economy in the sectors of iron, steel and coal (the basic materials of a war effort) could be allowed to regain its former powerful position without endangering the future peace of Europe. The answer was a French plan, elaborated by Jean Monnet and put forward by Robert Schuman in May 1950. The *Schuman Plan* was essentially political in character. It sought to end the historic rivalry of France and Germany by making a war between the two nations not only unthinkable but also materially impossible. This was to be achieved in a manner which ultimately would have the result of bringing about that European federation which is indispensable to peace. The answer was not to nationalize or indeed to internationalize the ownership of the means of production in coal, iron and steel, but to create, by the removal of customs duties, import quota restrictions and similar impediments on trade and factors, a common market in these products. Every participating nation in such a common market would have equal access to the products of these industries wherever they might be located, and, to reinforce this, discrimination on the grounds of nationality was to be forbidden.

The plan had a number of attractive features. First, it provided an excellent basis for solving the *Saar* problem: the handing back of the Saar region to West Germany was more likely to be acceptable to the French if Germany was firmly locked in such a coal and steel community. Second, the plan was extremely attractive to Germany since membership of the community was a passport to international respectability; it was the best way of speeding up the end of occupation and avoiding the imposition of dampers on the expansion of the German economy. Third, the plan was also attractive to the federalists who had found the OEEC far short of their aspirations for the Council for Europe,[5] and, in any case, the prospects for the OEEC were not very good since by 1952 the four-year period of the Marshall Plan would be over and the UK attitude was that thereafter the OEEC's budget should be cut and some of its functions passed over to NATO.

As it turned out, however, the ECSC was much more to the federalists' taste since its executive body, the *High Authority*, was given substantial direct powers which could be exercised without the prior approval of the Council of Ministers. Note that the ECSC also had a *Council of Ministers*, a *Parliamentary Assembly* and a *Court of Justice*.

The plan received favourable responses from Belgium, France, Italy, West Germany, the Netherlands and Luxembourg (the Six). The UK was invited to join but refused. Clement Attlee, British Prime Minister at the time, told the House of Commons: 'We on this side [of the House] are not prepared to accept that the most vital economic forces of this country should be handed over to an authority that is utterly undemocratic and is responsible to nobody'. However, the Six were not to be deterred, and in April 1951 the *Treaty of Paris* was signed. The ECSC was born and it embarked on an experiment in limited economic integration, albeit a sectoral one, on 1 January 1952.

The next stage in the development of European unity was also concerned with Germany. When the Korean War broke out in 1950 the USA put pressure on the Western European nations to do more to defend themselves against possible attack by the USSR. This raised the issue of a military contribution from West Germany, the implication being that Germany should be rearmed. However, this proposal was opposed by France, which was equally against Germany's becoming a member of NATO. This was not a purely negative attitude. Indeed, René Pleven, French Prime Minister at the time, put forward a plan which envisaged that there would be no German army as such, but that there would be a *European Army* to which each participating nation, including Germany, could contribute.

Britain was not against this idea but did not itself wish to be involved. The Six were positively enthusiastic and discussion began in 1951 with a view to creating a *European Defence Community* (EDC). It was envisaged that there would be a *Joint Defence Commission*, a Council of Ministers, a Parliamentary Assembly and a Court of Justice. In other words, the institutions of the EDC were to parallel those created for the ECSC. The Six made rapid progress in the negotiations and the *EDC Treaty* was signed in May 1952.

Having gone so far, there were a number of reasons for further integrative efforts. First, the pooling of both defensive and offensive capabilities inevitably reduced the possibility of independent foreign policies; it was logical to follow integration in defence with measures which serve to achieve political integration as well. Second, it was also desirable to establish a system whereby effective control could be exercised over the proposed European army. Third, there was also the Dutch desire that progress in the military field should be paralleled by more integration in the economic sphere as well. Therefore, the foreign ministers of the Six asked the ECSC Assembly, together with co-opted members from the Consultative Assembly of the Council for Europe, to study the possibilities of creating a *European Political Authority*.

In 1953, a draft of a *European Political Community* (EPC) was produced in which it was proposed that, after a period of transition, the political institutions of the ECSC and the proposed EDC be subsumed within a new framework. There would then be a *European Executive* responsible to a *European Parliament*,[6] a *Council of Ministers* and a *European Court* to replace the parallel bodies created under the ECSC and EDC treaties.

This was a watershed in the history of the European Movement. The Six had already successfully experimented in limited economic integration in the fields of iron, coal and steel; had now signed a treaty to integrate defence; and were about to proceed further by creating a community for the purposes of securing political unity. Moreover, the draft treaty proposed to push economic integration still further by calling for the establishment of a general common market based on the free movement of commodities and factors of production.

However, on this occasion the success that had attended the Six in the case of iron, coal and steel was not to be repeated. Five national parliaments approved the EDC Treaty, but successive French governments felt unable to guarantee success in asking the *French Assembly* to ratify. Finally, the Mendès-France government attempted to water down the treaty but failed to persuade the other five nations. The treaty as it stood was therefore submitted to the French Assembly which refused to consider it and in so doing killed the EPC too.

There were a number of reasons for the refusal of the French Assembly to consider the treaty. First, there was opposition to the supra-national elements which it contained. Second, the French 'left' refused to consider the possibility of the rearmament of Germany. Third, the French 'right' refused to have the French army placed under foreign control. Fourth, British aloofness was also a contributing factor: one of the arguments employed by those who were opposed to the treaty was that France could not participate in the formation of a European army with Germany if the UK were not a member.

It is perhaps worth noting that the failure of the EDC was followed by a British initiative also aimed at dealing with the problem of rearming Germany in a way acceptable to the French. A series of agreements was reached in 1954 between the USA, the UK, Canada and the Six under which the BTO was modified and extended: Germany and Italy were brought in and a new intergovernmental organization was formed – the *Western European Union* (WEU). These agreements also related to the termination of the occupation of Germany and its admission into NATO. As a counterbalance to the German army, the UK agreed to maintain specified forces on the continent. In short, the gist of the agreements was to provide a European framework within which Germany could be rearmed and become a member of NATO, while also providing for British participation to relieve French fears that there would be no possible German predominance. It should be pointed out that the response of Eastern Europe to these agreements was a further hardening of the East/West division in the shape of the formation of the *Warsaw Pact*.

Unity via the back door

The year 1954 was a bad year for European unity since those advocating the creation of supra-national bodies had suffered a reverse and the establishment of the WEU, an organization cast more in the traditional intergovernmental mould, had thereafter held centre stage. However, such was the strength then of the European Movement that by 1955 new ideas were being put forward. The relaunching initiative came from the BENELUX countries. They produced a memorandum calling for the establishment of a general common market and for specific action in the fields of energy and transport.

> The year 1954 was a bad year for European unity since those advocating the creation of supra-national bodies had suffered a reverse

The basic idea behind the BENELUX approach was that political unity in Europe was likely to prove difficult to achieve. It was the ultimate objective but it was one which could be realized in the longer run. In the short and medium terms the objective should be overall economic integration. Experience gained in working together would then pave the way for the achievement of political unity, i.e. *political unity should be introduced through the 'back door'*. The memorandum called for the creation of institutions which would enable the establishment of a *European Economic Community* (EEC).

These ideas were considered at the meeting of the foreign ministers of the Six at Messina, Italy, in June 1955. They met with a favourable response. The governments of the Six resolved that work should begin with a view to establishing a general common market and an atomic energy pool. Moreover, a committee should be formed which would not merely study the problems involved but should also prepare the texts of the treaties necessary in order to carry out the agreed objectives. An intergovernmental committee was therefore created, and significantly enough, Paul-Henri Spaak, then Foreign Minister of Belgium, was made its president; what a triumph for members of the European Movement.

The Messina resolution recorded that since the UK was a member of the WEU and had been associated with the ECSC, through an *Agreement of Association* in 1954, it should be invited to participate in the work of the committee. The position of the other OEEC countries was not so clear. In fact, the question of whether they should be allowed to participate was left for later decision by the foreign ministers of the Six.

The Spaak Committee held its first meeting in July 1955. British representatives were present and then and subsequently played an active role in the committee's deliberations. However, as the committee's discussions continued, differences between the Six and the UK became evident. The UK was in favour of a free trade area arrangement, while the Six were agreed upon the formation of a customs union; the Messina resolution had explicitly called for this type of arrangement. Moreover, the UK felt that only a little extra machinery was needed to put the new arrangement into effect: the OEEC, perhaps somewhat strengthened, would suffice. This view was bound to anger the federalists who put emphasis on the creation of supranational institutions which should help achieve more than just economic integration. These differences culminated in the withdrawal of the UK representatives from the discussions in November 1955.

Meanwhile, the Spaak Committee forged ahead, although not without internal differences. For example, the French had apprehensions about the transition period allowed for the dismantling of the intra-member tariffs, escape clauses, the harmonization of social charges and the height of the common external tariffs (CETs); they wanted high CETs while the BENELUX nations desired low ones.

In April 1956, the Spaak Committee reported and its conclusions were considered by the foreign ministers of the Six in Venice in May of the same year. However, the attitudes among the Six were not uniform. On the one hand, the French liked the idea of an atomic energy community, but were not keen on the proposition for a general common market, while, on the other, the remaining five had reverse preferences. Nevertheless, in the end the Six agreed that the drafting of two treaties, one to create a general common market and another to establish an atomic energy community, should begin. Treaties were subsequently signed in Rome on 25 March 1957. These were duly ratified by the national parliaments of the Six. The *EEC* and *Euratom* came into being on 1 January 1958. Thus, in 1958 the Six belonged to three separate entities: the ECSC, the EEC and Euratom.

Initial aims

With history still in the background, one needs to ask about the initial objectives of the EEC. These are stated in Article 3 of its treaty and can be summarized as:

1 The establishment of free trade between the member nations such that *all* impediments on intra-union trade are eliminated. The EEC treaty did not simply ask for the elimination of tariffs, import quota restrictions and export subsidies, but for all measures which had an equivalent or similar effect (now generally referred to as *non-tariff trade barriers* – NTBs). Moreover, that treaty called for the creation of genuine free trade and therefore specified rudiments of common competition and industrial policies.

2 The creation of an intra-union free market for all factors of production by providing the necessary prerequisites for ensuring perfect factor mobility. These include taxes on, and subsidies to, capital, labour, enterprise, etc.

3 The formation of common policies with regard to particular industries which the members deemed it necessary to single out for special treatment, namely, agriculture (hence the *Common Agricultural Policy* – CAP) and transport (hence the *Common Transport Policy* – CTP).

4 The application of procedures by which the economic policies of the member nations could be co-ordinated and disequilibria in their balances of payments can be remedied.

5 The creation of a *European Social Fund* (ESF) in order to improve the possibilities of employment for workers and to contribute to the raising of their standard of living.

6 The establishment of a *European Investment Bank* (EIB) to facilitate the economic expansion of the EEC by opening up fresh resources.

7 The establishment of a common commercial policy vis-à-vis the outside world, i.e. the creation and management of the CETs, the adoption of a common stance in multinational and multilateral trade

negotiations, the granting of a *Generalized System of Preferences* (GSP) treatment to imports of certain manufactured and semi-manufactured products coming from the least developed countries (LDCs) and the reaching of trade pacts with associated nations.

It should be noted that a period of transition of 12 years, divided into three four-year stages, was granted for the elimination of intra-EEC trade barriers and for the establishment of the CETs.

Since in 1957 the Six belonged to the three entities, the aims of the EEC treaty should be supplemented by those pertaining to:

8 A common market for, and equitable access to, steel, iron and coal as expressed in the ECSC treaty.

9 A common approach to energy as expressed in the Euratom treaty.

Development of the EC

Each one of the three entities had its own institutions. These centred on a Council of Ministers (Council, hereafter) and a Commission (High Authority in the case of the ECSC: see earlier), backed by a European Parliament or Assembly and a Court of Justice. Although there were some differences of legal competences, it later became convenient to consider the three entities as branches of the same whole and, in this, the EEC became the dominant partner. When the *Merger Treaty* was passed in 1965, it seemed more logical to refer to the whole structure as the European Communities, or simply the European Community (EC), whose main constitutional base was the Treaty of Rome creating the EEC.

By the 1970s, however, it was clear that the EC needed institutional strengthening. Having completed the early tasks laid down in the treaties (see El-Agraa 2000, Ch. 25), further internal objectives had to be formulated and a way found to ensure that the EC could act more effectively on the international stage. The result was to bring national political leaders more closely into EC affairs by the introduction of summit meetings. These were formalized under the name of the *European Council* in 1974, but the first summit was held in 1969 (the end of the transition period), in The Hague, when the member states agreed that they were then so interdependent that they had no choice but to continue with the EC. That decision provided the necessary political will to reach agreement on the development of the CAP, on budgetary changes, on embarking on, yes, *economic and monetary union* (EMU) and, most importantly, on the need to work on enlargement. At that time, this meant settling the teasing question of relations with the UK, which, as we have seen, had vexed the EC from the very beginning.

Moreover, it was recognized that the EC needed institutional development to match its growing international stature. Its existing international responsibilities neither matched its economic weight nor allowed effective consideration of the political dimensions of its external economic relations. Individual members still conducted most of their external affairs themselves and could easily cut across EC interests, and this was apart from the issue of whether the EC should begin to move into the field of wider foreign affairs. Since the member states had very different interests and often different views on relations with the USA, with the USSR and on defence, it was clear that the EC was

> # Member states agreed that they were so interdependent that they had no choice but to continue with the EC

not ready to take over full competences. However, the foreign ministers were asked to study the means of achieving further political integration, on the assumption of enlargement, and to present a report. Consequently, the EC began gingerly to move into political co-operation with an emphasis on foreign affairs. This did not lead to a common foreign policy, but it did mean efforts were to be exerted to identify common aims and it led to further institutional innovation alongside the institutions of the EC rather than as part of them, although the new and the old gradually came together.

A second landmark summit was held in 1972 (in Paris) and was attended by the three new members: Denmark, Ireland and the UK. It devoted considerable attention to internal affairs and notably to the need to strengthen the social and regional aims of the EC as part of an ambitious programme designed to lead to EMU, thus to a full 'European Union'. It also saw a continuous need to act externally to maintain a constructive dialogue with the USA, Canada and Japan and for member states to make a concerted contribution to the *Conference on Security and Co-operation in Europe*. Foreign ministers were to meet more frequently to discuss this last issue. This meeting marked the realization that the heads of governments would have to meet more frequently than in the past. At first sight this seemed to strengthen the intergovernmental structure of the EC at the expense of the supra-national element, but this was not really the case. Rather, it showed that the future was a joint one, that the international climate was changing and often bleak and that if the members dealt with their internal economic difficulties alone then this could undermine the efforts of the EC to strengthen its economies. Informal discussion of general issues, whether economic or political, domestic or worldwide, was a necessary preliminary to action which often seemed stronger if it were to be EC based. Through the summit meetings and the *Political Co-operation Procedure* (ECP) the subject matter coming to the EC steadily enlarged (Collins 2000).

Indeed, the 1969–72 period can be described as one of great activity. Apart from what has just been mentioned, in 1970 the Six reached a common position on the development of a *Common Fisheries Policy* (CFP), although total agreement was not to be achieved until 1982. Also, at another Paris summit in 1973, agreement was reached on the development of new policies in relation to industry and science and research. Moreover, the summit envisaged a more active role for the EC in the area of regional policy and decided that a *European Regional Development Fund* (ERDF) should be created to channel EC resources into the development of the backward EC regions. Furthermore, later in the 1970s, the relationship between the EC and its ex-colonies was significantly reshaped in the form of the Lomé Convention. It is obvious from all these developments that the EC needed financial resources not only to pay for the day-to-day running of the EC but also to feed the various funds that were established: the ESF, the ERDF and, most important of all, the *European Guidance and Guarantee Fund* (EAGGF), to finance the CAP. In 1970, the EC took the important step of agreeing to introduce a system that would provide the EC, and specifically the EC general budget, with its 'own resources' (see Chapter 11), thus relieving it of the uncertainty of annual decisions on national contributions for its finances as well as endorsing its political autonomy in this respect. Another step of great importance was the decision that the European Parliament (EP, discussed later) should be elected directly by the people, not by national parliaments. In addition, the EC decided to grant the EP certain powers over the EC general budget, which proved to be a very significant development. Finally, but by no means least, there was the development of the political co-operation mechanism. It is important not to forget that the dedicated members of the European Movement had always hoped that the habit of co-operation in the economic field would spill over into the political arena, that is, into foreign policy matters.

By the 1980s, it was clear that the political and economic environment in which the EC operated was changing fast. Tumultuous events in the former USSR and the countries of the *Warsaw Pact* threw the institutional arrangements of Western Europe into disarray and brought the need to reassess defence requirements, the role of NATO and the continuance of the US defence presence. The unresolved issue of whether the EC needed a foreign policy, or at least some halfway house towards one, was bound to be raised once more. Meanwhile, the economic base upon which the EC has been able to develop had become much more uncertain. Recession, industrial change, higher unemployment (see Table 2.2), slower growth (see Table 2.3) and worries about European competitiveness undermined previous confidence.

Table 2.2 Unemployment rates for the EU and a selection of comparable economies (%)

Country	1973	1981	1985	1990	1995	2000
EU15	—	—	—	—	10.5	9.5
Austria	—	—	—	3.2	4.3	3.7
Belgium	3.0	11.0	14.0	7.2	9.3	11.3
Denmark	1.0	9.0	12.0	8.3	7.0	5.4
Finland	—	—	—	3.2	15.5	10.0
France	2.0	8.0	12.0	9.2	11.6	10.5
Germany[a]	1.0	5.0	7.0	4.7	8.1	8.7
Greece	—	—	8.0	7.0	9.1	10.8[b]
Ireland	6.0	11.0	15.0	13.0	12.2	11.1
Italy	5.0	8.0	12.0	11.4	11.5	11.0[c]
Luxembourg	*	*	*	1.6	2.9	2.4
Netherlands	2.0	8.0	12.0	7.4	7.1	2.7
Portugal	—	—	9.0	4.7	7.2	4.4[c]
Spain	—	—	22.0	16.0	22.7	15.1
Sweden	—	—	—	1.8	9.0	5.7
UK	2.0	8.0	16.0	6.8	8.6	5.9
Other						
Norway	—	2.0	5.5	5.1	4.9	3.3
Switzerland	—	—	1.2	0.5	3.3	2.4
Japan	—	2.2	2.1	2.1	3.2	4.9
Canada	—	7.5	10.2	8.1	9.4	6.8
United States	—	7.5	6.6	5.6	5.6	4.1

Notes: [a] Until 1990 the data are for the former West Germany only; [b] data are for 1998; c data are for 1999; * data included in Belgium's; — means not available

Sources: World Bank's *World Development Report* (various years); Eurostat's *Basic Statistics of the European Union* and *Statistical Yearbook*; ILO; *The Economist*

The twin issues of constitutional development and institutional reform continued to exercise EC circles but little progress was possible and the EC seemed to be running out of steam. The deepening of the integrative process required action which governments found contro- versial; the new members, now including Greece, Spain and Portugal, inevitably made for a less coherent group, while the recession hardened national attitudes towards the necessary compromise required for co-operative solutions. EC finances were constrained so that new policies could not be developed and this, in turn, led to bitter arguments about the resources devoted to the CAP. Internal divisions

Table 2.3 Average annual GDP growth rates for the EU and a selection of comparable economies (%)

Country	1960–70	1970–80	1980–90	1990–98
EU15				
Austria	4.5	3.4	2.2	2.0
Belgium	4.8	3.0	2.0	1.6
Denmark	4.7	2.2	2.3	2.8
Finland	4.6	3.0	3.3	2.0
France	5.7	3.2	2.3	1.5
Germany[a]	4.4	2.6	2.2	1.6
Greece	6.9	4.9	1.8	2.0
Ireland	4.2	4.9	3.2	7.5
Italy	5.3	3.8	2.4	1.2
Netherlands	5.5	2.9	2.3	2.6
Portugal	6.2	4.3	3.1	2.3
Spain	7.3	3.5	3.0	1.9
Sweden	4.4	1.9	2.3	1.2
UK	2.9	2.0	3.2	2.2
Other				
Norway	4.9	4.8	2.8	3.9
Switzerland	4.3	0.5	2.0	0.4
Japan	10.5	4.3	4.0	1.3
Canada	5.6	4.6	3.3	2.2
United States	4.3	2.8	3.0	2.9

Note: [a] Until 1990 the data are for the former West Germany only

Source: World Bank's *World Development Report* (various years)

were compounded by fears of a lack of dynamism in the EC economy, threatening a relative decline in world terms. Such worries suggested that a significant leap forward was required to ensure a real common market, to encourage new growth and at the same time to modernize EC institutions.

The single market

As the debate progressed, a major division emerged between those who were primarily interested in the political ideal of political union and who wished to develop the EC institutions accordingly and those, more pragmatic in approach, who stressed the need for new policies. It was not until 1985 that the lines of agreement could be settled. These were brought together in the *Single European Act* (SEA) which became operative on 1 July 1987. The SEA contained policy development which was based upon the intention of creating a true single market (usually referred to as the Single European Market – SEM – and *'internal market'*), by the end of 1992 (hence, EC92) with free movement of goods, services, capital and labour (the so-called *four freedoms*) rather than the patchy arrangements of the past. The SEA also introduced, or strengthened, other policy fields. These included responsibilities towards the environment; the encouragement of further action to promote health and safety at work; the promotion of technological research and development (R&D); work to strengthen economic and social cohesion so that weaker member nations may participate fully in the freer market; and co-operation in economic and monetary policy. In addition, the SEA brought foreign policy co-operation into scope and provided it with a more effective support than it had in the past, including its own secretariat, housed in the council building in Brussels. Institutionally, it was agreed that the Council would take decisions on a qualified majority vote (QMV: see pp. 53–4) in relation to the internal market, research, cohesion and improved working conditions and that, in such cases, the EP should share in decision making. These developments were followed later by agreement regarding the control of expenditure on the CAP, which, as we have seen, has been a source of heated argument for a number of years, and, most importantly, a fundamental change in the EC general budget.

At this juncture, given that the euro has been justified on the grounds that it is vital for the internal market, it is necessary to state that, according to the official EU Commission estimates (see Cecchini 1988 and Emerson *et al.* 1988), the single market was expected to increase EC GDP by between 2.5 and 7 per cent and employment by between 2 and 5 million jobs, and Baldwin (1989) believes the former figure might be between 11 and 35 per cent when allowance is made for the changes in the rate of growth implicit in the Cecchini calculations. In spite of the fact that the assumptions on which these forecasts were based left a lot to be desired (El-Agraa 2000), nevertheless, the single market provided a goal for the next few years and the EC became preoccupied with the necessary preparations (300 directives had to be passed and then incorporated into national law for this purpose), giving evidence of its ability to work together as one unit. However, it also brought new complications. It raised the question of how much power should be held by the EC institutions, presented member states with heavy internal programmes to complete the changes necessary for the single market, and exposed the very different economic conditions in member states which were bound to affect their fortunes in the single market. Meanwhile, the unification of Germany fundamentally changed its position within the EC by giving it more political and economic weight, but at the same time it required it to expend considerable effort eastwards.

A further challenge at the time came from new bids for membership; so far there has been one withdrawal: the position of Greenland was renegotiated in 1984, but it remains associated and has a special agreement to regulate mutual fishing interests. The single market policy finally convinced the doubters in Western Europe that they should try to join. This was both a triumph and an embarrassment for the EC in that it was preoccupied with its own internal changes and a belief that it had not yet fully come to terms with the southern enlargement which had brought in Greece, Portugal and Spain. An uncertain reaction was shown in that some member states wished to press on with enlargement as a priority, while others wished to complete the single market and tighten internal policies before opening the doors. A closer economic relationship was negotiated between the EC and the EFTA countries, except for Switzerland, to form the EEA which was widely assumed to be a preliminary step towards membership. Austria, Finland, Sweden and Switzerland all formally applied between 1989 and 1992 and Norway shortly followed them; Switzerland's application remains on the table

> **The single market policy finally convinced the doubters in Western Europe that they should try to join**

(see 'An overview' above). Hungary, Poland and Czechoslovakia signed association agreements and hoped that they might join in a few years' time. Turkey and Morocco applied in 1987, although the former application was laid aside then and the latter rejected. Cyprus and Malta applied in 1990. Later, most states in Central and Eastern Europe expressed their desire to join and formal negotiations were opened with those most likely to succeed. However, the instability in the Balkans and the war in Kosovo showed the need to hasten the process and, at Helsinki in December 1999, it was agreed to open accession talks with the group originally thought of as being in the second round (see 'An overview'). There is now the active list of the 13 candidates mentioned earlier in this chapter, which include Turkey, and a recent change in regime has brought Croatia closer to joining this group.

It may not seem easy to generalize about the issues involved in admitting such a variety of countries for membership, but the brief history shows that integration was almost meant to apply to all of Europe. However, the EU has a series of agreements with the applicants through which it provides aid and advice on development and reform. In particular, as mentioned earlier, the EU is looking for economic reform, the development of democratic political institutions and the protection of minority and human rights as necessary preconditions for closer relationships before full membership. Partnership and co-operation agreements with Russia and the newly independent states also exist, but they do not aspire to join.

Clearly, an organization with such a large and varied membership would be very different from the original EEC of the Six, and the application challenged received wisdom as to its nature. This is one reason why pursuing the question of enlargement was made consequent upon the finalizing of the Maastricht Treaty (see later) and agreement upon new financial and budgetary arrangements for the existing member states. Continuing issues about defence and the appropriate reaction to conditions in Central and Eastern Europe, the Gulf War and the collapse of Yugoslavia all suggested that further consideration of foreign and defence capabilities was important.

It was, therefore, against a troubled background that the EC set up two intergovernmental conferences (IGCs) to prepare the way for a meeting of the European Council in Maastricht in December 1991 which produced a new blueprint for the future. It aimed to integrate the EC further through setting out a timetable for full EMU, introduced institutional changes and developed political competences, the whole being brought together in the *Treaty on European Union* (or Maastricht Treaty) of which the EC should form a part of a wider European Union.

It is not surprising that the treaty's ratification process, for which some have argued not a great deal of time was allowed, produced furious argument across Western Europe. Although each nation had its own peculiar worries, a general characteristic which the treaty made obvious was the width of the gap between political elites and the voters in modern society. Even though political leaders rapidly expressed contrition that they had failed to provide adequate explanation for their moves, they seemed less able to accept that there were strong doubts about many of the proposed new arrangements as being the best way forward and that a period of calm reflection, with less frenetic development, might in the end serve the EC and its people better (Collins 2000).

Hence, Maastricht left contentious problems for the Amsterdam conference to tackle. Although the hard core, comprising changes to the voting system in the Council and the size of the Commission, was not tackled (but the 2000 Treaty of Nice does so – see later), the 1997 Treaty of Amsterdam was useful in updating aims and policies, in clarifying the position regarding foreign and defence policies and justice and home affairs, and in strengthening the social side. The treaty itself modified the existing treaties, notably those on the EEC and Union, and these, together with the *acquis communautaire* (legislation deriving from the treaties), can be considered as the constitution of the EU. Supplementary treaties must be used when developments go beyond the existing ones. Past examples include changes in budget procedures, agreements to admit new members and the single market (see earlier). In addition, a unique arrangement was attached to the Maastricht Treaty in 1991: an agreement and protocol were annexed because the UK could not accept changes in the social field endorsed by the other members. The EC, i.e. EEC, ECSC and Euratom, forms the most developed section of the Union and its legislation takes precedence over national decisions in the appropriate field. A moment's reflection will show that this is a necessary precondition for the EC to work at all; it would otherwise be impossible to create a single economic unit, to establish the confidence needed between members or to handle external relations.

The European Union

The Amsterdam Treaty gives the EU a more coherent structure and a modern statement of its aims and policies and brings some necessary improvements in the working of the institutions. Naturally, it highlights the new aspects, but these are not necessarily more important than more long-standing policies – for example, publicity is given to provisions on foreign and defence policy, yet they remain far less developed than arrangements in the economic sphere. Despite being thought of as a tidying up of the Maastricht loose ends (Collins 2000), the treaty is a substantial document, but naturally greatly overlaps Maastricht's. Thus, it has three parts on substantive amendments to previous treaties, their simplification and modernization and their renumbering, ratification procedures and official language versions. In addition, there are an annexe, 13 protocols, often dealing with very difficult issues, 51 declarations and eight declarations by individual member states.

The post-Amsterdam EU has broad objectives, but again these naturally overlap with those in the Maastricht Treaty. The classic aim, set out long ago, is to lay the foundations of, and subsequently develop, the 'ever closer union'. It promotes economic and social progress, an aim which includes the abolition of internal frontiers, better economic and social cohesion to assist the less-developed members to catch up with the EU average (facilitated by the creation in 1993 of a *Cohesion Fund*) and an EMU, complete with a single currency (see Chapter 3). It wishes to assert an international identity through a common and defence policy and new provisions are designed to enhance this and to draw closer to the WEU (see earlier), which has been dormant since it was launched in 1954 and will become the equivalent of an EU defence force. Thus for the first time the EU is set to have a common defence policy with the implication that the WEU will eventually be responsible for implementing decisions of an inevitable political union. Appreciation for (or is it accommodation of?) NATO was reiterated by stating that the revival of the WEU is to be linked to NATO, thus ensuring a continued alliance with the USA and Canada for the defence of Europe. It has not only introduced a formal Union citizenship, but taken steps to strengthen the commitment to democracy, to individual rights, to promote equality and to combat discrimination. It has a procedure to be followed should a member state appear to breach human rights. The treaty has also established the EU as an area of free movement, security and justice and is attempting to establish clearer and more uniform rules in these fields. These goals are supplemented by those of the EEC treaty (see 'The initial aims'). Internally, the EU has general economic objectives relating to the single market, agriculture and transport, the aim of economic and social cohesion and a new emphasis on policy making in employment, social and environmental matters. The need for enhanced competitiveness for EU industry, the promotion of R&D, the construction of trans-European infrastructure, the attainment of a high

level of health protection, better education, training and cultural development all find their place. Recognition is given to development
policies, to consumer protection and to measures in energy policy,
consumer protection and tourism. There are, of course, a host of
subsidiary and supporting objectives.

After many arguments, the concept of flexible integration has been
brought out in the open. Articles 40, 43 and 44 (EU) allow some member
states to establish closer co-operation between themselves with the aim
of developing Union policies which not all members wish to pursue, but
subject to veto by dissenting members. This was fully endorsed in the
2000 Nice Treaty by stating that groups of eight or more member
countries may pursue greater integration in certain areas. Such a move
must be supported by a majority of members, not harm the interests of
others and allow the non-participating members to be involved in the
discussion of developments, but not to vote on them. There are some
important examples of policies which are less than fully inclusive. They
include membership of the single currency, the Danish opt-outs from the
free-movement provisions although accepting the Schengen principle
and from decisions with defence implications, and the British and Irish
non-acceptance of the abolition of border controls.

The Maastricht conference touched fears of the creation of a super-
state, which it attempted to counter by introducing the doctrine of
subsidiarity, and the Treaty of Amsterdam tried to clarify this further.
Article 5 (EC) explains that, where the EC does not have exclusive
competence, it may only proceed if the member states cannot pursue
the action themselves and it is an objective better achieved by
Community action. A protocol attached to the treaty has tried to clarify
how this concept should be applied and, in particular, insists that the
reasons for action must be stated, Community action must be simple
and limited and a report must be given to Community institutions on
what has been done. These provisions are meant as a check on an
insidious growth of Community power, allowing it to slip in a direction
which has never been agreed. This brake is supported by the right of
member states to bring a case in the Court of Justice arguing that the
EC is extending its powers unjustifiably.

An element in the debate about subsidiarity is doubt concerning the
remoteness of decision making in Brussels. There is a need to make the
EU more responsive to the needs of the general public and more
sensitive to the effects of the intrusiveness that EU legislation appears
to bring. The 'democratic deficit' is an issue that has long been
discussed and there are several ways of addressing it, of which greater
powers to the EP is one. Individuals have long had the right to petition

the EP and this has been supported by the appointment of an ombudsman, chosen by the EP but independent of it.

A particular issue is the undermining of national parliaments, especially those that have an important legislative function and that have found it hard to find ways of exercising control over the EC. In practice, they have been limited to scrutiny of proposals which, once they are in the advanced stage, are very difficult to change. Some efforts have also been made, through scrutiny committees, to discuss general issues, thus helping to suggest policy positions for the future, while Denmark, in particular, has tried to define the parameters within which ministers may negotiate. A protocol of the Amsterdam Treaty tries to increase the influence of national parliaments. It requires that all Commission consultation papers be forwarded promptly, that proposed legislation should be made available in time for parliaments to consider it and that there should be a six-week gap between a legislative proposal's being submitted to the EP and the date it is sent to the Council. A great deal is, of course, up to national parliaments to keep abreast of events and to improve contacts with the EP. Associated with this was the general acceptance of the need to keep the public better informed and to provide access to Community documentation. A declaration attached to the treaty stresses the importance of transparency, access to

> ## The right to petition the EP was buttressed by the establishment of an ombudsman, appointed by the EP, but independent in investigation

documents and the fight against fraud, Article 255 (EC) giving citizens a right to access official documents. A further declaration accepts the importance of improving the quality of drafting in legislation. Over the years, efforts have been made, too, to help individuals question the EC. As mentioned, the right to petition the EP was buttressed by the establishment of an ombudsman, appointed by the EP, but independent in investigation. A further change, directly affecting individuals, was to confer the citizenship of the Union on the nationals of member states. Although such changes are intended to encourage a greater openness in decision making, it will take time for them to be implemented. Actual decision making in the Council remains private.

Flexible policies and subsidiarity have been tackled together, although they deal with very different circumstances, because they both suggest that the EU is still uneasily balanced between the two opposing views on how to organize Western Europe which have been so eloquently expressed since the end of World War II. The treaty, to some observers, is one more step towards a federal Europe, but to others, it is a means of keeping a check upon this drive and retaining a degree of national governmental control. The final outcome is still uncertain.

Unfounded allegations

The rest of these developments are either too recent to require mentioning (the Treaty of Nice both amends QMV – see later – and extends it to new areas, including trade in services; asks the larger member nations to drop their second commissioner after 2005; limits the total number of commissioners to 20 after 2007; and proclaims the Charter of Rights, but without legal force) or are covered in Chapter 3, but adequate ground has been covered to substantiate two points. First, those who wanted, and continue to desire, a United States of Europe have been seeking mainly a voice for Europe, i.e. they wanted a nation able to compete on equal terms with the USA and Japan, not one to be the next hegemon, hence the assertion by Wyplosz (1997) that the EU wants the euro to replace the dollar has no factual basis. Second, the driving force behind European unity is the achievement of eternal peace in Europe. Feldstein (1997) questions the wisdom of the creation of one nation for peace purposes in the modern age, but his argument is unconvincing, especially since he does not distinguish between *voluntary* and *enforced* unity and also switches from long-term positions:

> **The euro is an essential ingredient in the process leading to the final goal of European political unity**

'War may seem unthinkable in the current age of weapons of mass destruction. Unfortunately, such a view was widely held before both World War I and . . . II' (p. 24) to projecting into the indefinite future unqualified short-term factors: 'Russia . . . is now relatively weak and focusing on achieving economic reform and industrial rebuilding' (p. 26) and 'The ethnic-based struggles in eastern Europe and the former Soviet Union and the splitting of Czechoslovakia . . . show that separation may be a more stable peace equilibrium' (p. 26). He cannot have it both ways and he is not justified in building straw men only to knock them down.

Hopefully, this short history of European unity has clearly demonstrated why the euro is an essential ingredient in the process leading to the final goal of European political unity. Also, contrary to claims by Feldstein (1997), it has shown that the achievement of this objective is not determined by France and Germany alone. Indeed, in this respect, one has to stress that EU decisions require either unanimity (in all major decisions such as fiscal harmonization and the admittance of new members) or simple or QMV, which used to cover 80 per cent of EU decisions, but as mentioned already has been extended to new areas. In the case of unanimity, obviously each member nation has a veto; hence no nation can be coerced into accepting positions it deems detrimental to its interests. Simple majority requires eight out of the present 15 member nations to agree to a decision; hence France and Germany cannot call the tune 'at the table'. Before the Nice Treaty, QMV required 62 votes out of a total of 87, where France, Germany, Italy and the UK each had 10, Spain 8, Belgium, Greece, the Netherlands and Portugal 5 each, Austria and Sweden 4, Denmark, Finland and Ireland 3, and Luxembourg 2; hence, even the four largest nations plus Spain could not have conspired to force a decision since they needed the support of at least three more members, making the total number of nations match that in the case of simple majority. However, the smaller nations actually had more say under QMV since the population of Germany is about 82 million and that of France, Italy and the UK about 58 million each; that of Denmark and Finland is each about 5 million, while Ireland's is less than 4 million. Thus, taking the votes for France, Italy and the UK as a point of reference (one vote per 5.8 million persons), Germany should have had 14, Spain a generous 7, Denmark and Finland a generous 1, and Luxembourg and Ireland none. Not only that, but EU rules dictated that if 23–5 votes could be mustered against an intended decision by QMV, the Council should endeavor to reach, within a reasonable time, a satisfactory solution that could be adopted by at least 65 votes, thus ensuring that Luxembourg could not have been a deciding factor in terms of the eight nations needed, and that the smallest nations needed to entice only two of the nations with five votes each to activate this condition. Furthermore, EU rules dictated that if a Council decision is to be taken on a proposal not originating from the EU Commission, the required 62 votes should be cast by at least 10 nations. Hence, the assertion that France and Germany will dictate what should happen is far from reality and confuses 'political clout' with 'ability to persuade' and 'being seen to set an example'. This general picture remains basically true after the Nice Treaty in spite of the increased votes for the larger countries (29 each for France, Germany, Italy and the UK; 27 for Spain; 13 for the Netherlands; 12 each for Belgium, Greece and

Portugal; 10 for Austria and Sweden; 7 for each of Denmark, Finland and Ireland; and 4 for Luxembourg), which, when the EU admits the 12 Eastern and Central European nations, would require 96 out of a total of 134 votes, with 39 for a blocking minority.

Has the EU been successful?

This is a question that is often being, and sometimes has to be, asked even though the coverage in this chapter would suggest that it is, to some extent, meaningless. As we have seen, the ultimate objective of those who founded the EU is to bring about the political unity of Europe. Even when all the member nations have adopted the euro, the EU would still not have reached this goal and in this sense it has not been successful. However, the EU neither started with the whole of Europe nor does it presently comprise it, and it has reached its total membership of 15 in stages, through three enlargements and an accession. Each one of these additions brought with it new problems which frustrated the progress that had been achieved before it. This was compounded by tumultuous changes in the world economy over which the EC could not be held responsible (see later). Thus, the very fact that the EU is still here and has been able to achieve all the developments that have been discussed, is a clear sign that it has been very successful, i.e. it has survived against all odds.

If by the question one is asking whether the EU has been able to achieve the goals it set itself for each policy area, then the answer would require a whole book (see El-Agraa 2000). Here, it suffices to state that although EU progress has been variable, it has to a large extent been successful, especially in the cases of enhanced intra-EU trade (see Tables 2.4 and 2.5 and allow for variable membership, Ireland's historical closeness to the UK and EU-EFTA intimacy through the EEA), the CAP and EMU.

However, the enhancement of intra-EU trade may be due to better allocation of resources ('trade creation' in technical jargon), at the expense of cheaper imports from outside the EU ('trade diversion') or both; one can never rest assured which one has been its major cause (see El-Agraa 1999). Moreover, there are not many analysts who would condone either the CAP achievements or the methods by which they have been reached. With respect to the EMU, as we shall see in Chapter 3, it was first adopted in the early 1970s and was to be introduced in three stages. Although important measures were subsequently introduced in order to achieve it (indeed the first stage was successfully negotiated and the second was progressing nicely), the goal of reaching this aim eventually failed. This was due to the global economic difficulties of the early 1970s (the Nixon and oil shocks) and to the first enlargement of the EC (as just mentioned, each of the three new member nations brought with it a new set of problems), not to any lack of real effort on the part of the total membership. Be that as it may, it is now the reality, with the euro as the common currency for 12 of the present 15 members of the EU.

With regard to the variable progress, one should, of course, point out that in contrast to this somewhat rosy picture, a number of NTBs either still remain or have sprung up in the process. However, as we have seen, the aim of the internal market is to abolish these either directly or indirectly via the harmonization of technical specifications which will promote the right environment for getting rid of them. All these NTBs are fully set out in the White Paper of 1984 and comprehensively discussed in Emerson *et al.* (1988).

If by the question one is enquiring whether the EU has been able to perform better in terms of both reduced rates of unemployment and

Table 2.4 Exports to EC6, EC9, EC12 and EU15 for various years (% share of total exports of exporting country)

Exporter	1957	1974	1981	1986	1990	1995	1998
EU15	—	—	—	—	66.9	64.0	62.9
Austria	—	—	—	60.1	67.9	65.8	62.9
Belgium[a]	46.1	69.6	70.0	72.9	80.0	77.1	75.8
Denmark	31.2	43.1	46.7	46.8	68.6	66.6	67.1
Finland	—	—	—	38.3	60.2	57.5	56.1
France	25.1	53.2	48.2	57.8	65.4	63.0	62.4
Germany	29.2	53.2	46.9	50.8	64.0	58.2	56.4
Greece	52.5	50.1	43.3	63.5	68.3	60.1	50.7
Ireland	—	74.1	69.9	71.9	78.6	73.9	70.1
Italy	24.9	45.4	43.2	53.5	62.8	57.3	56.2
Netherlands	41.6	70.8	71.2	75.7	81.5	79.9	78.8
Portugal	22.2	48.2	53.7	68.0	81.2	80.1	81.6
Spain	29.8	47.4	43.0	60.9	67.7	67.9	70.5
Sweden	—	—	—	50.0	62.1	59.6	57.9
UK	14.6	33.4	41.2	47.9	57.4	58.2	58.0

Notes: [a] Includes Luxembourg; — means not available

Sources: Eurostat's *Basic Statistics of the European Union* and *Statistical Yearbook*

enhanced rates of GDP growth, then the answer is also mixed. As Table 2.2 shows, the unemployment rates for the EU are not easy to interpret. For example, if one were to compare 2000, the latest year for which there are comparable data, with 1995, the time of the last enlargement, then except for Belgium and Germany, all EU nations have managed to reduce their unemployment rates. However, one cannot attribute this to EU membership except arguably for the three countries joining then. For the others, comparison must be made with reference to the time when they joined the EC and then the picture is far from clear. If one were to compare relative to the USA, then the EU nations must be deemed to have failed the test. If the comparator has to be Japan and Switzerland, then although all EU nations except for Luxembourg have higher rates, these two countries have been experiencing increases in their rates; hence the EU has performed better. This deduction is reinforced in relation to Japan when one hastens to add that many analysts believe the rate for Japan does not reveal all since a number of those in employment would not be classified as such if one were to standardize the system for recording the data (see El-Agraa 1988).

Table 2.5 | Imports from EC6, EC9, EC12 and EU15 for various years (% share of total imports of importing country)

Importer	1957	1974	1981	1986	1990	1995	1998
EU15	—	—	—	63.2	64.2	64.1	62.5
Austria	—	—	—	69.3	71.4	75.9	73.3
Belgium[a]	43.5	6.16	59.3	73.5	74.3	72.8	70.9
Denmark	31.2	45.5	47.9	70.4	69.7	71.8	70.3
Finland	—	—	—	57.6	60.1	65.0	65.7
France	21.4	47.6	48.2	67.6	68.2	68.5	67.0
Germany	23.5	48.1	48.2	61.6	62.1	60.4	58.3
Greece	40.8	43.3	50.0	61.3	67.8	70.1	65.1
Ireland	—	68.3	74.7	76.1	73.9	64.9	61.5
Italy	21.4	42.4	40.7	59.5	62.0	60.9	61.6
Netherlands	41.1	57.4	52.4	64.5	63.8	63.2	57.7
Portugal	37.1	43.5	38.0	62.1	72.1	73.9	77.2
Spain	21.3	35.8	29.0	54.4	62.3	68.5	68.5
Sweden	—	—	—	65.5	63.1	68.6	69.2
UK	12.1	30.0	39.4	56.3	56.5	54.6	53.3

Notes: [a] Includes Luxembourg; — means not available

Sources: Eurostat's *Basic Statistics of the European Union* and *Statistical Yearbook*

With regard to the rates of GDP growth, a comparison of the data provided in Table 2.3 for 1960–98 indicates that, except recently for Ireland, all the countries concerned have, on the whole, experienced a consistent decline. Thus, one is left with an equally ambiguous answer.

If by the question one is asking whether or not the EU has been able to perform better in the world economy as a result of being one trading bloc, then no answer is possible. As shown elsewhere (see El-Agraa 1999), the measurement of changes in economic variables before and after integration, a must for answering such a question, is so fraught with difficulties that it does not matter how advanced econometric techniques may become: no such answer can ever be achieved. Some analysts have attempted an answer by simply looking at the performance of the EU relative to its major competitors in a controlled market (see Winters 1993), but their conclusion that the EU has not been successful in this respect cannot be taken seriously, given what has just been stated and the fact that the EU has been having variable membership. In short, the appropriate question in this particular respect should have been: have the EU member nations done better as a result of membership of the EU than they would have done in isolation or in alternative blocs? However, given what we have seen in this chapter and the ultimate aspirations of the EU, this is a question that we shall never be able to answer.

Conclusion

One cannot escape the conclusion that although the EU has not yet arrived, it has gone a long way towards achieving the dream of its founding fathers: the creation of a United States of Europe. The long march is easily explicable in terms of the difficulties inherent in securing the necessary compromises needed for going forward and accommodating new members and the tackling of unforeseen economic and political problems, from both within and without. It does not really matter when the EU will realize its dream since what is important is that one

> **The creation of a powerful united European economy is an achievement in its own right**

should never forget that that vision has been the guiding light without which disaster might have struck at any time. It behoves of all those who would like to think of the EU as, or dearly want to reduce it to, a trading bloc to think twice, even though the creation of a powerful united European economy is an achievement in its own right.

Notes

1 See El-Agraa (1997) for a comprehensive coverage of all such clubs, their practical experience, theoretical rationale, empirical problems and adherence to the rules of the World Trade Organization (WTO), i.e. Article XXIV of the General Agreement on Tariffs and Trade (GATT), WTO's predecessor. For a technical coverage, see El-Agraa (1999), and for the particular case of the EU, see El-Agraa (1998, 2000).

2 As we have seen, in some quarters this meant a *United States of Europe*.

3 Belgium, the Netherlands and Luxembourg agreed in 1944 to form a customs union, which did not become effective until 1948.

4 Its critics called it a debating society.

5 Its unanimity rule and the fact that no powers could be delegated to an independent commission or *commissariat* were extremely frustrating for them.

6 Which would consist of a *People's Chamber* elected by direct universal suffrage and a *Senate* elected by national parliaments.

References

Baldwin, Richard E. (1989) 'The growth effects of 1992', *Economic Policy*, 9.

Cecchini, P. (1988) *The European Challenge 1992: The Benefits of a Single Market*. London: Wildwood House.

Collins, C. Doreen E. (2000) 'History and institutions' in El-Agraa 2000.

Commission of the European Communities (1970) *Report to the Council and Commission on the Realization by Stages of Economic and Monetary Union in the Community* (The Werner Report), *Bulletin of the European Communities*, Supplement 11. Brussels.

Commission of the European Communities (1975) *Report of the Study Group 'Economic and Monetary Union 1980'* (The Marjolin Report). Brussels.

Commission of the European Communities (1997) *Report of the Study Group on the Role of Public Finance in European Integration* (The MacDougall Report). Brussels.

Commission of the European Union (1997) *Agenda 2000: For a Stronger and Wider Union*. Brussels.

Eichengreen, Barry (1993) 'European monetary unification', *Journal of Economic Literature*, XXXI, September, pp. 1321–57.

El-Agraa, Ali M. (1980) *The Economics of the European Community*. Oxford: Philip Allan; New York: St. Martin's Press.

El-Agraa, Ali M. (1988) *Japan's Trade Frictions: Realities or Misconceptions*. London: Macmillan.

El-Agraa, Ali M. (1989) *The Theory and Measurement of International Economic Integration*. London: Macmillan; New York: St. Martin's Press.

El-Agraa, Ali M. (1998) *The European Union: History, Institutions, Economics and Policies*. Hemel Hempstead: Prentice Hall Europe.

El-Agraa, Ali M. (1999) *Regional Integration: Experience, Theory and Measurement*. London: Macmillan; New York: Barnes & Noble.

El-Agraa, Ali M. (2000) *The European Union: Economics and Policies*. London: Pearson Education, Prentice Hall and Financial Times.

El-Agraa, Ali M. (ed.) (1997) *Economic Integration Worldwide*. London: Macmillan; New York: St. Martin's Press.

Emerson, M., Aujean, M., Catinat, M., Goybet, P. and Jaquemin, A. (1988) *The Economics of 1992: The EC Commission's Assessment of the Economic Effects of Completing the Internal Marketing*. Oxford: Oxford University Press.

Feldstein, Martin (1997) 'The political economy of the European Economic and Monetary Union: political sources of an economic liability', *Journal of Economic Perspectives*, 11, 4, Fall, pp. 23–42.

Fleming, John M. (1971) 'On exchange rate unification', *The Economic Journal*, 81, pp. 467–88.

Kenen, Peter B. (1968) *Managing Exchange Rates*. London: Routledge.

Krugman, Paul R. (1990) 'Policy problems in a monetary union' in R. de Grauwe and L. Papademos (eds) *The European Monetary System in the 1990s*. Harlow: Longman.

Lipgens, Walter (1982) *A History of European Integration*. Oxford: Oxford University Press.

McKinnon, Ronald I. (1963) 'Optimum currency areas', *American Economic Review*, 53, pp. 717–25.

Mundell, Robert A. (1961) 'A theory of optimum currency areas', *American Economic Review*, 51, September, pp. 657–65.

Robson, Peter (1990) *The Economics of International Integration*. London: Allen & Unwin.

Winters, L. Alan (1993) 'Goals and own goals in European trade policy', *The World Economy*, 15.

World Bank (2001) *World Development Report 2000/2001*. Oxford: Oxford University Press.

Wyplosz, Charles (1997) 'EMU: why and how it might happen', *Journal of Economic Perspectives*, 11, 4, Fall, pp. 3–22.

The euro and EMU

3

EMU and the euro

Ali M. El-Agraa

Introduction

On 2 May 1998, the 15 member nations of the European Union (EU) decided that 11 of them would adopt the euro on 1 January 1999 as their common currency. Now that the euro is a reality as an official currency and will begin to circulate as everyday money by the beginning of the year 2002 in 12 EU nations (Greece joined in 2001), this decision is regarded as one of the most, if not *the* most, significant events of the 20th century. This is because the

> The majority of people equate currencies with national sovereignties and they cannot comprehend why EU nations wanted to sacrifice them

majority of people equate currencies with national sovereignties and deem both sacrosanct; hence they cannot comprehend why EU nations wanted to sacrifice them. In this chapter, I want to consider why the EU nations wanted the euro, to describe how it came about and to prognosticate on its significance now and in the future.

Before doing so, however, one should draw attention to the fact that the euro is part of *EMU*, a strange 'bird', which in the field of 'international economic integration' generally stands for 'economic and monetary union', but in the particular case of the EU, refers to 'European monetary unification'. Therefore, the chapter begins by defining the term itself and clarifying the difference in its usage, before going on to describe the road taken by the EU to achieve it.

What is EMU?

For a proper understanding of EMU, a brief reference to international economic integration may be helpful. This area of international economics, which has been growing in importance for about five decades, is concerned with the formation of 'clubs' between nations. Such clubs can take various forms, but all of them have a common element: the elimination of restrictions on trade in goods and services between the members. If that is all they intend to do, the club would be called a 'free trade area' (FTA), examples of which are the European Free Trade Association (EFTA) and the North American Free Trade Agreement (NAFTA), although NAFTA's arrangements also extend to investment. However, if the members decide also to have a common commercial policy towards the non-member nations, the club would be labelled a 'customs union' (CU). If members of a CU also agree to extend free movement to their people, companies, technology and capital, their club would be named a 'common market' (CM). If a CM decides to adopt common monetary and fiscal policies, it would be termed an 'economic union' (EcU). It is interesting to note that certain Asia-Pacific nations have been demanding that all such clubs should also extend their privileged arrangements to non-members, resulting in what is now coined 'open regionalism', and believe that the Asia Pacific Economic Co-operation (APEC) forum is such a club. However, many analysts cannot comprehend how a discriminatory association can be non-discriminatory.[1]

Within this club context, the EU is more than an economic union, given that 12 of its members have adopted the single currency, the euro. Moreover, when the euro is in full circulation at the start of 2002, the EU would look very much like a political union since all that would be needed to transform into a single nation is to galvanize its common defence policy and introduce appropriate changes to its institutional and political structure: it is as simple or difficult as that!

EMU, as generally used in international economic integration, has two essential components: an exchange rate union and capital market integration. An exchange rate union is established when member countries have permanently and irrevocably fixed exchange rates among themselves. When exchange rates are so fixed, the member nations will have in effect one currency, which is the EU version of EMU, but a single currency is not a necessity. Capital market integration refers to capital convertibility, which means the permanent absence of all exchange controls between the member nations for both capital and current transactions, including interest and dividend payments. Note that convertibility for trade transactions is needed by all the mentioned clubs if they are to promote free trade among themselves. In the context of the EU, the harmonization of relevant taxes and measures affecting the capital market is also essential since capital mobility in its own right is enshrined in the EU treaties; recall that the EU is partly a common market.

In practice, this definition of monetary integration should specifically include the following:

- an explicit harmonization of monetary policies
- a common pool of foreign exchange reserves
- a single central bank.

There are important reasons for including these elements. Suppose union members decide either that one of their currencies will be a reference currency or that a new unit of account will be established. Also assume that each member country has its own foreign exchange reserves and conducts its own monetary and fiscal policies. If a member finds itself running out of reserves, it will have to engage in a monetary and fiscal contraction sufficient to restore the reserve position. This will necessitate the fairly frequent meeting of the finance ministers or central bank governors, to consider whether or not to change the parity of the reference currency. If they do decide to change it, all the member currencies will have to move with it. Such a situation could create the sorts of difficulty which plagued the *Bretton Woods System*:

- Each finance minister might fight for the rate of exchange that was most suitable for his/her country. This might make bargaining hard; agreement might become difficult to reach and the whole system might be subject to continuous strain.
- Each meeting might be accompanied by speculation about its outcome. This might result in undesirable speculative private capital movement into or out of the union.

- The difficulties that might be created by the first two items might result in the reference currency's being permanently fixed relative to outside currencies, e.g. the US dollar.

- However, the system does allow for the possibility of the reference currency's floating relative to non-member currencies or floating within a band. If the reference currency does float, it might do so in response to conditions in its own market. This would be the case, however, only if the union required the monetary authorities in the partner countries to vary their exchange rates so as to maintain constant parities relative to the reference currency. They would then have to buy and sell the reserve currency so as to maintain or bring about the necessary exchange rate alteration. Therefore, the monetary authorities of the reference currency would, in fact, be able to determine the exchange rate for the whole union.

- Such a system does not guarantee the permanence of the parities between the union currencies that is required by the appropriate specification of monetary integration. There is the possibility that the delegates will not reach agreement or that one of the partners might finally choose not to deflate to the extent necessary to maintain its rate at the required parity or that a partner in surplus might choose neither to build up its reserves nor to inflate as required and so might allow its rate to rise above the agreed level.

In order to avoid such difficulties, it is necessary to include in monetary integration the three elements specified. The central bank would operate in the market so that the exchange parities were permanently maintained among the union currencies and, at the same time, it would allow the rate of the reference currency to fluctuate, or to alter intermittently, relative to the outside reserve currency. For instance, if the foreign exchange reserves in the common pool were running down, the common central bank would allow the reference currency, and with it all the partner currencies, to depreciate. This would have the advantage of economizing in the use of foreign exchange reserves, since all partners would most likely not tend to be in deficit or surplus at the same time. Also surplus countries would automatically be helping deficit countries, which would make Keynes smile in his grave, since he fought hard, but to no avail, to establish this as a working principle for the international financial order that created the IMF.

However, without explicit policy co-ordination, a monetary union would not be effective. If each country conducted its own monetary policy, and hence could engage in as much domestic credit creation as it wished, surplus countries would be financing deficit nations without any incentives for the deficit countries to restore equilibrium. If one country ran a large deficit, the union exchange rate would depreciate, but this might put some partner countries into surplus. If wage rates were rising in the member countries at different rates, while productivity growth did not differ in such a way as to offset the effects on relative prices, those partners with the lower inflation rates would be permanently financing the other partners.

Without explicit policy co-ordination, a monetary union would not be effective

---

Monetary integration which explicitly includes the three require-ments specified will therefore enable the partners to do away with all these problems right from the start. Incidentally, this also suggests the advantages of having a single currency.

Gains and losses from EMU membership

Economic analysis points to both economic gains and losses from EMU membership. The gains can be briefly summarized as follows:

1 The common pool of foreign exchange reserves already discussed has the incidental advantage of economizing in the use of foreign exchange reserves since member nations will not be likely go into deficit *simultaneously* and intra-union trade transactions will no longer be financed by foreign exchange. In the context of the EU this will reduce the role of the US dollar or reduce the EU's dependence on the dollar.

2 The adoption of the euro should transform the currency into a major world medium able to compete with the US dollar or Japanese yen on equal terms, and afford the EU income from seigniorage. Indeed, Cooper (1999) argues that the creation of the euro 'raises the possibility that in the longer run it will not only replace the [German] mark and the [French] franc in their international roles, but will also compete more effectively with the dollar and the yen as international currencies, *even to the extent of eventually displacing them* as well' (p. 1; italics added). And Bergsten (1997) suggests that within a decade as much as $1000 billion held in foreign currency balances around the world, mainly

68 | PART II THE EURO AND EMU

in US dollars, at the time of the adoption of the euro, may shift into euros, with profound consequences for the exchange rate between the dollar and the euro and possibly for macroeconomic performance as well.

3 Another source of gain could be a reduction in the cost of financial management. The euro should enable the spreading of overhead costs of financial transactions more widely. Also, some of the activities of the institutions dealing in foreign exchange might be discontinued, leading to a saving in the use of resources.

4 There also exist the classical advantages of having permanently fixed exchange rates, symbolized by the euro, among members of the EMU for free trade and factor movements. Stability of exchange rates enhances trade, encourages capital to move to where it is most productively rewarded and ensures that labour will move, if it is inclined to do so at all, to where the highest rewards prevail. It seems unnecessary to emphasize that this does not mean that *all* labour and *all* capital should be mobile, but simply enough of each to generate the necessary adjustment to any situation. Neither is it necessary to stress that hedging can tackle the problem of exchange rate fluctuations only at a cost, no matter how low that cost may be.

5 The integration of the capital market has a further advantage. If an EMU member country is in deficit, it can borrow directly on the union market or raise its rate of interest to attract capital inflow and therefore ease the situation. However, the integration of economic policies within an EMU ensures that this help will occur automatically under the auspices of the common central bank. Since no single area is likely to be in deficit permanently, such help can be envisaged for all the members. Hence, there is no basis for the assertion that one country can borrow indefinitely to sustain real wages and consumption levels that are out of line with that nation's productivity and the demand for its products.

6 When an EMU establishes a central fiscal authority with its own budget, then the larger the size of the budget, the higher the degree of fiscal harmonization (see the *MacDougall Report*, Commission of the European Communities 1977). This has some advantages: regional deviations from internal balance, defined as acceptable unemployment and inflation rates, can be financed from the centre and the centralization of social security payments financed by contributions or taxes on a progressive basis would

have some stabilizing and compensating effects, modifying the harmful effects of EMU.

7 There are negative advantages in the case of the EU in the sense that EMU, especially with the euro, is necessary for maintaining the EU as it exists; for example, realizing the 'single market' would become more difficult to achieve and the common agricultural prices enshrined in the *Common Agricultural Policy* would be undermined if exchange rates were to be flexible (see El-Agraa 2000, Chapters 8 and 11).

These benefits of EMU are clear and there are few economists who would question them. However, there is no consensus of opinion regarding their extent, but the EU's own estimates suggest a minimum of 0.4 per cent of EU GDP for savings in currency convergence transactions costs alone (see Emerson *et al.* 1990), but this could be about 1–1.5 per cent. However, some analysts believe that such a saving is not worth the effort, given the expected costs (see, *inter alia*, Eichengreen 1993 and Feldstein 1997).

The purely economic costs of EMU are too technical to discuss here (see El-Agraa 2000 for a full coverage). I shall, therefore, confine myself to a popular version of their presentation. Note that I use the term 'purely economic' since the literature under consideration deals with only the economic conditions necessary for countries to adopt permanently fixed exchange rates; the terminology used by the profession is 'optimum currency areas' (see Mundell 1961; and Fleming 1971, Chapters 4 and 8), some implications of which are known within the EU as the 'impossible trilogy' or 'inconsistent trinity' principle.

The principle states that only two out of the following three are mutually compatible:

1 completely free capital mobility

2 an independent monetary policy

3 a fixed exchange rate.

This is because with full capital mobility, a nation's own interest rate is tied to the world interest rate, at least for a country too small to influence global financial markets. More precisely, any difference between the domestic and world interest rates must be matched by an expected rate of depreciation of the exchange rate. For example, if the interest rate is 6 per cent in the domestic market, but 4 per cent in the world market, the global market must expect the currency to depreciate by 2 per cent this year. This is technically known as the 'interest parity condition', which implies that integrated financial markets equalize expected asset returns; hence assets denominated in a currency expected to depreciate must offer an exactly compensating higher yield.

Under such circumstances, a country that wants to conduct an independent monetary policy, raising or lowering its interest rate to control its level of employment or unemployment, must allow its exchange rate to fluctuate in the market. Conversely, a country confronted with full capital mobility and wanting to fix its exchange rate must set its domestic interest rate to be exactly equal to the rate in the country to which it pegs its currency. Since monetary policy is then determined abroad, the country has effectively lost its monetary independence.

The loss from EMU membership can be calculated in terms of the employment sacrificed or increased unemployment due to fixing the exchange rate between EMU members. The extent of this loss is evaluated relative to three criteria, which are known as the Mundell–McKinnon–Kenen criteria, under which two or more countries can adopt a common currency without subjecting themselves to serious adverse economic consequences. These criteria relate to elements which render price adjustments through exchange rate changes less effective or less compelling. They are:

● openness to mutual trade
● diverse economies
● mobility of factors of production, especially of labour.

Greater openness to mutual trade implies that most prices would be determined at the union level, which means that relative prices would be less susceptible to being influenced by changes in the exchange rate. An economy more diverse in terms of production would be less likely to suffer from country-specific shocks, reducing the need for the exchange rate as a policy tool. Greater factor mobility enables the economy to tackle *asymmetric shocks* (those that affect the member states differently) via migration, hence reducing the need for adjustment through the exchange rate.

The EU nations score well on the first criterion since the ratio of their exports to their GDP is 20–70 per cent while that for the USA and Japan is, respectively, 11 per cent and 7 per cent; the US being the preferred reference nation on the assumption that it is an optimum currency area. They also score well in terms of the second criterion, even though they are not all as well endowed with oil and gas resources as Denmark and Britain. As to the third criterion, they score badly in comparison with the USA since EU labour mobility is rather low due to the Europeans' tendency to stick to place of birth, not only nationally, but also regionally. Indeed, while in the USA an employee who moves to San Francisco after being made redundant in Nashville enters the national statistics as a happy example of internal mobility, an Italian who moves to Munich after losing a job in Milan is seen in a different light. To the Italian government, emigration would have overtones of domestic policy failure and to the German government, the inflow of Italian workers might be seen as exacerbating Germany's unemployment problem (see McAleese 1990, p. 421). In the EU, there is also the language factor, but Europeans are increasingly bilingual, with English being the dominant tongue. Moreover, in the EU, casual observation will reveal that it is the unskilled from the south who tend to be relatively less immobile in terms of moving north in search of jobs, i.e. they move because they have no other choice.

Although there is no definitive estimate of the costs due to the relative lack of labour mobility, most economics specialists suggest that it is very high and assert that even if it is not, it must be far in excess of the benefits in the EU's version of EMU; hence they cannot comprehend why the EU nations wanted to have the euro. I do not intend to dwell on this matter here since if one takes a historical perspective, one can argue that the purely economic approach is misguided: it ignores the wider dimension of unity via the back door, a process in which the adoption of the euro is a vital tactical manoeuvre. Although some EU nations insist that EMU is for purely economic reasons, those in the driving seat know very well that that is not the case. Nonetheless, even on purely economic grounds alone, the longer-term perspective will not lend support to the economists' pessimistic assessment. Consider, for example, Krugman's (1990) model, which utilizes such a perspective when examining the costs and benefits of EMU. In Figure 3.1, the costs are represented by CC and the benefits by BB and both costs and benefits are expressed in relation to GDP. The benefits from the single currency are shown to rise with integration, since, for example, intra-EU trade, which is expected to increase and has been doing so for a long time (El-Agraa 2000 and Chapter 2), with integration over time, will be conducted with lesser costs, while the losses from giving up the exchange rate as a policy variable decline with time. To put it in modern economic jargon, as we have seen, changes in the exchange rate are needed to absorb asymmetric shocks, but these will decline with time, owing to the shocks' becoming less asymmetric as integration proceeds and becomes more intensive. In short, the essence of Krugman's analysis is that as the member economies become more integrated, the use of the exchange rate instrument for variations against member nations' currencies would become less and less desirable. Thus, for countries seriously and permanently involved in an EMU, sooner or later, a time will come when the benefits will exceed the costs: the two lines are bound to intersect at some future point in time, indicating 'bliss' thereafter. One should add, however, that Krugman advances this analysis to depict which countries can expect gains from EMU membership, which would depend on where they stand relative to t^* (for more on this see Figure 4.3, p. 99).

One should add that those who ignore the political dimension, and also insist on the net outcome's being a negative sum, are not only relying on pure gut feeling, but are also ignoring the fact that the EU has 'structural funds' (see Chapter 11) aimed at assisting the poorer regions and member nations. Admittedly, these funds are presently small relative to EU GDP, but they are set to rise with further integration. Moreover, when the European Central Bank (ECB), to which I shall soon turn, becomes well established and the EU general budget is increased due to fiscal harmonization and further integration, deviations from the desired levels of economic activity can be catered for from EU central coffers (see the *MacDougall Report*, Commission of the European Communities 1977).

Figure 3.1 | Krugman's (1990) cost–benefits of EMU

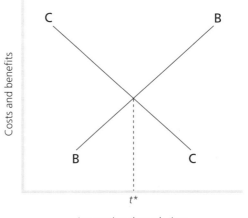

Integration through time

The road to EMU

The aim of achieving EMU, although enshrined in the Maastricht Treaty of 1992 and incorporated in Amsterdam and later treaties, is not a new phenomenon for the EU (see El-Agraa 2000). Here, I would like to provide a historical perspective on EMU by travelling, albeit along the fast lanes, on the route taken by the EU in this direction. However, a thorough understanding of this issue requires an appreciation of how the EU came about and what it has achieved to date and for this my advice to the reader who has skipped Chapter 2 to at least read the section 'A short history of European unity'.

> The aim of achieving EMU, enshrined in the Maastricht Treaty of 1992, is not a new phenomenon for the EU

The Werner Report

In 1969, during The Hague summit, the original six member nations (the Six) decided that their club, which became the European Communities (EC) after the Merger Treaty of 1967, should progressively transform itself into an EMU, and set up a committee, led by Pierre Werner, then Prime Minister of Luxembourg, to consider the issues involved. The 'Werner Report' was endorsed by the Council in February 1971. According to the Council resolution, the EC would:

1 Constitute a zone where persons, goods, services and capital would move freely – but without distorting competition, or creating structural and regional imbalances – and where economic undertakings could develop their activities on a Community scale.

2 Form a single monetary entity within the international monetary system, characterized by: the total and irreversible convertibility of currencies; the elimination of fluctuation margins of exchange rates between the [members]; and the irrevocable fixing of their parity relationships. These steps would be essential for the creation of a single currency and they involve a Community-level organization of central banks.

3 Hold the powers and responsibilities in the economic and monetary field that would enable its institutions to ensure the administration of the economic union. To this end, the necessary

economic policy decisions would be taken at Community level and the necessary powers would be attributed to Community institutions.

The Community organization of central banks would assist, in the framework of its own responsibilities, in achieving the objectives of stability and growth in the Community.

These three principles would apply to:

● the internal monetary and credit policies of the union

● monetary policy vis-à-vis the rest of the world

● policy on a unified capital market and capital movements to and from non-member countries

● budgetary and taxation policies, as related to the policy for stability and growth

● structural and regional action needed to contribute to the balanced development of the Community.

As progress was made in moving closer to the final objectives, Community instruments would be created whenever they seemed necessary to replace or complement the action of national instruments. All actions would be interdependent; in particular, the development of monetary unification would be backed by parallel progress in the convergence and then the unification of economic policies.

The Council decided that EMU could be attained during that decade, if the plan had the permanent political support of the member governments. Implementation was envisaged to be in three stages, with the first beginning in 1971 and the final completed by 1980. The Council made quite clear how it envisaged the process leading to full EMU (emphasis added):

● The first phase should begin on 1 January 1971 and could technically be completed within three years. This phase would be used to make the Community instruments more operational and to mark the beginnings of the Community's individuality within the international monetary system.

● The first phase should not be considered as an objective in itself; it should be associated with the complete process of economic and monetary integration. *It should therefore be launched with the determination to arrive at the final goal.*

● In the first phase consultation procedures should be strengthened; the budgetary policies of the member states should accord with

Community objectives; some taxes should be harmonized; monetary and credit policies should be co-ordinated; and integration of financial markets should be intensified.

Thus, it should be clear that the EMU launched by the EC in 1971 was consistent with and satisfied all the requirements for a proper EMU. What is of significance for our purposes, however, is that EMU is not a new venture for the EU since it goes back about three decades. Yet, the 1971 venture did fail after an earlier than expected completely successful negotiation of the first phase and some progress during the second, but the failure was not due to lack of commitment, determination or both: the Nixon shock, which resulted in worldwide monetary upheavals in the early 1970s, the first oil shock of the same period, which led to great disruption of industrial activity, and the first enlargement shock, which added three new members (Denmark, Ireland and the UK), each bringing with it its own unique problem, especially a UK facing complete industrial decline and vast regional problems, were the real culprits.

The EMS

In some quarters, the European Monetary System (EMS)[2] was considered as the next EC attempt at EMU, but in reality the EMS was no more than a mechanism devised to check the monetary upheavals of the 1970s by creating a 'zone of monetary stability'. Nevertheless, one needs to be familiar with it before making a decision.

In essence, the EMS was, and continues to be, concerned with the creation of an EC currency zone within which there is discipline for managing exchange rates. This discipline is known as the 'exchange rate mechanism' (ERM), which asks a member nation to intervene to reverse a trend when 75 per cent of the (initially) allowed exchange rate variation of ± 2.25 per cent is reached; this is similar to that which was practised within the 'snake' arrangements that preceded the EMS. In the beginning, however, the ERM did not apply to all the member nations of the EMS, since wider margins of fluctuation for those not participating in the snake were allowed for (± 6 per cent). The European Currency Unit (ECU), which was similar to its predecessor the European Unit of Account (EUA) in that it was a basket of *all* EC currencies, lay at the heart of the system; it is (was) the means of settlement between the EC central banks. The EMS was supported by a European Monetary Fund (EMF) which (supposedly within two years) was to absorb the short-term financing arrangement operating within the snake, the short-term monetary support agreement which was managed by the European Monetary Co-operation Fund (EMCF) and the medium-term loan facilities for balance of payments assistance. The EMF was backed by approximately 20 per cent of national gold and US dollar reserves and by a similar percentage in national currencies. The EMF issued ECUs which were used as new reserve assets. An exchange stabilization fund able to issue about 50 billion US dollars was to be created.

It is clear from this that the EMS asks neither for permanently and irrevocably fixed exchange rates between the member nations nor for complete capital convertibility. Moreover, it does not mention the creation of a common central bank to be put in charge of the member nations' foreign exchange reserves and to be vested with the appropriate powers. Hence, the EMS is not EMU, and although it could be seen as paving the way for one, the 1992 crisis, which resulted in the complete withdrawal of Italy and the United Kingdom from the ERM and the widening of the margin of exchange rate fluctuations to ± 15 per cent, completely erased such a vision, even though member currencies have recently been performing within the original ±2.25 per cent margin, but mainly for reasons related to the conditions set in the following section.

The Delors Report and the Maastricht Treaty

The EC summit which was held in Hanover on 27 and 28 June 1988 decided that, in adopting the Single European Act (SEA), the EC member states had confirmed the objective of 'progressive realisation of economic and monetary union'. The heads of state agreed to discuss the means of achieving this in their meeting in Madrid in June of the following year and to help them in their deliberations then they entrusted to a committee of central bankers and others, chaired by Jacques Delors, President of the EC Commission at that time, the 'task of studying and proposing concrete stages leading towards this union'. The committee reported just before the Madrid summit and its report is referred to as the Delors Report on EMU.[3]

As agreed, the Report was the main item for discussion in the EC summit which opened in Madrid on 24 June 1989. In that meeting member nations agreed to call a conference which would decide the route to be taken to EMU. This agreement was facilitated by a surprisingly conciliatory Margaret (now Lady) Thatcher, the British Prime Minister then, on the opening day of the summit. Instead of insisting (as was expected) that the UK would join the ERM 'when the time is ripe', she set out five conditions for joining: a lower inflation rate in the UK and in the EC as a whole; abolition of all exchange controls (at the time, Italy, France, and Spain had them); progress towards the single EC market; liberalization of financial services; and agreement on competition policy.

Since these were minor conditions relative to the demands for creating the EMU, all member nations endorsed the Report and agreed on 1 July 1990 as the deadline for the commencement of the first of the three stages leading to full EMU. Indeed, the economic and finance ministers of the EC at a meeting on 10 July 1989 agreed to complete the preparatory work for the first stage by December, thus giving themselves six months to accommodate the adjustments that would be needed before the beginning of the first stage. The three-stage timetable for EMU did start on 1 July 1990 with the launching of the first phase of intensified economic cooperation during which all

A single currency, to be managed by an independent ECB, was to be introduced as early as 1997

the member states were to submit their currencies to the ERM. The main target of this activity was the UK, whose currency was not subject to ERM discipline; the UK joined in 1991 while Thatcher was still in office, but withdrew from it in 1992, as did Italy.

The second stage is clarified in the Maastricht Treaty. It was to start in 1993. During this stage the EU was to create the *European Monetary Institute* (EMI) to prepare the way for a European Central Bank (ECB) which would start operating on 1 January 1997. Although this was upset by the 1992 turmoil in the EMS, the compromises reached in the Edinburgh summit of December 1992 did not water down the treaty too much. Be that as it may, the treaty already allows Denmark and the UK to opt out of the final stage when the EU currency rates were to be permanently and irrevocably fixed and the single currency floated. However, in a separate protocol, all the then 12 EC nations declared that the drive to a single currency this century is 'irreversible'. Denmark, which supports the decision, is an exception because its constitution demands the holding of a referendum on this issue; the UK likewise because, apart from its cultural and institutional differences from the rest of the EC, it has always been the black sheep of Europe (see Young 1998)!

A single currency (the euro), to be managed by an independent ECB, was to be introduced as early as 1997 if seven of the then 12 EC nations passed the strict economic criteria required for successful operation and in 1999 at the very latest. These conditions are as follows:

1 *Price stability*. Membership requires 'a price performance that is sustainable and an average rate of inflation, observed over a period of one year before the examination, that does not exceed by more than [1.5] percentage points that of, at most, the three best performing' EC member countries. Inflation 'shall be measured by means of the consumer price index on a comparable basis, taking into account differences in national definitions'.

2 *Interest rates*. Membership requires that 'observed over a period of one year before the examination, a Member State has had an average nominal long-term interest rate that does not exceed by more than two percentage points that of, at most, the three best performing Member States in terms of price stability. Interest rates shall be measured on the basis of long-term government bonds or comparable securities, taking into account differences in national definitions.'

3 *Budget deficits*. Membership requires that a member country 'has achieved a government budgetary position without a deficit that is excessive' (Article 109). However, what is to be considered excessive is determined in Article 104c(b), which simply states that the Council shall decide after an overall assessment 'whether an excessive deficit exists'. Given the general trend at the time, one could argue that the deficit should be less than 3 per cent of GDP.

4 *Public debt*. The Protocol does not state anything on this, but by present standards it is interpreted to mean that membership requires a ratio not exceeding 60 per cent of GDP.

5 *Currency stability*. Membership requires that a member country 'has respected the normal fluctuation margin provided for by the [ERM] of the [EMS] without severe tensions for at least two years before the examination. In particular, [it] shall not have devalued its currency's bilateral central rate against any other Member State's currency on its own initiative for the same period.'

One is, of course, perfectly justified in asking about the theoretical rationale for these convergence criteria. The answer is simply that there is none; for example, the inflation criterion is not even based on non-accelerating inflation rate of unemployment (NAIRU); i.e. inflation bears no relationship to that consistent with a natural rate of unemployment and there is no way to evaluate whether or not a 60 per cent of GDP public debt is better or worse than, say, a 65 per cent of GDP rate. The only rationale is that 3 per cent of GDP happened to be the average level of public investment at that time, and considering it acceptable it has to be financed by a budget deficit of that amount, and calculating this at the steady state of equilibrium and a compound rate of interest of 5 per cent per annum results in a public borrowing of 60 per cent of GDP (see Buiter, Corsetti and Roubini 1993). Also, these criteria were consistent with Germany's, so adopting them implied that the ECB would be as solid as the Bundesbank in controlling inflation, which is the sole role attributed to the ECB – i.e. the ECB cannot offer credit or make bailouts; the exchange rate will be the responsibility of the Council of Ministers.[4] The important point is that the performance of the member countries must not diverge so much as to make it difficult for the EMU to operate and for the euro to be stable, and the members, in their wisdom, decided that the convergence criteria agreed upon are the ones that will insure against such an outcome.

It is interesting to note that if one had conducted this test then, only France and Luxembourg would have scored full marks, i.e. five points each. The others would have scored as follows: Denmark and the UK four points each; Belgium, Germany and Ireland three points each; the Netherlands two points; Italy and Spain one point each; Greece and Portugal zero points each. Hence, the EMU could not have been introduced since seven countries needed to score full marks for this purpose. After the 1992–93 EMS crisis, the currency stability criterion lost its meaning for a number of the member nations, hence that item can be ignored in a September 1994 score sheet. As to the other four criteria, Luxembourg kept its perfect record, but was joined by Ireland, while France failed on the budget deficit. Greece, Italy and Portugal maintained their zero score and were joined by Spain. Of the rest, only Belgium maintained its previous score. Both Denmark and the UK failed on the budget deficit, the Netherlands on inflation and Germany on public debt, but reversed its score on both inflation and budget deficit. The position at the end of 1996 was even worse since only Luxembourg qualified (see Figure 3.2). These developments need to be borne in mind when considering the data on which the final decision rested (Table 3.1) since they give a clear indication of what the member states had to achieve in order to make the euro a reality. However, writing before the event, I mentioned that one should hasten to add three provisos regarding this test (see El-Agraa 1998). The first is that it is an extremely severe one since it is based on the most demanding scenario stated in the Protocol. The second is that not only has the text been written in a vague manner, but the vagueness has been enforced by Article 6 of the Protocol which states that the (italics added):

Council shall, acting unanimously on a proposal from the Commission and after consulting the European parliament, the EMI or the ECB as the case may be, and the Committee referred to in Article 109c, adopt appropriate provisions to lay down the details of the convergence criteria referred to in Article 109j of the Treaty, *which shall then replace this Protocol.*

The third proviso is that the day of reckoning was yet to arrive, but the data on which the decision on 2 May 1998 was based indicated that, in the opinion of the EU Commission, 11 nations had passed the test (see Table 3.1).

Of the remaining four, three (Denmark, the UK and Sweden) had already decided not to join in the first wave and Greece has never tried. Note that the Commission's interpretation of the government's performance is consistent with my 'flexible' interpretation:

Fourteen member states had government deficits of three per cent of GDP or less in 1997: Belgium, Denmark, Germany, Spain, France, Ireland, Italy, Luxembourg, the Netherlands, Austria, Portugal, Finland, Sweden and the United Kingdom. Member states have achieved significant reductions in the level of government borrowing, in particular in 1997. This remarkable outcome is the result of national governments' determined efforts to tackle excessive deficits combined with the effects of lower interest rates and stronger growth in the European economy. The Commission's report critically examines the one-off measures which have contributed to some member states' 1997 figures. In particular it analyses budget measures for 1998 and other factors to assess whether the budgetary situation is sustainable. *The report concludes that the major part of the deficit reductions are structural.*

In 1997 government debt was below the Treaty reference value of 60 per cent of GDP in four member states – France, Luxembourg, Finland and the United Kingdom. According to the Treaty, countries may exceed this value as long as the debt ratio is 'sufficiently diminishing and approaching the reference value at a satisfactory pace'. This was the case in almost all member states with debt ratios above 60 per cent in 1997. Only in Germany, where the ratio is just above 60 per cent of GDP and the exceptional costs of unification continue to bear heavily, was there a small rise in 1997. In 1998, all countries above 60 per cent are

Figure 3.2 | Performing to the convergence criteria in 1996

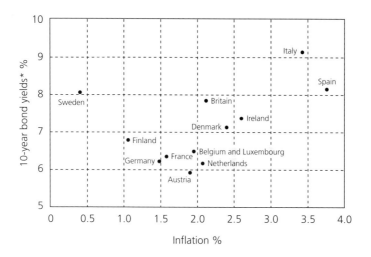

*Data were unavailable for Portugal and Greece

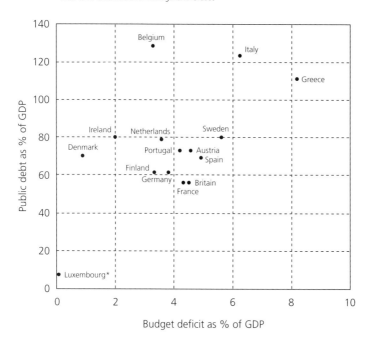

*Luxembourg has a budget surplus of 0.7% and public debt of 6.2%

Table 3.1 EU member states' performance to the convergence criteria

| | Inflation | Government budgetary position | | | | | | | Exchange rates | Long-term interest rates[d] |
| | HICP[a] | Existence of an excessive deficit[b] | Deficit (% of GDP)[c] | Debt (% of GDP) | | Change from previous year | | | ERM participation | |
	January 1998		1997	1997	1997	1996	1995		March 1998	January 1998
Reference value	2.7[e]		3	60						7.8[f]
Austria	1.1	Yes[g]	2.5	66.1	-3.4	0.3	3.8		Yes	5.6
Belgium	1.4	Yes[g]	2.1	122.2	-3.7	-3.3	-2.2		Yes	5.7
Denmark	1.9	No	-0.7	65.1	-5.5	-2.7	-3.9		Yes	6.2
Finland	1.3	No	0.9	55.8	-1.8	-0.4	-1.5		Yes[k]	5.9
France	1.2	Yes[g]	3.0	58.0	2.4	2.9	3.2		Yes	5.5
Germany	1.4	Yes[g]	2.7	61.3	0.8	2.4	7.8		Yes	5.6
Greece	5.2	Yes	3.0	108.7	-2.9	1.5	0.7		Yes[h]	9.8
Ireland	1.2	No	-0.9	66.3	-6.4	-9.6	-6.8		Yes	6.2
Italy	1.8	Yes[g]	2.7	121.6	-2.4	-0.2	-0.7		Yes[j]	6.7
Luxembourg	1.4	No	-1.7	6.7	0.1	0.7	0.2		Yes	5.6
Netherlands	1.8	No	1.4	72.1	-5.0	-1.9	1.2		Yes	5.5
Portugal	1.8	Yes[g]	2.5	62.0	-3.0	-0.9	2.1		Yes	6.2
Spain	1.8	Yes[g]	2.6	68.8	-1.3	3.6	2.9		Yes	6.3
Sweden	1.9	Yes[g]	0.8	76.6	-0.1	-0.9	-1.4		No	6.5
UK	1.8	Yes[g]	1.9	53.4	-1.3	0.8	3.5		No	7.0
EU (15)	1.6		2.4	72.1	-0.3	2.0	3.0			6.1

Notes: [a] Percentage change in arithmetic average of the latest 12 monthly harmonized indices of consumer prices (HICP) relative to the arithmetic average of the 12 HICP of the previous period; [b] Council decisions of 26.09.94, 10.07.95, 27.06.96 and 30.06.97; [c] a negative sign for the government deficit indicates a surplus; [d] average maturity 10 years; average of the last 12 months; [e] definition adopted in this report: simple arithmetic average of the inflation rates of the three best performing member states in terms of price stability plus 1.5 percentage points; [f] definition adopted in this report: simple arithmetic average of the 12-month average of interest rates of the three best performing member states in terms of price stability plus two percentage points; [g] Commission is recommending abrogation; [h] since March 1998; [i] average of available data during the past 12 months; [j] since November 1996; [k] since October 1996

Source: *EU Commission Services 1998*

expected to see reductions in their debt levels. *The Commission concludes that the conditions are in place for the continuation of a sustained decline in debt ratio in future years* (EU Commission Services 1998; italics added).

Significance

The euro's present and future significance is not confined to the EU since it extends beyond it to the whole world. First, an economically united EU with a strong single currency should be a formidable economic force at the international level. This should enable the EU to have the equal voice in international economic affairs that it has always sought. Many analysts and commentators have misinterpreted this dimension through thinking that what Europe wants is to become the next economic hegemon; that is far from the truth since all that most of the member nations of the EU have been seeking is to have an 'equal voice' in this field.

Second, a euro backed by a solid EU economy should eventually be able to match the US dollar. This is because, as stated earlier and partly corroborated in Chapter 6, the adoption of the euro has created the possibility that in the longer run it will compete more effectively with the dollar and the yen as international currencies, 'even to the extent of eventually displacing them' (Cooper 1999, p. 1). Indeed, Bergsten (1997) suggests that within a decade as much as $1000 billion held in foreign currency balances around the world, mainly in US dollars, may shift into euros, with profound consequences for the exchange rate between the dollar and the euro and possibly for macroeconomic performance as well. This will realize gains for the EU from seigniorage, but such gains are not the object of the exercise (see later). However, one should add that world monetary history shows that it would take decades for a new currency to dominate the international financial markets (just recall how long it took the dollar to replace the pound sterling as the world's number one currency); thus, in the short term, the USA has nothing to fear from the euro.

Third, a solid and fully integrated EU economy would have significance for the USA too. A truly equal economic partner will relieve the USA of many of its global responsibilities – including those in Europe itself, e.g. US forces stationed there – and hence lower the tax payments by US citizens. Thus, unless one is prepared to argue that the USA would want to continue indefinitely to be the major provider, through NATO, of European defence for the mere sake of doing so, the relief should be most welcome by all. Moreover, as just mentioned, it would take decades for the US dollar to lose, if ever, its dominance; hence, even if the euro became the dominant partner, the transition for the USA would be a very slow and painless one.

Fourth, it is difficult to accept the argument that a euro to match the US dollar would have adverse effects on the rest of the world. The rest of the world should welcome the choice. After all, who would prefer to continue to put all their eggs in one basket?

Finally and controversially, the adoption of the euro has brought the EU nations much closer to realizing the dream of the founding fathers. After the member nations have become familiar and comfortable with the euro, the ECB has demonstrated its ability to match the performance of the Bundesbank, and the various governments have behaved responsibly in terms of maintaining appropriate exchange rate parities with the outside world, all that would be needed for the creation of a politically united Europe would be a mere step in the right direction. Of course, such a step could be a short one or a quantum leap, depending on what form political unity takes: some are thinking of a 'federal Europe', others of a 'united Europe of states', yet others of a 'United States of Europe'. No one would dismiss the real difficulties to be encountered in achieving such unity; indeed, it could be asserted that the thought of overcoming them is no more than an adolescent's dream. However, the overall progress achieved to date (see El-Agraa 2000) plus the expected smooth transition within the next few years and the open utterances by President Jacques Chirac of France (on the 10th anniversary of German unification held in Dresden in October 2000 and at the German Parliament earlier in June), Chancellor Gerhard Schröder of Germany (responding in Dresden) and his Foreign Minister Joschka Fisher before him suggest otherwise.

> It is difficult to accept the argument that a euro to match the US dollar would have adverse effects on the rest of the world

Conclusions

With regard to EMU, the point to stress is that there is almost complete consensus among economists regarding its benefits to the participating nations, but that there is no agreement as to the extent of such benefits. The EU Commission itself estimates the savings from only currency convergence transaction costs to be about 0.4 per cent of EU GDP. As to EMU costs, there is a wide divergence of opinion, ranging from utterly prohibitive to nothing of significance. The bottom line is that costs depend on how much importance should be attached to a member nation's retention of its ability to vary its exchange rate and the yardstick to be used in measuring this loss. In the case of the original ERM, intra-EU exchange rate changes were confined to 75 per cent of the allowed margin of ±2.25 per cent; i.e. within the EU context, one is not referring to absolute freedom to vary exchange rates.

The costs and benefits of EMU notwithstanding, an important consideration is the significance of the euro, but for this one is referred to the previous section.

Notes

1 See El-Agraa (1997) for a comprehensive coverage of all such clubs, their practical experience, theoretical rationale, empirical problems and adherence to the rules of the World Trade Organization (WTO, i.e. Article XXIV of the General Agreement on Tariffs and Trade (GATT), WTO's predecessor). For a technical coverage, see El-Agraa (1999) and for the particular case of the EU, see El-Agraa (2000).

2 The route to EMS was a fairly short one: the Bremen Declaration on 6 and 7 July 1978 was followed by its affirmation in Bonn on 16 and 17 July and then by its adoption by the Council, in the form of a resolution 'on the establishment of the European Monetary System (EMS) and related matters', on 5 December of the same year.

The EMS was introduced with the immediate support of six of the EC nations at the time. Ireland, Italy and the UK adopted a wait-and-see attitude; 'time for reflection' was needed by Ireland and Italy and a definite reservation was expressed by the UK. Later, Ireland and Italy joined the system, while the UK expressed a 'spirit of sympathetic co-operation'. The EMS was to start operating on 1 January 1979, but France, which wanted assurances regarding the MCA system, delayed that start to 13 March 1979. The main features of the EMS are given in the annexe to the conclusions of the EC presidency (see *Bulletin of the European Communities*, 6, 1978, pp. 20–21):

(a) In terms of exchange rate management, the . . . [EMS] will be at least as strict as the 'snake'. In the initial stages of its operation and for a limited period of time, member countries currently not participating in the 'snake' may opt for somewhat wider margins around central rates. In principle, intervention will be in the currencies of participating countries. Changes in central rates will be subject to mutual consent. Non-member countries with particularly strong economic and financial ties with the Community may become associate members of the system. The European Currency Unit (ECU) will be at the centre of the system; in particular, it will be used as a means of settlement between EEC monetary authorities.

(b) An initial supply of ECUs (for use among Community central banks) will be created against deposit of US dollars and gold on the one hand (e.g. 20% of the stock currently held by member central banks) and member currencies on the other hand in an amount of a comparable order of magnitude.

   The use of ECUs created against member currencies will be subject to conditions varying with the amount and the maturity; due account will be given to the need for substantial short-term facilities (up to 1 year).

(c) Participating countries will coordinate their exchange rate policies *vis-à-vis* third countries. To this end, they will intensify the consultations in the appropriate bodies and between central banks participating in the scheme. Ways to coordinate dollar interventions should be sought which avoid simultaneous reserve interventions. Central banks buying dollars will deposit a fraction (say 20%) and receive ECUs in return; likewise, central banks selling dollars will receive a fraction (say 20%) against ECUs.

(d) Not later than two years after the start of the scheme, the existing arrangements and institutions will be consolidated in a European Monetary Fund.

(e) A system of closer monetary cooperation will only be successful if participating countries pursue policies conducive to greater stability at home and abroad; this applies to deficit and surplus countries alike.

3 The committee was of the opinion that the creation of the EMU must be seen as a single process, but that this process should be in stages which progressively led to the ultimate goal; thus the decision to enter upon the first stage should commit a member state to the entire process. Emphasizing that the creation of the EMU would necessitate a common monetary policy and require a high degree of compatibility of economic policies and consistency in a number of other policy areas, particularly in the fiscal field, the Report pointed out that the realization of the EMU would require new arrangements which could be established only on the basis of a change in the relevant Treaty of Rome and consequent changes in national legislation.

The first stage should be concerned with the initiation of the process of creating the EMU. During this stage there would be a greater convergence of economic performance through the strengthening of economic and monetary policy co-ordination within the existing institutional framework. The economic measures would be concerned with the completion of the internal market and the reduction of existing disparities through programmes of budgetary consolidation in the member states involved and more effective structural and regional policies. In the monetary field the emphasis would be on the removal of all obstacles to financial integration and on the intensification of co-operation and co-ordination of monetary policies. Realignment of exchange rates was seen to be possible, but efforts would be made by every member state to make the functioning of other adjustment mechanisms more effective. The committee was of the opinion that it would be important to include all EC currencies in the exchange rate mechanism of the EMS during this stage. The 1974 Council decision defining the mandate of central bank governors would be replaced by a new decision indicating that the committee itself should formulate opinions on the overall orientation of monetary and exchange rate policy.

In the second stage, which would commence only when the treaty had been amended, the basic organs and structure of the EMU would be set up. The committee stressed that this stage should be seen as a transition period leading to the final stage; thus it should constitute a 'training process leading to collective decision making', but the ultimate responsibility for policy decisions would remain with national authorities during this stage. The procedure established during the first stage would be further strengthened and extended on the basis of the amended treaty, and policy guidelines would be adopted on a majority basis. Given this understanding, the EC would achieve the following:

● Establish 'a medium-term framework for key economic objectives aimed at achieving stable growth, with a follow-up procedure for monitoring performances and intervening when significant deviations occurred'.

● 'Set precise, although not yet binding, rules relating to the size of annual budget deficits and their financing.'

● 'Assume a more active role as a single entity in the discussions of questions arising in the economic and exchange rate field.'

In the monetary field, the most significant feature of this stage would be the establishment of the European System of Central Banks (ESCB) to absorb the previous institutional monetary arrangements. The ESCB would start the transition with a first stage in which the co-ordination of independent monetary policies would be carried out by the Committee of Central Bank Governors. It was envisaged that the formulation and implementation of a common monetary policy would take place in the final stage; during this stage exchange rate realignments would not be allowed except in exceptional circumstances.

The Report stresses that the nature of the second stage would require a number of actions, e.g.:

● National monetary policy would be executed in accordance with the general monetary orientations set up for the EC as a whole.

● A certain amount of foreign exchange reserves would be pooled and used to conduct interventions in accordance with the guidelines established by the ESCB.

● The ESCB would have to regulate the monetary and banking system to achieve a minimum harmonization of provisions (such as reserve requirements or payment arrangements) necessary for the future conduct of a common monetary policy.

The final stage would begin with the irrevocable fixing of member states' exchange rates and the attribution to the EC institutions of the full monetary and economic consequences. It is envisaged that during this stage the national currencies would eventually be replaced by a single EC currency. In the economic field, the transition to this stage is seen to be marked by three developments:

● EC structural and regional policies may have to be further strengthened.

● EC macroeconomic and budgetary rules and procedures would have to become binding.

● The EC role in the process of international policy co-operation would have to become fuller and more positive.

In the monetary field, the irrevocable fixing of exchange rates would come into effect and the transition to a single monetary policy and a single currency would be made. The ESCB would assume full responsibilities, especially in four specific areas:

- the formulation and implementation of monetary policy
- exchange market intervention in third currencies
- the pooling and management of all foreign exchange reserves
- technical and regulatory preparations necessary for the transition to a single EC currency.

4 The ECB has a Board of Governors, which comprises an Executive Board (consisting of the President, Vice-President and four others, all appointed for eight years), 15 national bank governors and, as non-voting members, the Presidents of the Commission and Council of Ministers. The ECB must issue quarterly reports and make annual submissions to the European Parliament, and can be called to testify before its committees. Within this context, Feldstein's assertion that those appointed to set policy at the ECB will continue to act in their national interest because they 'would be political appointees of their national governments' (Feldstein 1997, p. 38) is a gross misrepresentation of EU political and constitutional reality: members of the EU Commission are so appointed, yet once in office, they are mandated to act in the interest of the EU as a whole and can be taken to the Court of Justice if they act otherwise, and on the whole they have always acted as mandated. If Feldstein has made an inappropriate use of the word 'appointees', meaning the national central bank governors, then his assertion is tantamount to stating that all the Council of Ministers' deliberations have been to no avail in terms of EU-wide interests, which would obviously be far off the mark.

References

Bergsten, Fred C. (1997) 'The dollar and the euro', *Foreign Affairs*, 76, July/August.

Buiter, W. H., Corsetti, G. and Roubini, N. (1993) 'Excessive deficits: sense and nonsense in the Treaty of Maastricht', *Economic Policy*, 16, pp. 57–100.

Commission of the European Communities (1970) *Report to the Council and Commission on the Realization by Stages of Economic and Monetary Union in the Community* (The Werner Report), *Bulletin of the European Communities*, Supplement, 11.

Commission of the European Communities (1975) *Report of the Study Group 'Economic and Monetary Union 1980'* (The Marjolin Report). Brussels.

Commission of the European Communities (1997) *Report of the Study Group on the Role of Public Finance in European Integration* (The MacDougall Report). Brussels.

Cooper, Richard, N. (1999) 'Key currencies after the Euro', *The World Economy*, 22, 1, pp. 1–23.

Eichengreen, Barry (1993) 'European monetary unification', *Journal of Economic Literature*, 31, pp. 1321–57.

El-Agraa, Ali M. (1980) *The Economics of the European Community*. Oxford: Philip Allan; New York: St. Martin's Press.

El-Agraa, Ali M. (1989) *The Theory and Measurement of International Economic Integration*. London: Macmillan; New York: St. Martin's Press.

El-Agraa, Ali M. (1997) *Economic Integration Worldwide*. London: Macmillan; New York: St. Martin's Press.

El-Agraa, Ali M. (1998) 'The euro: Why? How? Significance?', *The World Economy*, 21, 5, pp. 639–57.

El-Agraa, Ali M. (1999) *Regional Integration: Experience, Theory and Measurement*. London: Macmillan; New York: Barnes & Noble.

El-Agraa, Ali M. (2001) *The European Union: Economics and Policies*. Hemel Hempstead: Pearson Education for Financial Times and Prentice Hall Europe.

Emerson, M., Aujean, M., Catinat, M., Goybet, P. and Jaquemin, A. (1988) *The Economics of 1992: The EC Commission's Assessment of the Economic Effects of Completing the Internal Market*. Oxford: Oxford University Press.

Feldstein, Martin (1997) 'The political economy of the European economic and monetary union: political sources of an economic liability', *Journal of Economic Perspectives*, 11, pp. 23–42.

Fleming, John M. (1971) 'On exchange rate unification', *The Economic Journal*, 81, pp. 467–88.

Kenen, Peter B. (1968) *Managing Exchange Rates*. London: Routledge.

Krugman, Paul R. (1990) 'Policy problems in a monetary union' in P. de Grauwe and L. Papademos (eds) *The European Monetary System in the 1990s*. Harlow: Longman.

McAleese, Dermot (1990) 'External trade policy', in Ali M. El-Agraa (ed.) *The Economics of the European Community*, 3rd edition. Oxford: Philip Allan.

McKinnon, Ronald I. (1963) 'Optimum currency areas', *American Economic Review*, 53, pp. 717–25.

Mundell, Robert A. (1961) 'A theory of optimum currency areas', *American Economic Review*, 51, pp. 657–65.

Robson, Peter (1990) *The Economics of International Integration*. London: Allen & Unwin.

Wyplosz, Charles (1997) 'EMU: why and how it might happen', *Journal of Economic Perspectives*, 11, pp. 3–22.

Young, Hugo (1998) *This Blessed Plot: Britain and Europe from Churchill to Blair*. London: Macmillan.

4

Can EMU survive unchanged?

Forrest Capie and Geoffrey Wood

Introduction

Although EMU, the economic and monetary union of (some parts of) Europe, has now proceeded to a stage where for many observers it is irrevocable, there is nevertheless still discussion of whether it might break up and of how it has to evolve, politically and economically, to ensure it does *not*. It has not, therefore, yet reached the status of that monetary union which comprises the United States of America; discussion of whether that will survive as a monetary union, or of what has to be done to keep it together, is essentially unknown. The US monetary union has become like the Rocky Mountains; its existence is for all practical purposes taken as given. EMU has not reached that state.

In this chapter we seek first to consider why the future of EMU is still seen as so unsettled as to be a subject worthy of frequent and intense analysis and discussion. Having set out why we consider that to be the case we then proceed to consider various aspects of monetary unions that existed in the past, some of which have survived and some of which have not. What factors contributed to survival? And what factors – if any, in addition to absence of those necessary for survival – contributed to break-up? That leads to a study of a monetary union already mentioned: how did the USA develop into a single currency area and how long was it before it functioned well as one? Further, how did it survive in the turmoils of the inter-war years, when so many similar monetary arrangements did not? Next, in the chapter's penultimate section, we turn to the role of fiscal policy in monetary unions. This has been discussed analytically and econometrically; but it has not been discussed in the light of the experience of an earlier monetary union in which explicit attention was paid to the public finances of the constituent parts. We then conclude by drawing out the common lessons from the episodes we have studied, and reflecting on what they suggest for both the future of EMU and for debate over whether Britain should join. In particular with regard to the latter, we consider whether the institutional structure of EMU is stable and whether history supports claims that political unity close to subordination of nationhood is necessary for EMU to survive.

There is a strong case for thinking that the formation of EMU is a 'regime change'

The methods used in this chapter are both analytical and historical. We do not attempt to build an econometric model to assess the likely future of EMU. We eschew that partly because it has been done several times in the fairly recent past. But we avoid it also for two other reasons. The first is that there is surely a strong case for thinking that the formation of EMU is a 'regime change'. Europe has moved from the ERM, in which a collection of national central banks followed the policy of the Bundesbank, a central bank with a clear reputation such that expectations about its future policies at any time, although of course uncertain in detail, were absolutely clear in outline. (See Capie and Wood 2001a, for discussion of the evolution of the Bundesbank.) Monetary policy in Europe is now run by a completely new central bank, with a low inflation mandate but with a completely untested constitution and no incentives to keep to its mandate.[1] Expectations are no longer anchored as they were under the Bundesbank; so, as argued in Lucas (1976), reactions to shocks such as policy changes are likely to be quite different from what they were in the past. Our second reason for pursuing the methods of this chapter is that discussion of EMU, while sometimes drawing on the history of monetary unions, has done so to only a modest extent. There is much more to be learned from that history. After all, history is the only laboratory economists have. We wish to use it.

Why is EMU still debated?

EMU is still debated, it will be argued here, because the body of analysis used to appraise EMU is based on Robert Mundell's (1961) paper, 'A theory of optimum currency areas'. Max Corden (1972) observed some years ago that that body of literature seems to relate not to the optimality of a currency area, but rather to its feasibility. In this section of the present chapter we review briefly the main contributions to the optimum currency area literature and set out why in our view it is indeed the case, as Corden (1972) conjectured, that it guides not on the optimality of an area, but rather, and that fairly imprecisely, on its feasibility. We conclude this section by explaining why we think this lies behind the continuing debate on EMU.

The best known early papers in the area are Mundell (1961), McKinnon (1963) and Kenen (1969). We consider them in that order, as well as looking at Mundell's important (but much less frequently discussed) 1973 contribution. The problems these reveal are then compared to the rather similar problems which beset another and quite different area of economic analysis, and some implications of this similarity are drawn out.

The optimum currency area concept (and the term) was invented by Mundell (1961). The crucial trade-off he identified for determining optimality is, to quote McCallum (1996), that 'an extension of the area over which a single currency prevails enhances [microeconomic] efficiency but reduces the possibility of monetary policy responses to shocks [or conditions] that affect various subareas differently' (p. 258). The wider the area, that is to say, the greater are the efficiency benefits of possessing a single medium of exchange and unit of account, but the smaller the area, the greater are the possibilities of tailoring monetary policy to (temporary) local conditions. Somewhere between one currency for the entire world and one for each city lies the optimum.

A textbook by Obstfeld and Rogoff (1996, pp. 632–34) develops this point by listing four main benefits and four main costs which accrue to a pair of countries as a result of having a common currency. These (in the words of Obstfeld and Rogoff) are as follows, with benefits listed first (B for benefits, C for costs):

B1 Reduced transaction costs from currency conversion

B2 Reduced accounting costs and greater predictability of relative prices for firms doing business in both countries

B3 Insulation from monetary disturbances and speculative bubbles that might otherwise lead to unnecessary fluctuations in real exchange rates

B4 Less political pressure for trade protection because of sharp shifts in real exchange rates

C1 Individual regions in a currency union cannot use monetary policy to respond to region-specific macroeconomic disturbances

C2 Regions in a currency union give up the option to use inflation to reduce the real burden of public debt

C3 Political problems arise in determining how member countries split seignorage revenues

C4 Avoiding speculative attacks in the transition from individual currencies to a common currency can be a major problem

A list of the Obstfeld–Rogoff type can be extended by noting that the existence of a common currency tends to bring a greater degree of integration to financial and non-financial markets in the two countries. (See last part of this section and Mundell 1973a.)

Merely stating that this optimization problem exists does nothing to solve it in any particular case. The relevant issue for the present section of this chapter is how the optimization problem should be handled in practice. In his original paper, Mundell (1961) emphasized factor mobility, especially labour mobility, as a crucial consideration. Subsequent contributions by McKinnon (1963), Kenen (1969) and others have proposed other criteria. McKinnon emphasized openness, measured by the share of tradeable goods in a country's output and Kenen focused on the extent of product diversification in production. McKinnon was concerned that an area could be 'too small' to sustain its own currency as a result of being so open to trade that any exchange rate change impacted directly and completely on domestic prices. Kenen, meanwhile, saw diversification as important for reducing susceptibility to shocks.

All the criteria are very sensible. None, therefore, can by itself define an 'optimum currency area'. Further, each of the criteria is extremely difficult to implement quantitatively. It seems impossible to avoid the conclusion that the optimal currency area (OCA) concept is in practice non-operational. The concept reflects an important and interesting trade-off, but in practice it seems that one cannot go beyond the conclusion that currency unions 'will be relatively more attractive for small, open economies that engage in a large volume of international trade (relative to their size)' whereas 'floating rates . . . are more suitable for large and relatively self-contained economies' (McCallum 1996, p. 225).

Bayoumi and Eichengreen (1996, 1997) have, however, been able to go a little further. In their 1997 paper they develop quantitative measures (or proxies for them) for size, trade linkages and dissimilarity of aggregate shocks for different European countries, each relative to Germany. An index of suitability for membership in the contemplated currency area is constructed (for each country except Germany) by using coefficients obtained in a cross-section regression whose dependent variable is the variability of bilateral exchange rates with Germany. This index indicates that Austria, Belgium, Ireland, the Netherlands and Switzerland would be relatively suitable for inclusion in the union, whereas Denmark, Finland, Norway, Portugal, Spain, Sweden and the UK would be relatively unsuitable. These groupings seem unexceptionable.

Bayoumi and Eichengreen have made significant progress towards operationalization of OCA theory. Nevertheless, their approach yields only rankings of suitability, not actual cost–benefit measures that would indicate where the line separating included from excluded countries should be. Accordingly, one could still maintain that true operationality of the OCA concept has not been achieved. To emphasize this point, it should be observed that if there were ever a situation that required application of the OCA calculus, it was the January 1999 creation of the European Monetary Union. But Bayoumi's and Eichengreen's (1996) review of numerous studies indicates that none actually provides estimates indicating which countries should, and which should not, be members of the euro area.

That the concept is operational only in this very limited sense is important for the arguments and approach of this chapter, so it is worth setting out and developing the conclusion a little further. Krugman and Obstfeld (1994, pp. 611–17) provide a diagram which lets the point be made with particular clarity. The construction of the diagram is in three stages (see Figures 4.1–4.3).

In Figure 4.1, the upward sloping GG schedule shows that a country's monetary efficiency gain from joining a fixed exchange rate area rises as the country's economic integration with the area rises. In Figure 4.2, the downward sloping LL schedule shows that a country's economic stability loss from joining a fixed exchange rate area falls as the country's economic integration with the area rises. And, finally, in Figure 4.3, the intersection

Figure 4.1 | Monetary efficiency gain

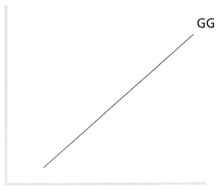

Monetary efficiency
gain for the joining country

GG

Degree of economic integration between the
joining country and the exchange rate area

Figure 4.2 | Economic stability loss

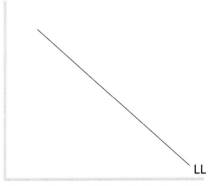

Economic stability
loss for the joining country

LL

Degree of economic integration between the
joining country and the exchange rate area

of GG and LL at point 1 determines a critical level of economic integration between a fixed exchange rate area and a country considering whether to join. At any greater level of integration, the decision to join yields positive net economic benefits to the joining country (see Figure 3.1 for an alternative understanding).

The analysis shows the relevant issues: but reading the labelling of the axes shows how far the theory is from being operational.

It may therefore be useful to approach the concept of an optimum currency area in a different way.

Rather than starting by listing the conditions which make a currency area optimal and seeing which areas satisfy these conditions, one could start with the following definition: the basic definition of a currency area of optimum size is that it can maintain itself indefinitely in competition with currency areas of other sizes.

> # The basic definition of a currency area of optimum size is that it can maintain itself indefinitely in competition with currency areas of other sizes

Figure 4.3 | Gains and joining

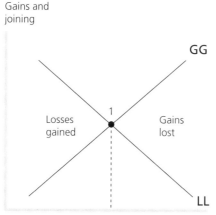

Gains and joining

GG

Losses gained   1   Gains lost

LL

Degree of economic integration between the joining country and the exchange rate area

That definition may seem familiar. Familiarity would not be surprising. The definition is taken, with one modification, from the 4th (1987) edition of George Stigler's *The Theory of Price*. The change is that 'currency area' has been substituted for 'firm'. Stigler produced that definition on the basis of concluding that 'the theory of the economies of scale has never achieved scientific prosperity' (1958, p. 4). He went on: 'A large cause of its poverty is that the central concept of the theory – the firm of optimum size – has eluded confident measurement' (1958, p. 14). He then argued that we should judge the optimum size by whether firms survive or not. Trying that led him to find a wide range of optimum sizes. We see the same when we look at currency areas which have survived without the protection of exchange controls.[2] What can we do with this concept? We can borrow from Stigler again and look at various factors popularly said to contribute to currency area size, as he did for firm size. (For example he looked and rejected advertising expenditure.) We could look at labour mobility; at price stability; at commodity composition of output. Given the reluctance of governments to abandon national currencies, we could focus on how competition led them to adopt policies necessary for their currencies' survival.[3]

The theory thus restated has an immediate application in considering EMU. We can consider any proposed currency area and ask if it falls within the range of existing areas. If, as the euro area does, the answer is 'not quite', we can then compare it with a successful currency area of almost the same size (considering both economic and geographical dimensions) and ask if it has the same attributes. The obvious comparison is with the USA. The answer from that comparison would appear to be that some factors are lacking and, if optimality develops over time (as Hugh Rockoff (2002) suggests that it does) the road to it could be bumpy. These points are developed in the following sections.

Our conclusion so far would therefore be that EMU remains debated because there is no body of analysis which can be used to consider whether or not EMU is an optimal currency area. Rather the literature suggests that there is a wide range of such optimal – or perhaps feasible (to use Corden's term) – areas. EMU is an outlier in that range (if it is in the range at all) and so discussion of it is particularly vigorous. Why, one might ask, is the USA not similarly discussed? The answer may be that its having survived for a long time has promoted almost unthinking acceptance of it. (Martin Feldstein (1997) has observed that if the USA were now separate currency areas – two to four, perhaps – no one would suggest forming it into one.) Further, it is one country.

All in all, then, our approach of drawing on a wide variety of precedents to see what lessons they teach for various aspects of EMU, rather than approaching EMU with a single model, seems unavoidable and fully justified. There is no single model appropriate to the task.

A neglected argument for unions

Mundell elaborated a further argument for the fixing of exchange rates between countries. To quote from Mundell (1973a): 'A fixed exchange rate system is a device for automatic cushioning of shocks without destroying the image of the international moneyness of the national money in the public mind' (p. 115).

He summarizes the argument behind this by a very simple example:

If we consider two different countries, one with internationally acceptable gold as money, and the other with inconvertible paper money, the state with the gold is better off since, other things equal, the gold can be spent abroad – used as an emergency reserve – if the rest of the world is on a gold standard and the state in question does not make up too large a share of the world (as measured by reserves). Inconvertible paper money is not a reserve for the state as a whole, except insofar as it can be marketed abroad. (1973a, p. 114)

Fixed exchange rates thus, Mundell argues, facilitate international borrowing and lending and help smooth out asymmetric shocks.

Now, that is indeed an argument for countries' having fixed exchange rates, or even a common currency, between them. It does not, of course, guide us in deciding the 'optimal' domain of a currency, except insofar as it suggests a presumption in favour of large rather than small domains (other things equal).

His view on how smoothly the system would work are summed up in the following quotation:

The adjustment mechanism if it is run correctly, works just like the interregional mechanism of adjustment between the twelve districts of the United States, which runs so smoothly that most people are not even aware that there are twelve Federal Reserve district currencies. (1973b, p.146)[4]

But in a penetrating and wide-ranging paper, Balassa (1973) set out how important 'others things equal' qualifications are in this case. In considering the regional adjustment mechanism within the USA, he observed as follows:

For one thing, the literature on interregional payment mechanisms leads to the conclusions that reserve flows are not solely responsible for the equilibrium of regional balances of payments and that short-term as well as long-term capital movements, income changes, government transfers as well as labour migration all contribute to it.' (p.174)[5]

So we are still left with 'optimality' not being a clear-cut phenomenon and Corden's 'feasibility' being perhaps the more accurate term for the issue examined in the literature on the appropriate domain of a currency.

Previous monetary unions

There is no strict historical precedent for the European Monetary Union, but there are some similarities with previous experience which can be instructive. Two important points need to be made at the outset, however, and should be held in view throughout. The first is that previous unions of any size or significance are found in the 19th century at a time when metallic monetary standards were almost universally used. This makes for considerable differences from any union that might take place now in a world of fiat money. The second point is that the 19th century was the century of the nation state, when there was widespread desire among small states for political union.

This section considers the principal attempts at political and monetary unions. In the first category are Switzerland, Germany and Italy. In the second are the Latin Monetary Union and the Scandinavian Currency Union.

Political union through common money

Switzerland

Although a territory recognized as Switzerland has been around for many hundreds of years, serious political union did not take place until 1848. There were 22 cantons in the union and many different currencies. There was discussion about how to rationalize such a system and the preference was for the French franc-based system which came into being in 1850. The Swiss silver franc happened to coincide with the French franc and by the early 1850s 80 per cent of Swiss coins originated in France. An act of 1860 allowed for the reduction of the metal content in coins and that led to some problems with Switzerland's monetary partners in the Latin Monetary Union (to which we will return). In the 1880s and 1890s the Swiss franc depreciated against the French franc and Swiss banks began losing silver.

Paper money was in use in Switzerland. But bank notes were not legal tender and their regulation was left to individual cantons. In 1876 a Konkordat was made agreeing to a rationalization of the bank notes and in 1907 the Swiss National Bank was founded following discussion and legislation of 1904. The Bank was given a monopoly on the issue of bank notes.

The main point to make about the Swiss experience is that the organization of the currency was simply a rationalization of a system that had come *after* political union had been achieved.

Germany

Germany is more interesting in the present context and at least at some levels would appear to have some striking parallels with the EMU – principally that substantial moves toward *economic* union clearly preceded political union; although it should be stressed that political union was the objective. There were hundreds of German states in the early 19th century. Some attempts were made at removing obstacles to trade; first of all in the formation of the Zollverein in 1834. The real starting point for the process of German unification, however, can be found at the Congress of Vienna in 1814. After that 35 principalities and four free cities had full sovereignty and, particularly, the authority to regulate their own money systems. They had independent fiscal systems too, but in most cases the power of princes to tax had been heavily circumscribed and customs duties remained an important source of revenue. In most of the territories a silver standard was in use. There was some government paper but it was not a significant proportion of the total stock of money. Fiscal needs were invariably the source of such paper.

In 1837 the Munich Coinage Treaty was signed. It was a step taken toward monetary union. Some states renounced their rights of monetary sovereignty. In 1838, following the Dresden Coinage Convention, each state was obliged to adopt either the Thaler or the Gulden. Additionally, to promote the idea of a unified system a common coin was minted (the Vereinsmünze, meaning 'union coin'). It was equal in value to two Thaler and 3.5 Gulden. What was tending to happen, however, was that the Prussian Thaler was beginning to penetrate all over Germany.

An important aspect of the Dresden Convention was that it established permanently fixed exchange rates between the two currency areas of the Zollverein. However, some states within the Zollverein had opt-out clauses and did not participate in these arrangements (e.g. Luxembourg) and other important German states were outside the Zollverein.

The political turmoil of 1848 brought some changes in Europe but the political movement for German unification failed. The Vienna Coinage Treaty of 1857 must be regarded as the next important further step towards German monetary union. It standardized the silver coinage system, laid down strict rules on the circulation and minting of gold coins and prohibited the conversion of gold to silver at a fixed exchange rate, so preventing a bimetallic system from emerging. It also touched on the issue of paper money. This was aimed at Austria, whose paper money was inconvertible. The treaty insisted on convertibility. Thus coinage was on a common standard after 1857.

> The political turmoil of 1848 brought some changes in Europe but the political movement for German unification failed

In 1871 the German Reich was founded. At that point there were still different coinage systems in place and paper money was highly diverse. But coinage acts of 1871 and 1873 unified the coinage across the Reich. The set of rules meant that in fact something close to a common currency existed; paper money remained a small proportion of the total.

There is some disagreement in the case of Germany over whether monetary union led or followed political union. There can be no doubt that political union was a desired objective, as it was for some other states. And it does seem that steps taken in that direction were frequently of an economic kind so that it could be argued that the path to monetary union was well advanced by 1871.

As to how this union performed over the next 30 years, it has recently been argued that because the central authority had limited taxing powers and limited income from the individual states, strains emerged and problems developed which led directly to World War I and on to the hyperinflation that followed. Ill-designed fiscal federalism (which happens to look surprisingly like that of the EU) proved fatal (Hefeker 2001).

Italy

The story of Italy can be treated at less length. The drive for political union was a romantic vision of the nation state that drove the separate kingdoms and territories along in the course of the 19th century, so that by 1861 unification under the King of Sardinia was achieved. When that union was completed it became necessary to remove many of the obstacles to trade, some of which came in the form of the many different currencies that were in existence. Steps therefore followed to convert the country to a monetary union as well. In 1862 a unified system based on the Sardinian lira was introduced. Sardinia was French oriented which accounts in part for the adoption of a system closely related to the French. A bimetallic standard was adopted in common with Italy's main trading partners and also to allow for the fact that silver coin predominated in the south of Italy. The main reason for not saying more here is that we turn next (and briefly again) to the Latin Monetary Union of which, of course, Italy was a founder member.

Common money pure and simple

Latin Monetary Union

In 1865 France, Switzerland, Italy and Belgium made an agreement to co-ordinate their monetary systems. It was this that became known as the Latin Monetary Union. Some have seen it as an attempt at establishing bimetallism but Redish has argued convincingly that it was not (Redish 1994). These countries all had strong monetary links and were on a *de facto* gold standard. It is not without significance that the union was formed soon after the rapid fall in the gold price that was consequent upon the Californian and Australian gold discoveries. This drove silver out of circulation. The four countries of the Latin Monetary Union had close connections but had different token coins and the union established a common token currency. The agreement between them also stated the type of token and the quantity that would be issued and the conditions of convertibility.

When the price of gold started to rise in the 1870s it might have been imagined that the *de jure* bimetallic standard would have restored a *de facto* silver standard. In fact union members abandoned bimetallism. Again the important fact was the 19th-century climate of economic integration.

Some background may be helpful. In 1798 the French had invaded the Netherlands and imposed the new French monetary system. When the

Belgian provinces revolted and went their own way they kept the French monetary system. In 1798 the French had also invaded Switzerland and instituted a system there, based on the franc. By 1852 the silver coins of France, Belgium and some Italian states were made legal tender. (Napoleon had already introduced the French system to Italy in 1793.) We noted earlier that when Italy was unified in 1861 it led to the adoption of the French system with which large parts of the country were already familiar. It was thus the case that the coins of Belgium, Switzerland and France all had legal-tender status. So by 1852 these countries all used the same unit of account and gave legal-tender status to each other's coins. It must be regarded as no great leap forward to form what they called a union – a currency union was in effect already in place.

Interestingly, Duisinberg recently drew the following lesson from this experience: 'Monetary unification of countries with different monetary systems is not easily attained; a treaty aimed at unification is ultimately doomed to failure if it is more or less imposed on the other signatories to the treaty' (quoted in van Thoor 1996).

Scandinavia

Much the same might be said for the Scandinavian countries Norway, Denmark and Sweden as for the Latin countries. These countries had a long history of close connection and had similar units of account – principally the riksdaler – and exchange of coins. They were on a silver standard. After long discussion and with a view to joining the increasingly prosperous club, these countries joined the gold standard – Norway and Denmark in 1874, and Sweden in 1874. In 1873 they formed a currency union and at that point the krona replaced the riksdaler. Gold and other coins circulated freely.

In the 1870s these countries had considered various proposals – of joining the LMU; of joining the German Union; of joining the sterling area. They opted for the less adventurous course of forming their own union. It must be said it was not so much imposed as the natural evolution of these similar countries' gradually using each other's coins. The main step taken to enlarge the union was in 1885 when the 'central banks' established inter-country drawing rights. This clearing arrangement cleared notes at par.

By 1901 bank notes circulated freely and the most complete form of the union came about. However, no sooner had that happened than political problems between Norway and Sweden in 1905 brought strains and the system was doomed in 1914 with the beginning of the end of the gold standard.

The principal points that can be made about these unions which are of interest from our point of view are as follows. First, some were principally driven by a desire for political union. Those that resulted in political union were successful and those that did not failed. Second, they were essentially currency unions among countries using the same metallic standard. As such it can hardly be regarded as a great advance to make the formal announcement that all their notes and coins were acceptable to one another. Third, they did not have fully developed central banks; but insofar as they did, they did not have an explicitly unified monetary policy.

The fact that it was the unions that were political unions that succeeded leads to the question, is it necessary for a monetary union to be supported by a fiscal union? Study of the USA bears on this issue.

The United States

A major part of the economic analysis of monetary unions is concerned with whether or not the territories covered make, in the jargon, an optimum currency area. As noted earlier this is not an easy concept to make operational. It is straightforward to list the basic requirements such as price flexibility, labour mobility, capital mobility and so on, but much more difficult to say at what stage the combined factors have defined an optimum currency area. The originator of the concept, Robert Mundell, has in fact come out in support of the idea that the different European states would certainly become an optimum currency area even if they are not one at present. There can perhaps be no denying that; but the questions would then be, how long would that take and might there be unacceptable costs to some parts of the territory along the way. This is a question that has been addressed in relation to the USA (Rockoff 2001). The USA was a political union from an early date and that may no doubt have smoothed the monetary experience. Nevertheless, the question can still be put – might some parts of the USA have been better off with their own currencies floating against the US dollar?

Rockoff traces US experience from the origins of the monetary union, which date from the ratification of the Constitution in 1788. Prior to that, currency differed among the different colonies. The central question that he puts is, might the USA have been better off if some of the regions had had their own currency? He shows that there were bitter disputes during the 150 years after ratification. Typically what happened was that one region would experience a shock – commonly a fall in demand for an agricultural product – and the local banking system would suffer, perhaps even collapse, leading in turn to falling money supply and a further fall in real income.

In the Civil War there were effectively three monetary regions: the East and the Mid West used greenbacks; the South had a Confederate dollar; and the Pacific coast stayed on gold. After the war there was a long struggle towards acceptance of monetary reunification. Rockoff shows too that in terms of optimum currency area criteria some regions differed highly from others and that in many ways they were separable currency areas.

The most extreme experience was the Great Depression of 1929–32. While the whole country suffered there were big differences. It was at that point, argues Rockoff, that important institutional changes were made, such as the development of federally funded transfer programmes which 'redistributed reserves lost through interregional payments deficits' (p. 35). These and the increasing integration of the labour market helped to bring the USA closer to an optimum currency area. But the answer he gives to the question 'How long did it take the United States to become an optimum currency area?' is roughly 150 years.

The experience of the USA in the 1930s is of considerable interest. An early contribution to this literature, albeit made for a different purpose, came from Hartland (1949). There was, of course, a fiscal union in place in the USA in the 1930s. But there was a danger of monetary break-up as a consequence of the loss of gold reserves by individual states following on from the collapse of a state's banking system. In fact no state's system collapsed entirely since there were transfers from federal resources to alleviate poverty. Hartland concludes that these transfers were essential to the system's survival.

She does not ask if fiscal transfers can offset asymmetric shocks, but her study does bear directly on the problem. By the inter-war years the USA had a common currency, a central fiscal authority, a central bank and, crucial for the study, no nationwide banking system other than the Federal Reserve itself. All other banks could do business across one state (at most); and some states, such as Illinois, prohibited even intra-state branch banking. Hartland used this combination of facts to consider how the USA, effectively on a gold standard, held together as a monetary system when the international gold standard broke apart. It may be said that there was complete confidence that it would. But there was nevertheless a good analogy to monetary break-up as a consequence of the loss of gold reserves. This was collapse of a state's banking system consequent upon a loss of gold reserves. Although many problems were experienced, no state's system collapsed entirely. Why not? Hartland examined the flows of reserves through the Fed's accounts (the only means of monetary movement apart from shipments of cash). When a state was experiencing a net loss of reserves on private sector accounts, this was offset by inflows from the central government's account, arising not as a financial stabilization measure but as a result of transfers from federal resources made to alleviate poverty and depression.

The conclusion was that these transfers were essential to the system's survival. It must be admitted that the counterfactual was not explicitly posed – what would have happened had there not been such transfers? Would confidence in the continued integrity of the USA as a currency area have been such that private sector funds would have responded? In response to that question, it has to be said that given the degree of economic diffi-culties of the time it seems unlikely. The risk would have been too great.

> # Would confidence in the continued integrity of the USA as a currency area have been such that private sector funds would have responded?

This all points strongly to the conclusion that while monetary union may not lead automatically to political and fiscal union, without such union a monetary union may well not last. This conclusion would appear to be particularly robust in that it does not depend on asymmetric shocks to cause problems before it becomes relevant. For in the 1930s the problem was quite plainly an asymmetric response to a common shock.

It seems, then, that as a matter of fact there has been a close connection between monetary union and fiscal union. Sometimes that has been a consequence of the assertion of political power. Whether they need to go together when the desire to assert political will is absent is another question. But the historical evidence looks highly suggestive. In some cases there seem to have been agreements over the sharing of seigniorage – paralleled in EMU. And the US experience suggests that a monetary union might only be viable if it is associated with a fiscal union.

Fiscal constraints in EMU

As well as agreeing to adopt a common money, the countries which participated in EMU agreed limits in public sector debt to income and public sector borrowing to income ratios (60 per cent and 3 per cent respectively – see Chapter 9, Section 'Fiscal policy' and Chapter 11, Section 'Euro area fiscal policy'). These have been criticized. Some query whether there will be enough 'room' to stimulate the economy should there be a recession. Some criticize them as non-optimal. But surely a basic question is why there need be any fiscal constraints on individual members in a monetary union. We start by considering two possible theoretical justifications.

The first was formalized in Sargent and Wallace's 'Unpleasant monetarist arithmetic' (1984). Their point is simple. Governments, like everyone else, face a budget constraint. Spending must equal revenue. They have three sources of revenue: taxes, borrowing and money creation.

Thus,

$$GS = T + \Delta B + \Delta MB$$

Spending is identically equal to taxes plus net bond sales plus net creation of base money. If bonds cannot be sold – because there may be doubts about redemption, or even just because the stock is so high that the terms are unacceptable – and no further tax can be raised, then only one source of revenue remains, money creation. This can lead to inflation.

In the instances of very high inflation studied by Capie (1986) this was exactly the problem. Governments desperate for revenue fell back on money creation, and inflation – in some cases, hyperinflation – resulted. As one of the countries to experience this was Germany, it is easy to understand why Germany should wish fiscal constraints to prevent money creation resulting from excess borrowing. But that is to neglect an important point. The ECB is supposedly independent: it has an inflation target and no EU government, or any EU agency, supposedly can give it instructions. Accordingly, then, the ECB's constitution should render 'unpleasant monetarist arithmetic' irrelevant.

There is, however, a body of theory, quite recent in origin, which suggests that fiscal policy can be sufficient – that is, without consequent monetary expansion – to cause inflation. The main papers in this literature are Woodford (1994), Sims (1994), Begrin (2000) and Cochrane (1998). The feature which differentiates these models from all those which suggest that inflation is a monetary phenomenon is that the price level follows a path very similar to that of the stock of government bonds and not at all like, or even connected to, the path of the monetary base. Further, and a particularly striking feature of the literature, the models used are generally of a type in which Ricardian equivalence usually holds. Usually when that holds, bond-financed tax changes have effects on no important macroeconomic variable. The results of the 'fiscalist' models are thus, to use McCallum's (2002) words, 'truly startling'.

It is hard to confront the fiscalist position empirically, for usually bonds and money both increase in a period of inflation and it then can be disputed how to disentangle the effects empirically.[6] But, using history as this chapter does, it is surely appropriate to remark on episodes from quite far back in time which seem relevant. British economic history contains two notable and useful examples of such episodes. Under Henry VIII, there was a major currency debasement, but no increase in the stock of government debt. Yet prices rose, broadly in line with the nominal quantity of money. Then, somewhat later, between 1688 and 1790, the debt-to-income ratio rose from zero to something over 100 per cent. There was insignificant movement in the price level.

Accordingly, the 'fiscalist' theory of inflation cannot provide a robust justification for the fiscal constraint in EMU. And even if it could in principle, we would be cautious in claiming that such a novel and complex theory as the explanation.

What can history suggest? There is an interesting, and actually quite close, precedent – the monetary union between Austria and Hungary, a well-known 19th-century union, discussion of which we have deferred until this point as it is particularly illuminating on the role of fiscal constraints.

The Hapsburg economic union lasted from 1867 to 1914, without significant disruption. It had much in common with today's EMU: the two independent countries had a common central bank (inherited from Austria) yet retained national sovereignty over fiscal matters. There was, however, no 'stability pact'. The only restraint on government borrowing – and both governments wished to borrow substantially – came from the markets. How did matters work out?

The Austro-Hungarian currency, an inconvertible paper one, was established in 1867. In September of that year, an agreement was reached between Hungary and Austria whereby the Hungarians promised not to allow any bank of issue in their part of the Empire. There was thus one money, one exchange rate and one bank of issue, and monetary matters were all run (from Vienna) by that bank of issue. Following a stock market crash and economic stagnation in 1873, there was agitation by Hungary for greater control over monetary matters. This was gained in 1878, when the bank became the Austro-*Hungarian* Bank. Then in the 1890s the currency, which had previously floated, was put on gold. This ended the (rather limited) ability the two separate governments had previously possessed to coin silver and thereby hardened up the governments' budget constraints. The main restraint on government borrowing was now the capital market. Hungary was a new borrower, with no reputation. (All previous borrowing had been by the Austro-Hungarian empire (managed from Vienna) or by Austria.)

It was recognized by both countries that the terms on which one borrowed influenced those available to the other. This led to the common central bank's acquiring considerable power. For the capital markets required higher rates on currencies without gold clauses than on those with such clauses. Managing a gold debt was harder when the currency floated than when it was on gold. Hence market discipline led via gold clauses to a gold standard and to a central bank which could impose a hard fiscal constraint on governments.

> **Economic analysis cannot say whether EMU is an 'optimal' or even a sensible currency area**

The question this poses in the present context is why the founders of the euro have explicit constraints on fiscal profligacy, rather than relying on the market discipline which worked in a previous situation with close structural parallels to EMU. Market discipline led to an accretion of power to the central bank. Was that feared by the founders of the euro? Or was it feared that market discipline would not trouble some traditionally high-inflation members, and that they, unconcerned by reputation, would drag the reputation of others down with them? Either way, it would appear that behind the fiscal constraints may well be a lack of trust: lack of trust in the constitution of the euro area, with fear of accretion of power to the ECB; lack of trust of member states; or both. Among these three the evidence is insufficient to suggest a choice.

Lessons that emerge

It is clear from the point of view of economic analysis just why there is still debate over EMU and its future. Economic analysis cannot say whether EMU is an 'optimal' or even a sensible currency area. That is why the prospects for EMU are still discussed among economists. But that said, both certain aspects of theory and an overview of the performance of past monetary unions suggest that if EMU is to survive, further institutional development of it is necessary.

Fiscal constraints are hard to rationalize unless one sees them as a way of constraining irresponsible EMU member states so as to prevent power accruing, via a 'hard' fiscal constraint, to the ECB. It is difficult to believe in the durability of a monetary union whose members trust each other so little and fear their central bank so much. Evolution to promote greater political trust is manifestly desirable from that point of view. Such evolution could, too, lead to the creation of a European political body of sufficient importance that the ECB could sensibly be made accountable to it.

Second, examination of the history of monetary unions shows that only those which become political ones survive. Focusing on the history of the USA as a monetary union reinforces that conclusion, showing that even as recently as the 1930s, over a century and half after the USA became a monetary union, it required the political cohesion of a long-established community to hold it together as a monetary union in the face of a large common shock.

It is thus clear that further political developments are necessary in the EMU zone; and it is equally clear that those who claim that there are profound political and constitutional implications for Britain should that country choose to join are abundantly supported by history in making that claim.

Annexe: A Brief History of the Austro-Hungarian Union

There is a fascinating study of this union by Marc Flandreau (2001). Flandreau is perhaps best known for his work on bimetallism and the working of the French monetary system in the middle of the 19th century; and that of course included the relationship with the Latin Monetary Union. He raises here the question as to how useful the study of historical experience can be for guidance on the sustainability of modern monetary unions. He points out, correctly in our view as we noted earlier, that most of the arrangements that went under the name of 'monetary unions' can be found in the 19th century when most countries adhered to some form of metallic monetary standard. So as we have seen, unions such as the Latin Monetary Union or the Scandinavian Monetary Union turn out on closer examination not to be monetary unions of the kind we currently have in mind but rather simply currency unions. The countries involved simply agreed to accept each other's currency. Given that these were coins with specified metal content there was little to get excited about and much of the activity was already taking place without any formal agreement. These unions had no common monetary policy and no common central bank. Where the driving force was political union things were different – different currencies had to be rationalized in order to facilitate political union or as a sensible practice after political union was achieved or some combination of both of these. Insofar as the European monetary union is supposed to be about separate states and not political union these latter examples should be of little interest to us. And yet as has been stressed by many contributors to this debate European monetary union is a political agenda and has been carried along with 'devilish cleverness by a politically astute clique intent on achieving their own ends' (Goodhart 2001).

Be that as it may, Flandreau tried instead to find an experience which might fit our purposes more closely – a monetary union between separate independent states; this is found in the alliance between Austria and Hungary. This was an arrangement whereby both countries surrendered monetary sovereignty to a common central bank but retained fiscal sovereignty. The Habsburg monarchy operated without the kind of agreement that exists in Europe today to keep public expenditure within certain limits. There were great pressures to raise public spending in the 19th century to promote economic development and it was left to the capital market to discipline the fiscal authorities. The 'compromise of 1867' was the agreement struck between the two countries for a period of 10 years and reviewed regularly until 1917. Flandreau traces the monetary and fiscal experience of this union. He shows how the two states were continuously concerned about their reputation in the market. There was some competition over reputation and as they standardized their debt instruments the market could better read the price signals.

Notes

1 See Wood (2001) on the ECB's constitution.

2 It also prompts questions such as 'What is an area?' Is it an economic concept (measured, say, by GNP) or a political or geographic area? How big a currency area is Australia?

3 When this approach is taken it becomes much harder to defend the claim that the clear association between the abolition of exchange controls and the downward trend in inflation as seen over the past two decades is just a coincidence.

4 The paper from which this quotation comes, which appears in the same volume as 1973a, is surely the reason Mundell is sometimes called the 'Father of European Monetary Union'. His earlier and better known 1961 paper would surely, if placing him in any group, place him in one opposed to European Monetary Union.

5 A pioneering and unjustly neglected paper by Hartland (1949) makes some of these points. See further discussion of this paper in the next section.

6 The position is certainly not free of problems at the theoretical level (see Buiter 1998 and McCallum 1998).

References

Balassa, B. (1973) 'Comment', in H. G. Johnson and A. K. Swoboda (eds.), *The Economics of Common Currencies*. Cambridge, MA: Harvard University Press, pp. 173–79.

Bayoumi, T. and Eichengreen, B. (1996) 'Operationalising the theory of optimum currency areas', CEPR Discussion Paper 1484.

Bayoumi, T. and Eichengreen, B. (1997) 'Exchange market pressure and exchange rate management: perspectives from the theory of optimum currency areas', in M. I. Blejer, *et al.*, *Optimum Currency Areas: New Analytical and Policy Developments*. Washington, DC: IMF.

Bergin, P. R. (2000) 'Fiscal solvency and price level determination in a monetary union', *Journal of Monetary Economics*, 45, 1, pp. 37–53.

Buiter, W. H. (1998) 'The young person's guide to neutrality, price level indeterminacy, interest rate pegs, and fiscal theories of the price level', NBER Working Paper 6396.

Capie F. H. (1986) 'Conditions in which very rapid inflation has appeared', Carnegie-Rochester Conference Series on Public Policy 24(d), pp. 115–68.

Capie, F. H. and Wood, G. (2001) 'The birth, life and death of a currency', *Economic Journal*, 472, 449–61.

Capie, H. F. and Wood, G. (eds) (2002) *Monetary Unions: Theory, History, Public Choice*. London: Palgrave.

Cochrane, J. H. (1998) 'A frictionless view of U.S. inflation', NBER Working Paper 6646.

Corden, W. Max (1972) 'Monetary integration' essays in *International Finance*, 93. Princeton, NJ: Princeton University.

Feldstein, M. (1997) 'EMU and international conflict', *Foreign Affairs*, 76, 6, pp. 60–73.

Flandreau, M. (2001) 'The economics of Cacania, 1867–1914: Austro-Hungarian monetary lessons for Euroland' in Capie and Wood (eds) (2001b).

Goodhart, C. A. E. G. (2002) 'The future of EMU: comments on Borodo and Jonung' in Capie and Wood (eds) (200b).

Hartland, P. (1949) 'Interregional payments compared with international payments', *Quarterly Journal of Economics*, 63, pp. 392–404.

Hefeker, C. (2001) 'The agony of central power: fiscal federalism in the German Reich', *European Review of Economic History*, 5, 1, pp. 119–42.

Kenen, Peter B. (1969) 'The theory of optimum currency areas: an eclectic view' in R. A. Mundell and A. K. Swoboda (1969) *Monetary Problems of the International Economy*, Proceedings of the Conference on International Monetary Problems, September 1966. Chicago, IL: University of Chicago Press, pp. 41–60.

Krugman, P. and Obstfeld, M. (1994) *International Economics*. New York: HarperCollins.

Lucas, R. E. (1976) 'Econometric policy evaluation – a critique', The Phillips Curve and Labor Markets Carnegie-Rochester Conference Series on Public Policy 1, pp. 19–46.

McCallum, B. T. (1996) *International Monetary Economics*. New York: Oxford University Press.

McCallum, B. T. (1998) 'Indeterminacy, bubbles, and the fiscal theory of price level determination', NBER Working Paper 6456.

McCallum, B. T. (2002) 'Theoretical issues pertaining to monetary unions' in Capie and Wood (eds) (2001b).

McKinnon, R. I. (1963) 'Optimum currency areas', *American Economic Review*, 53, pp. 717–25.

Mundell, R. (1961) 'A theory of optimum currency areas', *American Economic Review*, 51, pp. 657–64.

Mundell, R. (1973a) 'A plan for a European currency' in H. G. Johnson and A. K. Swoboda (eds) *The Economics of Common Currencies*. London: Allen & Unwin.

Mundell, R. (1973b) 'Uncommon arguments for common currencies' in H. G. Johnson and A. K. Swoboda (eds) *The Economics of Common Currencies*. London: Allen & Unwin.

Obstfeld, M. (1996) 'Models of currency crises with self-fulfilling features', *European Economic Review*, 40, pp. 1037–48.

Obstfeld, M. and Rogoff, K. (1996) *Foundations of International Macroeconomics*. Cambridge, MA: MIT Press.

Redish, A. (1994) 'The Latin American union' in M. Bordo and F. H. Capie (eds.), *Monetary Regimes in Transition*. Cambridge: Cambridge University Press.

Rockoff, H. (2002) 'How long did it take the USA to become an optimum area?' in F. H. Capie and G. E. Wood (eds) (2002b).

Sargent, T. and Wallace, N. (1984) 'Some unpleasant monetarist arithmetic', in B. Griffiths and G. E. Wood (eds.), *Monetarism in the United Kingdom*. London: Macmillan.

Sims, C. A. (1994) 'A simple model for the study of the determination of the price level and the interaction of monetary and fiscal policy', *Economic Theory*, 4, 3, pp. 381–99.

Sims, C. A. (1997) 'Fiscal foundations of price stability in open economics', Working Paper presented to Hong Kong Meeting of the Far Eastern Region of the Econometric Society, 24 July 1997.

Stigler, G. J. (1958) 'The economies of scale', *Journal of Law and Economics*, pp. 54–71.

Stigler, G. J. (1987) *The Theory of Price*. New York: Macmillan; London: Collier Macmillan.

Van Thoor, Wim. F. V. (1996) *European Monetary Union since 1848*. Chettenham: Edward Elgar.

Wood, G. (2002) 'Is the ECB too independent?' in P. Schacht (ed.), *Studies in Money, Banking and Finance: Essays in Honour of S. F. Frowen*. London: Palgrave.

Woodford, M. (1994) 'Monetary policy and price-level determinacy in a cash-in-advance economy', *Economic Theory*, 4, 3, pp. 345–80.

Woodford, M. (1995) 'Price-level determinacy without control of a monetary aggregate', Carnegie-Rochester Conference Series on Public Policy 43, pp. 1–46.

Woodford, M. (1998) 'Public debt and the price level', Working Paper prepared for Bank of England Conference: Government Debt Structure and Monetary Conditions, 18–19 June 1998.

5

Policy co-ordination and economic adjustment in EMU: will it work?

David G. Mayes and Matti Virén[1]

The euro area is running policies directed at macroeconomic objectives of price stability, growth, equality and employment in a rather different manner from most large federal states. It has a Single Monetary Policy and stage 3 of economic and monetary union (EMU) will be completed in the first part of 2002 when the euro notes and coin are put into circulation and the existing national currencies withdrawn. Fiscal policy, however, remains the preserve of the national governments although subject to a set of constraints imposed by the Stability and Growth Pact (SGP) together with some constraints on the nature and level of taxation and expenditures. Planned and actual policies are assessed regularly by the European Commission and infringements of the Pact are subject to sanction. Employment policy also remains largely the preserve of the member states but with a framework of

> The euro area is running policies directed at macroeconomic objectives of price stability, growth, equality and employment in a rather different manner from most large federal states

priorities and targets following annual plans that are also assessed by the Commission. Here, however, there is no compulsion to conform and no power of sanction. A similar process is being applied to other 'structural' policies seeking to remove regulatory rigidities and distortions. These areas are brought together in the development of Broad Economic Policy Guidelines on an annual basis, drawn up from the Economic and Financial Committee (EFC) and agreed by the Council of Economic and Finance Ministers (ECOFIN). This rather loose-sounding process has been labelled 'open co-ordination'.

Other macroeconomic policy areas such as trade policy have been dealt with centrally by the Commission since the inception of the Common Market, while competition policy also involves a strong role for the Commission, not just as adjudicator but as the imposer of sanctions. The whole structure of regulation of markets, particularly agriculture, has been shifted towards common rules, developed by the Commission. While each rule may be microeconomic in itself, the changes as a whole are directed towards macroeconomic efficiency and have consequences for the flexibility of the macroeconomy. The necessary co-ordination extends beyond the policies themselves, for instance into the co-ordination of the definition and collection of statistical information about the member states through Eurostat.

Issues relating to equality are dealt with differently. In general, issues of income and wealth distribution are the preserve of the member states and there is no attempt at co-ordination. However, the summit at Nice in December 2000 made moves towards implementing similar ideas of open co-ordination in the field of social protection. Most importantly, the automatic transfer of incomes and wealth through taxes, benefits and discretionary public expenditure between the regions, sectors and households that are doing well and those that are faring worse across the national boundaries is virtually non-existent. The total EU budget (see Chapter 11) amounts to less than 1.2 per cent of GDP and most of that is not directed towards structural issues of relative disadvantage. The largest part goes towards the Common Agricultural Policy (CAP) which, as Franzmeyer et al. (1991) note, if anything makes the national discrepancies worse rather than smaller. However, the small size of the structural funds should not be belittled as they are highly focused on areas of the greatest perceived problems – long-term and youth unemployment and regions that are lagging well below the EU average or seriously affected by the closure of traditional industries. The great success of the Irish economy over the last 10 years is in part due to the major inflow of funds from the rest of the EU over an extended period to support infrastructural investment, training and the development of a competitive environment (O'Donnell 1998). However, it is rather more debatable what proportion of the convergence of the disadvantaged regions as a whole in the EU has been due to the structural funds rather than to the wider removal of barriers between members of a 'growth club' who would have performed more similarly in the past without the constraints (Quah 1993).

Co-ordination among macroeconomic policies has two elements to it. The first is co-ordination among the members of the EU over any one policy, to achieve goals that would not be attainable if they merely pursued their national interests separately. Different forms of co-ordination may be appropriate for different policies – if only because the extent of the possible externalities from the actions of the member states on each other are different for different policies. Such co-ordination is required on the one hand because policies with respect to common problems may differ and could conflict. On the other hand, the economic shocks to the member states may affect some more than others, hence the states have to decide how to handle the different needs of the parts of the area under common policies. In the main, it is the arrangements for the first problems of co-ordination that we have just listed, policy by policy. However, macroeconomic policies are inter-dependent, and hand in hand with co-ordination within policies runs co-ordination *across* policies. Although the Broad Economic Policy Guidelines are a form of co-ordination both within and across policies, this is an area where the level of co-ordination in the EU is more informal than in many countries.

Monetary policy and fiscal policy are not co-ordinated by having a common body responsible although the Eurogroup of the 12 ministers of finance from the euro area countries is joined by a representative of the ECB at its meetings, and the chairman of the Eurogroup and a representative from the Commission can attend ECB Governing Council meetings (without a vote). Co-ordination comes from the rules of the game laid down in the treaty and in the SGP. The ECB is charged with maintaining price stability – it does not have the multiple objec-tives of the US Federal Reserve (Fed) – and having regard to the economic policies of the EU is only to be observed subject to the maintenance of that price stability. The SGP similarly imposes rules of fiscal rectitude on the member states, ensuring not just an upper limit to debt and the pursuance of sustainable policy but the avoidance of excessive automatic or discretionary volatility in the fiscal balance over the cycle. Both parties can therefore act in the knowledge of what the others are likely to do. In some respects the degree of mutual knowledge is greater than in the USA, where the 1935 Banking Act, which created the Federal Open Market Committee (FOMC), simultaneously removed both the Secretary of the Treasury and the Comptroller of the Currency from the Federal Reserve Board. Nowadays the link is maintained *inter alia* through a weekly meeting between the Secretary and the Chairman of the Board (Meyer 2000).

Some co-ordination among policies has emerged from practice. Although the generalized arrangements for exchange rate policy remain the preserve of the Council of Ministers it is clear that the existence of the price stability mandate for the ECB means that the ECB will run the practice of exchange rate policy. Otherwise the two could readily conflict. When the euro declined against the US dollar in its first year of existence there were initially some suggestions by finance ministers that something should be 'done' about it. However, within the first few months of 1999 the primacy of the role of the ECB in this regard was established and hence the nature of the 'co-ordination' between monetary and exchange rate policy. Thus the foreign exchange interventions in the second half of 2000 were undertaken by the ECB as they saw the depreciation of the euro compared with perceived fundamentals threatening price stability.

The governance of the ECB and the Eurosystem is itself an exercise in co-ordination and determination of an agreed policy. The structure of the Governing Council by having the governors of the 12 participating national central banks (NCBs) and the six members of the Executive Board of the ECB (who are directly appointed by the agreement of the member states) differs from that in other large currency areas, although it has a lot in common with the structure of the Bundesbank.

All these arrangements are relatively untried and several of them are unique to the EU. Novelty and uniqueness do not have any intrinsic implications for success or failure. Simply having a decision-making body of 18, which will of course expand if new members join the euro area, is regarded as being unwieldy by some outside observers (Buiter 1999; Crooks 2001). However, such objections may merely reflect a disagreement with the actual decisions taken or a disagreement with the underlying view of how the economy works or the objectives for policy. The time period for judgement is very short. As Alesina *et al.* (2001) note in the third CEPR review of the progress of ECB: 'The ECB has shown, overall, good judgment in its actions' (p. xv). The debate is much wider. Contrary to the general thrust of the literature that co-ordination tends to be beneficial, Alesina *et al.* go on to say (p. xiv): 'Formal meetings between the monetary and fiscal authorities designed to co-ordinate policies are either unnecessary or harmful.'

In this chapter we seek to provide an initial assessment of just some of the aspects of this new framework for macroeconomic policy. In the second section we consider monetary policy, in the third section employment policy and in the fourth fiscal policy. The fifth section considers co-ordination issues and concludes. We begin by developing the overall framework.

Framework for macroeconomic policy in the euro area

The framework for macroeconomic policy in the EU, set out in Table 5.1, shows that a variety of approaches are applied. Indeed no branches of policy are run with identical structures. The picture is further complicated by the fact that Denmark, Sweden and the UK have not joined stage 3 of EMU and hence are not part of the Single Monetary Policy, even though they are full participants in the rest of the process of co-ordination. This means that discussions about what the

Table 5.1 | Framework for macroeconomic policy in the EU

Policy area	Form	Administration of co-ordination
Monetary	Single policy	Governing Council of ECB
Fiscal	Constrained national with sanctions	ECOFIN (Eurogroup) on commission assessment
Tax	National with limits	ECOFIN advice, regulation
Structural funds (regional)	Joint Commission and national	Commission
Employment	Open co-ordination	Employment Committee on Commission assessment
Structural	Open co-ordination	ECOFIN on Commission assessment
Broad economic policy	Open co-ordination	ECOFIN on Commission assessment
Competition	Commission with national sanctions	Commission including sanctions
Inter-country transfers	Not agreed	
Macro	Dialogue	Informal Council/Commission
Exchange rate	Single	ECB implementation ECOFIN regime
Commercial policy	Single	Commission

12 participants in the euro area should do over fiscal policy and related issues cannot be undertaken in the normal meeting of ECOFIN where all 15 countries are present. They have to take place through the 'Eurogroup' meetings of just the 12 participating finance ministers in a somewhat unofficial arrangement.

It would be easy to conclude that this hybrid was the typical product of a committee and that the more normal arrangement in federal countries, where the participating states play a reduced role in matters of fiscal, structural and employment policy, would apply without the national political constraints. A weaker criticism would be that the arrangements were the results of constructive economic and political pragmatism. In this view the EU has gone as far as it can politically towards a more centralized scheme and the arrangements are near optimal subject to those constraints. However, an even more charitable construction can be put on the arrangements by suggesting that in practice they come close to what might be optimal from an economic point of view, given that the EU is still relatively diverse. Greater uniformity of policy and central direction of it might in this view actually be counterproductive.

Clearly any such interpretation, given the nature of the negotiations over the last decade or more, is likely to be a matter of ex-post rationalization rather than clear-sighted planning from the outset. This does not, of course, make it invalid. A single currency and the attendant monetary policy need to be run by a single decision-making body. Furthermore, the time consistency literature (Walsh 1998, 2000) suggests that the institutions for monetary policy need to be clearly independent of short-run political concerns if inflation bias is to be avoided. They also need to be given an unambiguous objective (in this case price stability), credible powers to achieve it and a legal framework, which makes changing these rules seem relatively unlikely. (Since financial stability is also an essential ingredient of macroeconomic stability (BIS 2001; Kindleberger 1992) it is also helpful to have the eurosystem address these issues.)

If monetary policy and the overall fiscal stance are to be run in a harmonious manner then fiscal policy needs to be constrained to run according to prudential principles. Otherwise they may try to offset each other in a costly struggle. Furthermore any uncertainty on the part of the central bank as to the intentions of the fiscal authorities may lead them to take a rather tighter policy stance on average. The same need for predictability applies to monetary policy from the point of view of the fiscal authorities. They need to be good at predicting how the monetary authority will respond to fiscal decisions.

However, beyond the dictates of prudence, which are normally thought to relate to sustainability and the avoidance of undue short-run volatility, it is arguable that further constraints on the content and management of fiscal policy may be unnecessary. The EU actually imposes a somewhat greater constraint on sustainability than is strictly required, as fiscal policy not merely has to be consistent with long- run stability but the ratio of debt to GDP must be less than 60 per cent. Provided the SGP is credible, it may in fact go as far as is needed, given that there are also limits to acceptable tax (and benefit) competition agreed by the EU (such as over the coverage and rates for VAT). Thus within the overall prudent constraints the member states are free to find detailed revenue and expenditure policies that will best meet their local institutional and struc- tural environment. It is argued by Melitz (2000) that while there may be some characteristics of fiscal policy that will or will not work in a variety of environments, the effectiveness of many policies depends on their context. Thus it is the whole system of reinforcing institutions and behaviour that has a major impact on the outcomes, and the particular balance of policies must take this into account to be efficient. To take a simple example, the transmission channels vary across countries. Where equity finance is more important than debt finance the effect of an interest rate change on output and inflation will be different. Hence in the face of a Single Monetary Policy the combination of other policies will have to be different to compensate (Leichter and Walsh 1999).

When it comes to employment policy and structural policies, under this favourable reading, there is even less need to provide constraints or uniformity at the European level, beyond fiscal prudence and the banning of anticompetitive practices. Thus ruling out certain forms of state aids and encouraging a common focus may be the necessary minimum. The EU approach of trying to improve the ability of the member states to learn from each other and the introduction of incen- tives for states to outshine each other in the successful pursuit of higher employment may then be seen as taking a positive step that other countries have not. By not taking uniformity too far they avoid imposing unnecessary costs and by speeding up the learning process and introducing an element of competition and rivalry among states they may be speeding up the adjustment process.

We could attempt to take this argument further by appraising competition and commercial policy but the argument is weakest in the area of fiscal federalism and the transfer of resources to disadvantaged areas. The EU has decided to keep the overall budget very small by comparison with individual countries and in the Berlin Council in 1999 also decided to limit the extent of net contributions/benefits still further _hapter 11). Thus the degree to which there is any redistribution ɔenefits from the faster development of the EU as a result of ᵼegration is strictly limited. This certainly goes further than any of the ɹdvocates of 'trickle down' benefits argue. However, even allowing for any counterproductive influences from the Common Agricultural Policy, EU 'structural' policy has been very heavily targeted on the areas of greatest need: low income per head, high unemployment, poor infrastructure. The argument presented (Commission 1999) is that in most cases the limits of the absorptive capacity of the regions being targeted have been approached and hence beneficial transfers of this sort were not being severely limited. In any case most systems of fiscal redistribution involve a large element of 'dead weight' and the net flows involved are considerably smaller than the gross.

In NIESR (1991) we estimated that regional spread of incomes per head in the EU could be reduced to the target level (none below 85 per cent) with a total transfer of only around 2.5 per cent of EU GDP. Even the more vigorous role foreseen in the 1977 MacDougall Report was only for a 7 per cent budget in total. A doubling of the budget in net terms is of course totally outside anything contemplated in the EU at present. So although the adjustment may seem small in national terms where tax changes equivalent to 1 per cent of GDP are common in a single year, it is completely inconceivable in an EU context and therefore differentiates the EU from common practice elsewhere. However, the sources of EU revenues are not in the form of income taxes (mainly customs duties and VAT) and hence are more difficult to use for stabilization policy as they are not progressive.

Nevertheless, taking all these facets of macroeconomic policy together it is not clear that the EU is running a system that is massively different from what might be thought appropriate in a more federal system. However, for such an enterprise to work adequately, it has both to be able to cope with the likely stream of economic shocks to the EU economy and to be credible. We deal with these questions sector by sector, starting with monetary policy.

The Single Monetary Policy

As with the other facets of the macroeconomic policy of the euro area it is far too soon to label monetary policy a success or failure. Only three years have elapsed since the creation of the ECB, even less since the start of the euro in money markets. The euro itself is being introduced in the form of notes and coin in January 2002 and the current national currencies will only be withdrawn a few months after that. It is only in the last year or so that any judgements have been made in a quantitative manner on the success of the longest running of the new monetary policy regimes, that of New Zealand (Huang *et al.* 2000; Svensson 2001). These come after 10 years and the estimates are both tentative and not very well determined. Similarly judgements on US policy in the 1970s and 1980s are only now beginning to come through with clarity (Orphanides 1999; Sargent 1999). It is therefore only possible to make judgements about the single monetary policy on the basis of institutional struc- tures and earlier experience of the euro area.

Of course, popular judge- ments are not inhibited by the lack of evidence and any monetary institution will be subject to criticism or praise according to whether the policy settings it follows

> ## As with the other facets of the macroeconomic policy of the euro area it is far too soon to label monetary policy a success or failure

match the forecasts that market commentators have made for their clients. There have also been some measured assessments by the CEPR (Alesina *et al.* 2001; Begg *et al.* 1999; Favero *et al.* 2000), by the Shadow Committee and by Gali (2001). While these have primarily been based on how the ECB has been addressing its task rather than on the particular policy settings, a modestly favourable assessment has been made of what the ECB has done. Criticism of the nature of the twin-pillar strategy is largely irrelevant for our present purposes as it does not in the main relate to the appropriateness of the framework for policy.

Here there are several issues that relate to the credibility of policy. We only concern ourselves with three:

- the structure of decision making
- the information available for the co-ordination of policy
- the strains placed on a single policy from the diversity of the member states.

It is not that the others are irrelevant, merely that similar arguments apply.

The structure of decision making

The treaty lays down that in the Eurosystem the governor of each of the participating central banks has a seat on the Governing Council along with the six members of the Executive Board, which includes the

President and Vice-President. The Governing Council is responsible for the running of the euro system of NCBs and the ECB, most importantly for monetary policy. Not only is the balance of power different from that of the FOMC, with the governors having, currently, twice as many votes as the Executive Board, but the range of responsibilities is much greater. Although the running of each NCB remains the responsibility of the individual governor the Eurosystem has delegated far less responsibility for the running of the ECB to the Executive than is the case in the USA. Governing Council meetings thus have monetary policy decisions as only a part of their agenda. Not surprisingly therefore, particularly since the Eurosystem is still in the initial learning phase, it meets fortnightly – three times as frequently as the FOMC.

These differences in structure and functions mean that direct comparisons between the Eurosystem and the Fed can be misleading. Even in response to equal news, meetings result in policy changes would occur in the Eurosystem roughly only one-third as often as in the USA. (Large shifts could be spread across meetings rather more readily in the Eurosystem.)

The Governing Council has come in for round criticism (Buiter 1999) and robust defence (Issing 1999) of its size; some consider it too large and hence unlikely to be able to take decisions efficiently. It is certainly the case that most central banks' monetary policy committees are smaller (nine in the UK, seven in Sweden and the Czech Republic and so on – see Svensson 2001). In the USA the FOMC has a voting membership of 12 (the seven Board members, the President of the New York Fed and four other Fed Bank presidents by rotation). However, the FOMC has effectively 19 members, as the other seven non-voting Fed Bank Presidents also come to all of the meetings and speak on equal terms but do not, of course, vote. The challenge for the ECB Governing Council would be if membership increases. It could increase to 21 if all the current members of the EU joined and eventually to 34 if all the current applicant countries successfully participated in EMU as well. This is not, however, a current problem, as on the present timetable, new members are not due for admission to the EU before 2004 and even if they were to qualify immediately it would require a further two-year transition period before they could join the Eurosystem.

Changing the voting arrangement would require a change to the treaty, something that would be highly contentious. Large countries would no doubt be rather unenthused about rotation on the US model; small countries would be unhappy about arrangements based on size, as that would enable them to have a vote only rarely. (That problem already applies to the Executive Board. If, which is not the case, members were to be appointed by rotation and seats available roughly by GDP or population, small countries would feel lucky to get one of the eight-year appointments each century.) Grouping countries geographically or by size to create constituencies perhaps along IMF or World Bank lines is also unattractive because it assumes that such groupings have some relevance for voting interests.

Unlike the FOMC the members of the Governing Council of the ECB have no brief to report on or represent the interests of their particular region. Their concern is to be solely for the maintenance of price stability in the euro area as a whole. Attributed individual views are not recorded and the minutes are not published. So the chances of members being able to air views which reflect solely their ideas on how the euro economy works and how people respond to policy, even when this would not be to the short-run interest of their region, are enhanced. (Obviously one cannot police the source of the members' views and some might still be concerned about nationally adverse views getting out.)

Hence most models based on median voter behaviour or other decisions based on supporting the interests of the countries from which governors or even the Executive Board members come should be rather irrelevant to the modelling of the decision making (Persson and Tabellini 2000). Any future groupings that would make best sense from the point of view of being representative of the range of opinion would be chosen by the governors among themselves in a search for colleagues with like-minded views. In any case it is not at all obvious why one should only look to reduce the number of voting NCB governors if the total is to be squeezed. Why should all six Executive Board members continue to have a vote? The General Council (on which the governors of all 15 NCBs sit) has only the President and Vice-President from the Executive Board. If there is going to be any well-thought-out and organized interest group whose views could be represented by some of their number it is likely to be the Executive Board, who are working next to each other every day. Such a reduction could prolong the date by which some other arrangement has to be made and maintain the idea of each country's having both a seat at the table and a vote. It is normal in corporations for executives to attend board meetings but not necessarily to have a vote. Clearly, somebody is going to be unhappy whatever the decision.

In any case, up until now the Governing Council has not voted on monetary policy issues but has proceeded by consensus. Some (Blinder et al. 2001, for example) have suggested that this also represents a departure from normal monetary policy committee behaviour and that it will lead to slower decision making by the ECB. However, this interpretation rests partly on three illusions. The first is that MPCs usually disagree on what to do. An examination of the voting records of the Fed (Meyer 1998) shows that normally the members of the Committee are either completely or almost completely agreed about what to do. The second illusion is that MPCs are normally discussing changing monetary policy at their meetings. Most meetings result in no change and having serious disputes about whether and by how much to change interest rates is unusual except round expected turning points. Lastly, it is also an illusion to believe that consensus means that everyone must agree. Not only will those in a small minority usually give in if they do not feel passionately about an issue but the large majority would want to enforce their will if they could see no virtue in the minority case. The number of occasions when those on the losing side want to register dissent, even in the UK, which appears to have a rather more contentious system than many, is small. In the ECB case there is very little downside to registering dissent. The rest of the Governing Council have no say over the appointment of other NCB governors and the members of the Executive Board cannot be reappointed. Holding clearly different views may grate with one's colleagues but it is not a career-threatening issue as it could easily be within an internal MPC or one where tenure is short and renewable.

Thus many of the suggestions in this regard that the ECB cannot operate in as effective or objective a manner as other central banks are therefore likely to be misplaced.

The information available for the co-ordination of policy

For co-ordination of policy to take place effectively a central bank has to be very 'transparent' and 'predictable'. It is not that other decision makers will know what policy is going to be but that they will understand how it will be formulated and what the central bank's current thinking is about the future. In Castrén and Mayes (1997) we set out what these conditions are (see also Mayes 1999). In summary:

- Outsiders need to be clear what the bank's objectives are.
- They need to understand what the bank's view of the future is, in terms of both the most likely outcome and the risks that the bank is taking into account.
- They need to know how the bank thinks the economy works.
- Finally they need to know how the bank intends to respond to unexpected shocks.

With this knowledge they can plan their own strategy in the light of their views about the outlook for the economy and how it works – which will probably differ from those of the bank. They can be fairly clear about how the bank will react to their decisions and hence plan for the future in a framework that allows not only for their own decisions but for the expected decisions of the bank as well (Tarkka and Mayes 1999).

These information requirements can be boiled down to three things:

- a clear discussion of the bank's objectives and strategy in meeting them
- an exposition of the bank's 'model' of how the economy works
- a full published forecast that covers likely risks over the time horizon relevant for policy.

These are quite exacting requirements. The Norges Bank and the Reserve Bank of New Zealand probably come closest to providing them, as do the Bank of England and the Sveriges Riksbank. The Fed does not go that far, in that its forecasts are not clearly published and its strategy and objectives are fairly vague. (Bernanke *et al.* 1999 and others advocate that it also should make changes along the lines we have suggested above.) The ECB is on the way to meeting these requirements and what it has published thus far largely represents the development of its work. It now publishes a forecast twice a year. In its Monthly Bulletin and four-weekly press conferences it is developing an exposition of its objectives and strategy so that an idea can be built up of how it responds to shocks. It has published one of its models (the area-wide model) and no doubt when its large multi-country model is completed that will also be published.

Not surprisingly this falls short of what the market would like – indeed it is unlikely that one could ever meet that. The forecasts are currently on the assumption that interest and exchange rates will remain constant. A range is shown for a limited number of variables (currently excluding the fiscal stance) rather than the Bank of England/Riksbank fan charts. The exact meaning of the price stability target is not yet as clear as those in the inflation-targeting countries. Indeed the ECB is keen to point out that it is not just following an inflation-targeting strategy but one with two pillars. The first pillar involves monetary aggregates, particularly a reference value for M3 growth, and the second likely price developments. The published forecast is part of the assessment of the second pillar and does not explicitly interact with the monetary aggregates. ECB watchers thus have a difficult task of judging how the ingredients are being put together. The main difference between the ECB and the Fed is not so much in terms of how much information is available but in the length of the track record. Having had the same Chairman for 14 years the Fed has been able to provide a lot of evidence on how policy is determined. With only three years of operation and data on the euro area only now emerging there is no means of providing a comparable basis. This can only come with time.

The question therefore is not so much whether the EU has optimal co-ordination arrangements for a world in which EMU is as mature as the USA or other large economies but whether it has something suitable in the current state of knowledge. Popular complaints about the ECB's not 'speaking with one voice' reflect partly that Governing Council members may be speaking for themselves and not just for the euro system but also that listeners are trying to dissect the detail to find out how the strategy and views of the future are being developed. Differences without substance will inevitably appear at that level of scrutiny. All central banks suffer from it. In one press conference in 1995 Don Brash, Governor of the Reserve Bank of New Zealand, remarked to a questioner: 'Please stop trying to read between the lines. There is nothing written there.'

Several other features make comparison between US and Eurosystem monetary policy more difficult than might appear at first blush. The difference in structure between the Fed and the ECB assist that misinterpretation aided by the use of titles. The Chairman of the Federal Reserve Board is by design a more central figure in the process of monetary policy formulation than is the President of the ECB. However, the titles of the office holders and their institutions imply exactly the opposite relationship. While the president of the ECB is the chairman of a decentralized system, explaining the views agreed by his colleagues, the chairman of the Fed, is the leader of a more centralized system. Second, as mentioned already, the difference in objectives means that the responses of the two organizations to similar shocks are likely to be different in both timing and extent. Such differences can be amplified by any perceived differences in the transmission mechanisms in the two regions. Expectations of one based on experience of the other will therefore tend to be incorrect.

The strains placed on a single policy from the diversity of the member states

There has been some concern in the literature that it would be difficult to run a Single Monetary Policy for a diverse region. Clearly, if monetary policy is more constrained than in the past, particularly in the sense that the exchange rate cannot be used as a means of adjustment between the member countries, other adjustment mechanisms will have to compensate. However, as Vanhala (2000) points out, it is an illusion for many of the existing members that they have any great loss of freedom of action. Since most of them were exchange rate targeting within the Exchange Rate Mechanism (ERM) of the European Monetary System (EMS) they were largely following German monetary policy and

> **Clearly, if monetary policy is more constrained than in the past, other adjustment mechanisms will have to compensate**

were deliberately trying not to have exchange rate variation, as that was deemed to be an important cost. Furthermore asymmetric shocks are a feature of existing economies, and sectors have always had to adjust without the 'benefit' of an adjustable nominal exchange rate.

However, our concern in Mayes and Virén (1998, 2000 and 2001) has been to explore the nature of the divergences within the euro area that policy has to cope with, rather than to question whether that coping is feasible. We have shown that there are four main difficulties for policy:

- The parameters for many of the main variables in the transmission mechanism vary considerably in size (by at least a factor of two).

- The speed of the transmission mechanism also varies by a factor of around two across the member states.

- There are clear non-linearities and asymmetries in the relationships between unemployment and inflation (the Phillips curve) and the rate of economic growth and unemployment (Okun curve).

- Behaviour will change progressively from being the sum of the individual countries' previous responses to that of a new more integrated economy.

Between them they have very clear implications:

- First of all, running policy off the arithmetic average for the euro area without regard to where the shocks come from will be inefficient.

- Second, until the price formation mechanism changes substantially, the euro area is likely to remain much more open than reference to the share of external trade in euro area GDP would imply.

● Third, the responsiveness to shocks will depend on the dispersion of unemployment across the area and the extent of co-ordination of the economic cycles (and not just the position in the economic cycle and the level of unemployment or the output gap).

● Responsiveness to policy differs clearly depending upon whether capacity is slack or under pressure.

None of these results is particularly surprising and they do not represent any particular difference from other economies, even small ones, as we show in Mayes and Virén (2000) for Finland, and, in Buxton and Mayes (1986) for the UK.

All our remarks are, of course, dependent on the degree to which observed behaviour in the recent past is a good indicator of likely behaviour in the coming few years. Our estimates in the main relate to behaviour over the period 1987 to 1998 as this represents a fairly coherent monetary policy regime aimed at price and exchange rate stability in what is now the euro area. However, stage 3 of EMU is deliberately aimed at changing behaviour. In the first place it is designed to try to anchor price expectations on stability. This will affect price and wage formation. Second, it is intended to reduce uncertainty and make the transmission of price signals across the euro area more efficient. While the former should reduce the inflationary impact of shocks and hence the impact on real activity, the latter should mean that shocks are transmitted more rapidly and that the euro area becomes more of a price setter and less of a price taker. These mechanisms alone will alter the behaviour of the euro economy.

However, the most important aspect is expected to be an increase in the sustainable rate of economic growth. The removal of the interest rate premium for the more inflation-prone countries should reduce the real rate of interest on average, *ceteris paribus*, thereby stimulating investment. The increased efficiency and the removal of structural rigidities that are in progress and planned should also form part of the basis for faster growth. (Of course, as expected returns increase, real interest rates will rise with them.) The ECB claims that these effects are yet to be observed (Hämäläinen 2001).

All these changes mean that macroeconomic policies and monetary policy in particular will have to evolve over the coming years, which will not help for some aspects of their predictability and transparency. Adjusting to changes in the underlying rate of growth is one of the most difficult processes to sort out as the experience of the Fed in adjusting to the 'new economy' in the USA in recent years demonstrates. Given the differences in size and role of the IT and related industries across the EU countries the assessment of the problem may be even more difficult.

Employment and the operation of open co-ordination

The open method of policy co-ordination is well described in Hodson and Maher (2001). Although the term was only formally adopted in the Lisbon Council in 2000 it is a description of the organized form of the three 'processes' set in motion by the Luxembourg (1997), Cardiff (1998) and Cologne (1999) Councils. The Luxembourg Process is addressed to the employment objectives of the EU and requires the member states to carry through an annual process of:

- drawing up employment guidelines in the Council to set priorities
- setting out national action plans by each member state to achieve the objectives
- assessment by the Commission and Council on the plans and the performance of the member states in achieving the objectives.

The main novelty in the process is that while the priorities are set out under the four headings of:

- employability
- entrepreneurship
- adaptability
- equal opportunities (for men and women)

the means of achieving them are not prescribed. Each country has the opportunity to set out its own ideas and it can choose how much effort to expend under each heading. Similarly, the assessments produce recommendations but not compulsion. The objectives are not merely qualitative but quantitative in nature. The process thus involves the opportunity for benchmarking against the best practice in the member states. As a result there is a clear element of competition among the member states to come out well in the assessment.

As Madsen and Munch-Madsen (2001) and Madsen *et al.* (2001) have set out, the various National Action Plans appear to cluster in three groups:

- A 'Nordic' group, which also includes the Netherlands, of countries that are undertaking a wide range of measures under all headings.
- A 'southern' group, which also includes Belgium, where the level of action is clearly more limited.
- A group with the somewhat ironic title of 'Anglo-Saxon' as it includes both Ireland and France, where the effort is somewhat more focused.

Not all countries fit easily within the framework and it is clear that the pattern is changing over time, with countries such as Ireland increasing their efforts noticeably. Efforts also vary with the extent of the problem. Success will tend to be marked by a reduction in spending as employment and participation ratios rise.

The Cardiff process extended the same ideas to what is described as 'structural policies'. These cover the whole range of markets for goods, services, labour and capital. Here the annual process involves the formulation of broad economic guidelines. This follows on an assessment by the member states of the state of play in the flexibility of operation of various aspects of the economic system. As we consider in more detail in the next section, the picture is completed by the Essen Process under the Stability and Growth Pact, where the co-ordination process is less soft and sanctions can be brought to bear on those who do not comply. However, as far as the broad economic guidelines are concerned, there is no matching set of sanctions as there is for the excessive deficit procedure under the SGP.

The Cologne Process integrates the Cardiff and Luxembourg Processes with the macroeconomic dialogue, which involves the 'social partners' (employer and trade union organizations), the ECB, the Commission and the Council in six-monthly discussions of the overall policy mix. This last exercise is a largely informal opportunity to gather information and exchange views. It does not make recommendations.

What the Lisbon summit did was codify these processes as a way forward for integration that could be applied to other areas of activity and should be used as part of a 10-year programme to turn the EU into a competitive, knowledge-based economy that combines sustainable growth with high employment and 'social cohesion'. As Hodson and Maher (2001) explain, these processes can be characterized by:

- the setting of guidelines with quantitative targets and timetables for achievement
- the establishment of performance indicators and benchmarks to allow comparison of best practice

- periodic monitoring and review, with an emphasis on mutual learning.

The open co-ordination process has been extended to the annual joint action plans developed with the accession countries to monitor and assist their progress towards membership. Here again there is a common framework, targets to work towards, assessment of progress by the Commission and the opportunity to learn from the others who are simultaneously having to set out their intentions and actions. Here of course the incentives to strong performance are obvious.

Of course, efficient and effective co-ordination in the field of employment and related policies does not mean that the policies themselves will be any more effective than in other countries. If the consequence of co-ordination were to be an agreement to restrict competition among the EU countries with respect to the replacement rate or the tax wedge then this would merely serve to limit incentives to increase employment across all the member states. Co-ordination *per se* is not necessarily a plus if the content of the co-ordination does not advance the macroeconomic objectives. In Gold and Mayes (1993, 1995) for example we explore the extent to which employment 'protection' measures, such as limitations on hours, restraints on firing etc. can conflict with achieving faster growth and efficiency.

Fiscal policy and the broad economic policy guidelines

Most attention is normally placed on fiscal policy under the terms of the SGP, as it is here that there are sanctions. The main concerns expressed are over whether the sanctions will actually be effective in restraining behaviour or indeed whether they will actually be applied, as the Council has discretion in applying the decision. However, the focus of our interest in the current framework is not so much on the avoidance of extremes, i.e. excessive deficits or failure to bring public debt levels down below 60 per cent of GDP, but more on whether there can in practice be voluntary agreements and prudent actions within the bounds.

For example, the system would not work well if the member states manage their fiscal position over the cycle in such a way that there is a serious threat of breaching the deficit limit (3 per cent of GDP in normal circumstances) every time there is a downturn. Buti *et al.* (1998) estimate that, if countries were to aim at a fiscal structure that generated balance across the cycle as a whole, then normal automatic stabilizers would be unlikely to generate excessive deficits in all but the worst downturns, such as the Finnish and Swedish crises of the early 1990s. The problem, therefore, is not so much with automatic stabilization as with discretionary changes and it is here that the first problem has emerged, in the case of Ireland. It is clearly in the interests of small countries that there should be co-ordination in the case of shocks as their ability to have much effect on their economies alone is decidedly limited. This is particularly the case for automatic stabilizers, as then it is not a matter of persuading other countries to act at the time. It just happens anyway because of the structure of their tax and benefit systems. (This is also an area where there is a clear difference from the USA. The forces for automatic stabilization, particularly at the state level, are much more limited there because of the lower tax and benefit rates. Greater reliance on discretionary policy is therefore required to have a similar effect.)

While in the case of structural policy the incentive for the member states to want to control each other is relatively limited, the argument is not the same for fiscal policy. In structural policy it will obviously help develop markets if each country can expand both its long-run ability to grow without generating inflation and its ability to respond relatively costlessly to shocks. Both will have favourable spillovers to the other member states. However, it would only be gross changes that would upset the balance of macroeconomic policy management over the course of the cycle in a programme implementing change over a 10-year period. Nevertheless, because it is the balance of fiscal policy that is the main concern, relatively limited changes in the structure of revenues or expenditures can have an effect that would elicit responses from the markets and from the ECB. Second, because of the progressive structure of direct tax systems both real growth and inflation require periodic adjustments if the share of the public sector is not to keep rising. The timing of these – discretionary – changes, especially if they are done in anticipation of particular growth or inflation outcomes, can affect the overall picture. Thus for the euro area as a whole, a reduction in the surplus of one country may have a similar effect to the increase in the deficit of another. So both are a matter for joint concern. (Note that this is subject to our remarks about non-linearity in the previous section. Actions that increase excess demand in one part of the euro area will have a greater effect on inflation than actions that reduce excess supply by a similar amount elsewhere (Mayes and Virén 2000).)

The case of Ireland illustrates this problem nicely. The Irish budget for 2001 foresaw a balance of tax cuts and expenditure increases that would reduce the fiscal surplus from 4.7 per cent of GDP in 2000 to 4.3 per cent of GDP in 2001 (see Hodson and Maher 2001). The actual outcome will, of course, depend crucially on the rate of growth that occurs and on the impact on the automatic elements of tax receipts and benefit payments. Following a report from the Commission, ECOFIN recommended that Ireland stick to a budget that was expected to keep the surplus constant (ECOFIN 2001). The basis of the recommendation was twofold: first some scepticism over the impact of the changes on real behaviour and second the view that when a country is showing clear signs of overheating fiscal policy should not add to the problem.

Both these sources of objection are important from the point of view of voluntary co-ordination. The first relates to a difference of view over the effect of measures and the second to a difference of view over what constitutes prudent policy. Governments (not just in Ireland) have a history of optimism over the outcomes of fiscal policy that impart an inflationary bias to policy over the medium term (Rogoff 1985, for example). The process of multilateral surveillance and opinion by the Commission offers a mechanism whereby a more 'objective' view can be elicited and hence more prudent policy be followed in the EU than is the case in most nation states that do not have any similar external controls – except of course through the verdict of the markets through interest and exchange rates. Since these are forward-looking judgements, one cannot know at the time which party has the more accurate assessment. The key is credibility of the regime. If national governments reject Council judgements then not only do these judgements tend to

> **When a country is experiencing problems of overheating, its year-by-year policies should not make the problem worse**

have less force in the future but it may encourage governments to be more inflation biased in their judgements about likely outcomes.

In a sense it does not matter if the Irish government has actually made the better forecasts. It is the principle that counts for credibility. Outcomes in any case are dependent on the unforecastable shocks that occur during the year. The second debate, about prudence, is even more important in this regard, as it reflects a difference of view about the way economies work and about how policy rules should be set. The simple approach that ECOFIN is following is that when a country is experiencing problems of overheating, its year-by-year policies should not make the problem worse. This is a simple rule but one with only a 12-month horizon. Ireland, by the same token, sets the general flavour of its macroeconomic policy according to a series of four-year agreements between the government, employers, trade unions and a wide range of interest groups in society (Hodson 2001). These agreements have formed a key part of Ireland's success (Kilponen *et al.* 2000). The 2001 Irish budget is part of that longer-term agreement, expected to elicit supply-side improvements that will enable the exceptional Irish performance to continue despite the constraints that are now being encountered. (In Mayes and Virén 2001, we suggest evidence in the EU framework that most EU countries would tend to benefit in terms of growth if they were to take the opportunity to ratchet the tax system downwards.)

Here the argument is reversed. Governments can only introduce medium-term improvements to the fiscal system involving tax cuts or expenditure increases at a time when the economy is doing relatively well. If they do it when things are going relatively badly then they will increase both debt and deficits. (When things are going relatively well they will slow the rate of debt repayment and decrease surpluses.) In any case when things are going relatively badly the automatic stabilizers will be operating to help reduce the impact (also increasing deficits and debt). Thus the basis of the Irish argument is that with a surplus of over 4 per cent of GDP they are already putting heavy downward pressure on the economy. By altering the structure of the economy towards enduring faster growth at a time when it is doing well they can help avoid an unnecessary downturn. The counter-argument is that by not having harsher downward pressure now they will only cause an even bigger cycle later and pass inflation costs on to the rest of the area in the short run and employment costs in the longer term when the downturn appears.

The plus side of open co-ordination is that it permits this debate to occur and allows a country to maintain its own point of view. Ireland will still have to face the terms of the excessive deficit procedure if it has made a bad judgement and enters a severe recession with too expansionary a budget structure. It will then have to tighten in a recession, something no government is likely to plan to do deliberately or even run as a plausible risk. On the negative side it emphasizes that the SGP is asymmetric and that, while the worst excesses may be avoided in recessions, there will not be equal concerns in booms, hence maintaining some of the inflationary bias of fiscal policy and thus placing a greater burden on monetary policy. This then reopens the debate about whether the EU arrangements deliver the appropriate policy mix.

The treatment of Ireland could represent a change in attitude of ECOFIN or possibly reflect the fact that Ireland is a small country. In 1999 Italy also got into difficulty in that a reduction in growth prospects made the Italian government suggest that it might be unable to meet its plans for deficit reduction. The Commission reacted unfavourably, recommending that Italy take extra measures to bring the expected deficit back on track. The Italian government (not surprisingly) contested this and the Council (Council 1999) chose not to follow the Commission's lead and toned the phraseology down using the word 'encourage' rather than 'recommend'. At the time, there was some feeling that this meant that when difficult circumstances emerged ECOFIN might tend to be conciliatory in its interpretation of the constraints of the SGP. Since then it has turned out that the Italians were pessimistic and were in fact able to do rather better than the original plans for reducing the deficit.

It remains that the evidence on the rigour with which the fiscal policy constraints will be applied has to rely on infra-marginal concerns. The 3 per cent deficit barrier has not yet been in serious danger of being breached by any of the member states. That is largely because in the initial period up until the first part of 1998 the member states also had qualification for stage 3 of EMU at stake as well as the potential censure from the SGP. Since then the phase of the economic cycle has been for recovery and then growth in excess of the longer-run average. The real test of the constraints in the SGP will only come in a downturn. On other occasions, member states who appear to be running their policies with insufficient margin in better times can hope that, like Italy, when the future actually comes it will turn out not to pose too harsh a test. They could thus gamble on not having to take strong measures but still be able to take them much closer to the onset of an excessive deficit, if this turned out to be essential.

Framework for co-ordination

The issue of the policy mix is where we conclude. Governments have tried to impose on themselves rules that avoid an inflationary bias to policy stemming from allowing short-run concerns to dominate longer-term prudence. These can be very effective through giving central banks clear targets for price stability and assigning them the independence and powers to achieve them. Fiscal responsibility acts in the same vein are not so common. (New Zealand adopted one in 1994 and the UK has adopted some of the same principles.) They are also much more difficult to achieve in practice as it is not possible to constrain real behaviour and the budgetary balance within such tight bands as it is inflation. Harsher fiscal constraints are of course imposed effectively on lower tiers of government in many countries. But there the central government stands ready to provide assistance should there be adverse shocks whether or not asymmetric to the particular region. This mechanism does not exist in the EU.

Following the usual Mundell–Fleming arguments (see Chapters 4, 5 and 9) there is actually a difference in the incentives for the member states compared with the euro area as a whole. With a fixed exchange rate between them there is an incentive for the member states to follow a more active fiscal policy. For the euro area as whole where the exchange rate is flexible the relative position is changed and a less active fiscal policy but a more active monetary policy becomes attractive (Marston 1985; Virén 2000). This therefore provides an interesting dilemma for the member states, which will want to be individually more active according to this analysis in response to asymmetric shocks but collectively will want to see a less active approach to fiscal policy.

The Maastricht Treaty probably represents the high-water mark (King 2000) of independence for central banks. It is difficult to see that any stronger framework for achieving price stability could be agreed in a democratic environment at present. On the fiscal side, the EU has also managed to impose limits and incentives for prudent behaviour within those limits (which may or may not be very effective in the terms of our previous discussion). However, the concerns are not just one-sided. There is a danger that both monetary and fiscal policy could err on the side of restraint. The asymmetry of the SGP means that it is designed to reduce debt to GDP ratios. With 5 per cent nominal GDP growth an average deficit of 3 per cent GDP would maintain a 60 per cent debt to GDP ratio. However, current policy is designed to reduce debt to GDP ratios (as several member states are still above 60 per cent and the problems of the ageing of the population *inter alia* are likely to put pressure on debt levels in the future) so the 3 per cent deficit is the upper limit not the average. Thus fiscal policy may be trying to improve the long-run structural position at the same time that it has some credibility problems (including those with the monetary authority).

The final question we address is whether those rules, on their own, impose sufficient co-ordination, as augmented by the bi-annual macroeconomic dialogue. Alesina *et al.* (2001) argue that not only are the rules sufficient but the dialogue runs the risk of weakening the credibility of the scheme. They argue that any opportunity for there to be discussions behind closed doors between the central bank and the fiscal authorities will weaken the public belief that the ECB will fulfil its price stability objective instead of coming to an implicit or unwritten agreement to limit monetary pressure for political reasons. They go on to suggest that credibility requires the ECB to be as transparent as possible and to make it very difficult for the Governing Council either to discuss deviations from the price stability objective or to react implicitly to external pressure. The absence of published minutes to meetings or any full 'inflation report' that ensures that no reasoning can be pushed under the carpet makes it more difficult for the Bank to give these assurances. The problem is that it does not matter if the ECB never in practice entertains such notions. What matters is that markets do not believe

> **Credibility is a reflection of outsiders' attitudes and the problem is to structure the system to assist the holding of this credibility as far as possible**

that any response to these pressures is possible. Credibility is a reflection of outsiders' attitudes and the problem is to structure the system to assist the holding of this credibility as far as possible.

In New Zealand for example (Mayes and Razzak 1998) the Reserve Bank deliberately distances itself from both the treasury and the government. Questions are regularly asked in parliament about how often the governor and the minister of finance have met or spoken over the telephone. Forecasts are not discussed with the treasury, nor secret information sought by either side in preparation of forecasts. The Bank is therefore able to be completely open about the assumptions for its forecasts. Any inconsistency about the difference between the assumptions and the forecast could be picked up (after the event) should anyone try to rerun the model. The Bank therefore has to be completely honest in its building up of the view of the future, otherwise it runs the risk of being caught massaging the numbers. Any such detection would be disastrous for its future credibility. Credibility comes from having plenty at stake from deviating from the agreed procedures. (Even in the New Zealand case a report by Svensson (2001) suggests that both parliament and the external non-executive board of the Bank should be given more resources so they can investigate the Bank's processes and the quality of its monetary policy formulation more closely. The Bank has supported these recommendations but the decision of the minister of finance has not yet been revealed.)

The ECB has not been so forthcoming, although limited forecasts are now published. Alesina *et al.* (2001) argue against the presence of the Eurogroup president at Governing Council meetings on the grounds that this could be thought to permit influence, especially in the absence of a written record. This line of argument thus runs somewhat against the traditional literature, under which co-ordination between the two authorities is thought to lead to better outcomes (Ardy 2000, for example) simply because it enables uncertainty to be reduced. The reason is that having these strict rules also enables a co-operative game to be run. Fiscal policy can be set in the knowledge of the likely monetary policy response and the known current strategy. At the same time, because of the constraints on fiscal policy from the SGP and the incentives for improving macroeconomic policy as a whole under the broad economic policy guidelines and open co-ordination, the monetary authorities can be more accurate in forecasting the inflationary impact of actual and future fiscal decisions.

It is clear from the ECB Governing Council's statements that it is a little sceptical about the fiscal authorities' likely zeal in following fiscal prudence and about the success of the process of open co-ordination in advancing the pace of deregulation and structural change to make the adjustment of the real economy less costly and increase the sustainable rate of growth. One might be forgiven for thinking that some EU finance ministers share exactly the opposite fear about the ECB (Lafontaine 2000). Their worry is that it will be too focused on its price stability objective. While such misgivings among the two authorities could lead to contradictory policies and hence cost from poor co-ordination, there is little indication thus far that the public voicing of concerns has been translated into a policy bias by either party.

The short time span means that it is impossible to draw definitive conclusions. Nevertheless, the experience thus far seems to be rather more promising than a simple examination of the sanctions (or lack thereof) might imply for the innovative co-ordination processes being employed in the EU. Time will tell, but the trend towards increasing transparency both by the ECB and by the process of multilateral surveillance against measurable benchmarks suggests that both the co-ordination and the credibility of the processes may also increase. Thus, while our analysis suggests no compelling reason for large institutional reforms to the EU system, clearly increased openness, more systematic policy rules and better expertise in assessments and forecasts will assist the effectiveness of these more open methods of co-ordination.

Appendix

In this appendix we present some empirical results that support our contention that there are already considerable favourable spillovers from the fiscal policy of the rest of the euro area to the individual countries. We show that this is somewhat greater than suggested in some previous work.

The degree of interdependence between countries can be evaluated by estimating the following common factor regression model:

$$x_{it} = a_i + b_i x_{ger,t} + u_t.$$

We use a dataset of 17 European countries (the EU less Luxembourg plus Switzerland and Iceland (i = 1, 2 . . . 16; ger stands for Germany) for the years (t) 1960–2000 to see how much the time-series variation of the key variables is explained by common (i.e. German) variation. In Table A5.1 we report results for a panel regression in which the coefficients a_i and b_i are set equal for all countries while in Table A5.2 individual country estimates are reported.

Moreover, we estimate a spillover equation of the type:

$$c_{it} - c_{ger,t} = \alpha + \beta_{it} + \gamma_{ger,t} + \theta(r_{it} - r_{ger,t}) + u_t$$

where c_i (g_i) denotes the growth rate of private (public) consumption in country i and r_i the real interest rate. This equation is estimated to find out the basic nature of fiscal policy spillover effects. A useful starting point for the analysis of these effects is the Obstfeld and Rogoff (1998) intertemporal open economy model. Assuming fixed exchange rates, this model predicts that an increase in public consumption in a foreign country will

Table A5.1 | Panel data estimates for 16 European countries

Variables	Constant	$x_{ger,t}$
GDP growth rate	.025 (12.13)	.227 (4.17)
Private consumption growth rate	.019 (8.19)	.371 (6.01)
Public consumption growth rate	.021 (10.76)	.412 (7.05)
Public consumption growth/GDP	.004 (12.12)	.346 (6.24)
Government deficit/GDP	−.008 (4.23)	.634 (11.58)
Inflation	1.141 (2.81)	1.376 (11.76)
Real short-term interest rate	−.203 (0.73)	.925 (11.79)
Real long-term interest rate	−.857 (1.32)	.966 (6.42)

Note: All values are SUR estimates. Conventional t-ratios are inside parentheses

increase private consumption in the home country while an increase in public consumption would drive down private consumption in the home country (the implications are shown in e.g. Caselli 1998). Thus in the estimating equation, â should be negative and ā positive. Finally, the interest rate differential is expected to have a negative effect on the difference in consumption growth rates.[2]

In a more conventional (Mundell–Fleming) model, the public consumption spillover effect (from foreign country to home country) is still positive but (in the absence of debt neutrality) the effect of public consumption growth on private consumption growth in the home country is also positive. In this case, we have to write the spillover equation in an unconstrained form:

$$c_{it} = \alpha + \kappa_{ger,t} + \beta_{it} + \gamma_{ger,t} + \theta(r_{it} - r_{gert}) + u_t$$

Now, we would expect all parameters κ, β, γ (except for θ) to be positive.

Table A5.2 | Individual country estimates for the slope parameter β

Country	Private consumption	Public consumption	Deficit/ GDP	Inflation	Short-term interest rate	Long-term interest rate
Austria	.414*	.208*	.754*	1.038*	.630*	.779*
Belgium	.499*	.750*	.820*	1.238*	1.109*	1.216*
Denmark	.490*	.613*	.107	1.392*	1.190*	.720*
Finland	.410	.542*	.677*	1.682*	.862*	1.185*
France	.518*	.142	.667*	1.555*	.764*	1.044*
Greece	.705*	.568*	1.033*	1.320*	−.531*	
Iceland	.423	.389*	−.206			
Ireland	.150	.494*	−.006	2.066*	1.708*	1.093*
Italy	.551*	.355*	.700*	2.071*	.392*	1.519*
Netherlands	.753*	.130	−.346	1.192*	1.164*	
Norway	.132	.505*	.256*	.916*	.772*	1.258*
Portugal	.207	.660*	.533*	1.771*	.547*	2.276*
Spain	.801*	.336*	2.608	1.618*	1.537*	1.492*
Sweden	.394*	.549*	.072*	1.245*	.358*	1.002*
Switzerland	.694*	.709*	−.272*	1.042*	.633*	.726*
UK	−.030	.276*	−.004	1.779*	1.225*	1.405*

*indicates that the respective t-ratio exceeds the 5% critical value

Table A5.3 | Estimates of the cross-country spillover equation

Data	g_i	g_{ger}	$r_i - r_{ger}$	p_i	R^2/SEE	DW
G	.162	−.175			.067	1.468
	(6.42)	(2.43)			0.028	
G; c_{EU}, g_{EU}	.123	−.120			.085	1.536
	(4.56)	(4.67)			0.025	
W	.753	−.919			.059	1.456
	(5.26)	(2.51)			0.029	
W, c_{EU}, g_{EU}	.613	−.601			.078	1.524
	(4.25)	(4.14)			0.025	
G,|dev|<1	.163	−.133			.196	2.124
	(1.80)	(1.76)			0.023	
G, |dev|<5	.129	−.124			.149	1.450
	(2.37)	(2.45)			0.024	
W, |dev|<5	.644	−.655			.147	1.442
	(2.23)	(2.30)			0.024	
G, |dev|<5	.117	−.148	−.017		.121	1.207
	(1.72)	(2.03)	(0.24)		0.023	
G, |dev|<5	.122	−.152	−.047	−.049	.122	1.201
	(1.78)	(2.10)	(0.65)	(0.88)	0.023	

	c_{ger}	g_i	g_{ger}	Y_i	R^2/SEE	DW
G	.345	.264	.100		.202	1.507
	(5.64)	(4.50)	(1.33)		0.026	
W	.354	1.224	.622		.190	1.483
	(5.81)	(3.88)	(2.31)		0.026	
G, |dev|<1	.329	.320	.055		.377	1.829
	(3.21)	(3.60)	(0.73)		0.019	
G, |dev|<5	.378	.234	.092		.328	1.418
	(5.35)	(4.55)	(1.67)		0.021	
Def	.268	.028	.335		.327	1.286
	(3.21)	(2.09)	(5.04)		0.023	
Def, |dev|<5	.300	.024	.281		.315	1.232
	(3.09)	(1.46)	(4.59)		0.019	
Def, |dev|<5	.226	.015	.025	.625	.578	1.801
	(4.64)	(1.47)	(0.55)	(14.52)	0.015	

Note: The dependent variable is $c_{it} - c_{ger,t}$ in the upper part of the table and c_{it} in the lower part. G denotes the growth rate of public consumption, W the growth of public consumption/GDP and DEF government surplus/GDP (negative values are deficits); p the rate of inflation and y the rate of GDP growth. \|dev1\|< indicates that only the data for such years that the exchange rate vis-à-vis DMARK appreciates/depreciates less than 1 per cent are included. Newey-West t-ratios are inside parentheses. The first four equations are estimated by the SUR estimator in the panel data setting. The remaining equations are estimated by OLS. All equations include country dummies.

The main problem with the empirical implementation of the analysis is the exchange rate regime. We tried to control the regime by using conventional classification of the fixed and flexible exchange rate periods. Because that turned out to be somewhat imprecise we adopted a more empirically oriented approach by classifying the periods (years) on the basis of observed exchange rate fluctuations. Thus, if the rates vis-à-vis the Deutschmark appreciated/depreciated less than 1 or alternatively 5 per cent we considered the period a fixed exchange rate period. Obviously, this approach is subject to much criticism but, after all, the periods which were computed this way seem to correspond quite closely to the conventional classifications.

Our conclusions from these three tables of results are as follows:

- Public consumption and deficits are more closely related to the German (European average) than is output.
- The relationships are much closer for interest rates and inflation (than for the fiscal policy indicators).
- The UK, Iceland and Ireland are quite clear outliers in terms of the relationship with the German (European average).
- To some extent Denmark and the Netherlands also produce a somewhat different pattern.
- Gross-country spillover effects do not seem to follow the pattern implied by the Obstfeld and Rogoff REDUX model.
- Rather, a more conventional Mundell–Fleming (Keynesian) model seems to be consistent with the data.

Notes

1 The views expressed are those of the authors and do not necessarily correspond with any that may be held by the Bank of Finland.

2 Instead of German values as 'foreign country' values we used the European averages (so that the 'home country' was always excluded). The corresponding values are markes c_{EU} and g_{EU} in Table A5.3.

References

Alesina, A., Blanchard, O., Gali, J., Giavazzi, F. and Uhlig, H. (2001) *Defining a Macroeconomic Framework for the Euro Area*. London: CEPR (No. 3 in the series Monitoring the European Central Bank).

Ardy, B. (2000) 'A question of fit? Policy and process in the fiscal domain', South Bank European Papers 2/2000.

Begg, D., De Grauwe, P., Giavazzi, F., Uhlig, H. and Wyplosz, C. (1999) *The ECB: Safe at Any Speed?* London: CEPR (No. 1 in the series Monitoring the European Central Bank).

Bernanke, B. S., Laubach, T., Mishkin, F. S. and Posen, A. S. (1999) *Inflation Targeting: Lessons from the International Experience.* Princeton: Princeton University Press.

BIS (2001) 'Procyclicality of the financial system and financial stability: issues and policy options'. BIS Papers No. 1.

Blinder, A., Goodhart, C. A. E., Hildebrand, P., Lipton, D. and Wyplosz, C. (2001) 'How do central banks talk?', Third Geneva Conference on the World Economy.

Buiter, W. H. (1999) 'Alice in Euroland', *Journal of Common Market Studies*, 37, 2, pp. 181–209.

Buti, M., Franco, D. and Onega, H. (1998) 'Fiscal discipline and flexibility in EMU: the implementation of the Stability and Growth Pact', *Oxford Review of Economic Policy*, 14, pp. 81–97.

Buxton, A. J. and Mayes, D. G. (1986) 'The persistence of unemployment', *Quarterly Predictions* 88 (December), pp. 29–37.

Caselli, P. (1998) 'Fiscal consolidations under fixed exchange rates'. Banca D'Italia, Termi di Discussione No. 336.

Castrén, O. and Mayes, D. G. (1997) 'Establishing a credible monetary policy: the importance of transparency and its role in maintaining independence and accountability', Bank of Finland.

Commission (1999) *Eleventh Annual Report on the Structural Funds.* Brussels.

Council (1999) *Opinion of 8 February in the Stability Programme of Italy, 1999–2001.* OJ C 68, 11/03.

Crooks, E. (2001) 'Weaker currencies help world weather US downturn . . . so far', *Financial Times*, 20 April.

ECB (2000) *Monthly Bulletin* November.

ECOFIN (2001) Press Release 696/01 on 2329th Council Meeting – ECOFIN. Brussels, 12 February.

Favero, C., Frexias, X., Persson, T. and Wyplosz, C. (2000) *One Money, Many Countries.* London: CEPR (No. 2 in the series Monitoring the European Central Bank).

Franzmeyer, F., Hrubesch, P., Seidel, B., Weise, C. and Schweiger, I. (1991) *The Regional Impact of Community Policies.* European Parliament Research Paper 17.

Gali, J. (2001) *'Monetary Policy in the Early Years of EMU'.* Conference on the functioning of EMU: the Challenge of the Early Years, March, EU Commission, Brussels.

Gold, M. and Mayes, D. G. (1993) 'Rethinking social policy for Europe' in R. Simpson and R. Walker (eds) *Europe for Richer or Poorer*. London: Child Poverty Action Group.

Gold, M. and Mayes, D. G. (1995) 'European economic co-operation, economic and monetary union and the need for European social policy' in P. Kosonen and P.K. Madsen (eds) *Convergence or Divergence? Welfare States Facing European Integration*. Luxembourg: Commission of the EC, pp. 59–76.

Hämäläinen, S. (2001) 'Is the new economy really new?', Jaakko Honko Lecture, Helsinki School of Economics, January.

Hodson, D. (2001) 'Social inclusion through social partnership: the case of Ireland' in D. G. Mayes, J. Berghman and R. Salais (eds) *Social Exclusion and European Policy*. Cheltenham: Edward Elgar.

Hodson, D. and Maher, I. (2001) 'The open method as a new mode of governance: the case of soft economic policy co-ordination'. Mimeo, South Bank University.

Huang, A., Margaritis, D. and Mayes, D. G. (2000) 'Monetary policy rules in New Zealand, 1989–98'. Paper presented to the Auckland, New Zealand, meeting of the Econometric Society, 3 March 2001.

Issing, O. (1999) 'The eurosystem: transparent and accountable, or "Willem in Euroland" ', *Journal of Common Market Studies*, 37, 3, pp. 503–19.

Kilponen, J., Mayes, D. G. and Vilmunen, J. (2000) 'Labour market flexibility in the euro area', *European Business Journal*, 12, 2, pp. 100–10.

Kindleberger, C. (1992) *Manias, Panics and Crashes: A History of Financial Crises*, 3rd edition. Cambridge, MA: MIT Press.

King, M. (2000) 'Monetary policy: theory and practice'. Address to the Boston Meeting of the American Economic Association, 7 January.

Lafontaine, O. (2000) *Das Herz schlägt links*. Oxford: Blackwell.

Leichter, J. and Walsh, C. (1999) 'Different economies, common policy: policy trade-offs under the ECB'. Mimeo.
http://econ.ucsc.edu/~walshc

MacDougall, G. D. A. (1977) *Report of the Study Group on the Role of Public Finance in European Integration*. Brussels: Commission of the European Communities.

Madsen, P. K. and Munch-Madsen, P. (2001) 'European employment policy and national policy regimes' in D. G. Mayes, J. Berghman and R. Salais (eds) *Social Exclusion and European Policy*. Cheltenham: Edward Elgar.

Madsen, P. K., Munch-Madsen, P. and Langhoff-Roos, K. (2001) 'How well do European employment regimes manage social exclusion?' in R.

Muffels, P. Tsakloglou and D. G. Mayes (eds) *Social Exclusion in European Welfare States*. Cheltenham: Edward Elgar.

Marston, R. (1985) 'Stabilisation policies in open economies' in R. Jones and P. Kenen (eds) *Handbook of International Economics*, Vol. II. Amsterdam: Elsevier, pp. 859–916.

Mayes, D. G. (1999) 'Evolving voluntary rules for the operation of the European Central Bank', *Current Politics and Economics of Europe*, 8, 4, pp. 357–85.

Mayes, D. G. and Razzak, W. (1998) 'Transparency and accountability: empirical models and policy making at the Reserve Bank of New Zealand', *Economic Modelling*, 15, pp. 377–94.

Mayes, D. G. and Virén, M. (1998) 'The exchange rate and monetary conditions in the euro area', Bank of Finland Discussion Paper 27/98. Weltwirtschaftliches Archiv, 136, pp. 199–231.

Mayes, D. G. and Virén, M. (2000) 'Asymmetry and the problem of aggregation in the euro area', Bank of Finland Discussion Paper 11/2000, forthcoming in *Empirica*.

Mayes, D. G. and Virén, M. (2001) 'Macroeconomic factors and policies and the development of social exclusion' in R. Muffels, P. Tsakloglou and D. G. Mayes (eds) *Social Exclusion in European Welfare States*. Cheltenham: Edward Elgar.

Melitz, J. (2000) 'Some cross-country evidence about fiscal policy behaviour and the consequences for EMU'. Mimeo.

Meyer, L. (1998) 'Come with me to the FOMC', Federal Reserve Board boarddocs/speeches/1998040022.

Meyer, L. (2000) 'The politics of monetary policy: balancing independence and accountability', Federal Reserve Board boarddocs/speeches/20001024.

NIESR (1991) *A New Approach to Economic and Social Cohesion after 1992*, European Parliament Research Paper 19.

Obstfeld, M. and Rogoff, K. (1998) *Foundations of International Macroeconomics*. Cambridge, MA: MIT Press.

O'Donnell, R. (1998) 'Ireland's economic transformation: industrial policy, European integration and social partnership', Centre for West European Studies Working Paper 2, December.

Orphanides, A. (1999) 'The quest for prosperity without inflation', ECB Working Paper 15.

Persson, T. and Tabellini, G. (2000) *Political Economy: Explaining Economic Policy*. Cambridge, MA: MIT Press.

Quah, D. (1993) 'Empirical cross-section dynamics in economic growth', *European Economic Review*, 37, pp. 426–34.

Rogoff, K. (1985) 'Can international monetary policy co-ordination be counterproductive?', *Journal of International Economics*, 18, pp. 199–217.

Sargent, T. (1999) *The Conquest of American Inflation*. Princeton, NJ: Princeton University Press.

Svensson, L. E. O. (2001) *Independent Review of Monetary Policy in New Zealand*. **www.rbnz.govt.nz**

Tarkka, J. and Mayes, D. G. (1999) 'The value of publishing official central bank forecasts', Bank of Finland Discussion Papers 22/99.

Vanhala, M. (2000) 'The first year of the euro'. Conference on the euro and the Nordic Welfare State, Copenhagen, 22 June.

Virén, M. (2000) 'Fiscal policy automatic stabilisers and policy co-ordination in EMU' in A. Brunila, M. Buti and D. Franco (eds) *The Stability and Growth Pact*. Basingstoke: Palgrave.

Walsh, C. (1998) *Monetary Theory and Policy*. Cambridge, MA: MIT Press.

Walsh, C. (2000) 'Accountability, transparency and inflation targeting'. Mimeo. **http//econ.ucsc.edu/~walshc**

6

Causes of euro instability

Philip Arestis, Iris Biefang-Frisancho Mariscal, Andrew Brown and Malcolm Sawyer

Introduction

This chapter is partially based on our paper entitled, 'Explaining the Euro's Initial Decline', *Eastern Economic Journal*, Fall (2001).

The euro was formally launched in January 1999 and only two years later its value against the dollar was substantially below its initial level. There was a general decline through the period, with a low reached in May 2000 and again in September 2000. A further, all-time low was reached in October 2000. Figure 6.1 provides the details. The purpose of this chapter is to examine the causes of this general decline in the value of the euro. The various explanations proffered in the literature are assessed. We add our own explanation of the falling euro which emphasizes the problems with the institutional set-up of the euro system, that is the European Central Bank (ECB) and the national central banks (NCBs). In the light of this assessment, the future prospects of the euro and of, more broadly, the euro area (the geographical area defined by the country members of the euro system) are drawn out.

The introduction of the euro and the associated operation of the ECB have been under considerable scrutiny which is reflected in a relatively large number of scholarly papers providing a detailed assessment of the performance of the euro, of the ECB and of the euro area macroeconomy more generally (for a recent example see OECD 2000). Although our assessment draws on these papers in a critical manner, we provide further explanations based on our own research and published output (see, for example, Arestis, Brown and Sawyer 2001).

The following section reviews the decline in the value of the euro. The third examines two obvious explanations and argues that neither mere 'bad luck' nor fundamentals such as interest rate differentials or measures of long-run equilibrium magnitudes explain the decline. The next two sections of the chapter attempt to construct a more satisfactory explanation. In the fourth section the argument, prevalent in the literature, that the decline in value of the euro is due to 'US strength', rather than to any inherent difficulties with its imposition, is thought to be rather undeveloped. We suggest that US strength is an important but partial factor in euro decline. The other side of US strength is, we stress, euro area weakness. The fifth section reviews the (poor) performance of the ECB and assesses the level of macroeconomic convergence of euro area countries. The early indications are that the divergent state of the euro area countries has not been reversed, indeed it may have worsened, since the inception of the euro. In the absence of monetary and fiscal co-ordination and of large-scale regional transfers, such divergence is a fundamental weakness in a single currency area. Yet, the institutions accompanying the euro preclude the co-ordination of macroeconomic policy, and the magnitude of regional transfers within the euro area is negligible. Thus, our conclusion suggests that a combination of euro area weakness, endogenous to the inception of the euro, and of US strength most plausibly explains the euro's decline in value. While the future value of the euro remains uncertain, the future prospects for the euro area are bleak as long as the current institutions underpinning the euro remain in place, with the associated tendencies towards deflation.

> # US strength is an important but partial factor in euro decline

Decline in the value of the euro

Contrary to the predictions of its proponents the euro has declined in value by over 25 per cent against the dollar (see Figures 6.1 and 13.2), 30 per cent against the yen and 13 per cent against pound sterling since its inception in January 1999. It declined by 20 per cent on the (narrow) ECB measure of its effective rate (ECB 2000). Several possible explanations are reviewed and found wanting in the following. Before we embark on them, we ask the question of whether the euro is in fact 'undervalued'.

The answer to the question whether the euro is undervalued requires some discussion of the notion of the 'right' value of the euro. We suggest that two types of benchmark are appropriate, namely the value of the currency that would correspond to a trade balance and a purchasing power parity level.

The euro area maintains a trade surplus (in 2000, quarter 1, the surplus of exports over imports, as a percentage of GDP, was 2.1 per cent). On the face of it this would suggest that the euro is undervalued relative to the exchange rate which would generate a balance of trade. Chinn (2000), Coppel *et al.* (2000) and Deutsche Bank Research (2000) provide some of the most recent attempts to gauge the 'real' value of the euro. Chinn (2000) estimates an econometric 'monetary model', augmented by the relative price of non-tradeables, using the value of the synthetic euro; Coppel *et al.* (2000) prefer more direct indices of the real 'long run' or 'equilibrium' effective exchange rates, such as relative unit labour costs, manufacturing prices and consumer prices and indicate that there has been a divergence between such indices and the movement of the exchange rate. Both papers also survey recent attempts to estimate the equilibrium exchange rate (see also the review of PricewaterhouseCoopers 2000, Ch. 3). The striking feature of their own and

Figure 6.1 | Daily exchange rates: US dollars per euro

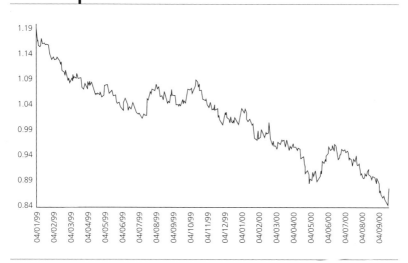

Source: Pacific Exchange Rate Service © 2000 Prof. Werner Antweiler

other such estimates is that the current level of the euro is, with few exceptions, found to be way below its supposed 'real' level, by a magnitude of 15 per cent or more, no matter what method is employed. Thus Deutsche Bank Research (2000) show that the euro moved more than 15 per cent away from their PPP measure of the real exchange rate in late 1999 onwards. Consequently, Duisenberg's comments, on announcing recent increases in euro area interest rates, that the euro is clearly undervalued,[1] are well supported by the relevant empirical work. It would seem then that the current value of the euro cannot be explained by appeal to any notion of its 'fundamental' value, whether that value is deemed to be purchasing power parity, fundamental equilibrium exchange rate or similar.

We now proceed to discuss a number of explanations of the fall in the value of the euro.

Obvious explanations

A number of explanations of the fall in the value of the euro suggest themselves. This section deals with the most obvious ones, which are the 'just bad luck' argument and interest rate differentials. We discuss both in this section and we find them not persuasive enough. We begin with the first.

Just bad luck?

It is widely recognized that a host of contingencies affect the short-run movements of the exchange rate, not least the vagaries of market sentiment. Thus it can be argued strongly that the fall in the value of the euro is simply 'bad luck' with little underlying significance. This point of view can be coupled with the argument that, in historical perspective, the decline is not dramatic and the current level is not unusually low (Buiter 1999b, Coppell et al. 2000, Corsetti and Pesenti 2000). It can start from the observation that the decline in the euro (say during the year of 1999) is not unprecedented. We have reported elsewhere (Arestis and Sawyer 1996) that over the period 1980 to 1995 the average ratio of the maximum level of sterling relative to the mark to the minimum level during a year was 1.13 and the corresponding figure for the dollar relative to the yen was 1.17 (with a figure of 1.28 in 1985 and 1.30 in 1986). The pound, for example, fell by around 25 per cent from 1984 to 1985 and by roughly the same percentage in the winter of 1992–93; similar or greater volatility is displayed by other comparable exchange rate series. This lends some weight to the view of Favero *et al.* (2000) that 'lamenting a weak euro is patently unjustified'. This can be further supported by the idea that the value of the euro was relatively high on its introduction. Hence a decline from a relatively high level may have been anticipated.[2]

The interesting question, however, is how this fall, even if there are precedents for its extent, should be interpreted. A first possibility is that this decline is indeed 'bad luck'. We may bet on the toss of a coin and let us say that tails represents a loss and heads a win. A string of tails arising from repeated tossing of a coin may represent 'bad luck' for us as the gambler but may not be unprecedented. If we regard the movement of the exchange rate as a 'random' event, then there will be 'runs' of generally negative movements in the exchange rate. However, although the decline in the euro is by no means unprecedented, many of the large movements in exchange rates do appear to have some underlying cause. For example, the rise and then fall of the dollar during the 1980s can be ascribed to tight monetary policies and then the impact of the Plaza Agreement.

> It is widely recognized that a host of contingencies affect the short-run movements of the exchange rate, not least the vagaries of market sentiment

A related possibility is that these declines in the value of the euro could be seen as an example of a self-perpetuating 'bubble' in financial markets in which expectations of price rises (falls) fuel those price rises (falls). A variant of the 'bubble' argument has been put forward recently by De Grauwe (2000). This contribution attempts to explain the apparent lack of a relationship between fundamentals and the falling euro by resorting to the uncertainty of the impact of fundamentals on the exchange rate and of the precise equilibrium value of the euro/dollar exchange rate. This uncertainty promotes 'beliefs' about the exchange rate which have nothing to do with fundamentals. Under these conditions exchange rate movements themselves become the focus and a signal to search for those fundamentals might explain the given exchange rate movement. So that when in early 1999 the euro began to fall against the dollar, it was interpreted as a signal that the US economy was strong and the euro area weak. Given the conflicting evidence of underlying strengths and weaknesses, such a search is normally successful. Those 'beliefs' have reinforced the euro fall since then.

Nonetheless, treating the decline of the euro as a 'bubble' may still raise the question of the cause of the start of the 'bubble' even if there are mechanisms by which the 'bubble' is perpetuated.

We would argue that the 'bad luck' argument captures an important but partial truth. The bulk of the literature is right to eschew the straightforward argument that the falling euro, per se, undermines the case of the euro's proponents. However, it is also correct to stress that, if the proximate causes of exchange rate movements are the beliefs of market participants and such beliefs have a random component, then, equally, beliefs are not *purely* contingent. Neither pure truth, nor pure whimsy, market beliefs do have some connection with economic reality. Thus, the historical and comparative precedents for the fall in the euro were not always a matter of 'luck'. On the contrary, in many cases, they have an underlying economic logic, as suggested earlier. It is significant that proponents of the euro had predicted that its value would *rise* from January 1999 (Buiter 1999b admits that he was one such proponent). Such predictions stemmed, not only from the relatively buoyant economic outlook at that time, but also from the view that the inception of the euro would *contribute* to the rosy economic future of the euro area. It is in this context that the decline in the value of the euro should be appraised. While it is true that the decline provides *prima facie* evidence against proponents of the euro, it is the underlying causes of the decline that provide the critical evidence for any assessment of the exchange rate debate. If the decline in value is most plausibly attributed to a change in the economic conjuncture that is external to the euro's inception, then the decline does not, after all, count against the euro. If such external causes are *not* sufficient to explain the decline, then the spotlight must fall on factors endogenous to the euro and its accompanying euro system institutions and the Stability and Growth Pact. One obvious candidate for explaining the decline is considered next, followed by other explanations subsequently.

Real interest rate differentials

The effects of interest rate differentials on the exchange rate appear at first sight to be paradoxical. A general presumption would be that raising the (domestic) interest rate would raise the exchange rate. The mechanism is quite simple: the higher interest rate makes acquiring financial assets in that currency more attractive and wealth holders acquire the currency in order to be able to acquire the financial assets. But uncovered interest rate parity indicates that the nominal interest rate differential is equal to the expected decline in the exchange rate. Thus a high interest rate differential foretells a declining exchange rate. These two ideas can be reconciled with an argument which is reminiscent of the 'overshooting' theories. The immediate impact of an (unexpected) increase in the domestic interest rate is a sharp rise in the exchange rate and the persistence of the interest rate differential is associated with a declining exchange rate. The extent of the initial rise in the exchange rate could be seen to depend on the expectations of the time period for which the interest rate differential persists. An interest rate differential of say 2 per cent expected to persist for five years would signify a cumulative decline in the exchange rate over those five years of (just over) 10 per cent.

The measure of interest rate differential depends, not surprisingly, on the interest rate chosen for the comparison and it cannot be assumed that the different interest rate differentials tell the same story. In terms of short-term interest rates, the differential between the USA and the euro area has been positive, fluctuating around 1.5 percentage points: the month-by-month movements in this differential are given in Figure 6.2a. But the differential in terms of long-term interest rates has generally fluctuated between negative values, particularly over the past 12 months, as shown in Figure 6.2b. Consequently, the picture over the sign and size of the interest rate differential between the USA and the euro area is a confused one. But the size of the differential is clearly not large enough to explain the rate of change of the value of the euro over this time period in terms of uncovered interest rate differentials.

With US interest rates moving roughly in parallel with euro rates and inflation rates likewise moving in rough parallel there has been little change in the real interest rate differential between the USA and the euro area since January 1999. This is true of both short-term (Figure 6.2a) and long-term (Figure 6.2b) real interest rates. Thus, Gros *et al.* (2000) report that the clear negative correlation between long-term interest rates and exchange rate movements, empirically robust in the past (as confirmed also by Coppel *et al.* 2000), has broken down from mid-1999. In the case of Japan, the real long-term interest rate differential was at the same level in April 2000 as it was in January 1999, with a 'hump shape' in between. Real short-term interest rates do drift against the euro area during 1999 (from 2 per cent to below 0.5 per cent), but they drift in the opposite direction during 2000 (moving back up above 1 per cent), with no reversal in the exchange rate decline (ECB 2000). Clearly, interest rate differentials do not explain the decline in the value of the euro.

Figure 6.2a | US–eurozone real 3-month money market rate differential

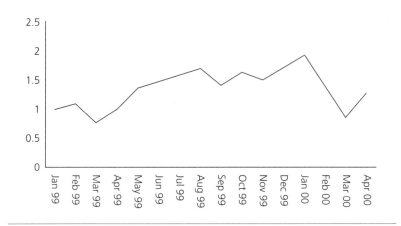

Source: ECB (2000)

Figure 6.2b | US–eurozone real 10-year bond yield differential

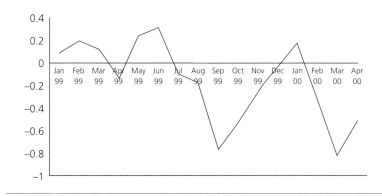

Source: ECB (2000)

US strength

There has been much focus on the euro/dollar exchange rate in general and in this chapter also. Clearly from that perspective the weakness of the euro can be treated as the other side of the coin of a strong dollar. The euro, however, has also declined against sterling and against the yen.

In the case of sterling, the decline of the value of the euro has been less pronounced. It is also the case that many of the arguments which have been applied to explaining the weakness of the euro against the dollar can be carried over to explaining the weakness of the euro against sterling. The UK economy has experienced relatively strong growth, and interest rates have been similar to US rates. Turning to the yen, its strength against the euro is more difficult to fit in with the explanations of the euro/dollar rate. The Japanese economy has experienced sluggish growth (and zero in the second half of 1999) and interest rates have been low – in fact, zero for most of the period under scrutiny. Although the explanation of the relationship between the euro and the yen is not the focus of this chapter, these observations are relevant to the arguments advanced later. Indeed, they contribute towards undermining the 'US strength' explanation of the euro's weakness. In this section we concentrate on explanations for the weakness of the euro by looking at the strength of the dollar and in turn we account for the perceived strengths of the US economy.

Expected and actual growth rate differentials

Buiter (1999b), Coppell *et al.* (2000), Corsetti and Pesenti (1999, 2000), OECD (2000), Deutsche Bank Research (2000), Eichengreen (2000), Favero *et al.* (2000) and von Hagen (1999) all point to the strong performance of the USA as being the fundamental cause of the decline in the value of the euro. The continuing strength of the USA in 1999 coincided with a rather slower growth than had been expected in the euro area during the first half of 1999. During the four quarters of 1999, the US GDP growth rate was, expressed at an annual rate, 3.9 per cent, 3.8 per cent, 4.3 per cent and 4.6 per cent. The corresponding figures for the euro area are 1.8 per cent, 2 per cent, 2.5 per cent and 3.1 per cent. In addition to the actual GDP figures, these authors offer striking graphical evidence (a graph first presented by Corsetti and Pesenti 1999) for the 'strong US' explanation. A very close fit obtains between the graph of the daily dollar/euro exchange rate and the graph of the difference between consensus 1999 GDP growth projections for the euro area and the USA; as can be seen (Figure 6.3), the fit holds very well through 1999. Thus, it is argued, the 'fundamentals', as expressed in actual and/or expected growth rate differentials, explain the decline in the value of the euro. However, difficulties remain in explaining the precise significance of the graph for the decline in value of the euro. So much so that Corsetti (2000), the co-originator of the graph, remarked recently that 'To be honest, it is hard

Figure 6.3 | Dollar/euro exchange rate and revisions to GDP growth forecasts

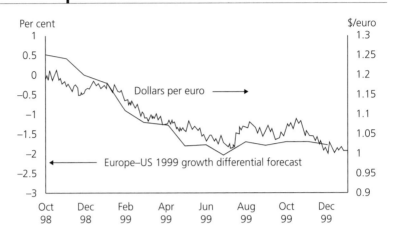

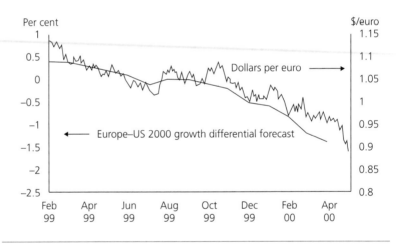

Source: *Consensus Economics*, European Central Bank, reproduced from Corsetti (2000)

to find a convincing interpretation of the recent evolution of the euro' (p. 32). The different interpretations will be scrutinised below.

Eichengreen (2000) interprets the differing expected, and actual, growth rate performance as follows: 'With demand growing relatively slowly and excess capacity pervasive in Europe, a weak Euro was the market's way of pricing European goods into international markets' (p. 2). Yet, Eichengreen offers no explanation as to why international currency markets should behave in the way he postulates. If trade in international goods is the key, then the euro area's trade surplus would lead to an appreciation rather than a depreciation of the euro. Buiter (1999b) provides a different interpretation. According to him, growth differentials affect the exchange rate through (i) money demand and (ii) the anticipated future path of short-term interest rates. On the first one, Buiter does not spell out the mechanism he has in mind, but we would interpret it as follows. Given the amount of money in existence and the level of prices, an acceleration in the rate of growth causes an increase in the demand for money, which in turn causes interest rates to rise (so that interest rates in the USA are expected to be higher than in the euro area). However, this view relies on the money supply's being regarded as exogenously given. In the (to our mind) more realistic case of endogenous money, an increased demand for money would lead to an increase in its stock without interest rates necessarily rising.

On Buiter's second point, interest rates may be anticipated to be higher in the future, but how does that lead to a rising exchange rate? Insofar as financial assets are held in the form of bonds, the anticipation of higher future interest rates is an anticipation of lower bond prices. Hence the anticipation of higher US interest rates would make US bonds less attractive now (than otherwise) and tend to generate a capital outflow rather than inflow. But financial assets may be held in the form of interest-bearing deposits. With low transaction costs, there is little reason to shift financial assets from one currency to another in this period for the prospects of higher future interest rates, but rather to shift when those higher interest rates materialize. Thus we are unconvinced that anticipated higher future interest rates can explain a rise in the value of the dollar (and hence decline in the value of the euro). In any case, and as noted already, it is clear that the *actual* interest rate differential has not moved substantially in favour of the USA (see earlier, and Figures 6.2a and 6.2b) at any time since the inception of the euro, neither is it currently expected to do so in the future (e.g. Deutsche Bank Research 2000).

Coppel *et al.* (2000) and Corsetti and Pesenti (1999) invoke the strong correlation of expected growth rate differentials and the dollar/euro exchange rate but they do not explain in detail just how the growth differential translates into a declining euro. Two explanations may be in order: (i) the vague notion of 'market confidence' whereby low growth prospects entail low 'confidence' and a movement of speculative capital to the strong USA – a possible 'self-fulfilling prophecy'; (ii) the view that a relatively stagnant eurozone cannot match the prospective earnings potential of the buoyant USA so that direct, and possibly portfolio, investment capital flows from the euro area to the USA. Despite being vague, these explanations tied in well only with the situation in the second half of 1999, when the decline in value of the euro appeared as little more than a reversal of a previous rise and when the recent growth performance of the euro was disappointing, especially relative to US strength. They have the effect of 'absolving' the euro, and its accompanying institutional structure, from blame. For they suggest that the decline in value is a purely *cyclical* phenomenon that will naturally reverse, in tandem with a future reversal of the relative cyclical positions of the USA and the euro. Thus, by focusing on the growth rate differential, it is possible to justify remaining sanguine about the fall in value of the euro. However, recent developments have served to cast doubt upon the cyclical explanation and led to a search for a clearer articulation of the relation between the expected US–euro area growth rate differential and the exchange rate.

> There is no reason to suppose that the parallel growth increase in the USA indicates a parallel increase in the earnings potential of direct investment

In fact, as already noted, the growth performance of the euro area started to pick up in the second half of 1999 and has continued on this upward path in the first quarter of 2000 (growing at 3.4 per cent annually), and growth at over 3 per cent is forecast for the euro area in 2001 (OECD, *Economic Outlook*, June 2000). Yet the value of the euro has not risen in tandem with the growth acceleration. On the contrary, it continued to decline and only began its (minor and short-lived) recovery in mid-May, which has been followed by severe falls again. It is now over 25 per cent below its value at its inception. Contrariwise, the US growth performance has matched the euro area quarterly increases (growing at 5.1 per cent annually in 2000 quarter 1), so that the *actual* growth differential has remained relatively stable in the five quarters since the inception of the euro (Figure 6.4). The point we would stress is that the 'cyclical' explanation is more convincing when the euro area is clearly sluggish, as was apparent during the first half of 1999. The subsequent pick-up in the euro area should, *ceteris paribus*, have led to profitable investment opportunities. There is no reason to suppose that the parallel growth increase in the USA indicates a parallel increase in the earnings potential of direct investment. Indeed the cheap euro should have provided the euro area with an advantage in this regard, now that the euro area recovery is well under way (Gros *et al.* 2000). These considerations are all the more pertinent for the case of Japan, given its below-zero growth in quarter 4 of 1999 (Figure 6.4). This may be one reason why, in the light of developments, Corsetti (2000) has considerably modified his explanation from that provided in Corsetti and Pesenti (1999). He now stresses that 'a growth-centered perspective of the euro-dollar exchange rate is far from being "cyclical" ' (p. 7). His more detailed explanations are considered next.

Corsetti (2000) shows that the consensus expected growth differential between the USA and the euro area in 2000 has shown a similar pattern to 1999 (Figure 6.3). The relationship with the yen has broken down in 2000, however, confirming that the expected or actual growth differential cannot be the main explanation of the euro's slide against the yen. If, given the argument of the preceding paragraph, Figure 6.3 cannot be interpreted to support a purely cyclical explanation of exchange rate decline, how, then, is it to be interpreted? Corsetti (2000) suggests that the high domestic US demand can explain the graph and as a result the exchange rate movement. In view of the fact that the US domestic demand growth outstrips US output growth (US consumption demand grew by 7.5 per cent in the first quarter of 2000), Corsetti argues that domestic US producers will export less product abroad, in order to satisfy domestic demand. For such a relative fall in exports to occur, the real price of US goods vis-à-vis foreign goods needs to rise, on this view (causing non-US consumers to substitute towards non-US products from US

Figure 6.4 | Eurozone, US and Japan growth rates

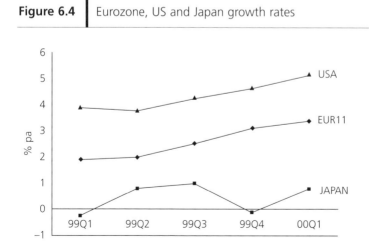

Source: ECB (2000)

products). This is no more than to say that the real exchange rate must appreciate. At the same time the current account will move (further) into deficit. By definition such an appreciation can occur through nominal exchange rate appreciation or through higher US inflation, or both. Thus, this explanation focuses entirely on the US side, irrespective of the situation in the euro area and so, like the explanations considered earlier, it has the effect of 'absolving the euro from blame' (though the explanation may be complementary to, rather than excluding, explanations that focus on the euro area).

In itself, Corsetti's theoretical argument is highly questionable. It relies upon the idea that US output is determined fully on the supply side and that it will be sold domestically, until domestic demand is saturated. We would argue, however, that aggregate demand is a spur to the growth of output. Clearly, such growth has not (yet) increased exports of goods and services to, over imports from, the euro area. It may be that such demand has, instead, 'sucked in' foreign direct investment. This would provide one alternative explanation for Corsetti's (2000) graphs showing a strong and positive correlation between the exchange rate and both the expected US–euro area consumption demand differential and the expected investment demand differential (though the strong association between growth expectations and demand expectations may, in any case, be a sufficient explanation). This alternative is focused upon later.[3]

Investment flows

Evidence on investment flows from the euro area highlights their potential importance in explaining the decline in value of the euro against the dollar (see Table 6.1).

Table 6.1 | Investments in the euro area and current account surplus (billions of euros)

	Direct investments	Portfolio investments	Current account surplus
1997	−48.1	−22.8	76.2
1998	−102.6	−85.3	63.4
1999	−147.3	−21.3	24.3

Source: ECB (2000)

Table 6.1 provides evidence that one *proximate* cause of the decline in the value of the euro is an outflow of direct and portfolio investment far in excess of the current account surplus (a number of recent publications concur with this view: ABN-AMRO Bank 2000; Gros *et al.* 2000; PricewaterhouseCoopers 2000). But what explains the net outflow of investment? A widely discussed possibility is that the outflow is due to the strong US equity market. However, as both Corsetti (2000) and Gros *et al.* (2000) note, the evidence from BIS (2000) is that 'the appreciation of the dollar coincided with the sell off in the US equity market, defying the view that US stock prices drive the dollar' (cited in Gros *et al.* 2000, p. 51). The negative correlation has continued to the present. We now have US equity 'downgrades' outstripping 'upgrades', supporting the pessimistic view about US equities which, nonetheless, has not affected the euro favourably (*Financial Times*, 4 October 2000). Interestingly enough, NASDAQ (the US high-technology stock market) reached its lowest for more than a year in the last week of November 2000, hardly affecting the euro/dollar exchange rate. However, it ought to be noted that by the end of December 2000, when NASDAQ lost more than 50 per cent from its 10 March 2000 high and other unfavourable US statistics, the dollar took a plunge with the euro appreciating, but not as much as the adverse statistics might suggest.

Moreover, the interest rate influence on the stock market and on the exchange rate provides the economic logic for such a correlation (an actual or expected interest rate increase could depress the stock market and raise the exchange rate simultaneously). Gros *et al.* (2000) note also that the net capital outflow cannot be explained by the selling of euro-denominated equity by investors outside of the euro area. The figures show that euro area investors purchased (around 60 billion euros) more foreign-denominated equity than euro-denominated equity in 1999. Gros *et al.* (2000) suggest, therefore, that the outflow of capital might stem from a structural (the outflow started before the inception of the euro) economic imbalance of long-term investment capital, rather than from more speculative sources. They suggest that the latter type of explanation may explain the portfolio investment outflow: the rise in the ECU prior to 1999 being attributed to a 'euphoria' that served to mask the underlying structural imbalance so that 'many wrong-footed investors who overinvested in the euro at the beginning of 1999 have had to "capitulate" since then, which may go a long way towards explaining the downward trend of the euro over the past fifteen months' (pp. 52–53).

Gros *et al.* (2000) thus provide, in our view, a more convincing argument than Corsetti (2000) as to just *why* relative US strength, as

expressed in actual and expected growth differentials, should contribute to the decline in value of the euro. However, in this case, US strength can be only half the story. A buoyant US economy will only attract foreign direct investment from the euro area if equally profitable opportunities for investment in the euro area are perceived to be unavailable. As argued earlier, the *actual* growth pick-up of the euro area would, *ceteris paribus*, suggest that suitable investment opportunities in the euro area are growing. It is true that the continued slide in the *expected* growth differential might be taken to suggest a growing lack of investor confidence in the euro area, but why should investors perceive the euro area to be weak? The import of this latter question is suggested also by a very different consideration: the validity of strong US growth figures has been the subject of significant doubt. Gordon's (1999) widely discussed analysis suggests that (i) strong US productivity growth is largely confined to just the IT sector; and (ii) in that sector changes in the statistical estimation of price declines and quality improvements serve to inflate greatly the true productivity growth. Finally, for the case of the decline in the euro against other currencies, such as the yen, US strength is clearly irrelevant and, as has been illustrated for the case of Japan, similar growth differentials do not obtain.

In conclusion, if Gros et al. (2000) are right, then the next important question to ask in order to get to the bottom of the decline in value of the euro is why has the euro area been perceived by investors to be weak? The timing of the investment outflow, which began about a year before the inception of the euro, is clearly consonant with the view that the inception of the euro itself has played a significant role in harming investor perceptions of the euro area. Indeed, this view is plausible even if a more cautious stance towards the interpretation of Gros et al. (2000) is adopted, so not taking the net ouflow of direct investment as necessarily fundamental. For it remains pertinent to ask just what market and speculative perceptions of the euro area have, for nearly a year and a half, helped to force down a range of currencies other than the US dollar. The extent of euro area weakness and the possible links of such weakness to the inception of the euro are discussed in the next section.

Euro and eurozone weaknesses

A number of writers such as Cohen and Loisel (2000) have provided explanations of the weak euro related to the policy mix introduced at the time of the euro's birth: tight fiscal policy imposed by the Maastricht Treaty and loose monetary policy following convergence of interest rates to the lower point of the range. This resulted in excess supply that was channelled abroad, through a depreciation of the currency. By contrast the USA has gone through a period of excess demand which, alongside the foreign capital attraction, produced currency appreciation. Others such as Feldstein (2000b) argue against the introduction of the euro, despite doubts expressed and reviewed earlier, concerning US strength, and given that the euro has declined against the dollar because of the perceived presence and effect of structural market rigidities and in particular labour market rigidity. Indeed, one does not have to go far in order to find the argument that the structural weakness of the euro area has caused the decline in value of the euro. Dornbusch (2000), George (2000), Price-waterhouseCoopers (2000) and (invoking high German labour costs) Gros *et al.*

> # The euro has, of course, ushered in a Single Monetary Policy

(2000), all point the finger at such 'rigidities'. Of course, the vague notion of 'labour market inflexibility' underlying 'eurosclerosis' has been around for over 20–30 years. Consequently, it raises the question of why 'the German mark surged against the dollar during the 1970s and later during 1985–89 when it doubled in value' at a time when 'rigidities in Germany were probably stronger than today' (De Grauwe 2000, p. 11). Consequently, even if the notion were to be accepted, it would require a great deal of further analysis in order to provide a satisfactory explanation of the decline in value of the euro.

In any case, we do not accept, on either theoretical or empirical grounds, the notion, widespread through the entire literature, that 'labour market inflexibility' is the cause of poor euro area economic performance (see also Arestis, Brown and Sawyer 2001). However, it is by no means necessary to accept the 'labour market rigidity' thesis in order to recognize that the economic and institutional arrangements accompanying the euro itself (their monetarist bias), along with the divergent state of the euro area, lead to the latter's weakness – a weakness that could plausibly cause outflows of both long-term and 'post-euphoric' speculative capital and that might, therefore, go some way to explaining the decline in the euro value (in conjunction with the considerations examined earlier regarding US strength).

The euro has, of course, ushered in a Single Monetary Policy. At the same time it has constrained national fiscal policy (via the Stability and

Growth Pact) and it has made exchange rate revaluation impossible for the individual euro area countries. This raises two critical questions: the first is the extent to which monetary policy can be run centrally by the ECB, while fiscal policy remains a matter for veto-wielding individual member states (the Stability and Growth Pact notwithstanding); the second is the extent to which the single currency regime can be effective in coping with what is a number of separate economies having widely differing needs in terms of economic policies. It is widely recognized that this single currency arrangement requires a high degree of convergence of the patently very diverse economies of the euro area. Without such convergence, it will enforce inappropriate economic policies on its member states, constrain automatic and discretionary fiscal stabilization, and negate room for manoeuvre in the face of economic asymmetries. In addition, a heavy burden of co-ordination is placed on the euro system, through the need to pursue a coherent monetary policy and to be perceived as so doing. The question of the performance of the euro system will be addressed first, then the issue of convergence will be taken up.

The performance of the euro system

It can be noted that the credibility of the euro system was set back, at the outset, by the 'fudging' of the Maastricht criteria. As we have demonstrated in detail elsewhere (Arestis, Brown and Sawyer 2001),

Figure 6.5 | Annual percentage change in eurozone M3

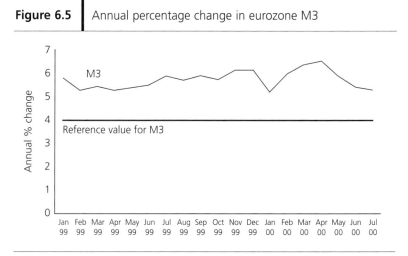

Source: ECB (2000)

various member states of the euro area resorted to accounting 'tricks' and the like in order to meet the criteria for entry into the single currency. This must have raised market concerns and also begs the question, to be explored later, of the extent to which divergence has taken place since the inception of the euro. Furthermore, the performance of the ECB, in terms of its presentation and the transparency of its decision making, has been widely condemned. Additional problems include: important ECB policy decisions have been leaked prior to official announcement; the speeches of different ECB bankers have given different signals regarding ECB policy; the ECB does not publish minutes or divulge information on its econometric models and forecasts;[4] the 4.5 per cent target for M3, which is one of the 'two pillars' of monetary strategy, has not been met at all (Figure 6.5), and yet it has been largely ignored (Arestis, Brown and Sawyer 2001, Ch. 3, elaborates on all these problems). Indeed, the ECB (2000, November) recognizes that this monetary strategy led to 'occasional misunderstanding of the ECB's policy framework' (p. 37).[5]

The ECB itself and sympathetic commentators, such as the OECD (2000) or Favero *et al.* (2000), argue, in defence of this performance, that the ECB and the euro area are very new and lack the historical time series and the relative stability that only time can bring. More significantly, for the question of the exchange rate decline, much of the academic literature plays down the significance of the problematic nature of the euro system, and ECB in particular, and other relevant institutional arrangements for the exchange rate fall, focusing, instead, on US strength. In the light of the foregoing arguments, we would agree that ECB weakness is by no means the whole, or even the main, story. However, as argued earlier, US strength is not sufficient to explain the exchange rate decline. The weakness of the ECB reflects the problems associated with trying to implement a single currency on as diverse an economic area as the euro area. It is one aspect of euro area weakness that is specific to the euro itself and therefore accords with the timing of the euro's decline in value. It could have contributed to the 'post-euphoric' speculative outflows and to long-term fears regarding the ability of the euro to cope with euro area divergence. Thus, we would argue that it is more important than the academic literature is willing to recognize. The issue of divergence is examined next.

The euro and the divergent euro area

Table 6.2 provides the current respective growth, inflation, unemployment, budget deficit, government debt and output gap figures for the euro area (Luxembourg is included in the table but ignored in the descriptive analysis in view of its small level of relative importance).

There is a relatively low growth camp consisting solely of Germany (2.3 per cent). There is also a high growth camp of Spain (4.2 per cent), Belgium (5.1 per cent) and, spectacularly, Ireland (11 per cent!). Inflation rates show Ireland to be way above the rest, once again, on 5.4 per cent, with Spain on 3.5 per cent, and at the other end of the scale, France on 1.9 per cent and Germany on 2 per cent. Unemployment rates vary greatly from 14.3 per cent in Spain to 3 per cent in the Netherlands. The budget deficit and output gap figures confirm the differing fiscal and cyclical positions of the euro area's members, with Ireland's deficit at +2 per cent, and output gap at +2.6 per cent, whereas the respective figures for Italy are −1.9 per cent and −2.5 per cent. Portugal and Austria also have relatively large deficits of

Table 6.2 Growth, inflation, unemployment, budget deficit, government debt and output gap figures for the euro area

Country	Growth rate (SA) % p.a. 2000Q1	Inflation rate (SA) % p.a. Jun 00	Unemployment rate (SA) May 00	Budget deficit 1999	Gross nominal consolidated debt as % of GDP 1999	Output gap 1999
Eurozone	3.4	2.4	9.2	−1.2	72.1	−1.1
Belgium	5.1	3	8.4	−0.9	114.4	−0.9
Germany	2.3	2	8.4	−1.2	61	−1.5
Spain	4.2	3.5	14.3	−1.1	63.5	−0.2
France	3.4	1.9	9.8	−1.8	58.6	−0.6
Ireland	11[Q3]	5.4	4.7	2	52.4	2.6
Italy	3	2.7	10.7[Apr]	−1.9	114.9	−2.5
Luxembourg	4.9+	4.4	2.2	2.4	6.2	N/A
Netherlands	3.9	2.5	3[Apr]	0.5	63.6	0.9
Austria	3.9	2.4	3.2	−2	64.5	0
Portugal	3+	2.8	4.5	−2	56.7	−0.3
Finland	5.1	3.1	9.5	2.3	47.1	−0.1

+% increase of 1999 period over 1998 period
Sources: Eurostat; OECD *Economic Outlook* June 2000; ECB (2000)

–2 per cent. Finally, both Italy and Belgium record debt levels of well over 100 per cent of GDP. Thus there are large differences of economic performance – even though it is early days for the euro, there is no sign that it has contributed to any diminishing of these differences. Still, the proponents of the euro could argue that the evidence thus far provides only a snapshot of the euro area economy. It is necessary, then, to look at the euro area economic performance through time, if questions regarding convergence, or divergence, are to be answered. First, the recent performance will be considered in its broad, historical context. Second, the most recent and detailed evidence on the impact of the euro will be examined.

Recent euro area performance in historical context

The importance of the historical trends for divergence/convergence is recognized by the ECB as reflected in two recent ECB studies, ECB (1999) and Angeloni and Dedola (1999). These papers will be considered along with an examination of the annual series for GDP, the output gap, unemployment and inflation. As a preliminary it can be noted that the 'degree of convergence' is difficult to measure since the relative weighting to be accorded to individual countries is difficult to decide upon. Both the spread (from highest value to lowest) and the standard deviation are, for example, dependent upon 'outliers', but, in fact, such outliers are, in some respects, of equal interest to countries of far greater size. Thus small countries, such as Ireland (which contributes less than 2 per cent of euro area GDP), should, to some extent, be given a greater weighting in analysis than mere regions of comparable size such as London. But just to what extent is not clear. In this circumstance, plotting the evolution of each country, side by side on the same graph, is preferable to merely quoting summary statistics, since the shape of the euro area as a whole can be discerned.

Figure 6.6 plots the annual growth in GDP rates of the past 17 years. Looking over the period as a whole, we would stress that a *divergent state* of the euro area is the norm. Even excluding the smallest and most volatile countries (Ireland, Finland, Portugal and Luxembourg), the difference between the highest and the lowest GDP growth rate, for each given year, for the most part fluctuates between the 1.5 per cent and 2.5 per cent levels. The difference has never fallen below the 1.3 per cent level and reaches a maximum of 4.2 per cent (1987). The most recent figure is 2.3 per cent in 1999. The inception of the euro has not, at this early stage, produced any outstanding change in the norm, but has maintained the euro area in a divergent state, with

Figure 6.6 Eurozone annual growth rates of GDP

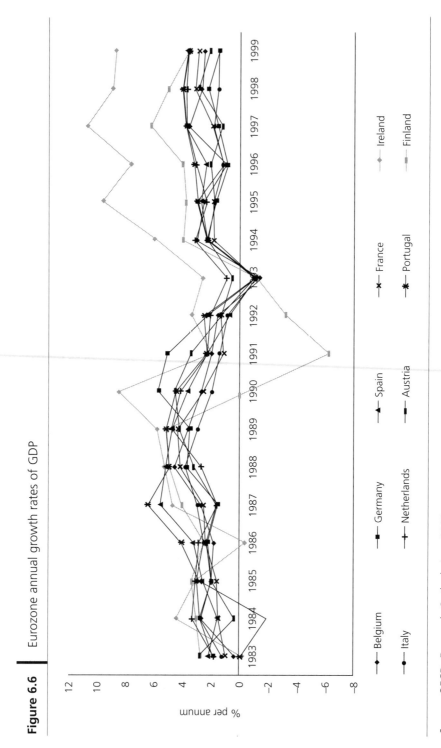

Source: OECD, *Economic Outlook*, June 2000

Ireland clearly threatening to overheat. Excluding the outliers of Ireland and Finland, a process of divergence is visible, from the unusually convergent state of 1995, through to 1997; this higher level of divergence has been maintained, though has not widened further, through 1998 and 1999.

Figure 6.7 plots the output gaps. The output gap is a measure of the difference between the actual and potential output of the country, here expressed as a percentage of the country's potential GDP. Thus it provides one indication of a country's cyclical position. The consistently wide spread between highest and lowest, and the many criss-crossing lines, suggest that the eurozone is in a continually divergent cyclical *state*, over the period, consonant with the growth rate data. There is an indication of a recent *process* of cyclical divergence with Germany and Italy falling further from potential output, in 1999, while France, and most other countries, move towards potential (further above potential, in the case of Ireland and the Netherlands). This evidence appears to contradict the suggestion of both the ECB (1999) and Angeloni and Dedola (1999) that there has been a generally high level of *cyclical convergence* over the time period, with a significant recent increase in the level of convergence. Both papers base their view on the decomposition of key indicators (GDP growth, industrial production growth, employment growth and inflation) into trend and cycle components using the Hodrick–Prescott filter (ECB 1999) or fourth-quarter difference in logs (Angeloni and Dedola 1999, who report that they achieve very similar results with the Hodrick–Prescott filter). For the period 1994–1998, the ECB (1999) find divergence in the growth rate of GDP *trend* but a correlation of around 0.7 to 0.8 (10-year rolling average) for most countries' *cyclical* GDP growth component with that of the euro area average; this compares with lower correlations (down to 0.4) in the early 1990s. Angeloni and Dedola's (1999) analysis confirms the ECB (1999) findings and suggests that German unification caused the divergence in the early 1990s (this is a point that the evidence on output gaps corroborates). For the early and mid-1980s, both papers find levels of cyclical convergence approaching the high levels of the mid- to late 1990s.

What explains the apparent contradiction of divergent output gaps and high measures of 'cyclical' correlation over the period? This is an important question for an assessment of the prospects for the euro, as currently implemented. We would suggest that the divergent spread of output gaps and growth rates, and the many criss-crossing lines evident on both graphs, reveal that the 'cyclical' correlation coefficient

Figure 6.7 | Eurozone output gaps

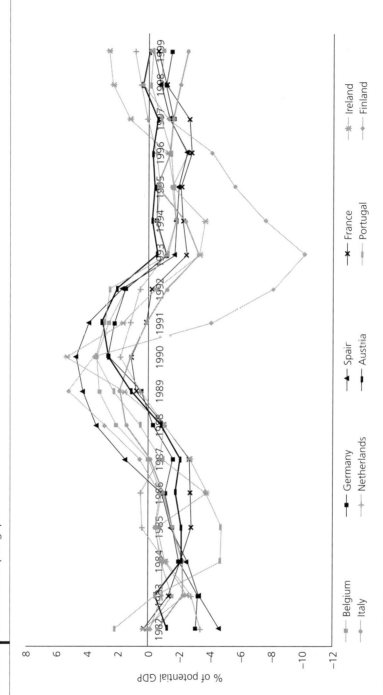

Source: OECD, *Economic Outlook*, June 2000

of 0.7 to 0.8 should not be considered 'high' in any absolute sense. Rather, it simply picks up the fact that there is a broad common cycle in the euro area. Within this broad cycle, however, there is clearly much room for a great deal of divergence, of a 'cyclical' as well as 'trend' nature. In any case, such divergence is of obvious policy relevance whatever its nature. For we reject the view that trend growth is a purely exogenous matter, of no concern to economic policy; on the contrary, the obvious quantitative significance of the 'trend' implies its policy significance. Overall, then, the GDP and output gap data reveal that the euro area remains in a divergent *state* with an evident recent *process* of divergence.

Figure 6.8 plots annual unemployment rates in the euro area from 1982 to the present. The outstanding feature is the continual divergent *state* of the euro area, with the diverse unemployment rates deviating relatively little in their ordering in terms of relative magnitude (Finland being a clear outlier, in this respect). In comparison with the previous graphs there are very few criss-crossing lines other than that of Finland. Spain is an outlier, remaining nearly 5 percentage points above the next highest country in 1999, at 15.9 per cent, having peaked at 24.1 per cent in 1994, when the rate was over 10 percentage points above the next country of substantial size, France.

Annual inflation rates, plotted on Figure 6.9, show strong convergence over the past two decades to the low magnitudes of around 1 per cent in 1999. This provides a much better outlook for the institutional mandate of the euro system in general and the ECB in particular (its prime goal being a low and steady euro area inflation rate), than would higher and more divergent rates. However, there are a number of downsides to this evidence. Wyplosz (1999) has pointed out that the Maastricht Treaty was conceived in the late 1980s, when neo-liberal monetarism held considerable sway over policy. Since then, however, the general lowering of inflation, evident on the graph, has downgraded the importance of inflation, certainly in the public perception. Wyplosz (1999) could also have pointed out that the sustained improvement in inflation performance across the euro area has coincided with a period of sustained sluggishness in terms of growth rates, as described earlier, and has also coincided with a general fall in the rates of inflation worldwide in industrialized economies. This provides some evidence that the prioritizing of inflation is misguided. Finally, it should be noted that the Harmonised Index of Consumer Prices (computed by Eurostat), only available for recent years, tells a slightly different story to the OECD measures for the period from 1998 to 1999. Whereas the non-standardized

Figure 6.8 | Eurozone unemployment

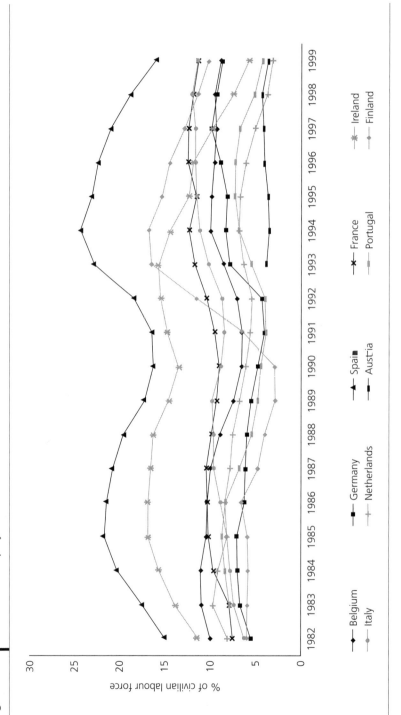

Source: OECD, *Economic Outlook*, June 2000

Figure 6.9 Eurozone annual inflation

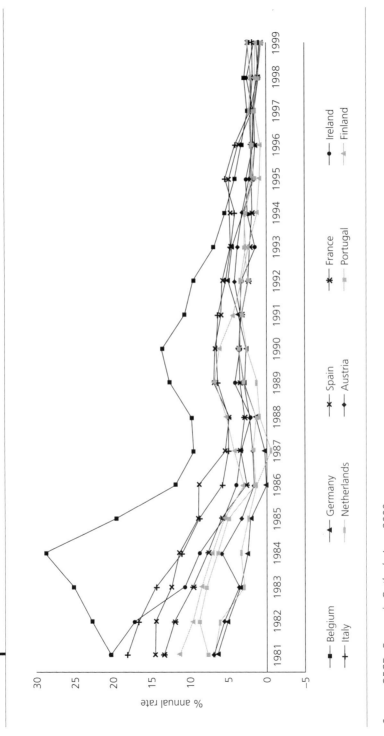

Source: OECD, *Economic Outlook*, June 2000

measure of the OECD shows some convergence for 1998 to 1999, the harmonized index shows divergence, with Ireland moving above the 2.5 per cent level and Spain pushing well above 2 per cent. This hints at the recent inflationary worries regarding Ireland and Spain, described in more detail later.

Before moving on to look at the impact of the euro on convergence in detail, it can be noted, finally, that 'optimum currency area' (OCA) theory, and the debate surrounding it (see Angeloni and Dedola 1999 and Chapters 4 and 8), suggest that the observable variables reviewed above are not the whole story. Rather, it is 'non-observable' shocks, either to aggregate demand (e.g. a shift in tastes) or to aggregate supply (e.g. a technology shift), that are ultimately of significance. This is because, essentially, OCA theory provides an assessment of the appropriateness of a single currency through a weighing up of the costs and benefits of its introduction. The benefits are reduced transaction costs and transparency of relative prices. The costs are the loss of exchange rate and national monetary policy as 'buffers' and adjustment mechanisms in the face of 'asymmetric shocks'. The important point is that these are *non-observable* shocks to aggregate demand, or to aggregate supply; the observable series reviewed thus far are only the outcomes of the unobservable demand and supply shocks.

Bayoumi and Eichengreen (1993) first attempted to identify and estimate the underlying shocks, concluding that their correlation for the euro area is, on average, smaller than that prevailing in the USA. Angeloni and Dedola (1999) update this work. They find that the correlation of shocks in the euro area is very low, i.e. it suffers from very asymmetric shocks. Corsetti and Pesenti (2000) have stressed the importance of this finding (in response to the ECB arguments regarding the observable cyclical convergence, discussed earlier). Our stance towards this evidence offers an opportunity to clarify our theoretical approach towards the evidence on convergence as a whole.

It is no secret that, as McCombie (1999) and, with gusto, Buiter (1999b) point out, the theoretical and econometric assumptions made in order to try to identify non-observable shocks are severe. On top of the well-known list of strong assumptions, we would add the following general point. The business cycle is not driven purely by economic 'shocks' to an otherwise smooth process towards general equilibrium, though, of course, exogenous shocks are very significant. Rather, the business cycle is an ongoing and endogenous economic process. On the financial side, Minsky (1975, 1978, 1982) has charted the inherent tendencies towards fragility of the unfettered capitalist economy. On the real side of the economy, Kaldor (1972, 1985) and Myrdal (1957) have analyzed the processes of cumulative causation and uneven development generated by the operation of unfettered markets. It is such endogenous processes that are the fundamental context for the single currency. The potential for increased regional asymmetries of demand and of resources unleashed by the single currency makes it imperative that the current monetarist structure behind the euro be transformed fundamentally. The evidence presented thus far, showing on the whole a divergent *state* and recent *process* of further divergence, corroborates this perspective. A more detailed look at the recent impact of the euro is now provided.

Impact of the euro: detailed evidence

The impact of the inception of the euro on the evolution of most recent and frequent series for inflation, growth, unemployment and the budget deficit will be assessed in turn.

Figure 6.10 plots the evolution of inflation, in annual percentage terms, from January 1999. In terms of the issue of convergence, the outstanding feature of the graph is the exceptionally high inflation rate of Ireland which moves from 2 per cent to 5.4 per cent, that is 1.9 percentage points above the next highest rate. Not since 1985 has the Irish inflation rate reached such a level so this evidence may well indicate inflationary pressures building up. If Ireland is excluded, then the rest of the countries show, in fact, a slight convergence. Nevertheless, two display notable acceleration: Spanish inflation has remained high relative to other countries, reaching its highest level, of 3.5 per cent in the latest month (June). Belgium has jumped to fourth highest out of the euro area, from third lowest in November 1999.

Figure 6.11 plots the quarterly GDP growth performance over 1999 of the euro area countries (data for Portugal are unavailable). Here, once again, the outstanding feature is Ireland, which is way above the other countries and which causes divergence of the countries as a whole. Again, if Ireland is taken out, there is slight convergence over 1999, as Germany and Italy slowly begin to recover and Belgium spurts, but there is divergence in 2000 quarter 1, owing to Germany growing at a constant rate while Belgium continues to accelerate and Spain picks up again.

Figure 6.12 plots the evolution of unemployment. Essentially the spread is wide and static, although Spain's rate has continued to fall from its very high level. The general recovery in the euro area, evidenced in the previous two graphs, has not served to reduce unemployment any more than a percentage point since early 1999.

Figure 6.10 Eurozone inflation rates measured by HICPs

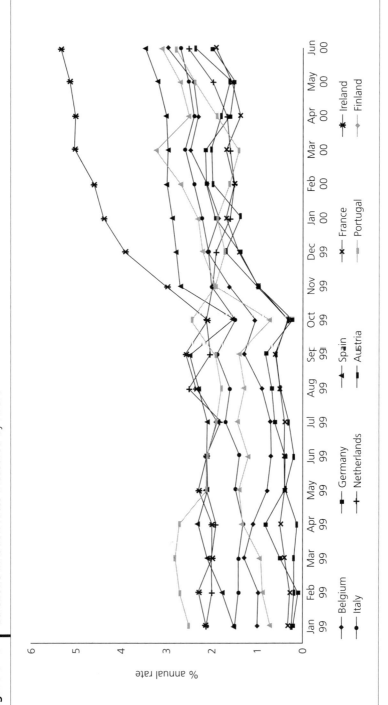

Source: Eurostat

Figure 6.13 plots the evolution of the budget deficits of the euro area from 1996. It shows the difficulties Italy has had in achieving the Maastricht criteria (–3 per cent of GDP limit), starting from below –7 per cent in 1996. The spread from 1998 to 1999 has shrunken slightly, as deficit countries have found that the recovery has eased them above the –3 per cent level. The graph, in conjunction with the previous graphs, shows how the slow recovery of 1999 and loose monetary policy of 1999 have generally served the euro area well, with Italy being the one country to experience fiscal difficulties.

Figure 6.11 | Eurozone GDP growth

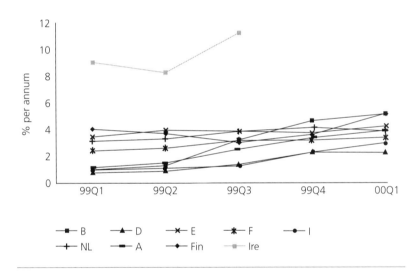

Sources: Eurostat; Bank of Ireland

Figure 6.12 Eurozone unemployment rates

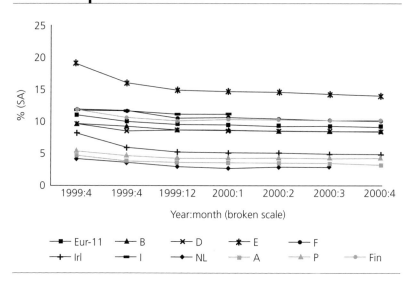

Source: Eurostat

Figure 6.13 Eurozone budget surplus/deficit (in national currencies)

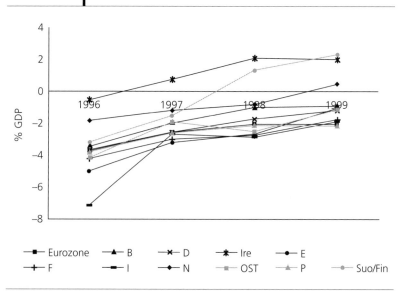

Source: Eurostat

Assessment

It is obviously early days for the euro and 18 months is not enough time to make clear-cut assessments regarding the issue of divergence. Clearly, Ireland is an exceptional case within the euro area, causing some overall divergence on the graphs. Undoubtedly, the Irish inflation rate is a cause for concern and may demonstrate the dangers of inflationary pressures' as policy has been tailored to suit an average from which Ireland is an outlier. Spain and Belgium show some danger of inflationary pressures' building up. But the recovery and the fact that it has been the larger countries, Germany and Italy, that have been at the bottom of their cycle suggest that the jury is still out on fears regarding the deficit levels and general deflationary bias of the single currency. It is hard to believe that, when the roles are reversed, and it is the more peripheral countries, such as Ireland and Finland, and countries such as Spain, that are at the bottom of their cycles, with Germany and Italy at the top of theirs, monetary policy will be loose. That will be the real test for the euro area.

> There remains a chronic problem of high unemployment and also large asymmetries within the euro area

What is clear is that there remains a chronic problem of high unemployment and also large asymmetries within the euro area; there has certainly been no significant trend towards convergence caused by the euro. Business cycles are by no means synchronized, though they do overlap. In terms of OCA theory, countries are likely to receive different shocks as well as being affected differently by shocks. The recent experience has shown that a truly *divergent* state of euro area economic cycles persists: few would argue that Germany actually requires the *same* monetary policy as Ireland! Growth has picked up, but there is no evidence that this is any more than a cyclical recovery around the low trend rate of growth. In terms of OCA theory, then, it is very clear that the euro area is not an OCA and the euro has not endogenously encouraged the necessary convergence for the euro area to become one. Neither has the euro overcome the long-standing difficulties of the euro area. When the economic conjuncture shifts the euro may well prove to harm them.

Summary and conclusions

The US economy has been growing faster than the euro area in the past few years and the general perception of the strength of the US economy relative to the euro area economies is likely to have contributed to the strength of the dollar and the weakness of the euro. However, there is no consensus as to just how US strength causes the value of the euro to fall. US strength cannot, of course, explain euro weakness against other currencies such as the yen. We have suggested that the most plausible explanation concerns long-term investment flows and (following Gros *et al.* 2000) shorter-term 'post-euphoria' flows of portfolio investment. This view stresses that the other side of the coin of US strength is euro area weakness. Reviewing the recent evidence, it seems clear that the introduction of the euro itself, with its restrictive monetarist institutional structures, to an area which is in a divergent *state*, which has recently been widened by a *process* of divergence, is ample reason for long-term investors, and, indeed, 'post-euphoric', short-term speculators, to regard the euro area as structurally weaker since January 1999. It is difficult to predict the future course of the euro; once portfolio investors have shifted fully back to their 'pre-euphoria' level of holdings of euros, then any number of contingencies may come into play, not least the possibility of the US bubble's bursting. As it stands, the low trend performance of the euro area and high unemployment are set to continue.

From the perspective established, the evidence and its policy implications provide a very different picture from that of most of the literature. The prevalent stress on the need for 'structural reform' and the existence of asymmetries can be seen as an attempt to express the idea that asymmetries and structural factors undermine the neoliberal institutional structures associated with the euro, as currently implemented. But this attempted expression is hamstrung by the prejudice towards the efficacy of unfettered markets and so is, ultimately, a failure. The problem with the euro and its associated institutions is not that it diverts attention from, or otherwise hinders, the 'needed labour market reforms'; asymmetries are not merely short-run, external 'shocks' to an otherwise smooth tendency towards a general equilibrium. Rather, policy must be enabled to play its vital role in overcoming aggregate demand asymmetries and uneven processes of cumulative causation through co-ordination of fiscal and monetary policy, within a transformed institutional setting. Thus we take the same phrase ('structural reform'), backed up by the same evidence (that is, high and divergent unemployment and growth rates), to mean utterly different things with radically opposed policy implications. If the markets are right to see problems with asymmetries and the need for 'structural reform' then they are hopelessly wrong in equating 'structural reform' with something called 'labour market flexibility' (and the like). What is needed is an expanded institutional setting, allowing the co-ordination of fiscal and monetary policy and large-scale regional transfers, guided by an alternative to the Stability and Growth Pact (see Arestis, McCauley and Sawyer 2000).

Notes

1 Duisenberg (2000a) states that the euro has 'clearly overshot a level which could be regarded as being in line with the fundamentals'. More recently (Duisenberg 2000b) he admitted that the euro exchange rate was 'a cause for concern' and reiterated that it had been out of line with fundamentals 'for a prolonged period of time'.

2 Relevant time series are available, beginning in the early 1990s on both narrow and broad measures of the effective rate, and, beginning in 1979, on a 'synthetic' euro construct (see ECB 2000; OECD 2000). The narrow ECB measure includes only the 13 main trading partners with the eurozone, whereas the broad measure includes 30 countries (ECB July 2000). The synthetic euro is based upon a weighted average of the respective exchange rates of the 11 euro area countries (with the dollar, for example), where the weights used are the country share in euro-wide GDP. It is calculated as a chain-linked index, taking the same value as the euro on 4 January 1999. The data show that the 'historical perspective' argument on the level of the euro was more persuasive in mid-October 1999 than now. Since mid-October 1999 the value of the euro declined by a magnitude of the order of more than 10 per cent.

3 An interesting, and relevant, episode is worth mentioning. In the first week of December 2000 the euro exhange rate with respect to the dollar increased, prompting commentators to declare that the euro was well on an upward direction. A few statistics may have suggested that the assessment may have had a grain of truth. The US GDP growth rate was 2.4 per cent in the third quarter of 2000 – the lowest for more than a year – against an expected 2.7 per cent. Consumer confidence in November was the lowest for more than a year, as a result of which durable goods orders were 5.5 per cent lower in October when in September they had been up by 2.4 per cent. These figures should have pushed the euro in relation to the dollar well above the level it actually reached at the time (it was at 0.8898 on 7 December from its lowest ever at 0.8828 on 26 November 2000).

4 The ECB publishes economic projections (not forecasts) over a two-year horizon as from December 2000. These take the form of ranges of prospective real GDP growth (and its components) and inflation for the euro area. They play 'an important but limited role' (Duisenberg 2000b) for the ECB's governing council, which 'is neither responsible for the content of these projections [produced by staff experts and not embodying the policy judgements of the council itself] nor should its performance be judged against them' (Duisenberg 2000b). The current projections are: 2.6 per cent–3.6 per cent (2001 GDP growth), 1.8 per cent–2.8 per cent (2001 HICP inflation), 2.5 per cent–3.5 per cent (2002 GDP growth), 1.3 per cent–2.5 per cent (2002 HICP inflation). These projections are so wide as virtually to eliminate the risk of the ECB's being proved wrong.

5 The 'two pillars' monetary strategy may be briefly summarized: the 'first pillar' is a commitment to analyze monetary developments for the information they contain about future price developments. This is the quantitative reference value for monetary growth (4.5 per cent of M3) referred to in the text. The 'second pillar' is a broadly based assessment of the outlook of price developments and the risks to price stability. This broad range of indicators includes: the euro exchange rate; labour market indicators, such as wages and unit labour costs; fiscal policy indicators; and financial market indicators, such as asset prices etc.

Acknowledgements

Generous financial support from the Levy Institute is gratefully acknowledged.

We should like to thank Professor Giancarlo Corsetti for permission to reproduce Figure 6.3.

References

ABN-AMRO Bank (2000) 'Euro suffers from capital outflows', *Euroland Economics Update*, Economics Department, April.

Angeloni, I. and Dedola, L. (1999) 'From the ERM to the euro: new evidence on economic and policy convergence among EU countries', ECB Working Paper, 4.

Arestis, P. and Sawyer, M. (1996) 'The Tobin financial transactions tax: its potential and feasibility', *International Papers in Political Economy*, 3, 3.

Arestis, P., McCauley, K. and Sawyer, M. (2000) 'An alternative to the Stability and Growth Pact', *Cambridge Journal of Economics*, 25, 1, pp. 113–30.

Arestis, P., Brown, A. and Sawyer, M. (2001) *The Euro: Evolution and Prospects*. Aldershot: Edward Elgar.

Bayoumi, T. and Eichengreen, B. (1993) 'Shocking aspects of European monetary unification' in F. Torres and F. Giavazzi (eds) *Adjustment and Growth in the European Monetary Union*. Cambridge: Cambridge University Press.

BIS (2000) *International Banking and Financial Market Developments*, February.

Buiter, W. H. (1999a) 'Optimal currency areas: why does the exchange rate regime matter?', Sixth Royal Bank of Scotland/Scottish Economic Society Lecture, Royal College of Physicians, Edinburgh, 26 October 1999.

Buiter, W. H. (1999b) 'Six months in the life of the euro: what have we learnt?', remarks prepared for a seminar on monetary and budgetary policy in the economic and monetary union, the Rabobank, 25 June 1999.

Chinn, M. D. (2000) 'The empirical determinants of the euro: short and long run perspectives', paper prepared for the Deutsche Bundesbank conference Equilibrium Exchange Rates of the Euro, 27–28 March.

Cohen, D. and Loisel, O. (2000) 'Why was the euro weak? Markets and policies', Centre for Economic Policy Research, Discussion Paper Series 2633.

Coppel, J., Durand, M. and Visco, I. (2000) 'EMU, the euro and the European policy mix', OECD Economics Department Working Papers 232.

Corsetti, G. (2000) 'A perspective on the euro', *CESifo Forum*, 1, 2, Summer, pp. 30–36.

Corsetti, G. and Pesenti, P. (1999) 'Stability, asymmetry and discontinuity: the outset of European Monetary Union', Brookings Papers on Economic Activity 2, December, pp. 295–372.

Corsetti, G. and Pesenti, P. (2000) 'The (past and) future of European currencies', *Cuadernos de Economia*, April.

De Grauwe, P. (2000) 'The euro–dollar exchange rate: in search of fundamentals'. Mimeo, University of Louven and CEPR, June.

Deutsche Bank Research (2000) *Economic and Financial Outlook*, 15 May.

Dornbusch, R. (2000) 'Euro Troubles', Euro Homepage, www.econ.yale.edu/~corsetti/euro/Euroit.htm

Duisenberg, W. (2000a) ECB Press Conference, question and answer session, Frankfurt am Main, 8 June.

Duisenberg, W. (2000b) ECB Press Conference, question and answer session, Frankfurt am Main, 23 December.

ECB (1999) 'Longer term developments and cyclical variations in key economic indicators across euro area countries', *Monthly Bulletin*, July, pp. 33–54.

ECB (2000) *Monthly Bulletin*, various issues, augmented by data available on the ECB website, **http://www.ecb.int**

Eichengreen, B. (2000) 'The euro one year on', *Journal of Policy Modelling*, 22, 3, pp. 355–68.

Eurostat (various) **http://europa.eu.int/eurostat.html**

Favero, C., Freixas, X., Persson, T. and Wyplosz, C. (2000) 'One money, many countries', *Monitoring the European Central Bank Volume 2*. London: CEPR.

Feldstein, M. (2000a) 'Europe can't handle the euro', *The Wall Street Journal*, 8 February.

Feldstein, M. (2000b) 'The European Central Bank and the euro: the first year', NBER Working Paper W7517.

George, E. (2000) Speech delivered to the Leeds and Bradford Chartered Institute of Bankers and Bradford Chamber of Commerce, 11 April.

Gordon, R. J. (1999) 'Has the "new economy" rendered the productivity slowdown obsolete?' **http://faculty-web.at.nwu.edu/economics/gordon/334.pdf**

Gros, D., Davanne, O., Emerson, M., Mayer, T., Tabellini, G. and Thygesen, N. (2000) 'Quo vadis euro? The cost of muddling through', Centre for European Policy Studies Macroeconomic Policy Group, Second Report.

Kaldor, N. (1972) 'The irrelevance of equilibrium economics', *Economic Journal*, 82.

Kaldor, N. (1985) *Economics Without Equilibrium*. Cardiff: University College Cardiff Press.

McCombie, J. S. L. (1999) 'Economic integration, the EMU and European regional growth' in P. Davidson and J. Kregel (eds) *Full Employment and Price Stability in a Global Economy*. Cheltenham, UK /Northampton, MA: Edward Elgar.

Minsky, H. P. (1975) *John Maynard Keynes*. New York: Columbia University Press.

Minsky, H. P. (1978) 'The financial instability hypothesis: a restatement', Thames Papers in Political Economy, Autumn.

Minsky, H. P. (1982) *Can 'It' Happen Again?*. New York: M.E. Sharpe.

Myrdal, G. (1957) *Economic Theory and Underdeveloped Regions*. London: Duckworth.

OECD (2000) *EMU One Year On*. Paris: OECD.

PricewaterhouseCoopers (2000) *European Economic Outlook*, May.

von Hagen, J. (1999) 'The first year of EMU'. Mimeo, Centre for European Integration Studies, University of Bonn.

Wyplosz, C. (1999) 'Economic policy co-ordination in EMU: strategies and institutions', presented at the German–French Economic Forum, Bonn, 12 January.

7

Did the successful emergence of the euro as an international currency trigger its depreciation against the US dollar?

Gerhard Fink and Gerhard Fenz

Introduction

The euro had a brilliant start as an international financing currency. Announced issues of international euro-denominated debt securities, the best indicator of judgements by market participants, increased dramatically in 1999. This pattern is also confirmed by net euro- and US dollar-denominated issues. The share of net issues of international bonds denominated in US dollars dropped from 60 per cent in 1998 to 46 per cent in 1999 while the euro share increased from 32 per cent to 46 per cent. Since the development was not a continuous process but characterized by a sudden jump in the volume of euro-denominated debt securities already in the first

> ## The euro had a brilliant start as an international financing currency

quarter of 1999, neither cyclical economic factors nor exchange rate movements serve as possible explanations. In addition, US borrowers used international euro-denominated security markets intensively for raising capital during 1999. Low interest rates in Europe made it very attractive for international borrowers to raise financial capital in euros. Our estimates indicate that net issues of international euro-denominated debt securities by US borrowers increased from 1998 to 1999 by 40 to 60 billion US dollars. According to the short-run portfolio model these shifts in the supply of euro- and US dollar-denominated international debt securities may well have triggered the depreciation of the euro against the US dollar. The pattern seems similar to what happened during the 'dollar glut' in the 1970s: attractive financing conditions motivated firms to raise capital in euros. Selling the euros afterwards led the currency to depreciate.

Functions of international currencies

The functions a national currency fulfils at the international level are similar to the functions of money within a country: it can serve as a medium of exchange, as a unit of account and as a store of value (see Table 7.1). In addition Krugman and Obstfeld (1993) distinguish between functions in the private and public sector. With respect to international transactions of the private sector an international currency is used to solve the 'double coincidence of wants' problem at the level of currency exchange by serving as a vehicle through which currency exchange is made indirectly at lower costs. If a currency is used for denomination purposes in international trade it serves as an international unit of account. The international store of value function in the private sector is associated with international financing and investment decisions.

Table 7.1 | Functions of international currencies

Functions	Private sector	Public sector
Medium of exchange	Vehicle currency	Intervention currency
Unit of account	Denomination	Currency peg
Store of value	Portfolio allocation	Reserve currency

Sources: Krugman and Obstfeld (1993); Hartmann (1998)

In the public sector currencies used by monetary authorities for interventions on foreign exchange markets fulfil the function as a medium of exchange. Closely linked to this decision is the store of value function determining the currencies suitable as international reserve. Finally, the international role as a unit of account is associated with currency pegs.

In this chapter we concentrate on the store of value function in the private sector. We analyze the role of the euro on international bond and money markets since its introduction in January 1999, especially in comparison with the US dollar. We focus on international financing decisions and their repercussions on the euro/dollar foreign exchange market. The following section deals with differences in the US and euro area financial systems and domestic security markets. In the third section we define the market for international debt securities. The fourth and fifth sections describe developments on international security markets during 1999 and 2000. Possible implications of the increased use of the euro as an international financing currency based on the portfolio asset approach are the topic of the sixth section. Finally, we draw conclusions in the last section.

Financial markets and the development of domestic debt securities

Both the USA and the euro area have well-developed financial markets. An appropriate measure of the degree of financial development should reflect the extent and efficiency of financial markets and cover all three important market segments, the credit, the bond, and the stock market. Since aggregate measures of the efficiency of financial market segments are difficult to construct we use financial depth as a measure of financial development, i.e. the sum of outstanding domestic credits, stock market capitalization[1] and outstanding domestic debt securities (Fenz 2000). In 1997 financial depth in per cent of GDP, indicating the quantity of external finance available, amounted to 367 per cent in the USA and 316 per cent in the euro area compared with 269 per cent in the USA and 249 per cent in the euro area in 1990. The sharp increase was mainly due to the rapid development on stock markets during that period. But the structures of US and euro area financial markets differ considerably (see Figure 7.1). The fluid US system is dominated by capital markets, the dedicated system in the euro area by credit markets. In the USA the share of credit markets in 1997 (1990) was 22 per cent (32 per cent), of bond markets 42 per cent (49 per cent), and of stock markets 36 per cent (19 per cent), while in the euro area credits had a share of 46 per cent (53 per cent), bonds of 35 per cent (36 per cent) and stocks of 19 per cent (11 per cent). The increasing shares of stock markets in both countries are driven by asset price inflation. During 1990–97 the trend to disintermediation has been more pronounced in the USA but may well indicate future developments in the euro area.

The difference between the financial systems is well illustrated by the development of domestic debt securities (see Appendix, Figure A7.1 and Table A7.1 for data). At the end of 1999 the US market was 2.5 times larger than its European counterpart. The fact that the volume of the European market seems to stagnate since 1995 also reflects exchange rate movements. Corporate issuers play a prominent role on US markets with a share of 18 per cent compared with less than 4 per

Figure 7.1 Shares of financial market segments

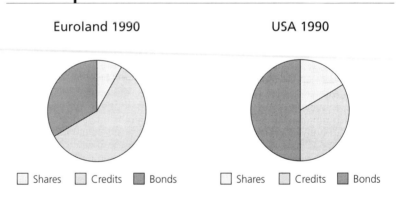

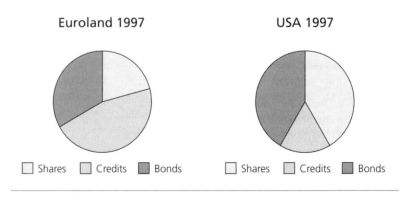

cent in Europe; US public issuers are losing market shares (60 per cent in 1990, 55 per cent in 1999) caused by reduced financing needs of the federal government, a development which due to the Maastricht criteria can be expected in the euro area for the next years. Issues by financial institutions are growing fast in the USA but are still less important (22 per cent) than in the euro area (35 per cent). The introduction of the euro so far had no significant influence on domestic securities markets. This stands in sharp contrast to developments on international debt securities markets.

Definition of international debt securities

In judging the success of the euro as an international financing currency we have to look at international rather than domestic debt securities markets. Before starting with a detailed analysis it is necessary to define which security market segments are covered by the term 'international debt securities'. We use data from the BIS international securities statistics and follow their definition. The BIS provides data for domestic and international debt securities which are further disaggregated along the categories of bonds and notes, and money market instruments (see Table 7.2).

The BIS definition of international debt securities includes eurobonds and euro notes (D + C) and traditional foreign bonds (B) plus the corresponding segments of money market instruments. Thus, only issues by residents in their domestic currency (A) are excluded.[2] The BIS provides data for outstanding amounts in current dollar terms and for announced and net issues in dollar terms of the date of announcement. Announced new issues are a good indicator of current judgements by market participants, net issues give the actual amount of new external financing volume

Table 7.2 | BIS definition of debt securities markets

	Issues by residents	*Issues by non-residents*
In domestic currency	A	B
In foreign currency	C	D

A = domestic bonds; B = traditional foreign bonds; C + D = eurobonds; B + D = external or cross-border bonds; B + C + D = international bonds

Source: BIS (1995)

and outstanding amounts measure the importance of debt securities during the recent past. A disaggregation by the currency of issue is available representing the most important statistical source for our analysis. Thus, for example, new net issues of euro-denominated international debt securities cover all euro-denominated issues except those by residents of the euro area (A). Additionally available are data for outstanding amounts, net issues and announced issues by nationality of issuer. International debt securities by US nationality issuer cover for example issues by US borrowers on the US market in foreign currencies (C); issues of US borrowers on a foreign market in the currency of that market (B, a euro issue in Frankfurt for example); and issues by US borrowers on a foreign market not in the currency of that market (D, a yen or US dollar issue in Frankfurt for example). Unfortunately these data are not further disaggregated by currencies

> The year 1999 could well turn out to be a watershed concerning the structure of international bond, note and money market instrument markets

But, assuming that segment B is an important component, an increase of US nationality issues would indicate additional US external financing activity in foreign currencies, most probably either in yen or in euros. A simultaneous increase euro-denominated international issues and in US nationality issues therefore indicates increased financing activities of US borrowers on euro- denominated international securities markets.

International security markets by currency

The volume of international securities markets amounts only to a tenth of domestic markets and its structure is markedly different. The year 1999 could well turn out to be a watershed concerning the structure of international bond, note and money market instrument markets. The euro successfully challenged the leading role of the US dollar as an international financing currency on international debt securities markets.

Our analysis is based on quarterly data from the Bank of International Settlements starting in the third quarter of 1993 until the fourth quarter of 1999 measured in current dollar terms. During the whole period outstanding amounts of international debt securities denominated in US dollars exceeded amounts in euros (see Appendix, Figure A7.2, and Tables A7.2–A7.4 for the actual data). Dollar bonds steadily increased their lead, which can only partly be explained by exchange rate movements. But this development was reversed in 1999. Announced euro issues, the best indicator of judgements by market participants, increased dramatically in 1999 (Appendix, Figure A7.3). In all four quarters announced issues were higher than in any other quarter during the analyzed time period. Despite the fact that activities on dollar markets were high as well and that the euro lost 18 per cent against the dollar within a year, announced euro issues almost equalled dollar issues in the fourth quarter of 1999. During the whole sample period the difference was never so small. This pattern is also confirmed by net euro and dollar issues (Appendix, Figure A7.4). Again the activity in each quarter of 1999 reached an all-time high and actual amounts raised on international euro-denominated markets surpassed dollar issues in the third and fourth quarters[3] (see Tables 7.3–7.5).

Due to the much more dramatic increase in euro issues, the market share of US dollar-denominated international bonds dropped from 60 per cent in 1998 to 46 per cent in 1999 while the euro share increased from 32 per cent to 46 per cent. In 1999 the volume of net issues in both currencies was almost identical at 469 billion US dollars.

Shifts in market shares are even more dramatic on money markets. But since these markets are much more volatile shares are not an appropriate indicator of long-run developments.

Table 7.3 | International bonds and notes: net issues by currency (billion US dollars)

	1Q 98	2Q 98	3Q 98	4Q 98	1Q 99	2Q 99	3Q 99	4Q 99
US $	113.6	143	80.8	66	131.2	154.1	114.3	69.1
Euro	59.9	69.9	56.5	30.2	86.4	142.4	141	99.1
Total	185.8	229.1	144.5	109.3	228.6	331.9	282	174.2

	1Q 00	2Q 00	3Q 00	1998	1999	2000
US $	122.1	105.5	133	403.4 (60.3%)	468.7 (46.1%)	360.6 (47.6%)
Euro	117.9	100.2	76.4	216.5 (32.4%)	468.9 (46.1%)	294.5 (38.9%)
Total	257.7	254.6	245	668.7	1016.7	757.3

Source: BIS (1999, 2000)

Table 7.4 | International money market instruments: net issues by currency (billion US dollars)

	1Q 98	2Q 98	3Q 98	4Q 98	1Q 99	2Q 99	3Q 99	4Q 99
US $	8.3	3.6	4.8	10.7	6.9	2.8	0.5	2.2
Euro	3.0	1.7	5.4	13.1	28.5	6.5	18	13.5
Total	10.3	0.1	10.9	11.5	35.1	8	22.8	18.7

	1Q 00	2Q 00	3Q 00	1998	1999	2000
US $	0.7	12.8	14.6	27.4 (83.5%)	12.4 (14.7%)	28.1 (70.3%)
Euro	−4.2	10.6	−0.3	23.2 (70.7%)	66.5 (78.6%)	6.1 (15.3%)
Total	1.2	24.4	14.4	32.8	84.6	40

Source: BIS (1999, 2000)

Table 7.5 | International debt securities (bonds, notes and money market instruments): net issues by currency (billion US dollars)

	1Q 98	2Q 98	3Q 98	4Q 98	1Q 99	2Q 99	3Q 99	4Q 99
US $	121.7	147.2	85.0	78.0	156.5	177.1	142.8	79.9
Euro	64.4	73.3	63.0	41.6	138.3	165.5	164.4	115.8
Total	196.1	229.2	155.4	120.8	263.7	339.9	304.8	192.9

	1Q 00	2Q 00	3Q 00	1998	1999	2000
US $	122.8	118.3	147.6	431.9 (61.6%)	556.3 (50.5%)	388.7 (48.8%)
Euro	113.8	110.8	76.1	242.3 (34.5%)	584.0 (53.0%)	300.7 (37.7%)
Total	258.9	279.0	259.4	701.5	1101.3	797.3

Source: BIS (1999, 2000)

Table 7.6 | International bonds and notes: net issues by nationality of issuer (billion US dollars)

	1Q 98	2Q 98	3Q 98	4Q 98	1Q 99	2Q 99	3Q 99	4Q 99
USA	59.5	96.3	62.7	57.9	126.9	139.5	134.7	79.8
Euro area	66.3	66.5	47.9	27	91.2	147.6	123.4	73.9
Total	187.4	232.1	144.3	107.2	271.7	370.5	318.6	188.3

	1Q 00	2Q 00	3Q 00	1998	1999	2000
USA	87.7	89.5	114.6	276.4 (41.2%)	480.9 (41.9%)	291.8 (38.5%)
Euro area	116.3	116.3	110.5	207.7 (31%)	436.1 (38%)	343.1 (45.3%)
Total	258.1	254.6	245	671	1149.1	757.7

Source: BIS (1999, 2000)

Table 7.7 | International money market instruments
net issues by nationality of issuer (billion US dollars)

	1Q 98	2Q 98	3Q 98	4Q 98	1Q 99	2Q 99	3Q 99	4Q 99
USA	−0.5	1.9	3	−0.8	2	−0.1	−3.3	2.3
Euro area	5.3	−4.3	4.2	−1.8	24.8	−3.2	13.8	19.4
Total	9.6	−0.2	11.8	−11	35	−8.5	22.6	17.3

	1Q 00	2Q 00	3Q 00	1998	1999	2000
USA	−0.9	2.7	5.5	3.6 (35.3%)	0.9 (1.4%)	7.3 (18.3%)
Euro-area	−1.8	22.5	6.7	3.4 (33.3%)	54.8 (82.5%)	27.4 (68.5%)
Total	1.2	24.4	14.4	10.2	66.4	40

Source: BIS (1999, 2000)

Table 7.8 | International debt securities (bonds, notes and money market
instruments): net issues by nationality of issuer (billion US dollars)

	1Q 98	2Q 98	3Q 98	4Q 98	1Q 99	2Q 99	3Q 99	4Q 99
USA	59.0	98.2	65.7	57.1	128.9	139.4	131.4	82.1
Euro area	71.6	62.2	52.1	25.2	116.0	144.4	137.2	93.3
Total	197.0	231.9	156.1	96.2	306.7	362.0	341.2	205.6

	1Q 00	2Q 00	3Q 00	1998	1999	2000
USA	86.8	92.2	120.1	280.0 (41.1%)	481.8 (39.6%)	299.1 (37.5%)
Euro area	114.5	138.8	117.2	211.1 (31;0%)	490.9 (40.4%)	370.5 (46.4%)
Total	259.3	279.0	259.4	681.2	1215.5	797.7

Source: BIS (1999, 2000)

International security markets by nationality of issuer

US and euro area issuers increased their financing activity on international debt securities markets (see Appendix, Figures A7.5–A7.7 and Tables A7.5–A7.7 for the actual data) right after the introduction of the euro. In particular US borrowers entered the euro-denominated international bond market to raise financial capital.

US borrowers issued bonds and notes worth 276.4 billion US dollars in 1998 and 480.9 in 1999, euro area borrowers 207.7 billion US dollars in 1998 and 436.1 in 1999. The increase in money market instruments by euro area borrowers was even more spectacular from 3.4 billion US dollars in 1998 to 54.8 billion US dollars in 1999. Net issues by US borrowers dropped from 3.6 billion US dollars in 1998 to 0.9 billion US dollars in 1999 (see Tables 7.6–7.8).

By way of contrast, as we demonstrated earlier the total volume of international bond issues denominated in US dollars increased only by 16 per cent (403.4 billion US dollars in 1998 and 468.7 in 1999) while those denominated in euros increased by a remarkable 117 per cent (1998: 216.5 billion US dollars; 1999: 468.9 billion US dollars): thus the increase in international financing activity by US borrowers was not matched by an equal increase in international US dollar-denominated bonds. Contrariwise, euro-denominated bonds increased more than the international financing activity by euro area nationality issuers.

In contrast to US borrowers, European borrowers made extensive use of international money market instruments in 1999

In contrast to US borrowers, European borrowers made extensive use of international money market instruments in 1999. Due to the volatility of these markets this cannot be interpreted as a long-run development. But even if money markets are taken into account, the fact that US borrowers entered euro-denominated international markets is also reflected in international debt securities data.

A rough estimate of the size of additional capital raised by US borrowers on international security markets in 1999 can be gained by a simple calculation: net issues of euro-denominated international debt securities increased by 341.7 billion US dollars from 1998 to 1999; net issues by European borrowers increased by 279.8 billion US dollars. Assuming that all additional issues by European borrowers were denominated in euros still yields a difference of 61.9 billion US dollars. The same considerations for US dollar issues and US issuers give a difference of –77.4 billion US dollars. Thus the supply change in euro-denominated issues that exceeded the additional supply by euro area borrowers – equal to 61.9 billion US dollars – was of similar size to additional issues by US borrowers over changes in international US dollar-denominated instruments – equal to –77.4 billion US dollars. Since US and EU11 borrowers accounted for 80 per cent of all international net issues and 103.5 per cent of all net issues were denominated either in US dollars or in euros, we can conclude that US borrowers used international euro-denominated security markets extensively for raising capital during 1999.

The active role of US borrowers on euro international bond markets can be confirmed by two additional sources. Merrill Lynch (2000) reports that: 'Non-EMU borrowers, mainly from the US and the UK, accounted for a third of 1999 large cap issuance.'[4] This is a marked increase compared to their share in outstanding bonds at the end of 1999 of 21 per cent. Estimates by the European Commission based on different statistics indicate that 7 per cent of all euro-denominated international bonds in 1999 were issued by the USA and 3 per cent by the pre-ins.[5] Thus according to the European Commission US borrowers raised 38 billion US dollars.

Several reasons were discussed as potential explanations of the successful start of the euro on international debt security markets as an international financing currency:

1 *The Asian and Russian crises.* In the wake of the Asian and Russian crises a flight to quality emerged, boosting demand for bonds supplied by issuers from well-rated countries such as the USA and the EU. Issues of emerging countries have been very low in 1999. This helps to explain the increased activity of US and European borrowers on international bond markets but not the shift in market shares from dollar to euro-denominated bonds.

2 *Disintermediation.* Similarly to **1**, the general trend to disintermediation can explain the increased volume of total international bond issues but hardly the marked relative increase of euro-denominated bonds. Nevertheless, the fact that disintermediation in Europe is far less advanced than in the USA could be – in the wake of a catching up process – a potential source of additional activity on European capital markets. As a matter of fact, the European corporate bond sector witnessed increased issues of debt securities and most of these offers were placed on international markets. Net issues of international corporate debt securities by euro area nationality borrowers were more than four times higher in 1999 than in 1998: they increased from 27.8 billion US dollars to 112.9. Domestic corporate issues, however, reached only 49.9 (21.7) billion US dollars in 1999 (1998). US net international corporate debt security issues almost doubled from 65.2 billion US dollars in 1998 to 124.9 in 1999 while US corporates issued domestic securities worth 255.5 (240.5) billion US dollars in 1999 (1998). Also international issues by European financial institutions experienced significant growth from 163.6 billion US dollars (1998) to 329.7 billion US dollars (1999), compared with 138.4 billion US dollars (1998) and 135.5 billion US dollars (1999) in the USA. In contrast net international issues of European governments dropped from 20.2 billion US dollars in 1998 to –4.5 billion US dollars in 1999 while US

$$\text{PPP: } e_{t+1} = e_t \ \frac{1 + \pi_{USA}}{1 + \pi_{EMU}}$$

$$\text{IFE: } e_{t+1} = e_t \ \frac{1 + i_{USA}}{1 + i_{EMU}}$$

e_t denotes the exchange rate (euro for 1 dollar), π the inflation rate and i the nominal interest rate.

Average interest rates (3 months' deposit rates) in the euro area and the USA were 3 per cent and 5.4 per cent, respectively; CPI-based inflation rates were 1.1 per cent and 2.2 per cent. According to relative PPP theory the dollar should have depreciated by 1.1 per cent, and according to the international Fischer effect by 2.3 per cent. Instead the dollar actually appreciated against the euro by 18 per cent (see Figures A.8, A.9). Also many market participants and exchange rate analysts were puzzled by the decline of the euro in the year of its introduction, especially as US saving rates were historically low and current account deficits high.

The gap between the euro as a success story as international financing currency and its more modest role as a currency for international investment may help to solve the puzzle.

As indicated earlier low interest rates in Europe compared to US levels and the creation of a new, liquid and deep international financial market by the introduction of the euro motivated US borrowers to become active on international euro-denominated markets. Most of the additional supply of euro-denominated securities was absorbed by European investors. The consequences of this financing strategy, not anticipated by market participants, were, *ceteris paribus*, the following:

1 Depreciation of the euro versus the dollar. A good deal of the additional euro-denominated financial capital raised by US borrowers was converted into US dollars on foreign exchange markets. Besides differences in productivity growth,[6] this was an important reason for the depreciation of the euro against the dollar. In 1999 the euro lost 18 per cent of its value relative to the US dollar.

2 Additional capital imports to the USA and a growing US current account deficit: the US current account deficit increased from 220 billion US dollars in 1998 to 338.9 billion US dollars in 1999 while the capital account displayed a surplus of 369.5 billion US dollars in 1999 compared with 216.6 billion in 1998.

3 An increase in the supply of euro-denominated debt securities tends to raise interest rates in the euro area: but differentials[7] in long-run interest rates (10-year government bond yields) did not change

much in 1999 and short-term interest rate differentials (3 months' deposit rates) even grew from 1.9 to 2.7 percentage points.

We will confront these empirical findings with theoretical results from the short-run portfolio asset model. We do not present the model in detail but provide a graphical analysis. For analytical details we refer to the corresponding literature.

Contrary to the monetary approach the portfolio asset model regards home currency securities as imperfect substitutes for foreign currency securities. Risk aversion of portfolio holders may motivate this pattern. Thus, uncovered interest rate parity does not prevail. As usual we assume a home asset preference. Differentials between home and foreign interest rates reflect mainly exchange rate risks.[8]

In traditional approaches to the portfolio model the outstanding amount of home currency securities either reflected cumulated government or cumulated current account deficits. In a world with integrated international financial markets this strict currency distinction is no longer valid. Especially large multinational enterprises can issue securities denominated in any international currency.

For our purpose it is convenient to view financing decisions and thereby the supply of home and foreign currency securities as exogenous and concentrate on the endogenous variables exchange rate and interest rate. They adjust to changes in the exogenous stock variables to clear markets.

In Figure 7.2 we present a graphical analysis of the portfolio asset model. In simulating the effects of the international financing and

Figure 7.2 | Effects in the short run-portfolio asset model

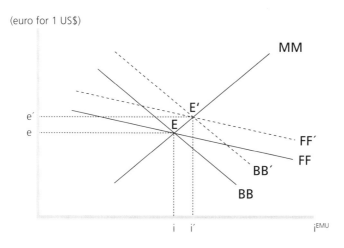

investing decisions we assume that other things being equal the issuing strategy of US borrowers increases the supply of euro-denominated debt securities (shifting the equilibrium condition for domestic bonds, the BB schedule, to BB′) and, second, reduces the supply of US dollar-denominated debt securities (shifting the equilibrium condition for foreign bonds, the FF schedule, to FF′). The MM schedule is unchanged since the money supply in EU11 is not affected by these portfolio shifts. The increase in the supply of home currency securities and the decrease in the supply of foreign currency securities are the exogenous shock we wish to analyze.

As shown, this leads undoubtedly to a depreciation of the euro against the US dollar (see Appendix, Figures A7.8 and 13.2). A devaluation of the home currency increases wealth (see the following equation 4) and thereby the demand for home currency securities (see the following equation 1). But the depreciation also increases the value of foreign bonds. Assuming preferences for a balanced portfolio concerning the value of stocks of foreign and domestic securities held by investors, the increased value of foreign bonds decreases demand for them. Thus we reach a new equilibrium at E′ with a depreciation of the home currency (euro) from e to e′. The effect on euro area interest rates is positive in our graphical example, the size of the increase depends on wealth and interest rate elasticities of the demand functions for money, euro currency bonds, and US currency bonds.

Home country (euro area)	Foreign country (USA)
1 $B = b(\overset{-}{r},\ r^* + \overset{+}{\bar{E}}(e),\ \overset{+}{\dot{W}})$	$B^* = b^*(r - \overset{+}{\bar{E}}(e),\ \overset{+}{r^*},\ e\overset{-}{\dot{W}}^*)$
2 $F = f(\overset{-}{\bar{r}}, r^* + \overset{+}{\dot{E}}(e), \overset{+}{W})$	$F^* = f^*(r - \overset{-}{\bar{E}}(e), \overset{+}{r^*}, e\overset{+}{\dot{W}}^*)$
3 $M = m(\overset{-}{\bar{r}}, \overset{+}{\dot{W}})$	$M^* = m^*(\overset{-}{r^*}, e\overset{+}{\dot{W}}^*)$
4 $W = B + eF + M$	$eW^* = B^* + eF^* + eM^*$
5 $B^T = B + B^*$	$F^{T-} = F + F^*$

B^T and F^T denote the total stocks of home and foreign currency bonds, b (b^*), f (f^*), m (m^*) denote home (foreign) demand for home currency bonds, foreign currency bonds and money. $E(e)$ and e indicate the expected exchange rate and the exchange rate, r and r^* the home and foreign interest rates, W and W^* home and foreign wealth.

Effects of the composition of wealth on the foreign exchange rate are a crucial feature of the portfolio asset model. Similar to the effects of a sterilized intervention by monetary authorities, a shift in the composition of wealth in the euro area from dollar- to euro-denominated bonds induces a depreciation of the euro.[10] (See Branson and Henderson 1990, Breuss 1998, and Isard 1995.)

Thus the model correctly predicts a depreciation of the euro. Since the real side of the economy is not modelled important factors determining exchange rates, for example inflation, current accounts and output growth, are not considered. Thus implications from this model are valid only in the short run.

It is not possible to determine the impact on the exchange rate. But as outlined earlier, if changing financing/investment behaviour resembles secret sterilized interventions by monetary authorities, we can use results from earlier studies on their effectiveness to derive a rough estimate. To our knowledge the latest study distinguishing between the portfolio effect (secret intervention) and the additional expectation effect (public intervention) was carried out by Dominguez and Frankel (1990) for the Deutschmark/US-dollar exchange rate. Using data for the period 1984–87 their findings suggest 'that a typical $100 million of "secret" intervention has an effect of less than 0.1 per cent [0.079] on the exchange rate'. Due to the fact that the euro's role on financial markets (especially on foreign exchange markets) is similar to the Deutschmark before 1999 and the volume of financial markets grew by approximately 300 per cent since 1985, the effect on the euro/dollar exchange rate at a rough estimate can be as high as 10 per cent.

Conclusions

The euro had a brilliant start on international financial markets as an international financing currency. Its share on international debt securities markets (net issues) increased from 34 per cent in 1998 to 49 per cent in 1999 while the share of dollar-denominated debt securities dropped from 61 per cent to 44 per cent. US borrowers were very active on euro-denominated international debt markets,

> The financing decisions of US borrowers may well have triggered the depreciation of the euro versus the dollar

attracted by low interest rates and the creation of a new, liquid and deep financial market. Our estimates indicate that net issues of international euro-denominated debt securities by US borrowers increased from 1998 to 1999 by 40 to 60 billion US dollars. Some comparative figures show that this is a considerable amount. For example total US goods exports in 1999 amounted to 702 billion US dollars; US current account deficit equalled 339 billion US dollars; and total reserves of the ECB plus EU11 national banks were 256 billion US dollars. So the financing decisions of US borrowers may well have triggered the depreciation of the euro versus the dollar. Theoretical results from the portfolio asset model support these findings.

Notes

1 IPOs are a better measure of external financing on stock markets. Since data are not available for all countries we use market capitalization instead as a measure of financial development on this market segment.

2 Due to the lack of data international notes cover only the segments C and D, i.e. euro notes.

3 In contrast to international bonds, domestic euro-denominated bond issues developed less spectacularly. Issues during the first three quarters in 1999 reached 273.3 billion US dollars, compared with 231 billion US dollars in the same period of 1998, US issues climbed from 940.7 billion US dollars (1Q-3Q 1998) to 964.9 billion US dollars (1Q-3Q 1999).

4 Issues > euro 500m.

5 The UK, Denmark, Sweden and Greece.

6 In 1999 the US economy grew at a rate of 4 per cent, the euro area at 2.2 per cent.

7 Differentials are measured as US minus euro area levels.

8 As in many empirical studies differences due to credit risk differentials between securities issued by foreign and home borrowers are ignored.

9 Graphically the effects are only shown for the euro area. The effects for the USA are a mirror image.

10 In this very simple version of the portfolio asset model the production side is not modelled. Therefore output and price changes are not analyzed.

References

Branson, W. H. and Henderson, D. W. (1990) 'Specification and influence of asset markets', in Ronald W. Jones and Peter B. Kenen (eds), *Handbook of International Economics*, Vol. 2. Amsterdam: North-Holland.

BIS (1995) *The BIS Statistics on International Banking and Financial Market Activity*, Basle, August 1995.

BIS (1999/2000) *Quarterly Review: International Banking and Financial Market Developments*, several issues, Basle.

Breuss, Fritz (1998) *Außenwirtschaft*, Band II. Vienna and New York: Springer Verlag.

Detken, Carsten and Hartmann, Philipp (2000) 'The euro and international capital markets', CEPR Discussion Paper 2461.

Dominguez, Kathryn and Frankel, Jeffery (1990) 'Does foreign exchange intervention matter? Disentangling the portfolio and expectations effects for the Mark', NBER Working Paper 3299

The Economist (1999/2000) 'Quarterly portfolio poll', several issues.

European Commission (2000) 'Quarterly note on the euro-denominated bond markets', N.12, January–March. **http://europa.eu.int/comm/ economy finance**

EZB (2000) *Annual Report*, Frankfurt.

EZB (1999/2000) *Monthly Bulletin*, several issues, Frankfurt.

Fenz, Gerhard (2000) 'Economic growth and financial development in the USA'. Mimeo.

Hartmann, Philipp (1998) *Currency Competition and Foreign Exchange Markets*. Cambridge: Cambridge University Press.

Isard, Peter (1995) *Exchange Rate Economics*. Cambridge: Cambridge University Press

Krugman, Paul and Obstfeld, Maurice (1993) *International Economics*. New York: HarperCollins

Merrill Lynch (2000) *Size and Structure of the World Bond Market: 2000*. Merril Lynch.

Obstfeld, Maurice and Rogoff, Kenneth (1996) *Foundations of International Macroeconomics*. Cambridge MA: MIT Press.

Appendix

Table A7.1 Domestic debt securities (billion US dollars)

	Amounts outstanding					Changes in stock				
	All issuers	USA	in %	Euroland	in %	All issuers	USA	in %	Euroland	in %
1989:12	14,191.9	6,825.8	48.1	2,792.2	19.7					
1990:12	15,861.4	7,432.2	46.9	3,730.3	23.5	1,468.0	606.5	41.3	517.0	35.2
1991:12	17,240.9	8,109.4	47.0	4,002.9	23.2	1,404.8	677.1	48.2	440.7	31.4
1992:12	19,388.9	8,722.2	45.0	4,755.9	24.5	1,799.4	612.9	34.1	568.2	31.6
1993:12	20,762.5	9,413.5	45.3	4,711.2	22.7	1,930.5	691.3	35.8	537.3	27.8
1994:03	21,234.2	9,592.7	45.2	4,757.1	22.4	461.2	179.2	38.9	74.1	16.1
1994:06	21,999.7	9,717.6	44.2	5,004.6	22.7	403.7	124.9	30.9	67.2	16.6
1994:09	22,626.8	9,872.9	43.6	5,244.3	23.2	377.5	155.4	41.2	93.2	24.7
1994:12	22,927.8	10,045.0	43.8	5,303.8	23.1	483.4	172.0	35.6	142.3	29.4
1995:03	24,433.8	10,271.0	42.0	5,804.0	23.8	534.0	226.0	42.3	145.2	27.2
1995:06	25,343.6	10,460.9	41.3	5,959.7	23.5	523.0	189.9	36.3	83.6	16.0
1995:09	24,901.6	10,628.4	42.7	5,992.5	24.1	440.5	167.6	38.0	97.5	22.1
1995:12	25,045.3	10,830.8	43.2	6,014.3	24.0	402.2	202.3	50.3	17.5	4.4
1996:03	25,393.6	11,041.4	43.5	6,060.6	23.9	648.2	210.7	32.5	156.3	24.1
1996:06	25,583.0	11,246.9	44.0	6,068.3	23.7	450.6	205.5	45.6	98.1	21.8
1996:09	25,920.7	11,468.1	44.2	6,155.7	23.7	416.2	221.1	53.1	90.9	21.8
1996:12	26,179.5	11,731.8	44.8	6,128.4	23.4	540.6	263.7	48.8	48.8	9.0
1997:03	25,696.8	11,932.3	46.4	5,736.9	22.3	443.3	200.5	45.2	87.1	19.6
1997:06	26,262.0	12,136.2	46.2	5,627.4	21.4	389.1	203.8	52.4	68.9	17.7
1997:09	26,171.2	12,341.2	47.2	5,592.7	21.4	318.7	205.0	64.3	37.2	11.7
1997:12	26,044.5	12,655.3	48.6	5,501.4	21.1	456.8	314.1	68.8	-9.5	-2.1
1998:03	26,491.4	13,065.5	49.3	5,405.6	20.4	682.8	410.2	60.1	76.8	11.2
1998:06	26,677.0	13,315.6	49.9	5,578.6	20.9	420.1	250.1	59.5	66.3	15.8
1998:09	27,727.9	13,601.4	49.1	6,114.3	22.1	444.2	285.8	64.3	92.1	20.7
1998:12	29,036.9	13,983.6	48.2	6,101.0	21.0	565.3	382.2	67.6	-17.7	-3.1
1999:03	28,915.7	14,419.7	49.9	5,750.4	19.9	784.6	436.1	55.6	143.2	18.3
1999:06	29,147.9	14,647.1	50.3	5,585.7	19.2	509.2	227.4	44.7	57.1	11.2
1999:09	30,558.4	14,982.4	49.0	5,847.0	19.1	509.8	335.3	65.8	79.3	15.6
1999:12	31,238.7	15,426.3	49.4	5,521.9	17.7	774.1	443.9	57.3	14.2	1.8
2000:03	31,203.8	15,649.2	50.2	5,312.5	17.0	511.8	222.9	43.6	61.9	12.1
2000:06	31,305.6	15,753.5	50.3	5,374.6	17.2	159.3	104.3	65.5	60.2	37.8
1998	29,036.9	13,983.6	48.2	6,101.0	21.0	2,112.4	1,328.3	62.9	217.5	10.3
1999	31,238.7	15,426.3	49.4	5,521.9	17.7	2,577.7	1,442.7	56.0	293.8	11.4
2000	31,305.6	15,753.5	50.3	5,374.6	17.2	671.1	327.2	48.8	122.1	18.2

Source: BIS (1999, 2000)

Table A7.2 International debt securities by currency (billion US dollars)

	Amounts outstanding					Gross issuance					Net issues				
	Total issues	US dollar	in %	Euro	in %	Total issues	US dollar	in %	Euro	in %	Total issues	US dollar	in %	Euro	in %
1993 Q3	2,015.4	816.5	40.5	505.3	25.1										
1993 Q4	2,025.2	832.0	41.1	501.4	24.8	210.6	109.5	52.0	47.9	22.7	61.9	15.4	24.9	25.9	41.8
1994 Q1	2,156.5	866.6	40.2	548.4	25.4	240.9	126.1	52.3	54.0	22.4	85.8	34.6	40.3	29.4	34.3
1994 Q2	2,249.0	875.7	38.9	588.9	26.2	198.1	101.5	51.2	39.9	20.1	41.4	9.2	22.2	16.6	40.1
1994 Q3	2,357.4	890.8	37.8	618.6	26.2	211.1	103.3	48.9	34.6	16.4	73.3	15.2	20.7	11.4	15.6
1994 Q4	2,393.7	897.1	37.5	637.9	26.6	203.4	104.2	51.2	41.8	20.6	66.1	18.7	28.3	26.9	40.7
1995 Q1	2,576.0	902.0	35.0	725.1	28.1	210.0	99.3	47.3	54.5	26.0	49.6	13.6	27.4	26.6	53.6
1995 Q2	2,663.4	918.5	34.5	747.1	28.1	228.0	104.9	46.0	52.9	23.2	62.5	16.5	26.4	19.6	31.4
1995 Q3	2,667.6	941.4	35.3	756.9	28.4	248.0	117.2	47.3	51.2	20.6	81.8	22.9	28.0	24.0	29.3
1995 Q4	2,709.4	965.3	35.6	772.1	28.5	233.6	113.0	48.4	51.2	21.9	68.2	23.9	35.0	21.7	31.8
1996 Q1	2,783.1	1,013.4	36.4	791.7	28.4	317.0	149.2	47.1	82.4	26.0	113.0	48.0	42.5	40.4	35.8
1996 Q2	2,888.0	1,093.8	37.9	801.6	27.8	326.0	178.8	54.8	64.5	19.8	141.6	80.4	56.8	32.6	23.0
1996 Q3	2,987.5	1,140.5	38.2	825.6	27.6	319.7	163.2	51.0	61.8	19.3	114.5	61.7	53.9	28.1	24.5
1996 Q4	3,130.2	1,224.8	39.1	857.0	27.4	363.8	181.3	49.8	78.3	21.5	168.6	84.3	50.0	44.4	26.3
1997 Q1	3,160.5	1,291.4	40.9	829.4	26.2	384.5	188.7	49.1	77.1	20.1	146.1	66.7	45.7	36.6	25.1
1997 Q2	3,329.3	1,389.7	41.7	829.0	24.9	381.5	216.3	56.7	66.7	17.5	157.7	98.2	62.3	33.3	21.1
1997 Q3	3,452.9	1,497.7	43.4	857.9	24.8	413.8	230.7	55.8	79.6	19.2	169.7	108.0	63.6	39.5	23.3
1997 Q4	3,494.3	1,553.8	44.5	879.4	25.2	338.7	180.7	53.4	69.9	20.6	94.3	70.2	74.4	33.0	35.0
1998 Q1	3,654.9	1,675.7	45.8	911.4	24.9	480.6	251.3	52.3	118.5	24.7	196.1	121.9	62.2	62.9	32.1
1998 Q2	3,864.5	1,822.4	47.2	998.4	25.8	440.3	254.7	57.8	102.0	23.9	229.2	146.6	64.0	71.6	31.2
1998 Q3	4,132.5	1,908.0	46.2	1,137.6	27.5	388.4	207.1	53.3	93.0	23.9	155.4	85.6	55.1	61.9	39.8
1998 Q4	4,293.9	1,963.2	45.7	1,167.2	27.2	384.4	194.7	50.7	94.3	24.5	120.8	76.7	63.5	43.3	35.8
1999 Q1	4,424.6	2,101.4	47.5	1,192.0	26.9	585.9	283.7	48.4	204.3	34.9	263.7	138.1	52.4	114.9	43.6
1999 Q2	4,688.4	2,252.7	48.0	1,281.9	27.3	605.5	274.6	45.4	219.8	36.3	339.9	156.9	46.2	148.9	43.8
1999 Q3	5,112.6	2,366.5	46.3	1,482.6	29.0	593.2	253.2	42.7	222.9	37.6	304.8	114.8	37.7	159.0	52.2
1999 Q4	5,226.2	2,433.4	46.6	1,512.1	28.9	469.1	181.2	38.6	178.0	37.9	192.9	71.3	37.0	112.6	58.4
2000 Q1	5,502.5	2,632.9	47.8	1,599.6	29.1	655.1	276.9	42.3	234.9	35.9	258.9	122.8	47.4	113.7	43.9
2000 Q2	5,762.5	2,751.2	47.7	1,709.4	29.7	655.3	278.6	42.5	215.8	32.9	279.0	118.3	42.4	110.8	39.7
2000 Q3	5,848.0	2,898.8	49.6	1,653.4	28.3	682.6	320.4	46.9	214.4	31.4	259.4	147.6	56.9	76.1	29.3
1998	15,945.8	7,369.3	46.2	4,214.6	26.4	1,693.7	907.8	53.6	407.8	24.1	701.5	430.8	61.4	239.7	34.2
1999	19,451.8	9,154.0	47.1	5,468.6	28.1	2,253.7	992.7	44.0	825.0	36.6	1,101.3	481.1	43.7	535.4	48.6
22000	5,848.0	2,898.8	49.6	1,653.4	28.3	1,993.0	875.9	43.9	665.1	33.4	797.3	388.7	48.8	300.6	37.7

Source: BIS (1999, 2000)

Table A7.3 International bonds and notes by currency (billion us dollars)

	Amounts outstanding					Announcements					Net issues				
	Total issues	US dollar	in %	Euro	in %	Total issues	US dollar	in %	Euro	in %	Total issues	US dollar	in %	Euro	in %
1993:09	1,906.5	730.5	38.3	494.9	26.0	130.1	47.4	36.4	41.2	31.7	61.7	15.4	25.0	24.7	40.0
1993:12	1,916.7	745.9	38.9	492.2	25.7	149.9	55.1	36.8	46.4	31.0	83.3	33.8	40.6	28.0	33.6
1994:03	2,045.3	779.7	38.1	538.7	26.3	109.4	34.6	31.6	31.1	28.4	37.6	8.8	23.4	14.6	38.8
1994:06	2,133.8	788.4	36.9	577.3	27.1	117.5	34.1	29.0	23.4	19.9	68.7	14.4	21.0	9.2	13.4
1994:09	2,237.3	802.8	35.9	604.8	27.0	115.7	41.5	35.9	29.4	25.4	59.7	12.5	20.9	22.3	37.4
1994:12	2,280.2	815.2	35.8	622.4	27.3	117.8	36.3	30.8	39.4	33.4	49.2	9.3	18.9	22.7	46.1
1995:03	2,461.6	824.5	33.5	705.5	28.7	131.5	42.7	32.5	35.3	26.8	55.4	16.4	29.6	14.7	26.5
1995:06	2,541.9	840.9	33.1	723.5	28.5	147.3	52.6	35.7	32.9	22.3	71.9	18.0	25.0	19.9	27.7
1995:09	2,536.3	858.9	33.9	730.7	28.8	134.1	48.8	36.4	35.6	26.5	66.9	22.8	34.1	18.7	28.0
1995:12	2,576.9	881.7	34.2	747.6	29.0	213.6	85.0	39.8	65.1	30.5	104.3	46.9	45.0	36.6	35.1
1996:03	2,642.2	928.6	35.1	766.4	29.0	208.9	102.9	49.3	48.8	23.4	124.6	65.7	52.7	30.2	24.2
1996:06	2,730.4	994.3	36.4	778.5	28.5	202.7	93.8	46.3	44.6	22.0	110.6	54.2	49.0	25.7	23.2
1996:09	2,833.9	1,048.5	37.0	802.4	28.3	233.9	109.5	46.8	53.6	22.9	150.5	78.7	52.3	35.2	23.4
1996:12	2,958.6	1,127.1	38.1	826.6	27.9	259.1	117.3	45.3	58.5	22.6	141.6	66.0	46.6	34.4	24.3
1997:03	2,985.9	1,193.1	40.0	798.6	26.7	254.9	139.4	54.7	50.4	19.8	152.5	90.8	59.5	35.2	23.4
1997:06	3,149.9	1,284.0	40.8	801.4	25.4	278.8	150.3	53.9	59.6	21.4	160.8	101.4	63.1	35.4	24.3
1997:09	3,265.2	1,385.4	42.4	827.2	25.3	209.8	108.1	51.5	50.0	23.8	90.6	63.2	69.8	30.8	34.0
1997:12	3,310.7	1,448.5	43.8	846.7	25.6	337.8	167.1	49.5	99.2	29.4	185.8	113.6	61.1	59.9	32.2
1998:03	3,461.5	1,562.1	45.1	880.4	25.4	308.5	174.8	56.7	82.9	26.9	229.1	143.0	62.4	69.9	30.5
1998:06	3,671.0	1,705.1	46.4	966.7	26.3	243.5	121.1	49.7	69.2	28.4	144.5	80.8	55.9	56.5	39.1
1998:09	3,927.0	1,785.9	45.5	1,101.3	28.0	252.4	124.8	49.4	65.9	26.1	109.3	66.0	60.4	30.2	27.6
1998:12	4,099.6	1,851.8	45.2	1,131.4	27.6	408.2	197.4	48.4	147.6	36.2	228.6	131.2	57.4	86.4	37.8
1999:03	4,196.1	1,983.1	47.3	1,128.3	26.9	445.6	193.9	43.5	175.1	39.3	331.9	154.1	46.4	142.4	42.9
1999:06	4,468.4	2,137.2	47.8	1,225.3	27.4	410.9	171.0	41.6	159.7	38.9	282.0	114.3	40.5	141.0	50.0
1999:09	4,869.0	2,251.5	46.2	1,407.5	28.9	310.2	111.9	36.1	127.2	41.0	174.2	69.1	39.7	99.1	56.9
1999:12	4,966.2	2,320.6	46.7	1,425.7	28.7	462.2	190.1	41.1	169.2	36.6	257.7	122.1	47.4	117.9	45.8
2000:03	5,252.9	2,519.4	48.0	1,518.3	28.9	450.7	183.1	40.6	146.3	32.5	254.6	105.5	41.4	100.2	39.4
2000:06	5,488.8	2,624.9	47.8	1,617.4	29.5	472.9	215.1	45.5	147.7	31.2	245.0	133.0	54.3	76.4	31.2
2000:09	5,562.5	2,757.9	49.6	1,563.8	28.1										
1998	4,099.6	1,851.8	45.2	1,131.4	27.6	1,142.2	587.8	51.5	317.2	27.8	668.7	403.4	60.3	216.5	32.4
1999	4,966.2	2,320.6	46.7	1,425.7	28.7	1,574.9	674.2	42.8	609.6	38.7	1,016.7	468.7	46.1	468.9	46.1
2000	5,562.5	2,757.9	49.6	1,563.8	28.1	1,385.8	588.3	42.5	463.2	33.4	757.3	360.6	47.6	294.5	38.9

Source: BIS (1999, 2000)

Table A7.4 International money markets by currency (billion US dollars)

	Amounts outstanding					Gross issuance					Net issues				
	Total issues	US dollar	in %	Euro	in %	Total issues	US dollar	in %	Euro	in %	Total issues	US dollar	in %	Euro	in %
1993 Q3	108.9	86.0	79.0	10.4	9.6	80.5	62.1	77.1	6.7	8.3	0.2	0.0	0.0	1.2	600.0
1993 Q4	108.5	86.1	79.4	9.2	8.5	91.0	71.0	78.0	7.6	8.4	2.5	0.8	32.0	1.4	56.0
1994 Q1	111.2	86.9	78.1	9.7	8.7	88.7	66.9	75.4	8.8	9.9	3.8	0.4	10.5	2.0	52.6
1994 Q2	115.2	87.3	75.8	11.6	10.1	93.6	69.2	73.9	11.2	12.0	4.6	0.8	17.4	2.2	47.8
1994 Q3	120.1	88.0	73.3	13.8	11.5	87.7	62.7	71.5	12.4	14.1	6.4	6.2	96.9	4.6	71.9
1994 Q4	113.5	81.9	72.2	15.5	13.7	92.2	63.0	68.3	15.1	16.4	0.4	4.3	1,075.0	3.9	975.0
1995 Q1	114.4	77.6	67.7	19.6	17.1	96.5	62.2	64.5	17.6	18.2	7.1	0.1	1.4	4.9	69.0
1995 Q2	121.5	77.6	63.9	23.6	19.4	100.7	64.6	64.2	18.3	18.2	9.9	4.9	49.5	4.1	41.4
1995 Q3	131.3	82.5	62.8	26.2	20.0	99.5	64.2	64.5	18.2	18.2	1.3	1.1	84.6	3.0	230.8
1995 Q4	132.5	83.6	63.1	24.5	18.5					15.7					
1996 Q1	140.9	84.8	60.2	25.3	18.0	103.4	64.2	62.1	17.3	16.7	8.7	1.1	12.6	3.8	43.7
1996 Q2	157.6	99.5	63.1	23.1	14.7	117.1	75.9	64.8	15.7	13.4	17.0	14.7	86.5	2.5	14.7
1996 Q3	153.6	92.0	59.9	23.2	15.1	117.0	69.4	59.3	17.2	14.7	3.9	7.5	192.3	2.4	61.5
1996 Q4	171.6	97.7	56.9	30.4	17.7	129.9	71.8	55.3	24.7	19.0	18.1	5.6	30.9	9.2	50.8
1997 Q1	174.6	98.3	56.3	30.8	17.6	125.4	71.4	56.9	18.6	14.8	4.5	0.7	15.6	2.2	48.9
1997 Q2	179.4	105.7	58.9	28.0	15.6	126.6	76.9	60.7	16.3	12.9	5.2	7.4	142.3	2.9	55.8
1997 Q3	187.7	112.3	59.8	30.7	16.4	135.0	80.4	59.6	20.0	14.8	8.9	6.6	74.2	4.1	46.1
1997 Q4	183.6	105.3	57.4	32.7	17.8	128.9	72.6	56.3	19.9	15.4	3.7	7.0	189.2	2.2	59.5
1998 Q1	193.4	113.6	58.7	31.0	16.0	142.8	84.2	59.0	19.3	13.5	10.3	8.3	80.6	3.0	29.1
1998 Q2	193.5	117.3	60.6	31.7	16.4	131.8	79.9	60.6	19.1	14.5	0.1	3.6	3,600.0	1.7	1,700.0
1998 Q3	205.5	122.1	59.4	36.3	17.7	144.9	86.0	59.4	23.8	16.4	10.9	4.8	44.0	5.4	49.5
1998 Q4	194.3	111.4	57.3	35.8	18.4	132.0	69.9	53.0	28.4	21.5	11.5	10.7	93.0	13.1	113.9
1999 Q1	228.5	118.3	51.8	63.7	27.9	177.7	86.3	48.6	56.7	31.9	35.1	6.9	19.7	28.5	81.2
1999 Q2	220.0	115.5	52.5	56.6	25.7	159.9	80.7	50.5	44.7	28.0	8.0	2.8	35.0	6.5	81.3
1999 Q3	243.6	115.0	47.2	75.1	30.8	182.3	82.2	45.1	63.2	34.7	22.8	0.5	2.2	18.0	78.9
1999 Q4	260.0	112.8	43.4	86.4	33.2	158.9	69.3	43.6	50.8	32.0	18.7	2.2	11.8	13.5	72.2
2000 Q1	249.6	113.5	45.5	81.3	32.6	192.9	86.8	45.0	65.7	34.1	1.2	0.7	58.3	-4.2	-350.0
2000 Q2	273.7	126.3	46.1	92	33.6	204.6	95.5	46.7	69.5	34.0	24.4	12.8	52.5	10.6	43.4
2000 Q3	285.5	140.9	49.4	89.6	31.4	209.7	105.3	50.2	66.7	31.8	14.4	14.6	101.4	-0.3	-2.1
1998	194.3	111.4	57.3	35.8	18.4	551.5	320.0	58.0	90.6	16.4	32.8	27.4	83.5	23.2	70.7
1999	260.0	112.8	43.4	86.4	33.2	678.8	318.5	46.9	215.4	31.7	84.6	12.4	14.7	66.5	78.6
2000	285.5	140.9	49.4	89.6	31.4	607.2	287.6	47.4	201.9	33.3	40.0	28.1	70.3	6.1	15.3

Source: BIS (1999, 2000)

Table A7.5 International debt securities by nationality of issuer (billion US dollars)

	Total	Amounts outstanding				Announced issues					Net issues				
		USA	in %	Euroland	in %	Total	USA	in %	Euroland	in %	Total	USA	in %	Euroland	in %
1993:09	2,014.9	175.6	8.7	549.7	27.3	213.3	23.8	11.2	59.0	27.7	61.4	2.2	3.6	26.3	42.8
1993:12	2,024.6	175.5	8.7	556.8	27.5	244.8	25.8	10.5	75.5	30.8	85.9	6.5	7.6	38.6	44.9
1994:03	2,156.1	184.2	8.5	611.2	28.3	200.9	31.4	15.6	56.9	28.3	41.8	7.2	17.2	17.9	42.8
1994:06	2,248.9	193.7	8.6	648.0	28.8	217.4	29.3	13.5	66.1	30.4	73.2	6.9	9.4	35.5	48.5
1994:09	2,357.1	202.3	8.6	698.0	29.6	205.1	26.3	12.8	70.1	34.2	52.1	2.3	4.4	34.4	66.0
1994:12	2,392.3	203.5	8.5	727.6	30.4	212.8	35.9	16.9	74.6	35.1	49.5	14.1	28.5	31.7	64.0
1995:03	2,574.2	224.1	8.7	813.8	31.6	231.8	31.9	13.8	81.1	35.0	61.9	9.1	14.7	33.6	54.3
1995:06	2,661.1	234.8	8.8	853.0	32.1	250.2	39.3	15.7	73.4	29.3	81.2	17.9	22.0	33.2	40.9
1995:09	2,664.9	248.8	9.3	865.0	32.5	237.9	39.4	16.6	81.9	34.4	67.5	14.3	21.2	33.9	50.2
1995:12	2,706.0	261.7	9.7	892.6	33.0	337.5	53.0	15.7	115.1	34.1	113.5	26.3	23.2	46.7	41.1
1996:03	2,780.6	286.0	10.3	922.6	33.2	397.0	62.6	15.8	123.6	31.1	134.6	32.8	24.4	47.7	35.4
1996:06	2,879.4	316.9	11.0	952.8	33.1	384.5	58.0	15.1	104.9	27.3	107.5	29.0	27.0	35.3	32.8
1996:09	2,980.1	345.5	11.6	985.4	33.1	362.9	62.2	17.1	110.2	30.4	163.7	42.1	25.7	47.3	28.9
1996:12	3,117.7	385.6	12.4	1,019.6	32.7	382.7	67.4	17.6	125.5	32.8	146.6	32.3	22.0	55.7	38.0
1997:03	3,148.9	411.3	13.1	1,023.7	32.5	378.0	71.8	19.0	110.2	29.2	158.2	45.9	29.0	40.6	25.7
1997:06	3,318.2	458.3	13.8	1,054.6	31.8	414.3	89.5	21.6	118.6	28.6	172.1	54.9	31.9	42.7	24.8
1997:09	3,444.3	510.4	14.8	1,083.4	31.5	336.7	72.6	21.6	105.9	31.5	86.6	43.0	49.7	33.2	38.3
1997:12	3,485.3	550.5	15.8	1,101.5	31.6	479.0	98.1	20.5	165.3	34.5	197.0	59.0	29.9	71.6	36.3
1998:03	3,646.9	607.2	16.6	1,153.0	31.6	450.3	125.0	27.8	137.0	30.4	231.9	98.2	42.3	62.2	26.8
1998:06	3,859.1	703.8	18.2	1,217.0	31.5	402.3	100.8	25.1	137.2	34.1	156.1	65.7	42.1	52.1	33.4
1998:09	4,127.3	777.6	18.8	1,329.0	32.2	387.2	100.1	25.9	134.9	34.8	96.2	57.1	59.4	25.2	26.2
1998:12	4,287.3	838.5	19.6	1,369.0	32.0	634.5	174.5	27.5	251.0	39.6	306.7	128.9	42.0	116.0	37.8
1999:03	4,460.1	957.7	21.5	1,415.9	31.7	646.7	180.4	27.9	256.7	39.7	362.0	139.4	38.5	144.4	39.9
1999:06	4,760.6	1,092.3	22.9	1,525.2	32.0	640.8	175.7	27.4	259.3	40.5	341.2	131.4	38.5	137.2	40.2
1999:09	5,222.4	1,232.4	23.6	1,708.7	32.7	504.8	110.2	21.8	221.0	43.8	205.6	82.1	39.9	93.3	45.4
1999:12	5,345.6	1,307.6	24.5	1,744.1	32.6	662.4	151.4	22.9	282.4	42.6	259.3	86.8	33.5	114.5	44.2
2000:03	5,499.3	1,386.3	25.2	1,801.1	32.8	655.3	145.3	22.2	303.8	46.4	279.0	92.2	33.0	138.8	49.7
2000:06	5,762.5	1,476.7	25.6	1,939.5	33.7	682.6	186.8	27.4	296.7	43.5	259.4	120.1	46.3	117.2	45.2
2000:09	5,848.0	1,583.0	27.1	1,954.0	33.4										
1998	4,215.7	838.5	19.6	1,369.9	32.0	1,718.8	424.0	24.7	574.4	33.4	681.2	280.0	41.1	211.1	31.0
1999	5,215.7	1,307.6	25.1	1,744.1	33.4	2,426.8	640.8	26.4	988.0	40.7	1,215.5	481.8	39.6	490.9	40.4
2000	5,848.0	1,583.0	27.1	1,954.0	33.4	2,000.3	483.5	24.2	882.9	44.1	797.7	299.1	37.5	370.5	46.4

Source: BIS (1999, 2000)

Table A7.6 International bonds and notes by nationality of issuer (billion US dollars)

	Amounts outstanding					Announced issues					Net issues				
	Total	USA	in %	Euroland	in %	Total	USA	in %	Euroland	in %	Total	USA	in %	Euroland	in %
1993:09	1906	163.2	8.6	521.8	27.4										
1993:12	1,916.1	160.5	8.4	531.1	27.7	132.5	11.1	8.4	41.2	31.1	61.6	-0.4	-0.6	28.2	45.8
1994:03	2,044.9	166.9	8.2	586.5	28.7	153.4	10.2	6.6	56.8	37.0	83.4	4.3	5.2	39.8	47.7
1994:06	2,133.7	171.7	8.0	622.8	29.2	111.8	11.9	10.6	37.8	33.8	38	2.5	6.6	17.5	46.1
1994:09	2237	181.6	8.1	669.3	29.9	123.7	13.1	10.6	43	34.8	68.6	8.3	12.1	31.8	46.4
1994:12	2,278.8	185.8	8.2	698.6	30.7	117	13	11.1	47.3	40.4	58.5	5.3	9.1	34.4	58.8
1995:03	2,459.8	208.2	8.5	778.4	31.6	120.4	22.5	18.7	45.4	37.7	49.1	16	32.6	25.3	51.5
1995:06	2,539.6	216.8	8.5	815	32.1	134.1	17.3	12.9	50.6	37.7	54.9	7	12.8	30.7	55.9
1995:09	2,533.6	231.6	9.1	821.3	32.4	148.4	25.5	17.2	40.6	27.4	71.3	18.6	26.1	27.3	38.3
1995:12	2,573.5	243	9.4	846	32.9	137.6	24.8	18.0	46.8	34.0	66.2	12.8	19.3	31	46.8
1996:03	2,639.7	268.8	10.2	873	33.1	222.1	38.5	17.3	75.1	33.8	104.9	27.8	26.5	43.6	41.6
1996:06	2,727.5	299	11.0	895.5	32.8	274.3	46.8	17.1	79.4	28.9	123.3	32.1	26.0	39.7	32.2
1996:09	2,832.3	329.8	11.6	930.6	32.9	267.7	44.1	16.5	63.8	23.8	111.7	31.2	27.9	37.7	33.8
1996:12	2,955.4	368.3	12.5	957.2	32.4	239.1	48	20.1	63.6	26.6	148.9	40.4	27.1	39.7	26.7
1997:03	2,983.4	394.3	13.2	957.5	32.1	263.8	53.2	20.1	82.1	31.1	142	32.5	22.9	50.9	35.8
1997:06	3,148.4	441.7	14.0	988	31.4	257.9	57.2	22.2	67	26.0	153.4	46.4	30.2	40	26.1
1997:09	3,265.6	491.4	15.0	1,010.8	31.0	286	72.9	25.5	66.6	23.3	162.8	52.4	32.2	36.4	22.4
1997:12	3,310.2	530.8	16.0	1026	31.0	213.4	55.9	26.2	54.9	25.7	89.8	42.3	47.1	29.9	33.3
1998:03	3,462.7	588.1	17.0	1,072.2	31.0	342.1	81.7	23.9	108.4	31.7	187.4	59.5	31.8	66.3	35.4
1998:06	3,675.1	682.8	18.6	1,140.6	31.0	324.3	106.8	32.9	88.6	27.3	232.1	96.3	41.5	66.5	28.7
1998:09	3,930.4	753.5	19.2	1,247.4	31.7	261.3	79.5	30.4	78.5	30.0	144.3	62.7	43.5	47.9	33.2
1998:12	4,101.2	815.2	19.9	1,290.1	31.5	258.7	82	31.7	77.1	29.8	107.2	57.9	54.0	27	25.2
1999:03	4,239.9	932.5	22.0	1,311.9	30.9	461.3	153.7	33.3	165.2	35.8	271.7	126.9	46.7	91.2	33.6
1999:06	4,549.5	1,067.2	23.5	1,424.9	31.3	491.1	159.7	32.5	182.4	37.1	370.5	139.5	37.7	147.6	39.8
1999:09	4,987.8	1,210.5	24.3	1594	32.0	463.8	158	34.1	171.5	37.0	318.6	134.7	42.3	123.4	38.7
1999:12	5,096.1	1,283.5	25.2	1,611.7	31.6	352.3	95	27.0	138.9	39.4	188.3	79.8	42.4	73.9	39.2
2000:03	5,249.7	1,363.1	26.0	1,671.3	31.8	469.5	131.4	28.0	182.3	38.8	258.1	87.7	34.0	116.3	45.1
2000:06	5,488.8	1,450.8	26.4	1,787.4	32.6	450.7	123.5	27.4	190.5	42.3	254.6	89.5	35.2	116.3	45.7
2000:09	5,562.5	1,551.8	27.9	1,797.1	32.3	472.9	159.7	33.8	184.4	39.0	245	114.6	46.8	110.5	45.1
1998	4,099.6	815.2	19.9	1,290.1	31.5	1,186.4	350	29.5	352.6	29.7	671	276.4	41.2	207.7	31.0
1999	4,966.2	1,283.5	25.8	1,611.7	32.5	1,768.5	566.4	32.0	658	37.2	1,149.1	480.9	41.9	436.1	38.0
2000	5,562.5	1,551.8	27.9	1,797.1	32.3	1,393.1	414.6	29.8	557.2	40.0	757.7	291.8	38.5	343.1	45.3

Source: BIS (1999, 2000)

Table A7.7 International money market instruments by nationality of issuer (billion US dollars)

	Amounts outstanding					Gross issuance					Net issues				
	Total	USA	in %	Euroland	in %	Total	USA	in %	Euroland	in %	Total	USA	in %	Euroland	in %
1993:09	108.9	12.4	11.4	27.9	25.6										
1993:12	108.5	15.0	13.8	25.7	23.7	80.80	12.70	15.72	17.80	22.0	-0.2	2.6	-1,300.0	-1.9	950.0
1994:03	111.2	17.3	15.6	24.7	22.2	91.40	15.60	17.07	18.70	20.5	2.5	2.2	88.0	-1.2	-48.0
1994:06	115.2	22.0	19.1	25.2	21.9	89.10	19.50	21.89	19.10	21.4	3.8	4.7	123.7	0.4	10.5
1994:09	120.1	20.7	17.2	28.7	23.9	93.70	16.20	17.29	23.10	24.7	4.6	-1.4	-30.4	3.7	80.4
1994:12	113.5	17.7	15.6	29.0	25.6	88.10	13.30	15.10	22.80	25.9	-6.4	-3.0	46.9	0.0	0.0
1995:03	114.4	15.9	13.9	35.4	30.9	92.40	13.40	14.50	29.20	31.6	0.4	-1.9	-475.0	6.4	1,600.0
1995:06	121.5	18.0	14.8	38.0	31.3	97.70	14.60	14.94	30.50	31.2	7.0	2.1	30.0	2.9	41.4
1995:09	131.3	17.2	13.1	43.7	33.3	101.80	13.80	13.56	32.80	32.2	9.9	-0.7	-7.1	5.9	59.6
1995:12	132.5	18.7	14.1	46.6	35.2	100.30	14.60	14.56	35.10	35.0	1.3	1.5	115.4	2.9	223.1
1996:03	140.9	17.2	12.2	49.6	35.2	115.40	14.50	12.56	40.00	34.7	8.6	-1.5	-17.4	3.1	36.0
1996:06	151.9	17.9	11.8	57.3	37.7	122.70	15.80	12.88	44.20	36.0	11.3	0.7	6.2	8.0	70.8
1996:09	147.8	15.7	10.6	54.8	37.1	116.80	13.90	11.90	41.10	35.2	-4.2	-2.2	52.4	-2.4	57.1
1996:12	162.3	17.3	10.7	62.4	38.4	123.80	14.20	11.47	46.60	37.6	14.8	1.7	11.5	7.6	51.4
1997:03	165.5	17.0	10.3	66.2	40.0	118.90	14.20	11.94	43.40	36.5	4.6	-0.2	-4.3	4.8	104.3
1997:06	169.8	16.6	9.8	66.6	39.2	120.10	14.60	12.16	43.20	36.0	4.8	-0.5	-10.4	0.6	12.5
1997:09	178.7	19.0	10.6	72.6	40.6	128.30	16.60	12.94	52.00	40.5	9.3	2.5	26.9	6.3	67.7
1997:12	175.1	19.7	11.3	75.5	43.1	123.30	16.70	13.54	51.00	41.4	-3.2	0.7	-21.9	3.3	-103.1
1998:03	184.2	19.1	10.4	80.8	43.9	136.90	16.40	11.93	56.90	41.6	9.6	-0.5	-5.2	5.3	55.2
1998:06	184.0	21.0	11.4	76.4	41.5	126.00	18.20	14.44	48.40	38.4	-0.2	1.9	-950.0	-4.3	2,150.0
1998:09	196.9	24.1	12.2	81.6	41.4	141.00	21.30	15.11	58.70	41.6	11.8	3.0	25.4	4.2	35.6
1998:12	186.1	23.3	12.5	79.8	42.9	128.50	18.10	14.09	57.80	45.0	-11.0	-0.8	7.3	-1.8	16.4
1999:03	220.2	25.2	11.4	104.0	47.2	173.20	20.80	12.01	85.80	49.5	35.0	2.0	5.7	24.8	70.9
1999:06	211.1	25.1	11.9	100.3	47.5	155.60	20.70	13.30	74.30	47.8	-8.5	-0.1	1.2	-3.2	37.6
1999:09	234.6	21.9	9.3	114.7	48.9	177.00	17.70	10.00	87.80	49.6	22.6	-3.3	-14.6	13.8	61.1
1999:12	249.5	24.1	9.7	132.4	53.1	152.50	15.20	9.57	82.10	53.8	17.3	2.3	13.3	19.4	112.1
2000:03	249.6	23.2	9.3	129.8	52.0	192.9	20	10.37	100.1	51.9	1.2	-0.9	-75.0	-1.8	-150.0
2000:06	273.7	25.9	9.5	152.1	55.6	204.6	21.8	10.65	113.3	55.4	24.4	2.7	11.1	22.5	92.2
2000:09	285.5	31.2	10.9	156.9	55.0	209.7	27.1	12.92	112.3	53.6	14.4	5.5	38.2	6.7	46.5
1998	186.1	23.3	12.5	79.8	42.9	532.4	74.0	13.90	221.8	41.7	10.2	3.6	35.3	3.4	33.3
1999	249.5	24.1	9.7	132.4	53.1	658.3	74.4	11.30	330.0	50.1	66.4	0.9	1.4	54.8	82.5
2000	285.5	31.2	10.9	156.9	55.0	607.2	68.9	11.35	325.7	53.6	40.0	7.3	18.3	27.4	68.5

Source: BIS (1999, 2000)

Figure A7.1 Domestic debt securities by country of issuer: amounts outstanding (billion US dollars)

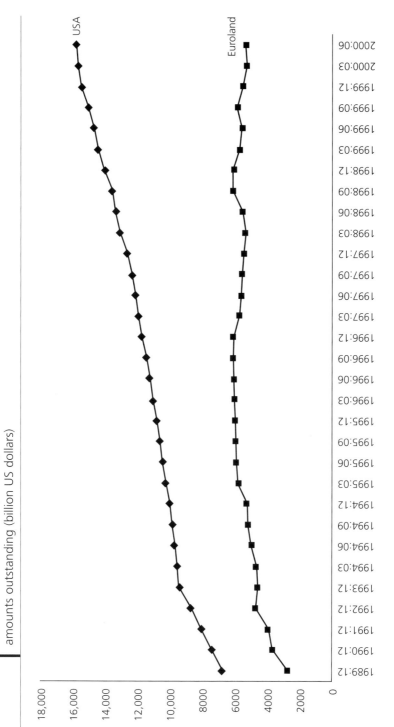

Source: BIS (1999, 2000)

Figure A7.2 | International debt securities by currency: amounts outstanding

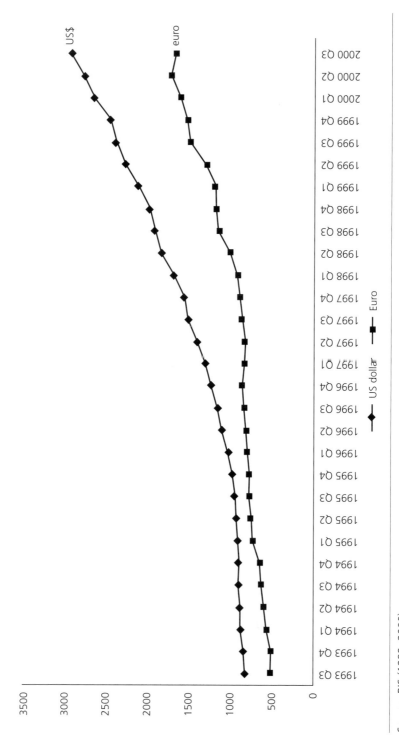

Source: BIS (1999, 2000)

Figure A7.3 International debt securities by currency: announced issues in billion US dollars

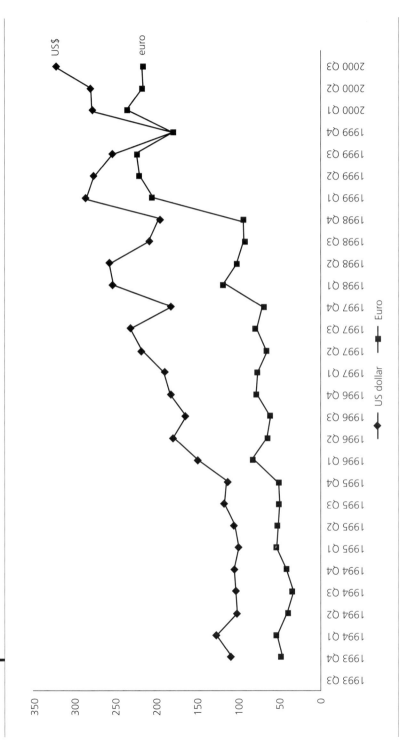

Source: BIS (1999, 2000)

Figure A7.4 International debt securities by currency: net issues in billion US dollars

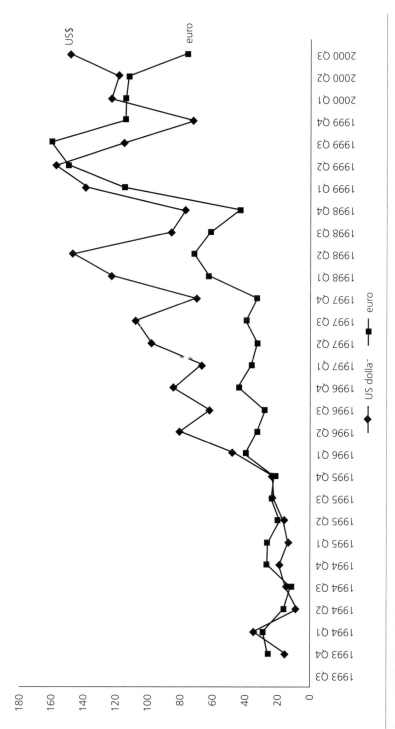

Source: BIS (1999, 2000)

Figure A7.5 International debt securities by nationality of issuer: amounts outstanding (in billion US dollars)

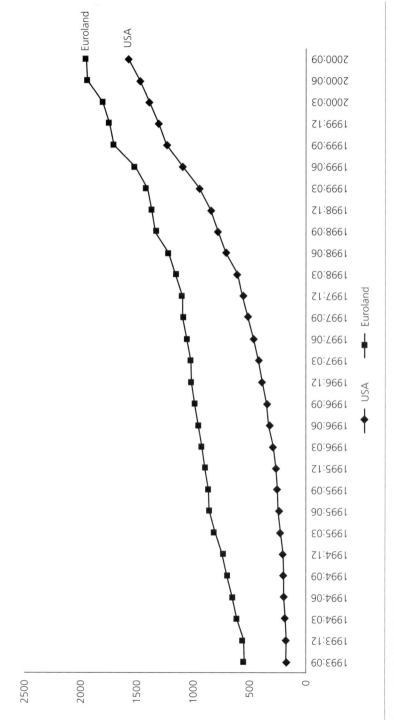

Source: BIS (1999, 2000)

Figure A7.6 | International debt securities by nationality of issuer: announced issues (in billion US dollars)

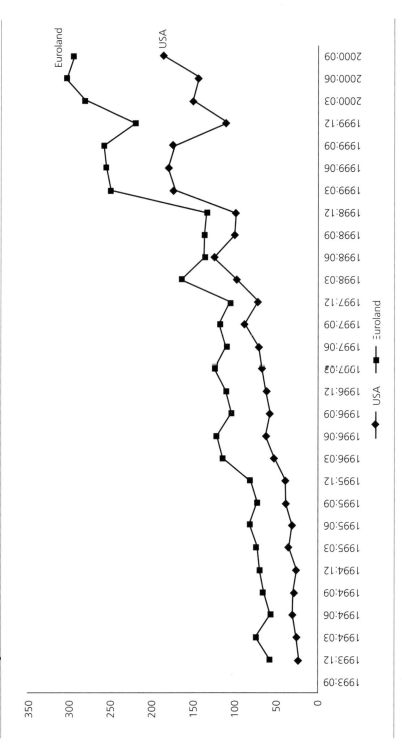

Source: BIS (1999, 2000)

Figure A7.7 International debt securities by nationality of issuer: net issues (in billion US dollars)

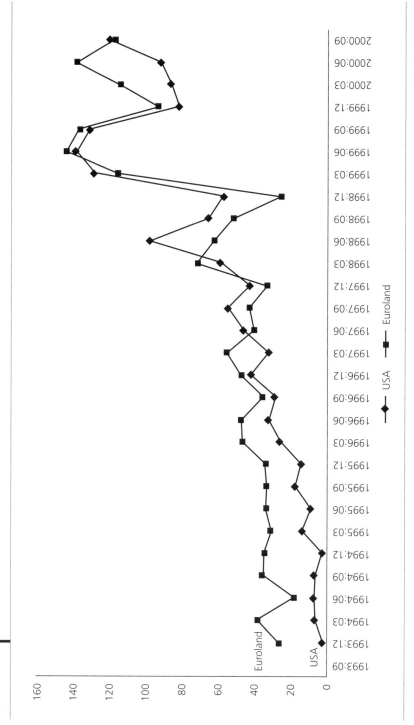

Source: BIS (1999, 2000)

Figure A7.8 | Exchange rate: euro versus US dollar

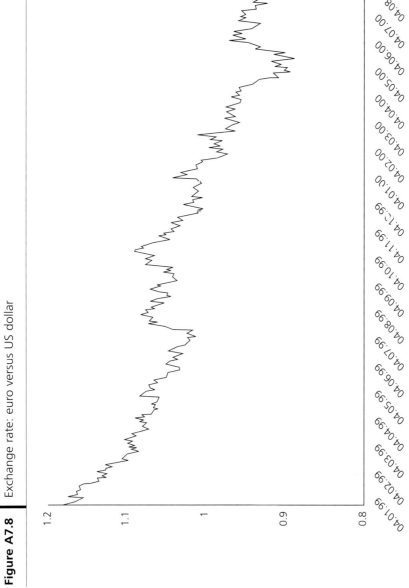

Source: ECB

Figure A7.9 Exchange rate: US dollar versus Deutschmark

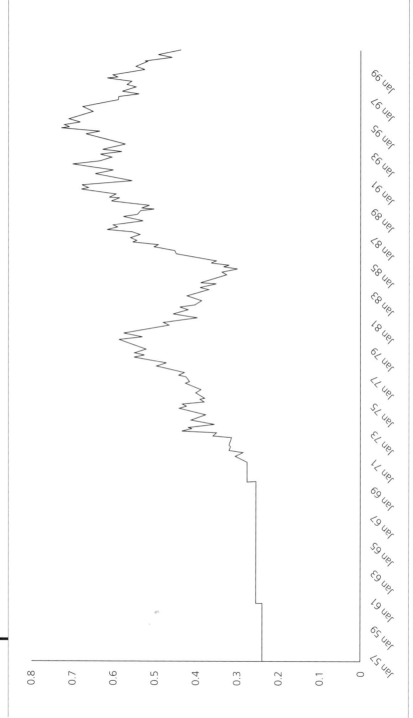

Source: ECB

III

Euro and
UK Concerns

8

Britain and the euro: a study in reluctance

Andrew Hughes Hallett

Introduction

During the 1990s the debate on economic integration in Europe – as opposed to that on the issue of participating in European integration more generally – had a relatively low profile in the UK. There were many debates that attempted to exploit the European issue, but they were largely conducted to advance the position of the domestic political parties – and tended to put little emphasis on the economic benefits of monetary union itself. Thus, the governing Labour Party has argued that, by being more pro-European, it could take a lead within the councils of the European Union. It has used this argument as a

> **During the 1990s the debate on economic integration in Europe had a relatively low profile in the UK**

means of widening the divisions within the Conservative Party; and as an appeal to the self-interest of big business in order to detach them from their traditional support of the Conservatives. Both moves would open up the centre ground as natural territory for Labour and preserve it in power for a long time. But it has nothing to do with a desire to be 'in' Europe.

The Conservatives meanwhile have used the Europe issue to paint Labour as being unable or unwilling to defend British interests and, by extension, as being willing to cede sovereignty and even aspects of democracy itself in their thirst for power and to be the 'controlling influence' within Europe. Given persistent and rising opinion poll majorities against joining the euro or further integration in Europe,[1] this strategy has been seen as the best way for the party to regain power against a government that otherwise adopts traditional conservative policies.

Neither party's strategy has much to do with the euro therefore. And if there is a silent majority with a genuine interest in the matter, it has not made its presence known. The perception that the EMU would bring only small benefits at best, and fragile benefits at that, has not persuaded this majority that the euro is worth campaigning for – although that was an argument used by the Danish Council of Economic Advisors in its report before the Danish referendum on the euro in 2000.[2]

As these developments reflect rather different attitudes to those held elsewhere in the eurozone countries, it is important to consider why these attitudes have developed in the UK, and how the performance of the euro since January 1999 has affected opinion and economic performance in the UK. And what are the lessons for the future? That is the agenda for this chapter. However, in trying to answer those questions, I shall stick to the economics of the issue – not the political arguments.

A political economy view of the UK position

Most people take the impetus behind EMU to be political rather than economic, their evaluation being that the net economic benefits over costs would be small and rather uncertain – a view that is consistent with the official estimates put forward from Brussels.[3] This is in contrast to the single market programme, where more significant gains – in the region of 5–7 per cent of GNP – are expected to arise from freer market access, increased competitiveness and scale economies.[4]

Consequently, the debate has been influenced more by risk aversion in the light of the euro's volatility, than by the positive aspects of the EMU programme. The question actually raised has been: How do you book the gains of the single market programme without risking the question marks which hang over EMU? And how do you join the euro without restricting the UK's 'locational competitiveness' via the social chapter or additional regulatory arrangements; and also without being excluded from EU decision making by an inner 'cabal' of core countries? We can try to answer those questions from several different points of view.

The Conservatives

As a party, the Conservatives had, until 1997, a better record in running the economy than their opponents. They had tighter links to business and finance and they have been through a period of ideological attachment to free market competition and deregulation. Hence, for them the issue is really a question of maintaining free market access and free market competition, without being burdened with the additional restrictions and regulations of EMU or the European industrial and social policies; but also without losing influence over EU decision making by sitting on the sidelines. They had less need of EMU, since, within the domestic market, their record of economic management did not lack credibility. Similarly, their attachment to free competition and flexible markets makes them more sensitive to the erosion of sovereignty (in terms of making one's own decisions versus 'interference' from Brussels).

The upshot is to make Conservatives into either sceptics or reluctant supporters of EMU as a necessary condition for preserving free market access. In the last analysis, market access and free trade are their first priority. If they lose influence over decision making, they will rest on the sidelines with their *à la carte* approach to integration. Certainly business and finance have already drawn their own conclusions, having found membership of the single market much more favourable than they had ever expected *after* leaving the ERM in 1992.

Labour

The Labour Party favours EMU because it has less attachment to sovereignty, but is acutely aware that it cannot manage the economy in isolation and without the discipline of European competition. It has therefore been more concerned about credibility. The interdependence of monetary and fiscal policy is well understood. Long-term credibility of their economic programme has been dependent on binding their policies into the framework of monetary and fiscal discipline offered by Europe. This was intended perhaps to remove any doubts over design faults, market-friendliness, or backsliding on their part, in fiscal and monetary discipline. However, this policy may have been too successful. Growth has been higher, inflation lower, fiscal discipline stronger, and monetary policy just as disciplined as in Europe – if not more so – but a good deal more transparent and hence more acceptable to the public. Meanwhile unemployment has fallen further; and neither the trade balance, nor foreign investment, nor the financial markets in London have been damaged by the introduction of the euro. In fact, if anything, all these indicators have shown improvements since 1999, despite a massive fall in the value of the euro and considerable financial volatility. Financial markets in London and Edinburgh continue to expand, foreign investment (especially from Europe) continues to grow at an accelerating pace and Britain now has a trade surplus with Euroland.

Thus the Labour Party has been deprived of one of the main reasons for being pro-euro. Economic performance has been weaker and more uncertain in Europe; and there appear to have been no losses from having stayed outside. Indeed, if anything, staying outside has proved beneficial. Politicians concerned with strategy have therefore been reduced to explaining to an increasingly sceptical public that Britain needs to be at the heart of Europe so that Britain can control Europe's development in some way. Given recent developments – both in terms of economic performance and financial stability, and in terms of the emerging two-speed system in Europe (of which the UK is not obviously a leading member) – that kind of rhetoric sounds increasingly self-seeking. The public has drawn its own conclusion – or so a political economy analysis would lead you to suppose.

The political debate

Lest this view should appear excessively cynical, it is important to stress that the problem actually lies in creating sufficient incentive to join the euro. The issue should be seen in terms of creating sufficient incentives for *all* participants, rather than just benefits for Europe on average. Thus British commentators would not say that the euro was not of any value. But they would say that it is of relatively little value when the British economy behaves rather differently from the European average. We go into some of the reasons for that later, but two political economy points will identify the source of the points being made. First, British attitudes are always influenced by the desire to adopt endogenous 'market solutions', rather than to impose some externally designed blueprint from outside. Long-run sustainability demands that everyone should have (and know that they have) a clear incentive for working within the system, and that the system should be responsive to changing market pressures. That implies a certain degree of market flexibility and structural reform, of course. Second, British debates follow the rules of parliamentary democracy – that is, the direct representation of popular views 'from bottom up'. It is not a matter of educating the people 'from the political elites down', as may happen elsewhere. Consensus is therefore reached by debating different views and then voting, rather than by imposing a series of rules and constraints on the range of decisions which are permissible.

A financial markets view

The standard criticism of monetary policy in Europe, and hence the euro, is that we do not know how, at the margin, the ECB will trade off inflation increases versus output stabilization or employment creation and that, although we know the ECB runs monetary policy based on 'two pillars', we do not know what exactly is in the second pillar – or how important that is compared to the first pillar.[5] That is a problem because the markets cannot then tell whether the ECB should be expected to make a policy change or not.

> ## We know the ECB runs monetary policy based on 'two pillars'

Then there is a question about how the ECB could – or should – design monetary policy to accommodate different performances in different parts of the union. That is to say, how will they end up designing one set of policies to deal with boom conditions in Ireland, Spain and the Netherlands, but also the depressed conditions in Germany or Italy?

There are also some important long-term concerns here. Perhaps the most interesting has to do with the potential for productivity growth and why that has not been exploited. Over the last two years the euro had fallen against the pound and dollar, and by late 2000 that fall was larger than the pound's collapse against the Deutschmark in September 1992. However, while everyone had expected an increase in inflation in the UK in 1992/93, there was none. Instead there was an immediate increase in growth and also an improvement in investment and the current account. But when the euro started falling in 1999, there was (after a time) a perceptible and significant increase in the inflation rate – but only minor increases in growth (which slowed again two years later) and a deterioration in investment and the overall current account. Why the difference?

The implication of these contrasting outcomes is that there was a difference in the underlying rates of productivity growth in the UK (after 1992) and in the euro area (after 1998). If there had not been such a difference, prices would have had to react in the same way on both occasions. The strong growth in the USA, without inflation after 1994, is another example. These outcomes then suggest that the fundamentals have not been so strong in Europe and that the markets do not anticipate that they will improve all that much in the near future. That does not say that the strong growth in productivity in the USA will necessarily continue or that the dollar will remain strong for ever. It almost certainly will not. But it does help explain why the euro has been so weak.

The lesson from these observations is that getting the fundamentals right may be at least as important as getting the regime right. After all, the same opportunities to invest in the new technologies, or in new ways of doing business, are open to everyone – European and non-European. So you might ask why Europe did not make the same productivity-improving investments that were made in the USA? One answer may be that there has been relatively little attempt to encourage price flexibility, labour market reform or institutional restructuring in many of the European economies. Without that flexibility the rate of return on such investments would necessarily have been lower in Europe (had they been made), compared to investments in the USA or Asia or possibly in the UK. Figure 8.1 shows the lower rates of return in Germany or Spain compared to those in the USA or UK. So the investments were not made – or, rather, they were made elsewhere, pushing the euro down as capital flowed out of Europe.

Figure 8.1 | Net rates of return (non-financial companies)

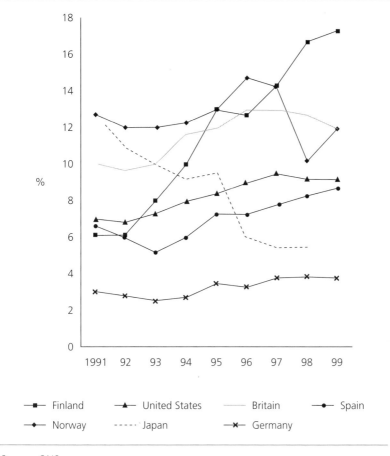

Source: ONS

Britain's economy since the euro

A statistical view

Britain's reluctance to join the euro can also be traced to her experience that staying out did not damage the British economy. The fact that much of the pro-euro debate had argued that Britain couldn't afford to stay out, when it now appears that the opposite may have been true, has certainly done a lot to undermine the credibility of the euro with the British public.

In fact, the British economy appears to have done better as an outsider than the economies of most of the insiders. In December 2000, two years after the introduction of the euro, Britain's growth was 3.1 per cent, compared to 2.7–2.9 per cent in the larger euro economies like Germany and France. Her annual inflation rate was 1.5 per cent or lower, compared with 2¾ per cent for the eurozone (6.8 per cent in Ireland and around 4–5 per cent for Spain, Portugal and the Netherlands). Unemployment had fallen to 5.5 per cent on the standardized measures, compared to 9–10 per cent in the eurozone . Similarly the budget was showing a surplus of 2 per cent of GDP whereas France and Germany remained in deficit. Even trade with the eurozone had moved to a small surplus, despite the strength of the pound and weakness of the euro. This has made it hard to argue that the UK actually needs the euro as such.

On the financial side, too, the passage has been easy. Foreign investment is up 50 per cent (of which one-third has been from eurozone countries); and while interest rates are lower in Europe, they are only lower by a limited amount and then only at the short end of the market. At the long end, the pound's rates are typically about 100 basis points lower. Then there is the fact that the pound has actually been more stable (in trade-weighted terms) than either of its main competitors. The euro had fallen from $1.18 to $0.88 by the end of March 2001 and from £0.74 to £0.61. That is a fall of 25 per cent against the dollar, and 18 per cent against the pound. The pound's fall against the dollar was only 8 per cent in the same period. Using ECB figures for the trade weights, this implies a standard deviation of 6–7 per cent for the fluctuations of the euro against its trading partners, but only 2 per cent or 3 per cent for the pound. That implies that there is a 30 per cent chance, on any day, that the euro will change its value by as much as 6 per cent – whereas the pound would only change 2 per cent with the same 30 per cent probability. It therefore has only one-third of the volatility of the euro, although a historical analysis might show that the volatility of both currencies was higher than normal. Hence there is some advantage in having a separate currency: one can steer a path between the fluctuations of the main competitor currencies, in order to minimize the (trade-weighted) volatility in one's own currency.

How well does the UK fit into the euro? An optimal currency area view

This has to be the fundamental consideration in assessing whether the UK might benefit from joining the euro. We know from first principles (see chapters 2 and 4) that a currency union will work well if:

● The countries forming that union are open to trade among themselves. This condition is clearly satisfied in Europe, given the single market, and it is reasonably well satisfied by the UK. British trade is roughly 50 per cent with the EU and 50 per cent outside, with trade being important at 28 per cent of GNP.

- The second condition is that capital should be very mobile between the partners. That is also clearly satisfied in Europe and by the UK.

- Third, there should be a high degree of labour mobility between countries. That is not satisfied in Europe. Eichengreen (1992) estimates that intercountry and interregional immigration in the EU is at least three times lower than in comparable monetary unions such as the USA. More recent estimates (MacLennan et al. 2000; Obstfeld and Peri 1998) confirm that figure for the four largest eurozone economies, although the UK itself has a somewhat more mobile labour force than elsewhere.[6] Decressin and Fatas (1995) argue that this lack of interregional migration has meant that shocks in national output have to be absorbed by changes in labour participation rates instead. As a result, unemployment plays little role in regulating the labour markets in Europe. Consequently, unemployment tends to persist in euroland and wages fail to adjust to clear the markets or to restore output and growth. That makes the euro economies harder to manage. Hence the pressure for market reform.

- However, it is also possible to substitute wage flexibility for labour mobility if the latter is not very high. But once again, the eurozone does not have flexible wages (or, more importantly, flexible non-wage labour costs) because of the high degree of labour market regulation – and, even if the UK is one of the better economies on this score, none of the European economies has the wage rate variations of up to 35 per cent (for the same job in different places) which the US economy seems to find necessary. And things are not likely to become much more flexible. Contrary to the idea of a social market economy, it would mean a much higher degree of uncertainty about incomes and less social welfare provision because payroll taxes would have to be cut in order to provide an equivalent degree of flexibility in unit labour. That is unlikely to prove acceptable in a eurozone which wishes to provide a social market economy. Indeed, globalization and closer market integration typically generate the opposite reaction, as governments and labour organizations attempt to provide employment protection in a world which is becoming increasingly uncertain. That is a natural reaction because governments are no longer able to control so many of the policy levers which affect output, employment and growth at home (Agell 1999). On the other hand, in the absence of sufficient market flexibility, we could expect greater boom and bust cycles and unemployment anyway. That, too, has its social costs. If you contrast current developments in Ireland with those in southern Italy, you can see the force of this dilemma.

● The fourth condition is that all participating countries should be subject to similar shocks, and have similar economic structures so that common shocks have common effects. We need that so that a common set of policies will be appropriate for all countries; not just appropriate for an average which may not be close to any of the member countries individually. And we also need all countries to respond in roughly the same way to those shocks or to any change in policy that is common to all of them.

Costs and benefits for the UK: a traditional view

Trade versus capital links

At this point I need to emphasize that the benefits of monetary union will depend on a lot more than just trade links. Even if there were suffi-cient capital mobility, labour flexibility and structural similarities, strong trade links are only a necessary condition for making a monetary union work. They are certainly not sufficient. It also matters who your investment partners are. They may be a different set of countries and require different patterns of integration.

So now we have a problem: we have to be sure to link not only with our trading partners, but also with our investment partners. This is important for the UK. She may trade predominantly with her European partners; but investment flows are clearly with the USA and Far East, and are predominantly dollar based. The bottom line here is that if the two sets of partners move apart, as the USA and Europe have done, then any currency link with either partner will imply extra costs. Ultimately, you have to decide which set of costs would be the smaller – and whether staying outside and steering a course between the two currencies would not actually bring the lowest costs and the greatest stability.

In fact, the case of the UK is quite interesting. She trades about 28 per cent of GDP, and roughly half of that goes to the EU countries and half does not (see Table 8.1). Sometimes we hear figures that are much larger than that, for example if we consider the proportion of trade in manufactures alone. But those are special cases. Across the economy as a whole, it is about half and half. That suggests there might be enough trade linkage to make it worthwhile to adopt the euro. But if we adjust those figures for investment income, the picture changes.

Table 8.1 | Trade dependence

- Trade as % GNP = 28% (exports of goods and services)

  of which 48%–51% is with the eurozone
- Investment income is 33% from the eurozone
- Hence the proportion of foreign currency earned from the EU area is 40.7%

Source: ONS, *Economic Trends*, December 1998

The proportion of foreign income derived from the EU area then falls to less than 41 per cent when investment incomes are included.

And if we go on to consider the position of foreign investments in the UK, we find an even stronger result. A good three-quarters of such investment flows come from *outside* the EU area, and only one-quarter from our European partners (see Table 8.2). So Britain clearly falls into that category of 'in-between countries' which are linked to one set of partners for trade, but to another set for investment.

> **Britain clearly falls into that category of 'in-between countries' which are linked to one set of partners for trade, but to another set for investment**

Table 8.2 | Foreign investment dependence

- Total investment as % GDP   1998 = 18.9

    1999 = 19.4

    2000 = 19.2
- Foreign direct investment was £51.3bn ≅ 6.5% GDP in 1999 or 34% of total investment
- Foreign investment from non-EU sources   =   78% by value

  =   75% by jobs created

  (of which ± 50% is from the USA and 24–29% from other non-EU countries)
- Foreign investment from EU countries   =   22% by value

  =   24% by jobs

Source: ONS, *Economic Trends*, 2000

Cyclical convergence

One way to assess whether you are sufficiently well linked overall (i.e. through both trade and investment) is to examine the correlations between aggregate demand factors and aggregate supply factors and between the monetary conditions in the different economies. However, simply extracting correlations from the raw business cycles is not very satisfactory since that conflates the supply and demand factors, and ignores the financial stability element.

In Table 8.3, I report some recent evidence on the correlation of the UK and European business cycles. They are not large – indeed in some cases they are even negative. However, that just involves composite shocks. In Table 8.4, I have divided up those correlations between the demand shocks, supply shocks and monetary shocks of the 1980s and 1990s. These correlations are not very high either, not even among the core countries such as France, Germany, Benelux, Austria, etc. On the other hand, they are not much lower among the 'periphery' countries (Spain, Italy, Portugal, Greece, etc.). In fact there is little clear pattern and they are all relatively small. However, what is interesting is that both Tables 8.3 and 8.4 show that the monetary shocks actually come from monetary policy movements which are negatively correlated to those in the UK. So in order to get even as far as this degree of symmetry, you would have to do opposite things with monetary policy in Europe and in the UK. What you *don't* need is similar policies. But that is what EMU would force.

Table 8.3 | Correlation of economic cycles: 1980–89/1990–95

	Demand	Supply	Money
UK with EU – core	.32/–.12	.13/–.04	–.27/.05
with EU – periphery	.29/.60	.11/.29	–.55/.09

Source: Demertzis *et al.* (1998)

Table 8.4 | Demand and supply shocks correlated with average or aggregate shocks, by country (1975 first quarter to 1995 second quarter)

Country:	Demand with			Supply with			Monetary with		
	Core	G	Per	Core	G	Per	Core	G	Per
AU	0.26*	0.56**	0.09	0	0.17	0.04	0.91+	0.28*	0.12
F	0.55**	0.23*	0.19*	−0.03	0.40**	0.03	−0.10	0.02	0.18*
G	0.68+	1	−0.06	0.17	1	−0.08	0.13	1	0.07
B	0.79+	−0.03	0.16	0.07	0.39**	0.02	0.50**	0.05	0.12
DK	0.73+	−0.14	0.34*	0.03	0.28*	0.04	0.27*	0.28*	0.09
LU	0.88+	−0.02	−0.01	0.23*	0.31*	0.02	0.13	0.10	0.04
NL	0.76+	−0.09	0.21*	0.11	0.29*	−0.10	0.10	0.01	−0.11

Periphery:	Demand with			Supply with			Monetary with		
	Per	G	Core	Per	G	Core	Per	G	Core
UK	0.60**	0.15	0.11	0.02	0.30*	0.12	−0.24	−0.01	−0.07
GR	0.90+	0.21*	0.30*	0.46**	0.08	0.20	−0.37	0.09	−0.30
IR	0.62**	0.16	0.08	−0.10	0.12	−0.10	0.32*	0.05	0.04
PO	0.76+	0.26*	0.09	0.16	0.14	0	−0.81	0	0.12
SP	0.68+	0.26*	0.03	−0.14	0.14	−0.19	0.05	0.08	0.11
FI	0.77+	−0.16	−0.02	−0.08	0.02	0.14	0.23*	−0.03	0.07
SW	0.81+	0.01	−0.12	−0.07	0.26*	−0.03	0.22*	0.29*	−0.07
IT	0.46**	0.24*	−0.06	−0.10	0.20*	−0.08	0.05	0.04	0.21*

* significantly larger than zero at the 5% level (critical value 0.18)
** not significantly different from 0.5 at the 5% level (critical value 0.37)
\+ significantly greater than 0.5 at the 5% level (critical value 0.63)

Note: Per = periphery, G = Germany

Source: Author's calculations

Size of the gains

Even if the UK does not satisfy the optimal currency area conditions, it does not follow that EMU is necessarily undesirable. The question we should ask is, are we so far away that joining the union would not be worthwhile? Could it not be combined with some domestic policies to make it work? To answer that we must look at the costs and benefits. If the benefits are very large, then the costs will not matter very much. But if the benefits are small, then monetary union is perhaps something that we ought not to risk since even small costs could then dominate the benefits.

The estimates of the benefits which appear in Table 8.5 are taken from the European Commission's own publication on the matter: 'One market, one money' (EC 1990). These benefits are significant, but quite small. And they are for the typical EU country which trades more with its European partners than the UK does. So the UK's benefits might be a little smaller than these figures.

The first benefit is a saving in transaction costs, i.e. the commissions which importers and exporters have to pay to change currencies. These savings are said to be worth 0.4 per cent extra in GNP per year. Then we have the benefits of greater price transparency – a single currency allows you to know the price of anything, free from any uncertainties about what movements in the exchange rate might do to those prices. That is said to be worth another 0.3 per cent of GNP. Then we have to worry about the fact that you get these gains every year. So we can take the net present value of these figures (at 5 per cent nominal growth, multiply by a factor of 20), then compute how much of that extra long-run income would get invested (one-fifth, if the investment ratio of national income is 20 per cent) and then how much extra output that extra investment would produce (one-quarter, using a capital–output ratio of 4). That yields a long-run increase of 0.3 + 0.4 = 0.7 per cent of GNP from those savings.

Putting those figures together, we are likely to get an increase in national income of somewhere between 1 per cent and 1.5 per cent. That is not very large. In fact shared across the population it is actually quite small given all the costs and risks entailed in getting it. To put this figure in perspective, it is about the same as one standard error of the typical error we make when forecasting national income one year ahead. Consequently, if our forecasting errors are roughly normally distributed each side of the average outturn (which they are) then the chances of getting a higher income as a result of joining EMU would be improved by about 20 per cent compared to the chances of getting a lower income out of joining the euro (Figure 8.2). In other words, we

Table 8.5 | Estimated benefits of EMU in Europe (% GNP)

Lower transaction costs in trade	0.4%
Eliminating information costs/price discrimination	0.3%
'Dynamic' effects of these on investment	0.7%
Reduced levels of foreign exchange reserves	0.05%
Seignorage if foreigners use the euro	—
Total	**Total** 1.4% GNP

Source: EC (1990)

could expect to get a higher income out of joining the euro in one year in five on average – or just once a parliament – compared to not joining. So clearly there are benefits, but they are small.

Figure 8.2 | Size of gains from EMU

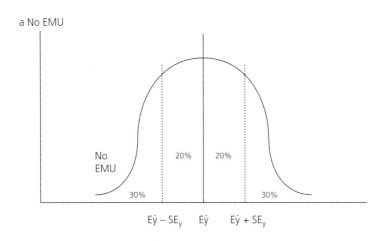

a No EMU

No
EMU

20%   20%

30%   30%

$E\dot{y} - SE_y$ $E\dot{y}$ $E\dot{y} + SE_y$

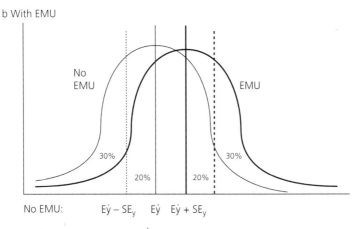

b With EMU

No
EMU

EMU

30%   30%

20%   20%

No EMU: $E\dot{y} - SE_y$ $E\dot{y}$ $E\dot{y} + SE_y$

With EMU: $E\dot{y} - SE_y$ $E\dot{y}$ $E\dot{y} + SE_y$

1 Hence P($\dot{y}$>E$\dot{y}$|No EMU)= 50%

2 But P($\dot{y}$=E$\dot{y}$|EMU)=P($\dot{y}$>E$\dot{y}$–SEy|No EMU)=70%

where E denotes an expected value, SE its standard error, and $\dot{y}$ the rate of growth of national income.

Costs

There are various costs and various risks involved in joining a currency union. Most of them have to do with a reduced ability to steer the economy and hence absorb the shocks which could damage output and cost jobs. These costs could be substantial, especially if the economy is susceptible to asymmetric shocks or to the asymmetric impacts of common shocks. I come to those next. However there are also set-up costs or 'changeover' costs. For the UK, they are estimated at £36 billion[7] or a little less than the entire annual expenditure on the National Health Service. That is not insignificant as an opportunity cost of money which might have been used in a different way. It is also nearly half of the value of all the benefits of EMU foreseen in Table 8.5.

> There are various costs and various risks involved in joining a currency union.

The single currency and the single market: the asymmetric relationship between the UK and the eurozone

A single market view

Now I want to turn to an interesting contrast: namely the fact that the single market and the single currency require rather different economic characteristics in order to be successful.

Evidently, the single currency needs a great deal of symmetry between the participating economies to be successful. But the single market needs strong asymmetries in the markets because, in order to get the full benefit, we must be able to exploit economies of scale and also the differences in comparative advantage in different countries. That is the point of having the single market and the extra trade it generates. So to some degree these two things – the single currency and the single market – are going to have, if not a conflict, a tension between them. In that case we need to worry about whether we will get more convergence between the economies if we adopt the euro (in which case we will get less out of the single market); or whether we will get more differences, in which case the single market will appear more important and the single currency could prove a problem. It is important to resolve this issue

because the Commission has estimated that the gains we might expect
from the single market are five times larger than those to be expected
from the single currency (4–7 per cent of GNP versus 1–1.5 per cent of
GNP respectively: Emerson *et al.* 1992).

It may be that this is the observation which lies behind Britain's reluctance to join the euro. It may be that membership of the single market
is more valuable than membership of the single currency. Indeed, the
single currency could generate costs which might eliminate the benefits
of the single market, given the differences in the UK's structure and
financial links. In that case, it would be natural to argue for membership
of the single market, but *not* of the single currency. One might then
counter with the idea that a single market needs a single currency. But
with the UK's experience since 1999, and with an opt-out incorporated
into the Maastricht Treaty, it is difficult to maintain that this is actually
true – either legally or logically. Given that, Britain's reluctance and the
tone of her political debate are easily explained.

Specialization versus diversification

The obvious question is, would the single currency not encourage
greater similarities between countries? Table 8.6 presents some simple
statistics for Europe, compared to the USA as a more mature monetary
union, to illustrate the point. There are four different regions and three
different kinds of industry in each case. One can see that the degree
of concentration in the mature monetary union is a lot more than the
degree of concentration in the monetary union now being formed. So
you might think that the natural development for Europe is that more
asymmetric structures will emerge from the single market.

Table 8.6 Distribution of industrial activity(%): USA and EU, 1989, 1990

	US(%) Cars	Steel	Textiles		EU(%) Cars	Steel	Textiles
Mid West	66.3	51.8	3.2	Germany	38.5	20.2	13.2
South	25.4	24.5	79.6	France	31.1	18.9	15.8
West	5.1	10.4	3.9	Italy	17.6	18.7	17.4
North East	3.3	13.4	14.2	UK	12.9	15.8	18.6

Sources: De Grauwe (1997); Krugman and Venables (1996)

History certainly supports that conclusion. De Grauwe and Vanhevebeke (1993) and Carlino and De Fina (1999) show that it happened in older monetary unions like Germany, Italy and the USA; Krugman (1993), Krugman and Venables (1996) and Puga (1999) have advanced theoretical models which show why this happens.

The next question has to be, where does the UK stand on this score? Tables 8.7–8.9 and Figure 8.3 now apply. Table 8.7 shows household liabilities as a percentage of GNP, across different European countries. The differences in the figures are largely due to mortgages; and the fact that the UK has higher stock of home ownership than others means that this disparity is not going to disappear overnight. You can see the range in the numbers if you compare Italy with the UK. It is huge. These figures imply that the demand-side responses to a change in interest rates would be very different in the UK, in terms of consumption expenditures, asset effects and hence in national income and employment.[8] Table 8.8 shows the degree to which corporate bonds are used to finance business. Once again the range between the different economies is large. So you would imagine very different economic

> # The effect of a 1 per cent tightening of the interest rates would be very different in the euro area compared to the UK

Table 8.7 | Financial liabilities of the household sector

	% GDP
UK	79
Norway	70
Spain	58
Germany	56
Sweden	54
France	50
Finland	41
Italy	24

Source: OECD balance sheets of non-financial sector (1995)

responses on the supply side too (for given changes in monetary conditions) in the UK compared to the other European economies. Table 8.9 shows the liabilities of public sector pension schemes in Europe: again the UK's liability is up to 10 or 15 times smaller than elsewhere. The future fiscal implications of that, again on the demand and supply sides, are potentially huge.

Finally, Figure 8.3 shows that, as a result of all those factors, the effect of a 1 per cent tightening of the interest rates would be very different in the euro area compared to the UK: the UK appears to respond twice as negatively as her partners. This just underlines the fact that there may be big differences in the way an economy reacts to a common policy change; and that that may lead you to the conclusion that EMU membership could carry significant costs. In short, some economies will fit more easily into a single currency framework than others, depending on the circumstances – the UK included.

Table 8.8 | Stock of corporate bonds outstanding in 1995

	% GDP
Sweden	69.5
Germany	61.2
Belgium	55.5
Austria	36.5
Switzerland	35.8
Norway	19.2
Finland	19.2
Italy	13.7
France	11.6
Iceland	9.6
Netherlands	7.6
Spain	6.1
Ireland	3.2
UK	2.9

Source: Merrill Lynch, 'The size and structure of world bond markets', October 1996

Table 8.9 | Net present value of public pension schemes as % of GDP

1994 evaluation (negative liability)

	Productivity growth (%)	NPV (at 3%)[a]
Germany	1	−111
	1$\frac{1}{2}$	−134
	2	−163
France	1	−185
	1$\frac{1}{2}$	−198
	2	−212
Italy	1	−135
	1$\frac{1}{2}$	−131
	2	−124
UK	1	−58
	1$\frac{1}{2}$	−6
	2	−9
Netherlands	1	−113
	1$\frac{1}{2}$	−124
	2	−137
Belgium	1	−257
	1$\frac{1}{2}$	−282
	2	−312
Spain	1	−252
	1$\frac{1}{2}$	−273
	2	−298

Note: [a] Excess of long interest rates over growth in national incomes
Source: OECD report (1996)

Figure 8.3 | Impact of 1% point rise in short rates on real GDP

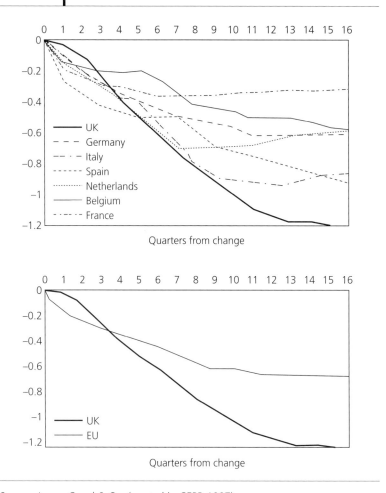

Quarters from change

Quarters from change

Source: James Capel & Co. (quoted in CEPR 1997)

Competitiveness in the UK: the contrary view

If there is a weakness in the British position, it probably lies in the competitiveness of British industry. Table 8.10 compares unit labour costs in manufacturing in the UK and Germany for the past five years. British unit labour costs have been lower than those in the core European economies for some time and this may account for Britain's robust performance in output growth and employment. But they have been rising since 1996 when the current decline in the value of the DM began and especially in the past two years as the euro has weakened.

Table 8.10 | Relative unit labour costs in manufacturing (index)

	UK	Germany	Ratio
1995	100	117.1	.85
1996	102.5	117.7	.87
1997	105.8	116.4	.91
1998	111.1	115.7	.96
1999	115.7	116.4	.99
2000	119.9	115.7	1.04

Source: HM Treasury

This could spell some difficulty for the UK, although labour costs for the economy as a whole are probably not as high as those in Table 8.10. Hughes Hallett (1998) and the Kiel Institute of World Economics put those costs at about 75–80 per cent of their German counterparts in 1995/97; that is 10 percentage points below the figures in Table 8.10. McKinsey (1998) also points out that capital productivity is higher in the UK than in Germany, offsetting the rise in unit labour costs reported in Table 8.10. Nevertheless, these production costs are a potential weakness which policy makers need to watch.

In fact Britain's position may be a little more difficult than those figures imply because, as Table 8.11 shows, payroll taxes and other employment costs are rather lower in the UK than elsewhere in euroland (Denmark and Ireland excepted). This may be rather favourable for output and employment, since the unit costs of labour will be lower than elsewhere. But it also means that there is less scope for the government to intervene in the labour markets in order to steer the economy when employment and growth are adversely affected – when Europe-wide monetary policy proves to be inappropriate for British conditions relative to the European average. Normally, in a world in which fiscal policy is constrained through the Stability and Growth Pact, governments would have to intervene to stabilize employment and growth by controlling labour costs directly. But Britain is in a poor position to do the same since the non-wage element is smaller than elsewhere. So, in order to have the same degree of control, Britain would probably be forced to adopt an old-fashioned prices and incomes policy instead.

Table 8.11 | Payroll tax rates in EU countries, 1998

	Blue-collar workers	White-collar workers
Austria	31.9	25.2
Belgium	37.7	34.9
Denmark	1.7	1.0
Finland	24.6	24.6
France	39.0	36.2
Germany	22.4	17.6
Greece	28.0	28.0
Ireland	12.0	11.2
Italy	45.8	43.0
Luxembourg	15.3	12.9
Netherlands	17.3	10.9
Portugal	24.5	24.5
Spain	33.0	33.0
Sweden	33.0	33.0
UK	10.0	10.0

Note: The payroll tax rates for blue-collar workers have been computed as the tax rates for the average wage for production workers in manufacturing and the payroll tax rates for white-collar workers as the tax rates for double this wage

Source: Swedish Employers' Federation, quoted in Calmfors (1998)

A conclusion

It is an irony that, because the economic benefits of joining the euro are almost certainly rather small, Britain appears to face a choice which is essentially political – but appears to want to take that decision on economic grounds. Most eurozone countries, however, have treated the matter as a political decision from the outset (political integration being the acknowledged goal in most cases: Issing 1996) without recognizing the possible economic costs.

Nevertheless, the analysis of this chapter shows that it is entirely logical that some countries would choose to join EMU, while others would not. Since this essentially turns on how flexible that economy's markets are compared to the eurozone average, a great deal depends, in the UK's case, on how much it can expect its European partners to undertake market reforms. Indeed the UK might well choose to stay out until that happens.

But would the eurozone ever create the necessary flexibility? One might guess not, because a form of 'Groucho Marx theorem' is going to reduce the incentives for reform. Given the need to have market flexibility, you would never want to join a monetary union whose markets are less flexible than your own – for, if you do, you will end up having to make all the necessary adjustments for yourself and for everyone else as well. So again the incentive is for the UK to stay out. But, by the same token, existing members would only want newcomers to join

---

The UK's fundamental dilemma with respect to the EU's single currency is unlikely to go away

---

who were more flexible than themselves. Hence the pressure on the UK to join. That has lead many to suspect that they would not like to join a union that is prepared to have them as a member.

Conversely, if you do decide to join such a union, the incentive is to become as inflexible (or as unreformed) as the least flexible member – in order not to have to shoulder an excessive amount of the adjustment burden on behalf of others. The UK's fundamental dilemma with respect to the EU's single currency is therefore unlikely to go away.

Notes

1 As of December 2000, opinion polls were putting 73 per cent of the population against entering the euro and the percentage among business people against entry at 62 per cent (in the employers' federation, CBI and other fora). These percentages appear to have risen from about 60 per cent and 30 per cent in 1998 and continued on an upward trend into 2001.

2 See **www.dors.dk/rapp/dors070.htm**, Chapter 2.

3 1 per cent to $1\frac{1}{2}$ per cent of GNP according to the European Commission (1990).

4 See Emerson et al. (1992).

5 The first pillar aims to maintain the growth in the nominal money supply at approximately $4\frac{1}{2}$ per cent a year.

6 The index of international and interregional mobility of MacLennan et al. puts the USA at 2.80 per cent of the population and the UK at 1.56, but Germany, France and Italy at 1.23, 1.07 and 0.50

respectively. Obstfeld and Peri have lower figures, with the UK, France and Germany at one-third or one-quarter of the US figure and declining.

7 The range for this figure was amended to £40–£60 billion in 2001 (Standard Life Annual Report, 27 March 2001).

8 It is often pointed out that because Italian institutions prevent houses from being used as collateral for loans and because Italian debt is almost entirely owned domestically, aggregate demand in Italy is almost immune to changes in interest rates. As a result this disparity in responses would not vanish if British borrowing behaviour shifted to mortgage, loan or employment contracts similar to those used in the rest of the EU. A more detailed analysis of these asymmetric responses to common (policy) shocks is contained in Hughes Hallett and Piscitelli (1999).

References

Agell, J. (1999) 'On the benefits from rigid labour markets: norms, market failures and social insurance', *Economic Journal*, 109, F143–64.

Calmfors, L. (1998) 'Macroeconomic policy, wage setting, and employment – what difference does the EMU make?', *Oxford Review of Economic Policy*, 14, 125–51.

Carlino, G. and De Fina, R. (1999) 'Monetary policy and the US states and regions' in J. von Hagen and C. Waller (eds) *Regional Aspects of Monetary Policy in Europe*. Boston and Dordrecht: Kluwer Academic Publishers.

CEPR (1997) *The Ostrich and the EMU: Policy Choices Facing the UK*. London: Centre for Economic Policy Research.

Decressin, J. and Fatas, A. (1995) 'Regional labour market dynamics in Europe', *European Economic Review*, 39, 627–56.

De Grauwe, P. (1997) 'Economics of monetary union', 3rd edition. Oxford: Oxford University Press.

De Grauwe, P. and Vanhevebeke, W. (1993) 'Is Europe an optimal currency area? Evidence from regional data' in P. Masson and M. Taylor (eds) *Policy Issues in the Operation of Currency Areas*. Cambridge and New York: Cambridge University Press.

Demertzis, M., Hughes Hallett, A. and Rummel, O. (1998) 'Is a 2-speed system in Europe the answer to the conflict between the German and the Anglo-Saxon models of monetary control?' in S. Black and M.

Moersch (eds) *Competition and Convergence in Financial Markets – the German and the Anglo-American Models*. New York: Elsevier North-Holland.

EC (1990) 'One market, one money', *European Economy*, 44, Luxembourg, EC Official Publications.

Eichengreen, B. (1992) 'Is Europe an optimal currency area?' in H. Borner and H. Grubel (eds) *The European Community after 1992: The View from Outside*. London: Macmillan.

Emerson, M., Anuean, M., Catinat, M., Goybet, P. and Jacquemin, A. (1992) *The Economics of 1992: The EC Commission's Assessment of the Economic Effects of Completing the Internal Market*. Oxford: Oxford University Press.

Hughes Hallett, A. (1998) 'Britain and the single currency: an assessment of the Chancellor's five economic tests' in the evidence of the Treasury Select Committee, *The UK and Preparations for Stage Three of Economic and Monetary Union*, Vol. III, 65–94, HMSO, April.

Hughes Hallett, A. and Piscitelli, L. (1999) 'EMU in reality: the effect of a common monetary policy on economies with different transmission mechanisms', *Empirica*, 26, 337–58.

Issing, O. (1996) 'Europe: Political union through common money?' Occasional paper 98, Institute of Economic Affairs, London.

Krugman, P. (1993) 'Lessons of Massachussetts for EMU' in F. Torres and F. Giavazzi (eds) *Adjustment and Growth in the European Monetary Union*. Cambridge and New York: Cambridge University Press.

Krugman, P. and Venables, A. (1996) 'Integration, specialisation and adjustment', *European Economic Review*, 40, 959–67.

McKinsey (1998) 'Driving productivity and growth in the UK economy', McKinsey Global Institute, October.

MacLennan, D., Muellbauer, J. and Stephens, M. (2000) 'Asymmetries in housing and financial market institutions and EMU' in T. Jenkinson (ed.) *Readings in Macroeconomics*. Oxford: Oxford University Press.

Obstfeld, M. and Peri, G. (1998) 'Regional nonadjustment and fiscal policy' in D. Begg, J. von Hagen, C. Wyplosz and K. Zimmerman (eds) *EMU: Prospects and Challenges for the Euro*. Oxford: Blackwell.

ONS: Office of National Statistics, London (various publications).

Puga, D. (1999) 'The rise and fall of regional inequalities', *European Economic Review*, 43, 303–34.

9

Macroeconomics of sterling and the euro

Philip Arestis and Malcolm Sawyer

There are a couple of inevitable consequences if the UK (or indeed any other country) were to adopt the euro and join the European Monetary Union (EMU). These are that taxes would have to be paid in euros, prices and wages would be denominated in euros and there would be a common monetary policy. It would be difficult to think of a monetary union which did not have a common monetary policy and a single unit of account. However, there would be many other changes and consequences for sterling joining the euro but those changes and consequences flow from the nature of the policies and institutions which have been put in place along with the EMU, but which are not inevitable features of a monetary union.

Different policies and institutional arrangements would bring different consequences. The desirability or otherwise of sterling's joining the euro crucially depends on those policies and institutional arrangements. The common monetary policy is an example. At present this policy takes the form of the setting of key interest rates by the 'independent' European Central Bank (ECB) in pursuit of the objective of low inflation. But the central bank does not have to be independent and monetary policy can be used to pursue objectives other than low inflation. A further example is that membership of the euro would commit a country to the *Stability and Growth Pact*, but alternative pacts (or no pact at all) can be envisaged.

This chapter focuses attention on two crucial aspects of the conditions surrounding the entry of sterling into the eurozone, namely the exchange rate at which sterling may join the European Monetary System and the macroeconomic policy regime within which the euro is embedded; in turn the macroeconomic aspects are divided into monetary policy and fiscal policy aspects.

Sterling exchange rate

An important issue, and one which would determine the economic performance of the UK for years ahead, is the value at which sterling entered the euro. Getting that exchange rate wrong and, in particular, setting the exchange rate too high would promise years (decades) of deflation. There are some interesting and revealing examples from the 20th-century experience of what might happen under these circumstances: the return to the Gold Standard in 1925 at the pre-World War I parity, and in 1990 when the UK joined the Exchange Rate Mechanism (ERM) at around 15 per cent overvaluation (we discuss these two episodes further later).

> An issue, which would determine the economic performance of the UK for years ahead, is the value at which sterling entered the euro

Following the launch of the euro in January 1999, its value fell almost substantially from circa $1.25 to circa $0.90 (see Arestis, Biefang-Frisancho Mariscal, Brown and Sawyer 2001 for a discussion of the possible reasons for this decline; and Chapter 6). The value of sterling relative to the euro has to some degree reflected this decline in the value of the euro, although the value of sterling had been relatively high (in terms of European currencies such as the Deutschmark) prior to the launch of the euro. At the time of writing (early 2001) sterling is circa 1.60 euros (equivalently 3.12 Deutschmarks). The euro is significantly undervalued against the dollar and sterling (Fred Bergsten, as reported in the Guardian of 22 January 2001, estimates the fundamental exchange rate at $1.25 = 1 euro), and sterling overvalued against the euro. Bubbles in exchange rates (for whatever cause) are well known and it can be expected that the present bubble involving high values for the dollar and sterling and low values for the euro will eventually burst and the exchange rates move to more reasonable levels. But given the nature of exchange rate markets it could be expected that there will be future bubbles and no doubt at some point in the future the talk will be of low value of the dollar and high value of the euro. The immediate concern, however, is with the effects of the current high value of sterling and the consequences of any decline in the value of sterling.

A recent estimate of the fundamental equilibrium exchange rate (Church 1999) based on the Treasury model was around 2.30 Deutschmarks to the pound for 1997, with the pound 18 per cent overvalued in 1997 and 23 per cent in the second quarter of 1999. Recent movements in the exchange rate will tend to leave sterling even further overvalued.

One of the conditions of the Maastricht Treaty criteria for a country to join the euro, and the only one which the UK currently clearly does not satisfy, is at least a two-year membership of the ERM with no significant change in the central exchange rate. But this may not be such a serious hurdle for the UK's entry. Consider the experience of other countries in the case of the Maastricht criteria in May 1997. In the event, as with other criteria, there was a degree of fudge when decisions were made in terms of country membership of the euro (see Arestis, Brown and Sawyer 2001, Ch. 3). Take, for example, the experience of Finland. This country had only been a member of the ERM for one year prior to being an initial member of the eurozone in January 1999. And yet Finland was deemed to have satisfied this particular criterion and thus became a full member of the EMU. It could be argued, however, that Finland had satisfied the substantive part of this requirement, namely stability of the exchange rate of its currency against the ECU. It is clearly possible that the UK's entry into the euro would similarly not require formal membership of the ERM. But the stability of the exchange rate prior to entry should be seen as an important requirement.

We can consider the implications of meeting this criterion of a stable exchange rate for two years prior to entry for the UK's joining the euro in three years' time, by which we mean the date at which the value of sterling would be locked to the euro. This could then be followed by a period of transition of two to three years similar to that currently being undertaken by the 11 eurozone members. Sterling might then disappear in five to six years' time.

It is helpful to consider three possible scenarios, while realizing that actual events may well lie somewhere between. The first is that sterling falls in value substantially over the next 12 months, followed by two years of exchange rate stability (vis-à-vis the euro) and hence, in effect, shadowing the euro. Whether or not sterling was in the ERM, it would satisfy the substantive requirement for entry into the euro and this could be seen as the dream scenario for such entry. It faces, however, the obvious, but serious problems of how to engineer the reduction in the value of sterling and the implications of a rapid devaluation for inflation. A 20 per cent devaluation overall could be expected to have a direct impact on prices of the order of 6 to 7 per cent. This could be more if domestic prices respond, although it could be modified if the euro were to rise against the dollar, leading to a devaluation in the effective exchange rate of less than 20 per cent.

The second scenario is that the value of sterling gradually declines in value over the next three years to reach a rate appropriate for entry. The interesting question would then be how this may be achieved. The obvious answer is through the rate of interest. But then this would contravene the objective of the Monetary Policy Committee (MPC) in view of their remit to achieve price stability and the 2.5 per cent target inflation rate. This is so since even if the MPC managed to lower the pound exchange rate, it may have such inflationary implications, which could very well imply an inflation rate above the target set by the Treasury. It would also require a bending of the criteria of the Maastricht Treaty to allow sterling to join. This would be the case in terms of both the inflation rate criterion (the UK would most certainly have under these conditions an inflation rate above the average of the three best-performing EMU countries in terms of their inflation rates) and the exchange rate criterion (two years of stable exchange rate without substantial devaluation, ruled out by definition).

The third scenario is that sterling remains overvalued, even if there is some decline in its value. The Maastricht Treaty requirement of a stable exchange rate vis-à-vis the euro would be satisfied, but entry occurs at an overvalued rate. This would be the nightmare scenario. Any benefits of lower transaction costs and reduced volatility of the value of the currency (zero, of course, against the rest of the eurozone) would be inconsequential against the cost of entry at an overvalued rate without any exit possibilities, or indeed any other policy to account for it. The consequences of the entry of sterling into the eurozone at an overvalued rate are clear. The current position is that the UK is running a substantial trade deficit, and the likelihood is that the UK would be entering the euro with a balance of trade deficit, a position that can only be sustained if others are prepared to lend to the UK. This can take the form of foreign direct investment, but then there is the obvious question of why all suddenly and under these conditions multinationals would wish to invest in the UK. The alternative is that prices in the UK would have to fall by say 20 per cent, with an accompanying fall in money wages. Even if this fall is relative to prices elsewhere in the eurozone, and could be achieved by lower inflation in the UK compared with the rest of the eurozone, this would be far from painless. Years of deflationary policies to push down inflation (and into deflation) could well follow.

In the 20th century, as previously mentioned, the UK suffered two major episodes of joining a fixed exchange rate system at too high an exchange rate. The first was the return to the Gold Standard in 1925 at the pre-World War I parity, implying an overvaluation of around 10 per cent. The second was in 1990 when the UK joined the ERM at around 15 per cent overvaluation. Both were associated with a period of economic depression and both ended ignominiously, in 1931 and 1992 respectively. The obvious difference between those two experiences and joining the EMU at an overvalued exchange rate is that in the case of the first two it was possible to end the overvaluation. There were clearly costs involved in doing so and during the time of overvaluation there were always those warning of the disasters of leaving the Gold Standard and ERM respectively. In the present case of the UK, joining the eurozone, there would be severe legal and political constraints on reversing the decision, and the only adjustment route would appear to be continuous deflation in the UK to reduce prices and wages.

Monetary policy

The introduction of a single currency inevitably involves the adoption of a single common monetary policy, but the introduction of the euro is within a particular institutional policy framework. There are three key elements to this institutional policy framework.

First, the ECB is the only effective federal economic institution. The ECB has the one policy instrument of the rate of interest (the 'repo' rate) to pursue the main objective of low inflation (as measured by the annual increase in the Harmonized Index of Consumer Prices, HICP) which for the euro area should be less than 2 per cent. This is to be achieved through the policy weapon of the rate of interest and by announced quantitative reference values for the growth of the broad M3 monetary aggregate set at 4.5 per cent. Being a reference level, there is no mechanistic commitment to correct deviations in the short term, although it is stated that deviations from the reference value would, under normal circumstances, 'signal risks to price stability'. It has also been agreed that a broadly based assessment of future price developments will be undertaken, but not publicly announced.

The setting of interest rates seems to be regarded by some as a technical matter: indeed part of the rationale for an independent central bank is that decisions on interest rates are depoliticized by being taken out of the hands of politicians. When, in contrast, interest rates have distributional consequences and have differential impacts on regions and industries (whether directly or indirectly through, for example, the exchange rate), the setting of interest rates should be influenced by those possible consequences. The board of directors of the ECB should be broadened through the explicit representation of different industrial sectors and of workers and consumers. An alternative would be for the board of directors to be appointed by the European parliament in a way which, at least informally, leads to a wide representation of interests.

Second, the ECB and the national central banks are linked into the ESCB with a division of responsibility between them. The ECB has the responsibility for setting interest rates in pursuit of the inflation objective and the national central banks responsibility for regulatory matters. In order to achieve its objectives, the ECB will conduct open market operations, it will offer standing facilities (overnight lending against eligible assets and deposit facilities to the institutions subject to minimum reserves with national central banks) and it will impose minimum reserve requirements. The latter will be interest rate bearing (at the repo rate) on institutions holding accounts with it. The reserve ratio will be 2 per cent of eligible liabilities[1] and the reserves will be lodged with national central banks. But a notable feature of the operation of the ESCB is the apparent absence of the lender of last resort facility.

Third, the ECB is intended to be independent of the EU Council and parliament and of its member governments. Thus there is a complete separation between the monetary authorities, in the form of the ESCB, and the fiscal authorities, in the shape of the national governments comprising the EMU. National governments are given the objective of keeping any budget deficit below 3 per cent of GDP according to the Stability and Growth Pact. It follows that there can be little co-ordination of monetary and fiscal policy. Apart from the separation of the monetary and fiscal authorities, there is also the requirement cited later that national governments (and hence the fiscal authorities) should not exert any influence on the ECB (and hence the monetary authorities). Any strict interpretation of that edict would rule out any attempt at co-ordination of monetary and fiscal policies.

The single policy instrument of the 'repo' interest rate cannot be set in a manner appropriate for different regions suffering from different shocks and/or at different points of the economic cycle. A particular concern here would be that the interest rate may be set more with regard to those regions which are viewed as 'overheating' rather than to those regions which are 'freezing'. It is clear that, in general, an interest rate level that is appropriate to an average will not be appropriate for the individuals that make up the average, especially in the case of 'outliers'. The setting of a uniform 'repo' rate to apply across the eurozone is, of course, an inevitable feature of a single currency (though the 'repo' rate may translate into differential rates of interest on loans and deposits across the eurozone). But it is not inevitable that the 'repo' rate is set with the single objective of low inflation, neither is it inevitable that monetary policy is the only eurozone-level policy instrument.

The use of monetary policy to target the rate of inflation draws on two broad sets of assumptions. The first is that monetary conditions are the cause and inflation the effect and that interest rates can affect monetary conditions. In the simple monetarist story, the money supply determines the rate of inflation. But if there is reverse causality, whereby inflation influences monetary conditions, then seeking to set the latter becomes much less attractive. The second broad assumption is the classical dichotomy under which there is a separation between the real and the monetary sides of the economy and under which the monetary conditions do not influence the real side of the economy, either in the short run or in the long run. The Non-Accelerating Inflation Rate of Unemployment (NAIRU) is a reflection of this notion, as it represents a supply-side equilibrium rate of unemployment, at which inflation is constant. In its usual representation, the NAIRU is settled by labour market factors and not influenced by capacity or by aggregate demand.

When there is the prospect (or actual experience) of rising inflation, the ECB will have no choice but to raise interest rates. The ECB may operate on evidence of prices rising faster or any evidence such as unemployment falling below the estimated NAIRU (or some combination of factors). Interest rates are likely to be a rather blunt instrument for this purpose. There are questions over how much impact a rise in interest rates will have on the rate of change of the money supply, and further whether changes in the money supply have a causal effect on changes in prices. It is also the case that increases in interest rates raise prices, whether directly through impact on mortgage payments (particularly significant in the UK – see Chapter 8,

Section 'Specialization versus diversification') or indirectly through impact on firms costs. The ECB, however, has no alternative to the use of interest rates and attempts to control the growth of the stock of money in the pursuit of the low inflation objective. The range of other economic policies which have or could be used to influence the pace of inflation are out of reach of the ECB. Thus, income policy, co-ordinated pay bargaining, the creation of a more balanced, less inflation-prone economy or even fiscal deflation are policy options which are simply not available to the ECB.

Monetary policy is often discussed in essential monetarist terms, namely that the stock of money can be changed (or targeted) by the Central Bank and the growth of the stock of money determines the rate of inflation, leaving output and employment determined on the supply side of the economy (invoking the classical dichotomy between the real and monetary sides of the economy). But whatever is the rhetoric, the reality is that the relevant stock(s) of money are bank deposits (whether narrowly defined as demand deposits or broadly defined to include time deposits) which are created by banks but remain in existence only when there is a demand to hold them. Further, and of particular significance here, is that monetary policy operates through interest rates. A change in the 'repo' rate works through the effect on the spectrum of interest rates and thereby on demand and supply of loans and the willingness of the public to hold money. From these rather obvious observations, three considerations arise.

> The ECB has no alternative to the use of interest rates and attempts to control the growth of the stock of money in the pursuit of the low inflation objective

First, the basis of the classical dichotomy is undermined and, in particular, it would be anticipated that variations in the rate of interest would have an impact on the level of investment (and thereby future productive capacity) and the exchange rate. Monetary policy in the form of interest rates is viewed as operating through the effect of the level of economic activity and thereby on the rate of inflation. Insofar as interest rate changes are effective in influencing the pace of economic activity, they can be seen to do so through exchange rates (and thereby on demand for imports and exports) and through investment.

Second, there are a range of reasons for thinking that monetary policy will have a differential impact across regions and countries. As the Monetary Policy Committee (1999) recognizes, monetary policy 'sets one interest rate for the economy as a whole and can only take account of the impact of official rate changes on the aggregate of individuals in the economy' (p. 7). Monetary policy is undifferentiated in that a single official rate will apply. But there are differences in financial structures between countries in the eurozone and, in particular, differences in the extent of variable and fixed rates of interest and in the effect of interest rate changes on economic activity. The effects of interest rate changes will be far from uniform across eurozone countries. An interest rate rise may succeed in slowing down economic activity in some countries but not in others; it may have little effect on inflation in some but act to speed it up in others.

Third, there is the question of how effective the interest rate is as an (or as *the*) instrument of demand management policy. The overall impact of interest rate policy is likely to be very difficult to predict, in the light of these considerations.

The euro could be embedded in a different monetary policy environment and one which, we would argue, would be much more conducive for economic performance. The objectives of the central bank should be changed to include the pursuit of full employment and economic growth as well as price stability (recognizing that there may be interdependence between the objectives, though not necessarily in the manner suggested by the Phillips curve). The central bank should also have the objective of the regulation of the financial system, with the further aim to provide an orderly functioning of the credit system. It is imperative, therefore, that the ECB is able and willing to assume the traditional role of any central bank, that of the lender of last resort. In this context there is also a requirement for more effective account-ability which requires mechanisms of democratic influence (if not control) over the central bank from the European parliament (and we would extend that to national parliaments). This accountability would reinforce the legitimacy of the institution and avoid at the same time dramatic conflicts between monetary policy and other EU objectives. A much wider membership of the board of directors than the present constitution, to include representatives of industry, trade unions, regions etc., would help a great deal on this score.

We have argued for a change in the objectives set for the ECB and a recognition of the channels of monetary influence with due regard being paid to the distributional effects of interest rate changes. Further, there is a need for the reformulation of the regulatory role of the ECB. In this respect, the ECB's most important function is that of ensuring that orderly conditions prevail in the money market. In order to achieve this, the reformulated ECB should be required to act as lender of last resort and not merely possess the potential to act as such. Moreover, the ECB should adopt a more proactive stance regarding bank surveillance and supervision. The proposal for the reformulation of objectives readily follows from what has been previously said: that is, the ECB should be charged with setting interest rates in a manner which encourages growth and full employment, rather than merely inflation.

Fiscal policy

The Stability and Growth Pact alongside the Maastricht Treaty creates four rules for economic policy: the ECB was granted independence from political influence; the rule of no bail-out of national government deficits was introduced; the monetary financing of government deficits was prohibited; and member states must avoid 'excessive' deficits (defined as more than 3 per cent of GDP).

The Stability and Growth Pact consists of three components: a single European Council Resolution and two Council Regulations. The Resolution commits all parties, member states, the Commission and the Council 'to implement the Treaty and the Stability and Growth Pact in a strict and timely manner'. The Council Regulations themselves, unlike the Resolution, have legal force and can be seen as composed of two complementary elements. First, the 'preventative' element: this resolution refers to the strengthening of budgetary positions and the surveillance and co-ordination of economic policies. It commits those member states which join the single currency to submit to the Commission a stability programme. These stability programmes will have to be updated annually and must detail the member state's medium-term budget objective, the main assumptions about economic developments, and the projected paths for both the deficit ratio and the debt ratio. Non-euro members should submit a 'convergence plan' which should be similar in outline to the stability programme. These programmes are intended to act as an early warning system and will signal when a member state is close to breaching the reference values detailed in Protocol 5 of the Treaty. The second Council Regulation is the 'deterrent' element. This is aimed at speeding up and clarifying the implementation of the excessive deficit procedure and it seeks to reduce the scope for discretion, which is allowed under the Maastricht Treaty.

The Stability and Growth Pact appears to be based on what we have elsewhere termed new monetarism (Arestis and Sawyer 1998). The essential features of new monetarism are:

- Politicians in particular, and the democratic process in general, cannot be trusted with economic policy formulation, with a tendency to make decisions which have stimulating short-term effects (reducing unemployment) but which are detrimental in the longer term (notably a rise in inflation). In contrast, experts in the form of central bankers are not subject to political pressures to court short-term popularity, and can take a longer-term perspective where it is assumed that there is a conflict between the short term and the long term. The logic underpinning this reasoning mirrors that found in the rules versus discretion debate. Policy makers' scope for using discretion should be curtailed and the possibility of negative spillovers from irresponsible fiscal policy must be reduced within the eurozone, hence fiscal policy will be permanently constrained by the Stability Pact, and monetary policy has been removed from national authorities and from political authorities and placed with the ECB.

- Inflation is a monetary phenomenon and can be controlled through monetary policy. The money supply is difficult (or impossible) to control directly, but the central bank can set the key interest rate (the 'repo' rate) to influence the monetary conditions, which in turn influence the future rate of inflation.

- The level of unemployment fluctuates around a supply-side-determined equilibrium rate of unemployment, that of NAIRU. The level of the NAIRU may be favourably affected by a 'flexible' labour market, but is unaffected by the level of aggregate demand or by productive capacity.

- Fiscal policy is impotent in terms of its impact on real variables and as such it should be subordinate to monetary policy in controlling inflation. It is recognized, however, that the government budget position will fluctuate during the course of the business cycle but in the context of an essentially passive fiscal policy.

The main feature of the Stability and Growth Pact is a requirement that the national budget deficit does not exceed 3 per cent of GDP, and failure to meet that requirement could lead to a series of fines depending on the degree to which the deficit exceeds 3 per cent.

A government which aims to avoid an 'excessive' budget deficit of more than 3 per cent of GDP would have to ensure that the 3 per cent limit is not breached during economic slowdown; and hence that the average deficit during the course of the business cycle would have to be much lower than 3 per cent. A country's budgetary data become available for the Commission to scrutinize on 1 March each year when the stability programmes are submitted. Each programme will contain information about the paths of the ratios of budget deficit to GDP and national debt to GDP. The Council (ECOFIN) will examine the stability reports and deliver an opinion on a recommendation by the Commission (within two months of the reports' submission). If the stability programme reveals that a country is significantly diverging from its medium-term budgetary objective, then the Council will recommend that the stability programme be strengthened. If the situation persists then the member state will have been judged to have breached the reference values. The Pact details 'escape' clauses which allow a member state that has an excessive deficit to avoid sanction. If there is an economic downturn and output has fallen by more than 2 per cent, then the member state will escape sanction automatically but the deficit should be corrected once the recession has finished. If output falls between 0.75 and 2 per cent then the Council can use discretion when making a decision on an 'excessive' deficit other factors will be taken into account, such as the abruptness of the downturn, the accumulated loss of output relative to past trends and whether the government deficit exceeds government investment expenditure.

When the Council has sifted through all relevant information pertaining to the country whose financial position is under review, it must decide whether an excessive deficit exists or not. In making the decision, the Council operates with a qualified majority and, under the Maastricht Treaty, all EU member states have a vote, including those countries that are not in the euro area and even the country which is under consideration. If a country is found to have breached the reference values, then it has four months to introduce the corrective measures suggested by the Council. If the country follows the Council's recommendations, then the 'excessive' deficit can continue, but the budget deficit must be corrected within a year following its identification. A country which chooses not to introduce corrective measures will be subject to a range of sanctions (Article 104c(11)); one or more must be imposed, of which one must be in the form of a non-interest-bearing deposit lodged by the national government. In this instance, it will fall upon EMU members, excluding the member country under consideration, to reach a decision on sanctions. The non-interest-bearing deposit consists of a fixed component (0.2 per cent of GDP) and a variable component (one-tenth of the difference between the deficit ratio and the 3 per cent reference value). If the budget deficit is not corrected within two years, the deposit is forfeited and becomes a fine, whereas if the deficit is corrected within two years the deposit is returned and the penalty becomes the foregone interest.

The penalty clause would add to the deficit it is meant to cure and as such it could generate national opposition. Von Hagen and Eichengreen (1996) and Eichengreen and Wyplosz (1998) argue that the Stability and Growth Pact tends to suppress the symptoms without treating the source of the problem. The constraints imposed by the Pact will severely reduce national fiscal independence and effectively preclude the use of national fiscal policy for demand management purposes. This is especially the case at present where countries have entered EMU at the upper limit of the Stability and Growth Pact; OECD (1998) estimates suggest that eight of the 11 countries (before Greece joined) have budget deficit targets in the range of 1–2 per cent of GDP over the next few years, which is not sufficient to allow automatic stabilizers to work under the Stability Pact. Bayoumi and Eichengreen (1995) suggest that this restriction on the workings of automatic stabilizers could lead to weaker fiscal stabilization and greater output volatility. Further, von Hagen and Eichengreen (1996) argue that if automatic stabilizers cannot function fully, then pressures will build for fiscal federalism to provide them.

> If automatic stabilizers cannot function fully, then pressures will build for fiscal federalism to provide them

This system of financial penalties for breaches of the budget deficit criterion implies that deflationary fiscal policies will continue and indeed intensify, as those countries which just met the 3 per cent requirement in conditions of cyclical upswing will have to tighten the fiscal stance to meet the 3 per cent requirement in times of cyclical downswing especially. It was indicated earlier that a clause was inserted into the Stability Pact which allows a country to have a larger deficit in the face of recession. However, even this formal recognition that automatic stabilizers and active fiscal policy could be hampered may not be sufficient to prevent the Stability and Growth Pact from operating to exacerbate recessions.

The dominant feature of the ECB's institutional structure is the complete separation between the monetary authorities (in the form of the central bank) and the fiscal authorities (in the shape of the national governments comprising the EMU), where the latter are constrained to keep their budget deficit below 3 per cent according to the Stability and Growth Pact. It follows that there can be little co-ordination of monetary and fiscal policy. Apart from the separation of the monetary and fiscal authorities, there is also the requirement that national governments (and hence the fiscal authorities) should not exert any influence on the ECB (and hence the monetary authorities). Any strict interpretation of that edict would rule out any attempt at co-ordination of monetary and fiscal policies. Indeed the primacy of monetary policy over fiscal policy is guaranteed because of the institutional structure and rules of the ESCB.

The budget of the EU itself is relatively small (see Chapter 11). It represents around 1.5 per cent of EU GDP and there is a requirement that it be in balance, with revenue from member governments determined so as to cover planned expenditure. The EU is, thus, constrained to run a balanced budget on an annual basis. Articles 199 and 201 of the amended Treaty of Rome (EC 1998) require that 'the revenue and expenditure shown in the [Community] budget shall be in balance' and that 'the budget shall be financed wholly from own resources'. Consequently, the scale and balanced budget nature of EU expenditure clearly mean that there is no role for fiscal policy at the EU level (even of a passive form whereby budget deficits vary with the business cycle).

In order to meet the upper limit of 3 per cent of GDP on national budget deficits during a recession, it is likely that member governments would need to run significant surpluses during economic upswings, and over the course of the business cycle the average budget deficit will be small or perhaps zero. The 3 per cent of GDP rule for budget deficits may well mean that over the business cycle the budget position is balanced or in surplus. This means that: 'National governments will need to aim at a balanced budget or surplus, or the deficit limit of 3 per cent could well prevent the proper working of fiscal stabilisers over the economic cycle.' It also means that 'governments could be required to raise taxes, or cut government spending, as the economy moves into recession, thereby exacerbating the downturn' (Currie 1997, p. 13). In the past decade, the budget position in the UK has swung from a surplus of 1 per cent of GDP to a deficit of nearly 8 per cent. If a comparable swing in the budget position occurred in the future, with the largest deficit constrained to 3 per cent, then the surplus would be 6 per cent, with an overall surplus averaging around 1 per cent of GDP. A more cautious government which aimed for say a maximum deficit of 2 per cent to provide a margin of error would clearly run a somewhat larger surplus.

The EMU approach to policy obviously means that there is *no* policy instrument at the EU level addressed towards the levels of employment and unemployment, and in effect (un)employment disappears as a policy objective. The loss of the exchange rate instrument means that shocks (positive or negative) which hit one EU country (or a small number of EU countries) cannot be offset by movements in the exchange rate. In particular, negative shocks to an economy which raise unemployment cannot be offset by a currency depreciation, although it can be noted that in the volatile floating exchange rate system there may be perverse responses by the exchange markets to a negative shock. The overall effect is likely to raise unemployment: there is a clear upper limit to the degree to which countries that experience a positive shock can benefit through lower unemployment, while countries with a negative shock may suffer a considerable increase in unemployment. In a similar vein, limited labour mobility means that there will not be a great deal of movement of labour from areas of high unemployment to those with low unemployment. The problem of unemployment will be particularly serious in those cases where governments have chosen the wrong exchange rate at entry. An overvalued entry exchange rate will mean an extended period of recession to accommodate its effects which emanate from the absence of the adjustable exchange rate safety valve. This is accentuated by the virtual absence of fiscal transfers, whether automatic or discretionary, from the relatively rich regions to the relatively poor ones. There is clearly no tax and social security system operating at the federal level which in other federal systems serves to make transfers between rich and poor in an automatic manner, and to provide an element of fiscal stabilization. The expenditures on regional aid and to a lesser degree agricultural policies do make some transfers from rich to poor, but on a very limited scale. In short, the European federal budget is not on a sufficient scale or of the right design to provide significant interregional insurance not present in the EMU (Fatas 1998). Eichengreen (1997) offered the suggestion that the European Investment Bank (EIB) can borrow off budget to perform these functions; however, this would exceed the EIB's remit. Article 198e of the Maastricht Treaty states that: 'The task of the EIB shall be to contribute, by having recourse to the capital market and utilising its own resources, to the balanced and steady development of the common market in the interest of the community.' Whether the functions of the EIB can be enlarged to include stabilization policy (distribution over time) is extremely questionable. It can entail redistribution across countries and it is specifically this function which should be expanded and strengthened from its present form where assistance is only in the form of loans and guarantees.

The economic analysis which lies behind these types of policy appears to be one in which macroeconomic demand conditions, including monetary and fiscal policies, cannot affect the (equilibrium) level of unemployment of labour and, more generally, the level of economic activity. The level of unemployment and of economic activity is viewed as solely a supply-side phenomenon.

At both national and European Union level, the use of fiscal policy is heavily constrained by the Stability and Growth Pact. It has already been indicated that the limit in the Stability and Growth Pact on budget deficits of no more than 3 per cent of GDP translates into a requirement for a budget which is in surplus or very small deficit averaged over the business cycle. A balanced budget implies (as a matter of an accounting identity) that the net sum of private savings minus investment plus trade deficit (borrowing overseas) is zero. There is little evidence that high levels of employment would necessarily generate an equality between savings and investment, and specifically it is expected that there would be an excess of savings over investment which needs to be mopped up by foreign lending or budget deficit. The limits on budget deficits would prevent this occurring and hence full employment would require a balance of trade surplus and the consequent foreign lending. At present, the European Union runs a significant trade surplus with the rest of the world, but the counterpart is, of course, that other countries run a trade deficit and are borrowing from the European Union. It is doubtful whether such a pattern of surpluses and deficits is sustainable in the long term with the consequent build-up of interest flows to service the borrowing.

We noted earlier that the 3 per cent of GDP limit on budget deficits in the Stability and Growth Pact is arbitrary and that this figure appears to have been plucked out of the air. In view of this argument and also of the ability to absorb shocks as well as to underpin high levels of aggregate demand, we would suggest that the figure of 3 per cent is highly inappropriate. In the absence of an EU-level fiscal policy, national governments should be allowed to pursue budget deficits as they think appropriate. Ideally, this should be seen as a temporary arrangement during a period in which a proper EU fiscal policy is generated. In the interim, national governments may well be constrained by the financial markets on how far they can borrow, and different governments may face different credit ratings in the financial markets (as different states within the United States of America do at present). There are no doubt 'externalities' of one country's fiscal policy on another in the context of the European Union, which can operate through the spillover effects of demand from fiscal policy and perhaps through the effects on interest rates. There is a paradox here in that interest rate is used as an instrument of monetary policy with the 'repo' rate set by the ECB and concern over the size of budget deficits through their impact on interest rates. There is then much to be said for co-ordinated fiscal policies, but in the context where that co-ordination is over the stances of active fiscal policies and where the policies themselves are aimed towards the achievement of high levels of economic activity. In view of the arguments of the European Commission (as in the MacDougall Report 1977), such co-ordination of fiscal and monetary policies become paramount. The euro will be greatly enabled to work under such circumstances.

We would argue for a new Stability and Growth Pact in a way that involves the objectives of both 'stability' and 'growth', not merely 'stability' (Arestis, McCauley and Sawyer 2001). This proposal emanates from the obvious recognition that within a single country there are substantial, often virtually automatic, transfers of income from the more prosperous to the less prosperous regions. The automatic elements come from the tax and social security system and other elements come through regional policy and allocation of funds to local government. Countries with federal structures have a significant share (say around half) of government expenditure at the national level with the national government having an ability to run deficits and operate fiscal policy, as well as to redistribute income between states. This is completely absent from the EU. Transfers from the operation of automatic stabilizers do not occur at the EU level and the discretionary transfers are relatively small. Hence the check on the decline of weak regions which emanates from these transfers is largely absent. The problems this entails will be particularly acute for those regions (countries) of the EMU and any entering the single currency with a trade deficit and high levels of unemployment (witness the high unemployment rates in some EMU countries as discussed earlier). Given the lower degree of labour mobility in Europe across national borders than within them, the complete loss of the exchange rate adjustment possibility requires an adequate policy of regional transfers through an EMU fiscal policy to accompany the proposed common EMU monetary policy. The absence of such co-ordination, indeed the non-existence of fiscal policy at the EMU level, implies that the interest rate variations necessary to achieve price stability become even more uncertain.

Two specific considerations inform our approach to fiscal policy. The first is the idea that there is no strong reason to believe that the private sector will generate sufficient demand to underpin full employment, and consequently full employment may well require a budget deficit which in effect mops up excess private savings. This is not to say that budget deficits are inevitable or in some way desirable in themselves, but, rather, may be a necessary element in the achievement of full employment. The second is the potency or otherwise of fiscal policy in stimulating aggregate demand. Here it is argued that, within the European Union, fiscal policy would be expected to be a more, rather than a less, effective policy as compared with fiscal policy at the national level. The European Union will constitute a relatively closed economy and as such there would only be small leakages of any demand stimulus. It is ironic to note that fiscal policy is being downgraded at a time when it may become more potent. In our discussion of fiscal policy, it should be clearly understood that we are not advocating any form of 'fine tuning' involving frequent (more than annual) changes in taxation and expenditure policies. Instead we would be advocating 'coarse tuning' under which budget deficits are used to support aggregate demand as necessary, given the levels of private demand.

> ## Rules which specify a fixed limit on government borrowing fail to recognize that it serves as a mechanism for distributing over time the cost of adjustment to shocks

Rules which specify a fixed limit on government borrowing fail to recognize that it serves as a mechanism for distributing over time the cost of adjustment to shocks and for smoothing the tax burden associated with public investment. We would argue that constraints on government borrowing reduce the flexibility of national governments' fiscal policy and make fiscal co-ordination extremely difficult. Moreover, we would suggest that the motivation behind the adoption of fiscal constraints by the Maastricht Treaty and their strengthening through the Stability and Growth Pact are questionable. Borrowing restrictions are not present in existing monetary unions (Eichengreen 1997). In fact, it could be reasoned that borrowing constraints would be justified only if the sub-central government had few or no tax-raising powers and was dependent on central government for most of its income because this increases the risk of a bail-out. In instances where a significant proportion of sub-central government expenditure was generated from its own tax base, the central government could force the sub-central government to take remedial action by either a decrease in expenditure or an increase in taxation, or indeed both, and government borrowing restraints should not be employed. The latter case applies to EMU: national governments still retain tax powers with a large tax base and can use this as a means to finance borrowing.

The separation of the monetary authorities from the fiscal authorities and the decentralization of the fiscal authorities will inevitably make any co-ordination of fiscal and monetary policy difficult. Since the ECB is instructed to focus on inflation while the fiscal authorities will have a broader range of concerns, there will be considerable grounds for conflict. This suggests a need for the evolution of a body charged with the co-ordination of these monetary and fiscal policies. In the absence of such a body, tensions will emerge in the real sector when monetary policy and fiscal policy pull in different directions (Begg and Green 1998, p. 131). The Stability and Growth Pact in effect resolves these issues by establishing the

> **Changes in the exchange rate can allow a country to offset differential shocks and differences in economic performance**

dominance of the monetary authorities (ECB) over the fiscal authorities (national governments). From this discussion, our proposals concerning fiscal policy would include three elements. First, the present constraints on national budget positions should be removed and national governments should be allowed to set fiscal policy as they deem appropriate in the light of economic circumstances and their perceptions of the costs and benefits involved. Second, institutional arrangements for the co-ordination of national fiscal policies must be strengthened. Third, European Union institutional arrangements are required for the operation of an EU fiscal policy and to ensure that monetary authorities do not dominate economic policy making.

The adoption of a single currency by eurozone countries clearly removes the possibility of variation in the value of their domestic currency. Changes in the exchange rate can allow a country to offset differential shocks and differences in economic performance. It may be questioned how far a country can determine its own exchange rate in the globalized financial markets, although, since an exchange rate is the relative value of one currency in terms of another, it is rarely the case that one country can completely determine the value of its own currency. It is also the case that exchange rates have been highly volatile since the breakdown of the Bretton Woods system and that exchange rates have diverged significantly from purchasing power parity (see, for example,

Krugman 1989 and Rogoff 1996). Nevertheless, variation in the exchange rate (whether in the context of a fixed or a flexible exchange rate system) does provide a safety valve to adjustment to differential shocks and economic performance, even though the safety valve may not always work quickly (in the case of fixed exchange rates) or may often be faulty (in the case of flexible exchange rates).

It is clear that there are few, if any, mechanisms with the Stability and Growth Pact and the single currency for a country or region to adjust to differential shocks and economic performance. There is a notable absence of automatic stabilizers at that level with the requirement of a balanced EU budget and the small scale of that budget. The ability of national governments to stabilize their own economies becomes more circumscribed through the requirements of the Stability and Growth Pact and the limits on the size of budget deficits. It is often pointed out that most single currency zones involve a central or federal government tax and public expenditure programme, which is substantial relative to national GDP and a government budget, which can run significant deficits.[2] The tax and public expenditure programme generally involves redistribution from richer regions to poorer ones, whether as an automatic consequence of a progressive tax and social security system or as specific acts of policy. The redistribution acts as a stabilizer with negative shocks leading to lower taxation and higher social security payments in the region adversely affected. With the removal of exchange rate varia- tions as an adjustment mechanism, it could be expected that economies would adjust to differential shocks and economic perfor- mance through a variety of other routes. These would include (in response to a negative shock) declines in economic activity, reduc- tions in living standards and outward migration. There is then a requirement for the development of a larger EU tax base within a progressive tax system and the use of the tax revenue in a redistrib- utive manner.

The problem of unemployment will be particularly serious in those cases where governments have chosen the wrong exchange rate at entry. An overvalued entry exchange rate will mean an extended period of recession to accommodate its effects, which emanate from the absence of the adjustable exchange rate safety valve. This is accentuated by the virtual absence of fiscal transfers, whether automatic or discretionary, from the relatively rich regions to the relatively poor ones. There is clearly not a tax and social security system operating at the European Union level which would make transfers between rich and poor in an automatic manner and to provide an element of fiscal stabilization. The expenditures on regional aid (structural and cohesion funds) and to a lesser degree agricultural policies do make some transfers from rich to poor, but on a very limited scale. In short, the European budget is neither on a sufficient scale nor of the right design to provide significant interregional insurance in the EMU (Fatas 1998).

Conclusions

We have raised serious concerns in this chapter of Britain's joining the EMU and thereby adopting the euro. We have concerns over the institutional framework supporting the euro, especially those relating to the ECB and the Stability and Growth Pact, as we have repeatedly argued elsewhere too (see, for example, Arestis, Brown and Sawyer 2001). In this chapter, however, we have emphasized the deleterious effects of Britain's joining at the wrong exchange rate, as 20th-century experience demonstrated vividly. We have suggested the conditions under which it would be in Britain's interest to join the euro. They inevitably imply different policies and different institutional arrangements from what we have had so far for the EMU. The main thrust of these suggestions is the avoidance of chronic unemployment, so that the objective of achieving and maintaining high levels of employment becomes realistic and of top priority within the EMU.

Notes

1 Eligible liabilities are: overnight deposits; deposits with agreed maturity up to 2 years; deposits redeemable at notice up to 2 years; debt securities issued with agreed maturity up to 2 years; and money market paper.

2 The CFA zone in Francophone West Africa is an exception.

References

Arestis, P. and Sawyer, M. (1998) 'New Labour, new monetarism', *Soundings*, 9, pp. 24–42; reprinted in *European Labour Forum* (1998–99), 20, pp. 5–10.

Arestis, P., Brown, A. and Sawyer, M. (2001) *The Euro: Evolution and Prospects*. Aldershot: Edward Elgar.

Arestis, P., McCauley, K. and Sawyer, M. (2001) 'An alternative stability pact for the European Union', *Cambridge Journal of Economics*, 25, 1, pp. 113–30.

Arestis, P., Biefang-Frisancho Mariscal, I., Brown, A. and Sawyer, M. (2002) 'Causes of euro instability', this volume, Chapter 6.

Bayoumi, T. and Eichengreen, B. (1995) 'Restraining yourself: the implications of fiscal rules for economic stabilisation', *Staff Papers*, International Monetary Fund, 42, 1, pp. 32–48.

Begg, I. and Green, D. (1998) 'The political economy of the central bank', in P. Arestis and M. C. Sawyer (eds) *The Political Economy of Central Banking*. Cheltenham: Edward Elgar.

Church, K. (1999) 'Properties of the fundamental equilibrium exchange rate in the Treasury model', *National Institute Economic Review*, July.

Currie, D. (1997) *The Pros and Cons of EMU*. London: HM Treasury.

Eichengreen, B. (1997) *European Monetary Unification: Theory, Practice and Analysis*. Cambridge, MA: MIT Press.

Eichengreen, B. and Wyplosz, C. (1998) 'The Stability Pact: more than a minor nuisance?', in D. Begg, J. von Hagen, C., Wyplosz and K. F. Zimmermann (eds) *EMU: Prospects and Challenges for the Euro*. Oxford: Blackwell.

European Commission (MacDougall Report) (1977) *Report of the Study Group on the Role of Public Finance in European Integration*. Brussels: European Commission.

European Commission (EC) (1998) *EURO 1999, Convergence Report*. Brussels: European Commission.

Fatas, A. (1998) 'Does EMU need a fiscal federation?', *Economic Policy*, 26, pp. 163–203.

Krugman, P. (1989) 'The case for stabilizing exchange rates', *Oxford Review of Economic Policy*, 5, pp. 61–72.

Monetary Policy Committee (1999) *The Transmission Mechanism of Monetary Policy*. London: Bank of England.

OECD (1998) *Economic Outlook*, December. Paris: OECD.

Rogoff, K. (1996) 'The purchasing power parity puzzle', *Journal of Economic Literature*, 34, 2, pp. 647–68.

von Hagen, J. and Eichengreen, B. (1996) 'Federalism, fiscal restraints and European Monetary Union', *American Economic Review*, AEA Papers and Proceedings, 86, 2, pp. 134–38.

10

UK banking and other financial services and the euro

Iain Begg and Sara Horrell

Introduction

The financial services sector has long been regarded as one of the jewels in the crown of the UK economy. Earnings from the City of London, in particular, have offset the relative long-run decline of manufacturing, and the prospects for financial services have been singled out in the chancellor's five economic tests for whether EMU membership is in the country's interest (HM Treasury 1997).

British ambivalence about European integration has been evident since the early

> Britain has championed the establishment of a single market for financial services, yet remains suspicious of the single currency

moves in the 1950s to construct what is now the EU. On the whole, the UK has been much more comfortable with measures to promote free trade than with monetary integration or 'deepening' of economic integration (Begg and Wood 2000). Banking, however, is in a curious position. Britain has championed the establishment of a single market for financial services, yet remains suspicious of the single currency, seen by many as the key to a genuinely integrated European financial area (see, for example, Trichet 2001).

As the EU has become more integrated, both formally (the Treaty on European Union and the various legally binding directives agreed at EU level) and as a result of market-led changes in industry structure, there has been a gradual but persistent trend towards integration of EU financial markets. Technological change and deregulation elsewhere have reinforced these trends and contributed to an intensification of competition at the European level (European Central Bank 1999a; White 1998). Yet, paradoxically, cross-border mergers and penetration of national markets by competitors from other EU member states have been conspicuous more by their absence than by their frequency (Altunbas and Chakravarty 1998; Danthine et al. 1999).

This chapter assesses the competitiveness of the UK financial services industry, focusing especially on its position within the EU, and considers how the advent of the euro might alter the picture. The next section presents summary statistics on the competitive strengths of UK financial services. This is followed by a comparison of the UK with other EU member states. We then turn to the impact of EMU and go on to sketch two scenarios for the possible evolution of UK financial services as EMU is consolidated. Concluding remarks complete the chapter.

The UK's competitive strength in financial services

The relative strength of any industry can be measured in a variety of ways, including shares of national output, rates of growth or net export performance. Strength in depth can also be ascertained from looking at the range of sub-sectors in the industry and their relative competitive positions. Starting with output, the entire financial and business services sector has been one of the most dynamic parts of the UK economy in recent years. From 1983 to 2000, the gross value added of the sector grew by 88.8 per cent, while the whole economy grew by 55.3 per cent and manufacturing by just 33.9 per cent. More disaggregated data suggest that the core financial services (banking and other credit institutions; insurance and securities) have not been as dynamic as the other segments of business services, especially in the last decade, but they have still been an important source of growth. Between 1990 and 2000, the output of 'financial intermediation' increased by 18.8 per cent, three times as fast as manufacturing, while the other parts of business services grew by two-thirds.

Employment figures also emphasize the vital contribution of financial and business services: between 1980 and 2000, employment in the sector rose by 80 per cent. By contrast manufacturing contracted, losing 42 per cent of its jobs between 1980 and 2000, while overall employment in the economy grew by just 3.8 per cent. The impact on the relative magnitudes is also striking. In 1980, the UK economy supported two and a half times as many jobs in manufacturing as in financial and business services. By the end of 1996, however, the level of employment in the two sectors was identical and there are now only 82 jobs in manufacturing for every 100 in financial and business services. Furthermore, the sector shows faster growth of labour productivity and total factor productivity than found for manufacturing or the whole economy in the recent past (see Table 10.1), emphasizing its importance as a source of growth.

Table 10.1 | Relative performance of financial services

	Whole economy	Manufacturing	Financial services
Growth of value added 1992–7 %, constant prices	8.6	13.5	16.7
% change in labour productivity (GDP/no. employed) 1992–7	2.4	11.3	17.8
% change in total factor productivity 1992–7	2.0	12.4	14.3

Source: National Statistics

UK trade in financial services

Detailed data on trade in services have only recently been published, making long-run comparisons on a consistent basis problematic. However, even a cursory look at these statistics shows that financial services make an important contribution to the UK's net exports. Exports of financial services constituted more than 10 per cent of total service exports in 1998 and, although only 0.8 per cent of GDP, the very small size of imports means that there is a substantial payment surplus. Moreover, exports of financial services grew 2.6 per cent in nominal terms between 1997 and 1998, the only two years for which data are available, while imports declined by 6.6 per cent resulting in a 2.9 per cent improvement in the trade balance. The share of financial services exported to the EU in 1998 was 34.7 per cent, up from 30.4 per cent the previous year, with particular increases evident in exports to France, the Netherlands, Belgium and Luxembourg (Figure 10.1). Against this, most of the decline in imports has been in financial services from the EU, 18.8 per cent of the total to 13.6 per cent. Although not too much can be read into two years' data, the difference in the magnitudes testifies to the competitive strength of the UK relative to its EU partners. There has been a corresponding drop in the share, and absolute amount, exported to North America, 31.8 per cent to 28.3 per cent, over the same period and it should be noted that other countries still constitute over a third of Britain's export market.

Longer-term trends exhibit similar growth but also highlight functions which have expanded in the recent past (Figure 10.2). The earnings of securities dealers and money market brokers have grown particularly fast between 1992 and 1998 (Figure 10.3), although fund managers' earnings have also grown faster than financial service exports as a whole. The earnings of banks, the largest individual sector, grew 56.0 per cent over the six years. In the recent past, 1997–98, this growth of the earnings of UK banks has been particularly evident for the EU. The net balance grew 66.9 per cent in nominal terms and the share sold to the EU grew from 25.4 per cent

Figure 10.1 | Exports of financial services by destination (% of total)

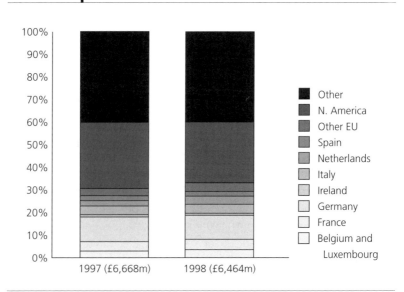

1997 (£6,668m)   1998 (£6,464m)

Other
N. America
Other EU
Spain
Netherlands
Italy
Ireland
Germany
France
Belgium and Luxembourg

Figure 10.2 | Exports of financial services by type (% of total)

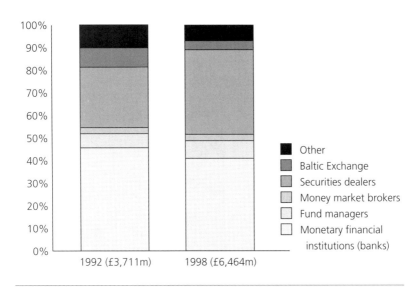

Figure 10.3 | Growth in financial service exports, 1992–98

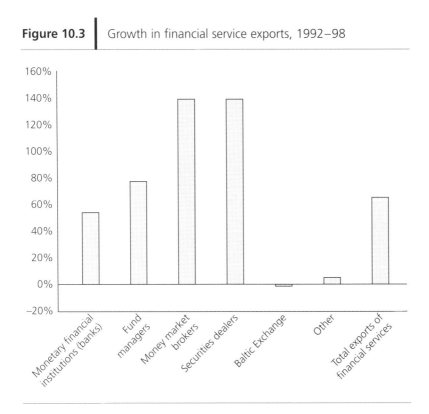

to 37.5 per cent (Figure 10.4). Again the earnings from Belgium and Luxembourg, the Netherlands and France showed the highest growth. All this suggests advancement and competitive strength in the UK financial services sectors in recent years.

Figure 10.4 | Service earnings of UK banks by destination (net credits, % of total)

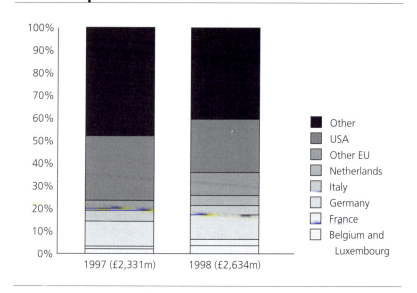

Banking in the UK and the rest of the EU compared

Differences in banking law, accountancy standards, market structures and regulation conspire to make direct comparisons of banks in different countries problematic. Both the OECD and Eurostat (the statistical office of the EU) have, however, made attempts to collect consistent data on banking and these are used in this section to compare the UK with the rest of the EU. It should be noted that despite efforts at harmonization of definitions, some of the figures need to be interpreted with caution.

Industry restructuring

Alongside the creation of a single market in financial services and the use of a single currency, the banking and finance sector has also been subject to forces for change from new technology, demographic pressures, concern for shareholder value and the altered role of the state in bank affairs. All these lead to an expectation of rationalization and increased efficiency within banking in Europe. Simple comparisons give the impression that continental European banks tend to be too small and have too many branches, so that they are ripe for concentration (White 1998).

The most obvious difference between the banking sectors in the UK and other larger EU countries is the number of credit institutions (Table 10.2). Germany, in particular, has a large complement of smaller banks with the result that its total number of banks is more than six times as high as in the UK, for a population just over one-third higher. The UK also stands out for the relatively low number of branches relative to population, the result not just of earlier rationalization but also of more rapid development of new forms of service delivery.

> Simple comparisons give the impression that continental European banks tend to be too small and have too many branches

It is particularly striking that small banks appear to retain a great deal of local monopoly power in other EU countries (de Bandt and Davis

Table 10.2 | Numbers of banks, branches and bank employees in EU countries

	Number of credit institutions 1999	Branches per million population 1999	Change in branches per capita 1990–99	Employees per thousand population 1999	Change in employees per capita 1990–99
			%		%
France	1,143	430	−4	7.03	−8
Germany	3,167	540	−14	9.22	−17
Italy	876	470	+51	5.99	0
Spain	383	1,000	+20	6.25	+1
Netherlands	101	400	−26	9.39	+19
UK	494	260*	−26*	8.26	−23

Note: Latest year 1998
Source: ECB 2000a

1999, p. 17). They also show that 'well over 80% of German and Italian banks have assets of under $1 billion, suggesting widespread inefficient scale' (p. 20). It remains the case that two-thirds of the income of the largest banks in the EU is earned in their home countries, with the balance evenly split between other EU countries and the rest of the world (Economic and Financial Committee 2000). But one of the paradoxes of European integration in financial services is that although it has promoted some rationalization, the bulk of this has occurred within rather than between member states. In 1998 there remained 8618 banks in the EU, representing a drop of 13 per cent since 1994 (Eurostat 2000). The numbers had fallen in 12 member states and the highest decreases were recorded in France, Portugal, Belgium and Spain. Although the number of mergers and acquisitions has tended to grow, only a relatively small proportion of the deals have been cross-border (ECB 2000a). Furthermore, similar tendencies have been observed elsewhere: the USA had a 16 per cent fall in the number of banks and Switzerland an 11 per cent fall, over the same period. Thus consolidation cannot be primarily attributed to integration and the introduction of the euro.

There has been relatively less merger and acquisition activity in the UK than in the other larger EU countries, reflecting the relatively more concentrated ownership of financial intermediaries. Thus, in the latter half of the 1990s, there were just 16 mergers or acquisitions per year in the UK, compared with 55 in France, 60 in Italy and 169 in Germany (ECB 2000a). However, the share of total assets held by the five biggest banks is relatively low in the UK at 29 per cent in 1999, compared with an EU average (unweighted) of 57 per cent, although the corresponding figures for the other larger member states are also below the average, at 48 per cent in Italy, 43 per cent in France and just 19 per cent in Germany (ECB 2000a).

The rationalization that has occurred may put some larger European banks in a position to benefit from the single currency and harmonized rules, but some observers still consider them less well placed than their US competitors. US mergers in investment banking have increasingly combined global producers of financial products with large distribution networks, making them a strong competitive force. Additionally, US banks may find it easier to capitalize on the advent of the euro as they have 'pan-European capabilities and mindset in greater measure than universal European banks' (White 1998, p. 22). At the retail level the large, global banks, such as Citicorp and, arguably, notionally UK banks such as HSBC, are also considered capable of taking on European markets, particularly if customers are willing to forgo traditional branch banking in favour of electronic transactions. Although the UK banking sector may exhibit more restructuring than its continental European counterparts, it will still have to compete in local markets with these global giants.

Prices, profitability and competition

European monetary union is likely to exacerbate the existing competitive trends and add impetus to rationalization, internationalization and geographical diversification with associated pressure on profit margins. Cost–income ratios should decrease as efficiency is increased and income and profit from foreign exchange wholesale activities will be reduced (ECB 1999a). However, British banks seem to be more profitable than their continental European counterparts (Table 10.3), a position that arises more from greater income-earning opportunities rather than lower costs.

Despite the large number of banks, there is some evidence of an increase in five-firm concentration ratios (Danthine *et al.* 1999; Economic Research Europe 1997), especially in the smaller member states. The growth in entry by foreign banks into many markets offsets any adverse effect of concentration in national markets and it can be argued that banking has in general become more competitive. This is reflected in a narrowing of intermediation margins, and has encouraged banks to diversify and to seek complementary income sources. In more mature

Table 10.3 | Bank profitability

		Large commercial banks			Switzerland	
	UK commercial	USA	Germany	France	Large commercial	Foreign
Operating expenses	63.8	64.2	66.4	74.6	58.3	57.8
Of which						
Staff costs	35.2	26.9	44.2	43.1	34.9	36.5
Profit						
Before tax	23.1	28.2	17.6	7.2	11.2	20.5
After tax	14.8	18.5	11.6	3.5	8.2	15.5
No. institutions included						
in 1996	44	100	3	5	4	141

Note: Figures averaged for 1992–96 and calculated as % gross income
Source: OECD, Financial statements of banks (1998)

financial markets, such as the UK, nearly 45 per cent of banking system gross income was generated from non-interest income sources by 1996. The ratio is either above or close to 40 per cent in other member states: Austria (38.7 per cent), France (39.4 per cent), and Sweden (42 per cent). However, much lower ratios elsewhere (Denmark with a ratio of 17.7 per cent and Spain 24.3 per cent, for example) show that there is still scope for diversification.

The single market

Before completion of the Single European Market the Cecchini Report (CEC 1988) identified the likely effects on prices of financial services across Europe. By comparing the price in each country of a variety of products with the lowest prices charged, it identified areas where increased openness and competition could result in improvements in efficiency and gains for customers. The UK came out of this comparison quite well. Although smaller price reductions could theoretically be available in Belgium, Luxembourg and the Netherlands (Table 10.4), it was only in the Netherlands that it was thought plausible that prices would see a smaller reduction.

The report identified products and market segments in the UK industry which either looked vulnerable to competition from EC producers or conveyed a competitive advantage for the UK in Europe. On this basis, mortgages were 20 per cent below the average in the UK

Table 10.4 | Potential falls in financial product prices as a result of completing the internal market

	Theoretical potential price reduction in banking (%)	Plausible price reduction (%)
Belgium	15	11
Germany	33	10
Spain	34	21
France	25	12
Italy	18	14
Luxembourg	16	8
Netherlands	10	4
UK	18	7

Source: Price Waterhouse, *European Economy*, 35, 1988.

and consumer credit was relatively expensive. The UK's prospects for expansion in corporate and wholesale finance and mortgage markets with completion of the internal market looked good, but any retail banking expansion was thought to be limited to specific product lines (Humphries *et al.* 1992). How have these positions evolved?

Subsequent work in a follow-up study of the effects of the single market (summarized in Monti 1996) was much less sanguine than Cecchini about the overall impact, claiming just a one percentage point increase in EU GDP, rather than 4–6 per cent. A study carried out for the European Commission as part of this review found that substantial differences in the costs of banking persist across member states (Economic Research Europe 1997). Although the study noted some increase in activity, it highlighted the dearth of cross-border activity involving larger banks. Instead, the main form of cross-border activity has been the acquisition by relatively large banks of smaller institutions, while most of the consolidation through mergers within member states have been adjudged to have been largely defensive. Competitive pressures have, however, obliged banks to focus on improving both their productive efficiency and their overall risk/return efficiency. Within countries, different institutional factors continue to characterize European banking systems (Altunbas and Chakravarty 1998).

Nevertheless, a recent comparison of bank margins and profitability for countries in the euro area (ECB 2000b) showed quite considerable reductions in margins on new lending to households and corporations since 1998 in most countries. Comparable figures for the UK revealed a similar trend. Lending margins had been reduced, most markedly to the personal sector in the area of consumer credit, but this was the continuation of a trend through the 1990s. In the euro area, deposit margins showed a different, u-shaped pattern that was largely due to short-term rates and which left overall margins more stable.

The narrowing of lending margins has been attributed to the ongoing tightening of pricing conditions owing to competition. Although some of this has occurred as a consequence of deregulation and the introduction of the euro, recent new entrants into, and technological developments in, the banking market have also intensified competition. For instance, in the UK the entry of foreign banks into both personal and corporate markets has been observed, supermarkets and insurance companies are offering banking services to households and internet and telephone banking developments have started to offer lower-cost banking facilities to many. These trends started in the UK in the mid-1990s and have been important in creating the squeeze on lending margins. In other European countries the advent of these types of competition is not always so evident. Only a few countries have had recent new entrants into the corporate sector and many have had no major entrants in the personal sector. The response of UK banks to these competitive forces has been to compete harder on price terms but also to segment the market in order to keep the most profitable customers. The entry of foreign banks into European markets suggests that regional cross-border competition is tightening in Europe, with the Nordic countries, the UK and Ireland being the clearest examples of where this is occurring. UK banks have encountered and adapted to new competitive pressures for some years

> In the UK supermarkets and insurance companies are offering banking services to households and internet and telephone banking developments have started to offer lower-cost banking facilities

and appear as able as any in Europe to respond to the changed conditions ushered in by the single currency.

London as a financial centre

London remains the pre-eminent financial centre in Europe and, although Britain's ambivalence about successive stages in European integration has regularly been cited as a threat to its position, it shows little sign of succumbing to the competition. However, London's main rival, Frankfurt, has undoubtedly been boosted by the location there of the European Central Bank, while certain other financial centres have managed to boost their shares of activity in niche areas such as fund management (Luxembourg and Dublin) or financial futures (Paris).

A survey of the prospects for European capital markets (Seifert *et al.* 2000) compares the positions of London, Frankfurt and Paris and shows the continued strong position of London. In terms of presence, London dominates. The Euromoney Bank Register (1999) indicates that London has nearly 5000 senior investment staff to Frankfurt's and Paris's 1000 apiece and nearly 1000 wholesale bank institutions to around 200 in each of the other centres. Possibly over half of the establishments in London are foreign banking institutions. In terms of performance of different financial products in the recent past the picture is more shaded. In products which are essentially homoge-neous, globalized and traded without substantial market infrastructure London has continued to dominate and has even increased its share and lead. Thus foreign exchange trading, cross-border lending, OTC derivatives and fixed-income trading continue to be centred in London. Continental successes such as German growth in OTC derivatives exist but have made little impact on the overall position. However, other products which rely more on local infrastructure, such as exchange-traded derivatives, equity trading and clearing and settlement, have shown greater gains for the European capital markets, particularly Frankfurt. Here the early adoption of electronic technology for trading, the development of a fully integrated stock exchange and encour-agement to other smaller, European stock exchanges to use this infra-structure have helped establish Frankfurt as a serious rival to London.

A third category of products – asset management, equity issuance and merger and acquisition advisors – contains a locational component relying on close knowledge of customers' requirements and the cultural and institutional constraints under which they operate. London, again, continues to lead in these product areas by a wide margin but the local nature of the business provides an opportunity for domestic providers to build up an expertise and capitalize in these areas. Indeed expansion has occurred, aided by both industrial restruc-turing and the launch of the euro. However, the trends are not all in one direction. Although the single currency, more liberal regulatory regimes and changes in corporate governance may all encourage business for local providers of financial services, the common currency has also encouraged a move away from country-based research, analysis and trading in equity and fixed-income sales. Instead teams now cover industrial and product sectors or sell by maturity date across geographical boundaries. London has moved rapidly to establish itself along these lines, such that by 1999 in the region of two-thirds of insti-tutional investors had moved to a sectoral approach. Furthermore London is recognized to have advantages of critical mass in terms of large numbers of practitioners, which encourages innovation, shared knowledge and continuing expertise, as well as the establishment of dedicated support services, in addition to its favourable tax and regulatory regimes. Thus London can benefit from the tendency of the single currency to have teams covering all of the EMU area from one location.

The report by Seifert et al. (2000) summarizes the competitive profiles of the three European financial centres across products. The UK has more than 50 per cent of the market share in six out of the nine product categories considered, is positioned first for seven of these products and has gained market share in some high-growth areas. Although Germany and, to a lesser extent, France have capitalized on the market changes occurring in these countries and achieved rapid growth in M&A activity and equity issuance, overall London's lead is lengthening. It concludes: 'London is the only truly international centre, exporting financial services on a vast scale, while also being largely self-sufficient in satisfying the demands of domestic clients. Frankfurt, and to a lesser extent, Paris, are its major clients' (Seifert *et al.* 2000, p. 87).

Indicators produced in a study for the Corporation of London (2000) show the importance of EU markets for the City of London and the significant contribution of the latter to the EU economy. According to the report, some 60,700 jobs in the City depended on demand from other EU countries, just over 20 per cent of total employment. The ratio is higher for international banking, corporate finance, derivatives trading and international equities, in which one in three jobs depends on EU demand. There is also a substantial presence of banks from other EU countries in the City, with 24 based in Germany and 13 from France out of an FII total of 108 in 1999. The report notes that around 10 per cent of City activity is denominated in the currencies of other EU countries. Because hardly any of the business is 'crosses' between currencies that now form the euro, the report dismisses fears that the jobs will be at risk from the introduction of the euro.

The report attempts to measure the impact of the City of London on the EU economy by assessing what would happen if the 'City-type' business currently disproportionately concentrated in London were to be dispersed. Although this exercise is necessarily somewhat speculative, the fact that over half of the relevant business is already concentrated in London means that the magnitudes involved are large. The calculations suggest that fragmentation of the business would lead to a loss of activity to non-EU financial centres and could result in a loss of GDP for the EU of just under 0.2 per cent.

Asset management and institutional investors

Detailed trade figures suggest a competitive strength for the UK in the area of fund management. Indeed, Danthine *et al.* (1999) argue that asset management is one area of financial services that is expected to become more Europeanized with the advent of the euro. In particular, they point out the potential for the achievement of economies of scale in this function, precipitating considerable merger and acquisition activity. Economies of scale can be realized through the acquisition of an increased stock of assets under management which more fully utilizes the human capital and expertise of a team of fund managers. Cross-border mergers are also encouraged. Managed assets and knowledge both tend to have a local bias, while cross-border acquisitions both increase and diversify the assets under management and the range of expertise within the team. Some evidence for this type of merger is already evident (Table 10.5). In recent years the amount of cross-border M&A activity among financial institutions has been greater than that within Europe, although a considerable amount of intra-European consolidation of banks is also evident.

The introduction of the euro will add a further impetus to cross-

Table 10.5 European M&A deals, 1985–97 (given as % of all M&A deals in sector, valued in US$bn)

| | Target institution | | | |
| | Intra-Europe | | Europe–non-Europe | |
Acquiring institution	Bank	Securities	Bank	Securities
Bank	44	26	29	9
Securities	13	17	31	31
Total value	33.8		50.3	

Source: Danthine *et al.* (1999, p. 55)

border consolidation of this function. Regulatory restrictions on the portfolio composition of pension and insurance funds across much of Europe have constrained fund managers in both the type and the currency denomination of assets in which they must invest. Prudential requirements for large proportions of assets to be held in the same currency as liabilities currently constrain many funds to assets denominated in the local currency (see Table 10.6). The use of the euro will allow these funds to expand to the European-wide holding of assets and some relaxation on rules about type of asset may also encourage a switch from government bonds into European equities. Such a move will be facilitated by the emergence of European-wide stock indices and, possibly in the future, a European stock market.

UK and US fund managers will be well placed to benefit from this diversification into European-wide stocks. The much less restrictive 'prudent man' regulation currently imposed on institutional investors in these countries means that fund managers already have wide experience of investing in foreign countries and equities (Table 10.7). Institutional investors manage a large proportion of the UK's wealth. Over two-thirds of the holdings for which they are responsible are held in equities and, in 1995, approximately 26 per cent was held in foreign equities.

The importance of institutional investment in the UK can be seen

Table 10.6 | Regulations governing institutional investors

Maximum % that insurance companies can invest in given classes of investment (non-life)		
	Foreign shares	Foreign bonds and other securities
France	65	—
Germany	6	5
Switzerland	25	20
UK	—	—
USA (Jersey)	restricted by size of liabilities in foreign countries	
USA (Delaware)	5	5

Summary of pension fund restrictions	
France	50% EU public bonds, no foreign assets
Germany	guidelines: 30% max. EU shares, 6% non-EU bonds, 20% foreign assets
UK	prudent management, 5% max. self-investment
USA	prudent management

Indication of maximum investment in foreign bonds and shares, assuming prudent management rules would allow 100% and equal sized pension and insurance funds	
France	41.3%
Germany	16.8%
UK	100%
USA	52.5%

Source: Constructed from OECD, *Financial Market Trends*, 71, November 1998

Table 10.7 | Institutional investors' financial assets, 1995

	Assets as % GDP	% held in equities
UK	162	69
France	75	22
Germany	46	12
USA	171	36

Source: OECD, *Economic Surveys, UK* (1998)

from the share register analysis (Table 10.8). Well over half of UK shares are held by institutional investors. Although these investors are the main players in the market, the main increase in recent years has been by overseas investors at the expense of individuals and companies. The USA constitutes some 51.1 per cent of these overseas shareholdings, the EU only 20.3 per cent.

Although not strictly comparable, the OECD figures for institutional

Table 10.8 | UK share register analysis, trends 1989–97 (%)

	1989	1994	1997
Total institutional investors	57.8	59.8	56.3
Of which			
Pensions and insurance	49.2	49.7	45.6
Overseas	12.8	16.3	24.0
Individuals	20.6	20.3	16.5
Other (charities and private non-financial			
companies)	8.8	3.6	3.2

Source: OECD, *Economic Surveys, UK* (1998); Hill (1999, pp. 31–53)

investors' shares of stock markets again demonstrate the much greater involvement of fund managers in equity trading in the UK than in some other European countries (Table 10.9). Business may come to the UK and US fund managers from Europe or their assets under management may be increased by acquisition. Alternatively cross-border mergers may make these teams an attractive acquisition, although the benefits of London as a location may mean business continues to be conducted within the UK, albeit by fund managers employed by non-UK banks and financial institutions.

Fund management activities could be further expanded as European

Table 10.9	Institutional investors' share of stock markets (%, mid-1997)

USA	UK	France	Germany
47.4	76.5	39.8	39.0

Source: OECD, *Economic Surveys, UK* (1998)

populations become more financially sophisticated. Currently the UK and USA have large proportions of their household assets managed by institutional investors. Most continental European countries have some considerable distance to go before similar levels are achieved (Table 10.10).

Table 10.10	Household assets managed by institutional investors (% total household assets, 1995)
France	27.3
Germany	28.9
Italy	9.0
Spain	24.4
UK	52.0
USA	45.0

Source: IMF (1997); Danthine *et al.* (1999, p. 67)

Consumer 'literacy' and sophistication

Indeed a breakdown for some countries of the types of wealth held and an index of 'financial literacy' (taken from Seifert *et al.* 2000, pp. 72–5) indicates the greater sophistication of the UK market with UK fund managers potentially being well placed to benefit from any increased involvement of household customers in investment activities.

Although total wealth holdings show some variation across countries the differences in holdings of financial assets are far more dramatic (Table 10.11). While US and UK households hold more than half their wealth in the form of financial assets, French and German investors appear more inclined to hold 'real' wealth, such as real estate. The returns on total wealth holdings reflect this mix. Returns are higher in the USA and, overall, the UK than found for the two European

Table 10.11 | Measures of consumer sophistication

	USA	UK	Germany	France
Total household wealth as % income, 1997	594	559	513	465
% wealth held in financial assets, 1997	64	60	28	45
Real returns on all assets				
Average 1985–97	3.0%	1.8%	N/A	0.4%
Average 1993–97	4.0%	0.8%	0.6%	0.4%
Leverage ratio (%)				
(financial assets/net financial wealth)	27.1	33.3	53.1	33.3
Savings rate (%)	2.2	11.0	11.0	14.6
Equity holdings (%)	61.5	48.9	4.9	43.5
Financial literacy index[a]	19	13	7	9

Note: [a] Financial literacy index constructed as rank score for each of the preceding three components (4 = highest, 1 = lowest with high saving and leverage taken to indicate higher costs and risks to the household respectively) plus the percentage of wealth held in financial assets and the percentage of assets held by institutions (from Table 10.10)

Sources: Constructed from OECD, *Economic Outlook* (1997); Seifert *et al.* (2000, pp. 69, 71, 74)

comparators. European investors appear to be missing opportunities. Measures of 'financial literacy' indicate that this does not arise because of inadequate leverage or low savings rates but instead appears to be related to levels of equity holdings and the involvement of institutional investors. The construction of a 'financial literacy' index demonstrates a clear correlation between the sophistication of investment channels open to households and rates of return on all assets.

But the importance of institutional investment in the USA and UK has not evolved in isolation. Tax relief on some retirement plans, various types of tax-exempt saving and investment schemes and wider holdings of equities encouraged by government privatization schemes and demutualizations have all encouraged increased access to and availability of more fruitful investment instruments to households. Similar moves on the continent, for instance the introduction of AS-mutual funds targeted at retirement saving in Germany, may point to opportunities for the alert institutional investor.

It can also be argued that one of the reasons that UK banking has done well is that the effects of competition have made consumers both more aware of opportunities and more willing to embrace new forms of product delivery. There is some suggestion that the UK is ahead of the game in, for instance, telephone and internet banking (ECB 1999h) while data on use of cards also support the view that UK consumers lead the way (Table 10.12).

Table 10.12 | Use of bank cards, 1997

	Cash cards, number per 1000 population	Change 1993–97 (%)	Debit or credit cards, number per 1000 population	Change 1993–97 (%)
France	515	36	473	27
Germany	N/A	N/A	1038	88
Italy	301	55	426	52
Netherlands	1540	80	163	98
Spain	910	9	897	8
UK	1641	27	1271	43
EU	741	33	786	41

Source: ECB (1999b)

Likely impact of EMU

There can be little doubt that monetary union will substantially c
the picture. Since the beginning of 2001, when Greece acceded, all 12
member states that wanted to be part of the single currency bloc were
'in', while the three that are reluctant (Denmark, Sweden and the UK)
look as though they will remain 'out' for the foreseeable future. A
recent report by the European Central Bank concludes:

> EMU is likely to act in the medium and long term as a catalyst to
> reinforce already prevailing trends in the EU banking systems. In
> particular, EMU is expected to reinforce the pressure for the
> reduction of existing excess capacity, to put profitability under
> pressure and to lead to increased internationalisation and
> geographical diversification, also outside EMU, as well as to
> increased conglomeration and mergers and acquisitions (ECB
> 1999a, p. 1)

The analysis in the report also anticipates a significant increase in
competition in banking within the euro area. Not surprisingly, the ECB
believes that a stable monetary environment will favour the banking
sector.

British experience to date is that the City has continued to prosper
outside the eurozone and, judging by the sanguine pronouncements
by the Governor of the Bank of England who said in September 2000
that 'the City of London is already making an important contribution
to this process of euro financial market integration', the outlook
remains favourable. However, the nature of the integrated financial
area will depend on how the rules governing financial intermediaries
evolve.

EU rules

Formally, it is in relation to the single market rather than the single
currency that the rules governing the financial services sector evolve,
although prudential supervision is explicitly mentioned as a function
that the ECB may become involved in (see Begg and Green 1996). In
essence, the regulatory regime for financial services that has evolved in
the EU is one that puts the onus on the member state in which a
financial intermediary is based to ensure that it is properly supervised
and regulated. Once the entity has acquired the so-called 'passport' it
is, in principle, free to conduct business in other EU member states. This

approach stems from the pro-competitive orientation of the single market in which the emphasis was on levelling the playing field. In practice, the degree of integration of markets for many financial services is much more limited, although a distinction has to be drawn between the wholesale markets and retail financial services aimed at final consumers.

> Once the entity has acquired the so-called 'passport' it is, in principle, free to conduct business in other EU member states

Recognizing that there is still some way to go before there is a genuine single market for financial services in the EU, the Commission has launched a programme to achieve it by 2005 (European Council 2000). This was approved at the 2000 Lisbon European Council and since then the European Commission has tried to accelerate the implementation of the Financial Services Action Plan (FSAP), in order to meet the 2005 deadline set by heads of state and government. The most immediate priorities identified are to create a single wholesale market for financial services, open and secure retail markets, state-of-the-art prudential rules and wider conditions for an optimal single financial market across the EU.

To advance these aims, various directives are proposed and the Commission will also resort to other 'soft law' devices to promote market integration. The FSAP was given further impetus by the agreement at the March 2001 Stockholm Council at which proposals on regulation by a group chaired by Lamfalussy, the former President of the European Monetary Institute, were endorsed.

On the whole, these developments augur well for the UK. Other countries have traditionally had tougher regulation and market entry rules that deter foreign-owned financial intermediaries. In addition, because domestic measures to open up financial services occurred earlier in the UK than in most other countries, the country is at an advantage for two reasons. First, it has already been through a more extensive process of restructuring than other countries, so that the threats are lesser. Second, the developments that have taken place in the UK mean that many of its leading players are in a strong position to exploit opportunities that might arise. The risk for the UK is, however, that eurozone members will press for new rules that are less in the UK's interest.

It is widely forecast that bond trading will concentrate in a few core centres, such as Paris, Frankfurt and, especially, London. More generally, EMU will intensify competition and can be expected to expose excess capacity in the banking industry. The notion of excess capacity in banking is, as Davis and Salo (1998) show, not an easy one to define. Assuming that the forecasts are correct, excess capacity in European banking will manifest itself in two ways. First, profitability in the sector will fall; and, second, there will be strong incentives to rationalize. A tough fight for ascendancy will, therefore, ensue.

Effect on London as the leading EU financial centre

Prior to the launch of the euro there was concern about the effects on London. The single currency would have the benefit of creating a large, unified pool of investable funds. Continental firms are making more use of equity and bond financing and are expected to increasingly tap this source of funds. The predicted consequence of this was that capital market business would migrate to continental centres with euro-denominated business being conducted within the euro area. Certainly the introduction of the euro has created a larger, more integrated capital market for some products and growth in the issuance of European corporate and high-yield bonds has been observed, but much of this business has been managed out of London (Bank of England 2000). The City has for some time been adept at handling multiple currencies: prior to 1999 the London Stock Exchange was conducting transactions in nine currencies and consequently had no problem conducting business in euros. Indeed, a greater percentage of trading on the London Stock Exchange was conducted in euros than pounds in 2000 (Bank of England 2000, p. 25).

Furthermore, London's position in trading and researching equities and bonds has been enhanced by the introduction of the euro, and the reorientation of sectors and maturities has meant the trading of all countries off the same desk. Indeed, a recent Bank of England report finds that London has fully maintained its market share since the launch of the euro. In its survey of key market firms it observes that international treasury and risk management, euro foreign exchange, international bond and equity trading and research, M&A, equity issuance and international fund management operations all continue to be conducted from London. Some equity and M&A business has been won by competitors in the euro area and the influence of global fund managers from the US is growing (Bank of England 2000). But, overall, London has not been disadvantaged by the introduction of the single currency and its prospects look good. Most firms continue to believe that London's role as an international financial centre does not primarily depend on whether the UK is inside or outside EMU, but believe instead that London's position depends on remaining internationally competitive. Key factors in retaining this competitiveness are identified as excellent financial skills, talent and support services, low corporate and personal taxation, a lack of restrictive labour laws and a fair and appropriately light and responsive regulatory framework.

Are there reasons to doubt this optimism? One is that, progressively, indigenous ownership of the British financial sector has been diminishing. Investment banking is dominated by the major US players, although a number of continental 'universal banks' have made inroads. Similarly, some long-established insurance companies have been taken over by larger entities from continental Europe. Banking, however, remains largely under indigenous control as, indeed, it does in other EU countries, although various alliances and a sprinkling of cross-border mergers suggest that a significant degree of change is on the cards. However, in this sector competition from new entrants and new technologies is likely to have a greater impact on the outcome than the single currency.

Second, other financial centres are bound to contest London's dominant position. Frankfurt, in particular, has the considerable pull of being the centre of decision making on monetary policy. It clearly lacks London's agglomeration advantages and the very considerable benefits from being the market leader. The English language together with a favourable regulatory and fiscal environment reinforces these competitive attributes, but it is recognized that there is a threat (McRae and Cairncross 1991).

Third, while the government leaves open the option of joining the single currency, sentiment towards the UK will remain relatively positive. But if hesitation becomes procrastination and begins to look like opposition, other member states could begin to develop policies that are inimical to UK interests. This could occur in areas such as regulation or taxation as well as the general conduct of policy. One illustration of the likely tensions was the long-running dispute – now settled on terms acceptable to the UK – over an EU-wide withholding tax. This was consistently rejected by the UK because of the perceived harm it would do to the competitive position of London as a financial centre and the fear that the business would be lost to offshore financial centres where the tax did not apply. Spats have also occurred over the rules for capital adequacy, notably the claim by UK fund managers that ratios for banks are inappropriate for what is a much lower-risk activity and thus competitively damaging. Measures in the pipeline include a European company statute, corporate taxation and possible new rules on corporate governance.

The UK decision

In setting out five economic tests that would have to be met for Britain to join the single currency, Chancellor Brown, in October 1997, singled out the financial services sector. The fourth of the five poses the question (HM Treasury 1997, p.5): 'What impact would entry into the euro have on the competitive position of the UK's financial services industry, particularly the City's wholesale markets?'

Unlike with other countries which had to satisfy the convergence criteria in order to join, the Chancellor's five tests effectively reverse the burden of proof. Yet it is worth asking whether the outlook for financial services might, ultimately, be an obstacle. It seems to us that although it is possible to envisage circumstances in which the UK financial services industry would be disadvantaged outside the euro, it is much harder to see how it would lose were the UK to join the single currency, although changes in the regulatory regime may have an impact. It has been argued that the flexibility of the regulatory regime has been important

> ## Allowing for the political process and the time needed to prepare a conversion, the earliest plausible entry date is now 2004

for the City's success. The FSA could be more rigid but has as one of its objectives the protection of 'innovation and international competitiveness' in the City, an objective that does not feature in the statutes of regulators on the continent. Joining the euro may imperil this flexibility as continental bankers tend to prefer interventionist mechanisms that have sometimes severely disrupted markets. But, as argued earlier, changes that are antithetical to the UK's interests are more likely to occur if it remains outside the euro and the associated decision-making fora.

Scenarios

The UK's decision on whether or not to join the single currency is bound to be one of the key influences on how the UK financial sector evolves in the next few years. Allowing for the political process and the time needed to prepare a conversion, the earliest plausible entry date is now 2004. Equally, if public sentiment continues to be 'anti', a referendum could either be delayed for several years or, if it resulted in a 'no' vote as in Denmark, postpone entry indefinitely. It is therefore instructive to construct scenarios for what these opposed outcomes might mean for the British financial sector. Two such scenarios are elaborated:

- *Early entry* in which a decision is taken and implemented as quickly as possible and the UK commits itself not only to sign up to the single currency, but also to embrace it enthusiastically.
- *Staying at arms' length* with the UK retaining the pound indefinitely and resisting attempts to augment harmonization beyond what is needed to ensure a more competitive single market.

Under the *early entry* scenario, the government would move rapidly to assess the five economic tests and find that the balance of advantage was, indeed, in favour of the UK's joining the single currency. With the introduction of notes and coins from 2002, the task of convincing public opinion becomes easier and a referendum is comfortably won, allowing the UK to become a full player in the management of the euro, with Sweden and Denmark also acceding. For financial services, the outcome is to accelerate the consolidation of the single market and the consequent restructuring of the industry. Critical uncertainties about the impact include how the pan-European regulatory environment develops and whether competitive forces push financial business into or out of the EU.

The presence of the UK at the heart of EMU would be expected to make it more likely that regulation and corporate governance develop in a manner that suits the financial services industry in the UK. As a result, the UK should be able to maintain its leading position in the EU market and find it easier to see off the challenges to the City of London from Frankfurt, Paris and other possible rivals. On the other hand, pressures to harmonize corporate taxation might lead to compromises that undermine the cutting edge of the City of London in international finance, with the result that other global players gain. The balance of advantage for the UK is thus dependent on which of these two trends dominates.

The *staying at arms' length* scenario starts from the presumption that UK public opinion on the single currency does not respond to the government's efforts to convert it. As a result, the referendum is either shelved or lost, and there is a resurgence of euroscepticism. The eurozone countries conclude that they cannot wait any longer and decide to bring forward measures to develop the institutional framework of the single currency, notably in the area of prudential supervision. Clashes with the UK contribute to a volatile exchange rate between the pound and the euro and the UK is unable to prevent measures from being agreed with which it disagrees, although the overall pace of change is slowed.

Disputes over the evolution of EMU would be expected to raise doubts about the UK's commitment to the EU and deter some inward investment. Hitherto, the threat to inward investment has largely been perceived as applying to manufacturing, but in view of the growth in the share of financial and business services, it can be argued that risks would also arise in the latter sector. By the same token, by staying outside the euro, the UK would find it easier to maintain forms of regulation of financial services that stimulate innovation and thus contribute to competitiveness. As a result, opportunities will arise for gains in global markets that might compensate for any losses within the EU.

Conclusions

The UK financial services industry is the best developed, most diversified and, arguably, most competitive in the EU. It has the manifest advantages of the City of London in its role as Europe's number one global financial centre and of having a regulatory environment that has encouraged innovation and helped to sustain competitive advantage. Although there have, inevitably, been challenges to this ascendancy that have seen some segments of financial services lured away to other centres, the gravitational pull of agglomeration has easily offset these losses. Moreover, the capacity that the City has exhibited to reinvent itself has seen it accommodate far-reaching changes in the structure and ownership of financial and business services. As McRae and Cairncross (1991) note, 'to write a book about the City is to shoot at a moving target' (p.1).

This background suggests that whether the UK is 'in' or 'out' of the euro, its financial services sector will continue to be competitive and should maintain its leading role in the EU. This, however, is not a foregone conclusion.

References

Altunbas, Y. and Chakravarty, S. P. (1998) 'Efficiency measures and the banking structure in Europe', *Economic Letters*, 60, pp. 205–208.

Bank of England (2000) *Practical Issues Arising from the Euro*, November.

Begg, I. and Green, D. M. (1996) 'Banking supervision in Europe and economic and monetary union', *Journal of European Public Policy*, 3, pp. 381–401.

Begg, I. and Wood, M. (2000) 'The creation of the single market and Britain's withdrawal from the EMS' in K. Larres with E. Meehan (eds) *Uneasy Allies: British–German Relations and European Integration since 1945*. Oxford: Oxford University Press.

Commission of the European Communities (CEC) (1988) *The Costs of Non-Europe in Financial Services, Costs of Non-Europe*, Vol. 9. Luxembourg: Office for Official Publications of the European Communities.

Corporation of London (2002) *The City's Importance to the European Union Economy*. Report prepared by the Centre for Economics and Business Research (CEBR). London: Corporation of London.

Danthine, J.-P., Giavazzi, F., Vives, X. and von Thadden, E.-L. (1999) *The Future of European Banking*. London: CEPR.

Davis, E. P. and Salo, S. (1998) 'Excess capacity in EU and US banking sectors: conceptual, measurement and policy issues', LSE Financial Markets Group Special Paper 105.

De Bandt, O. and Davis, E. P. (1999) 'A cross-country comparison of market structures in European banking', European Central Bank Working Paper 7. Frankfurt: ECB.

Economic and Financial Committee (2000) 'Report on financial stability', Economic Paper 143. Brussels: Directorate-General for Economic and Financial Affairs, European Commission.

Economic Research Europe (1997) *A Study of the Effectiveness and Impact of Internal Market Integration on the Banking and Credit Sector*. London: Kogan Page.

European Central Bank (ECB) (1999a) *Possible Effects of EMU on the EU Banking System in the Medium to Long Term*. Frankfurt: ECB.

European Central Bank (ECB) (1999b) *The Effects of Technology on the EU Banking Systems*. Frankfurt: ECB.

European Central Bank (ECB) (2000a) *Mergers and Acquisitions Involving the EU Banking Industry – Facts and Implications*. Frankfurt: ECB.

European Central Bank (ECB) (2000b) *EU Banks' Margins and Credit Standards*. Frankfurt: ECB.

European Council (2000) Lisbon Presidency Conclusions.

European Council (2001) Stockholm Presidency Conclusions.

Eurostat (2000) 'EU banking: growing consolidation in a profitable sector', news release 117/2000, 13 October.

Hill, I. (1999) 'Ownership of UK quoted companies at the end of 1997', *Economic Trends*, February, pp. 31–3.

HM Treasury (1997) *UK Membership of the Single Currency: An Assessment of the Five Economic Tests*. London: HM Treasury.

Humphries, J., Horrell, S. and Rubery, J. (1992) 'The single European market and employment in the banking sector' in R. M. Lindley (ed.) *Women's Employment: Britain in the Single European Market*. London: HMSO.

IMF (1997) *International Capital Markets*. Washington, DC: IMF.

McRae, H. and Cairncross, F. (1991) *Capital City: London as a Financial Centre*. London: Methuen.

Monti, M. (1996) *The Single Market and Tomorrow's Europe*. London: Kogan Page.

Seifert, W. G., Achleitner, A.-K., Mattern, F., Streit, C. C. and Voth, H.-J. (2000) *European Capital Markets*. Basingstoke: Macmillan Business.

Trichet, J.-C. (2001) 'The euro after two years', *Journal of Common Market Studies*, 39, pp. 1–13.

White, W. R. (1998) 'The coming transformation of European banking', Bank for International Settlements Working Paper 54, June.

11

The UK, the EU budget and EMU[1]

Brian Ardy

Introduction

Problems with the EU budget loomed large during the UK's early membership of the EU. The UK problem was largely resolved by an agreement in 1984 (Council of the EC 1985) but the EU budget still rankles with sections of the British public and the media. Already it has been suggested that the budget will expand with EMU and that UK taxpayers could end up financing German pensions. Monetary unions

> **The EU budget still rankles with sections of the British public and the media**

historically have only persisted for nation states[2] (Bordo and Jonung 2000) and they are, therefore, associated with comparatively large federal/central government budgets. These budgets, besides financing the provision of government goods and services, also enable fiscal policy to be used to stabilize the economy and to transfer resources between different regions[3] within a country. Economic and monetary union (EMU) in the EU is different, as there is no federal government endowed with a large budget. EU member states have only ceded control over government expenditure and taxation reluctantly and to a very limited extent. Most EU policies have developed on the basis of creating a framework of legislation with little EU expenditure. This is true of EU policies such as EMU, the single market, environmental policy, competition policy etc.[4] EU expenditure is further limited by the fact that the operation of policies remains largely the responsibility of the member states.

This chapter examines the current UK position with the EU budget and how EMU may affect this. The analysis begins with a comparison between the EU budget and those of nation states, considering the rules under which it operates and the characteristics of revenue and expenditure. The way in which these arrangements affect member states in general and the UK in particular are analyzed next. In particular the extent to which the EU budgetary rebate continues to be justified is considered. The focus then switches to the macroeconomics of the budget: the role of central government budgets in monetary unions. Thus, the stabilization function for the monetary union as a whole and intertemporal stabilization, inter-regional insurance and redistribution at the regional level are analyzed. Since the EU budget is not able to fulfil these functions, an assessment is made of the extent to which these functions need to be replicated in EMU and of the alternative mechanisms for their achievement such as the Stability and Growth Pact. Finally the implications for the EU budget and for UK membership of EMU are examined.

The EU budget and national government budgets: a comparison

EU budgetary rules

The EU budget differs from that of national governments in four fundamental ways: it is more tightly regulated; it is much smaller; the pattern of expenditure is completely different; and the sources of finance are distinct. These differences demonstrate the extent to which member states wanted to limit EU competence in this sensitive area of government activity. Recent controversy in the UK over an EU-wide tax on saving[5] and further EU tax harmonization has emphasized the political salience of this issue. Thus the EEC Treaty budgetary rules have been designed to ensure maximum control by member states and minimum discretion of EU institutions over expenditure and revenue. There are five basic principles derived from the treaties (European Union 1997): annuality, balance, unity, universality and specification.

Annuality means that the budget is only for the one year, that authorization cannot be given beyond this one year. This prevents the build-up of long-term commitments but has caused some problems because much EU expenditure is now on multi-annual programmes. The practical reconciliation of these two conflicting requirements has been by the use of commitments for future years, which strictly do not have to be honoured but which in practice usually are. Balance ensures that revenue covers expenditure and deficit financing is not permitted.[6] Unity requires that all expenditure be entered in a single budget document. Universality follows, with all EU revenue and expenditure being included in the budget, so that there are no self-cancelling items. Specification requires that expenditure be allocated to a particular objective and be used for the purposes the budgetary authority intended. There is, however, some possibility for transfers between categories for the effective execution of the budget.

Budgetary revenue

The EEC began financing its operations like other international organizations with national contributions as fixed shares of the overall budget. In 1970 with policies – especially the Common Agricultural Policy (CAP) – developing and expenditure rising, a system of 'own resources' as provided for in the EEC Treaty was set up. 'Own resources' were the proceeds from the Common Customs Tariff (CCT), agricultural and sugar levies[7] and VAT up to a maximum rate of 1 per cent[8] on the harmonized base. The revenue from these resources represented the upper limit of EC budgetary expenditure. In 1988 a fourth GNP-based resource was added and the overall budgetary limit was expressed as a proportion of EU GNP, currently 1.27 per cent.[9] This maximum level of expenditure can be changed but to do so requires the unanimous agreement of the member states. In agreeing to the latest seven-year financial framework for the EU budget in 1999 (European Council 1999) the member states showed not only that they were not prepared to raise this ceiling, but that they wanted expenditure constrained at a lower level (Begg 2000).

Revenue from the CCT and agricultural levies, the so-called traditional own resources (TOR), has been declining with reductions in protection and falling agricultural imports. So as can be seen from Table 11.1, over 80 per cent of budgetary revenue now derives from VAT and the GNP resource. The GNP resource paid by each country is calculated by taking the difference between overall EU expenditure and the revenue from TOR and VAT, and multiplying this by the country's share of EU GNP. So it is

Table 11.1 | EU revenue sources

% of own resource revenue

	1997	1998	1999
Agricultural levies	1.2	1.3	1.4
Sugar levies	1.5	1.3	1.5
Customs duties	18.1	16.4	15.8
Costs of own resources	−2.1	−1.9	−1.9
VAT	45.5	40.3	37.9
GNP	35.7	42.6	45.3
Total revenue ECU/euro millions	**75,292.9**	**82,249.2**	**82,532.7**
Total Revenue % of EU GDP	**0.94**	**1.08**	**1.13**

Source: ECA (1998, 1999, 2000)

Table 11.2 | National central government total revenue, 1997

% GDP

	Income tax	Corporation tax	Social security	Taxes on goods and services	Other	Total
			Federal states			
Australia	11.7	4.1	0.0	4.9	3.1	23.8
USA	8.9	2.2	6.5	0.7	2.0	20.3
Switzerland	3.1	2.3	12.5	5.4	0.4	23.7
Germany	3.9	0.6	15.5	6.3	5.3	31.6
			Unitary states			
France	6.0	2.1	17.2	11.8	4.7	41.9
Sweden	2.7	3.2	13.6	11.2	10.2	41.0
UK	8.9	4.2	6.1	11.6	5.0	35.8
			EU			
EU	—	—	—	—	0.9	0.9

Sources: IMF (1999b), ECA (1998)

simply a way of calculating a national contribution, which bears no relation to any particular tax. The VAT contribution has also been somewhat arbitrary because no country actually used the harmonized base. Gradually, to increase the fairness of the budget, it has become even more arbitrary so that the VAT base cannot exceed 50 per cent of GNP. At Berlin in 1999 it was agreed that the maximum rate of VAT should be reduced to 0.5 per cent and that the cost of collecting TORs retained by member states should be raised from 10 to 25 per cent of the revenue collected. When these changes are fully implemented two-thirds of budget revenue will be provided by GNP contributions.

Although the EU does have legally independent finance its revenue is derived principally from national governments' taxes and is tightly controlled by those governments. What the EU does not have is autonomy over any tax instruments. Thus, the typical revenue resources of federal governments, such as income tax, corporation tax, sales taxes and social security contributions (see Table 11.2), are not available to the EU. In nation states the federal/central government generally controls the most significant revenue resources and provides significant finance for lower tiers of government, whose expenditure is also limited. In the EU's case, it is the lower tier – the member states' central governments – that controls the vast majority of taxes and derives the revenue from them; thus the EU is financed by national governments and its expenditure is subject to strict limitation.

Budgetary expenditure

EU budgetary expenditure is concentrated on a narrow range of policies that are not significant for national governments (see Table 11.3).

Table 11.3 | EU budgetary expenditure

	% of budgetary expenditure		
	1997	1998	1999
CAP markets	50.3	48.1	49.5
Structural operations	32.8	35.1	33.2
Research	3.8	3.9	3.2
External action	4.9	5.0	5.7
Administration	5.1	5.2	5.6
Other	2.7	2.6	2.7
Total expenditure ECU/euro millions	**80,236**	**80,713**	**80,3010**
Total expenditure % of EU GDP	**1.01**	**1.06**	**1.10**

Source: ECA (1998, 1999, 2000)

Agricultural plus structural/regional policies alone account for more than 80 per cent of total expenditure. The only other significant areas of expenditure are research, external action and administration. Research covers EU funding of collaborative scientific projects under a series of framework programmes. External action expenditure reflects the EU's growing role in external relations, particularly in relation to Central and Eastern Europe. Administrative expenditure is a significant part of the budget because one of the most important roles of the European Commission is monitoring the operation of policies and regulations implemented by the member states.

Even the federal governments of very decentralized nation states such as Switzerland and the USA have levels of central government expenditure many times that of the EU (see Table 11.4). In the EU national central governments have large public sectors with total expenditure amounting to 40–50 per cent of GDP. The highest tier of government accounts for most of that expenditure even in a federal state such as Germany (see Table 11.5). The largest categories of national government expenditure are social security, health, education, defence and debt interest, none of which is significant for the EU.

Table 11.4 | National central government expenditure by function, 1997

% GDP

	Defence	Education	Health	Social security	Debt interest	Other	Total
Federal states							
Australia	1.7	1.8	3.4	8.7	1.7	1.0	**18.4**
USA	3.2	0.4	4.3	6.0	3.1	1.4	**18.4**
Switzerland	1.5	0.6	5.5	14.1	0.9	0.0	**22.6**
Germany*	1.3	0.2	6.4	16.9	2.4	5.3	**31.9**
Unitary states							
France**	2.5	3.3	10.0	17.9	2.7	6.6	**43.0**
Sweden	2.3	2.4	0.1	21.0	5.4	7.6	**38.8**
UK	2.7	1.6	5.5	14.0	3.5	3.2	**30.5**
EU							
EU	0.0	0.0	0.0	—	—	1.0	**1.0**

Note: Germany* 1996, France** 1993
Sources: IMF (1999b); ECA (1998)

Table 11.5 | EU GNP, budgetary contributions, expenditure and net contributions, 1997 (per capita ECU)

	GNP	Own resource contribution	Expenditure per capita		Net contribution
			Including administrative	Excluding administrative	
Luxembourg	40,012	422.8	2,213.8	366.3	−56.5
Denmark	29,837	296.9	310.3	304.3	7.4
Austria	25,222	271.6	178.5	177.0	−94.7
Germany	24,950	269.0	130.3	128.6	−140.4
Sweden	24,717	271.4	139.6	137.9	−133.5
Belgium	23,812	303.7	414.0	196.2	−107.5
France	23,390	234.1	220.2	217.0	−17.1
Netherlands	23,305	322.6	170.8	168.2	−154.4
UK	22,815	157.5	125.8	124.3	−33.2
Finland	22,801	215.0	226.3	223.6	8.6
Italy	19,735	156.8	155.7	154.1	−2.7
Ireland	17,768	195.3	956.0	952.5	757.2
Spain	13,734	142.0	299.1	298.4	156.4
Greece	10,786	116.6	549.0	547.8	431.3
Portugal	10,221	113.5	400.3	399.1	285.6

Source: European Commission (1998)

There are very major differences between these policies in different countries, reflecting their varied histories, cultures and preferences. This diversity is part of the reason for the very great reluctance to transfer these policies to the EU and thus they remain firmly under national control. The EU, therefore, has a pattern of expenditure that is totally different from that of national governments.

The UK and the EU budget

Despite the relatively small size of the budget, it remains politically controversial. This is because the total amounts of revenue and expenditure are very large in absolute terms. Unlike national government revenue and expenditure, payments and receipts are across national boundaries and so they subtract from, or add to, national income and affect a country's balance of payments. The fact that payments and receipts are readily measurable makes them an easily accessible assessment of the effect of EU membership.[10] EMU has perhaps added to the significance of the budget, especially via the Growth and Stability Pact. Net contributions[11] to the budget are a drain on the national finances, which are already strained by the requirement of a 'medium-term objective for the budgetary position close to balance or in surplus' (Council of the EU 1997a, Article 7.2(a)). Thus the concerns of Austria, Germany, the Netherlands and Sweden over net contributions at the 1999 Berlin summit were not just a result of the rigours of meeting the convergence requirements of EMU at a time of high

> # It is likely that EMU will ensure continued sensitivity over net contributions to the EU budget

unemployment. It is likely that EMU will ensure continued sensitivity over net contributions to the EU budget.

The UK's original problems with the EEC budget were the result of a revenue and expenditure system, which meant that despite the fact that the UK was one of the poorer member states, it was the second largest net contributor. The 1984 agreement and the compensation mechanism that it established resolved the UK's grievance. Is the rebate mechanism still appropriate, given the considerable changes in EU budgetary arrangements since 1984? The introduction and growing importance of the fourth resource, and restrictions on the size of the VAT base have meant that contributions to the EU budget have become more closely related to GNP, but the relationship remains somewhat imperfect (see Table 11.6).[12] The UK rebate mechanism does ensure that the UK contributes proportionally less than other countries. Italian contributions are also low but those of the Netherlands and Belgium are high because of the Rotterdam effect.[13] The relationship of contributions to GNP will be further tightened by the changes to own resources agreed at Berlin in 1999.

The major inequalities in the budget have, however, been the result of the distribution of expenditure rather than of contributions. Here again changes should have made the distribution of benefits fairer. The relative importance of agricultural expenditure has declined and that of the structural policies has increased. The greater concentration of structural policy expenditure in poorer regions will also have tended to concentrate expenditure in poorer countries. Receipts from the budget, however, are not related to GNP per capita if administrative expenditure is included.[14] This is because two of the richer member states, Belgium and Luxembourg, receive most administrative expenditure. This expenditure is not, however, comparable with expenditure on structural policies, agriculture and other internal policies, which could be regarded as replacing similar domestic expenditure.[15] Administrative expenditure is paid for the use of resources, labour, land and buildings, and so the benefits to the recipient country are much less than the expenditure.[16] Excluding administrative expenditure, Ireland, Greece and Portugal receive particularly high levels of expenditure. For the other member states there is no relationship between expenditure and GNP per capita.[17] The UK has the lowest level of EU budgetary expenditure per capita.

Net contributions[18] reflect predominantly the distribution of expenditures, so the cohesion states (poorer) are substantial net beneficiaries from the budget (see Table 11.6). Ireland, despite being the most

Table 11.6 | GNP and net contributions to the EU budget, 2006 ECU (per capita)

| | GNP | Net contributions | |
		Including admin. expenditure	Excluding admin. expenditure
Luxembourg	45,961	2351	−20
Denmark	34,273	−21	−29
Austria	28,972	−81	−83
Germany	28,660	−123	−125
Sweden	28,392	−94	−96
Belgium	27,352	152	−146
France	26,868	−1.9	−23
Netherlands	26,771	−139	−143
UK	26,207	−51	−53
Finland	26,192	−2	−6
Italy	22,670	−26	−28
Ireland	20,410	378	373
Spain	15,776	182	181
Greece	12,389	490	488
Portugal	11,740	326	324

Source: Ferrer and Emerson (2000)

prosperous of the cohesion states, does particularly well. Denmark and Finland are marginal net beneficiaries but all the remaining member states are net contributors. The net contributions from the Netherlands, Germany and Sweden are particularly large.[19] Even after the rebate the UK is still a net contributor to the budget. The changes made at the 1999 Berlin summit do not alter the situation fundamentally (Ferrer and Emerson 2000). The financing of the EU becomes more closely related to ability to pay as the GNP resource becomes preponderant. Structural policy expenditure becomes a little more closely concentrated in poorer member states. The impact of agricultural price reductions compensated for by direct subsidies, however, tends to favour countries that are more prosperous. Overall predicted net contributions are more closely related to GNP per capita (see Table 11.6).[20] The major change is that Ireland, although still a large net beneficiary, has its net benefits halved, while other cohesion countries' net benefits have been increased. The Netherlands, Germany, Sweden and Austria have slightly smaller net contributions and other countries' increase marginally.[21]

The UK's budgetary rebate remains anomalous but without the rebate the UK would still be the second largest absolute net contributor after Germany. Unlike the Netherlands and Belgium, the UK net contribution does not include taxes on imports whose incidence falls on the citizens of other countries. The UK also incurs a significant food cost associated with the operation of the CAP because it is a net importer of high-priced food from other EU member states (Ardy 2001). So although the UK rebate seems anachronistic, arguably it is still justified and remains so after the Berlin agreement. A fundamental reform of the CAP, e.g. the nationalization of the financing of direct subsidies, will be required to reduce the UK's net contribution to a more appropriate level without the correction mechanism.

Macroeconomics of the EU budget

There are two macroeconomic roles for the budget in a federation: fiscal policy and transfers between regions. Fiscal policy is the manipulation of the balance between government expenditure and revenue so as to influence aggregate demand in the economy. The discretionary use of fiscal policy fell out of favour with the end of the post-war boom and the increasing ascendancy of monetary economics. 'While active budgetary policy-making to sustain the cycle may be useful under particular circumstances, a number of undesirable features cannot be ignored: timing problems, non-reversibility of budgetary expansions, model uncertainty, delay of structural reforms etc.' (European Commission 1999, p. 5). This proposition derives from various studies (Alesina and Perotti 1995; Buti *et al.* 1997; IMF 1999a) suggesting that budgetary policies have not always been anti-cyclical,[22] because of technical problems,[23] as a result of the constraints of large debt and deficits,[24] or for political reasons.[25] There is still, however, a role for fiscal policy in the form of automatic stabilizers[26] (Buti and Sapir 1998). Whether federal fiscal policy is discretionary or automatic, three requirements need to be satisfied for its effective operation. First, the federal/central budget should be large in relation to the economy; otherwise, changes in the budgetary position will have little impact. Second, it must be possible to change the balance between expenditure and revenue in a counter-cyclical manner.[27] A balanced budget is of no use for stabilization purposes. Third, fiscal and monetary policy should be co-ordinated so that both elements of macro-economic policy are pulling in the same direction (Blake and Weale 1998; Hall *et al.* 1999).

Regions within a monetary union which face asymmetric shocks can no longer use the exchange rate as a shock-absorbing mechanism. One process that mitigates the impact of asymmetric shocks on regions in nation states is a system of automatic transfers from the central/federal budget. Central/federal fiscal policy will act as a means of interregional risk sharing by transferring resources between regions. These transfers perform three types of function (Fatás 1998): intertemporal stabilization, interregional insurance and interregional redistribution. The first two stabilize regional income; the third reduces inequalities in income levels between regions. Intertemporal stabilization seeks to smooth fluctuations in income levels by compensatory movements in the public-sector deficit, the Keynesian stabilization function. Thus in a recession government borrowing and debt expand and in the future, when the economy is growing more quickly, this borrowing can be repaid. Interregional insurance can occur when economic cycles are imperfectly correlated between regions. Under these circumstances tax revenue from fast-growing regions can be transferred to slow-growing regions to finance public expenditure and so smooth the economic cycle. Interregional redistribution involves the transfer of resources from more prosperous to less prosperous regions, so it is related to levels rather than changes in income. Such transfers might be justified in terms of the solidarity of the nation state, to achieve a fairer individual distribution of income or to enhance overall economic efficiency.[28]

The delineation of these transfers in theory and their separation in reality are another matter; in national monetary unions transfers between regions fulfil all three functions. For example, national progressive taxation used to finance social security will automatically achieve some interregional insurance, intertemporal stabilization and interregional redistribution. The large size of the central government budget relative to that of the regions and restrictions on regional budgets[29] mean that intertemporal stabilization, interregional insurance and redistribution in national monetary unions are a central government responsibility. The difference between interregional insurance and redistribution largely hinges on the persistence of the shock. Thus, if two regions had similar per capita income levels but one suffered a temporary shock reducing income, transfers from the growing to the contracting region would be interregional insurance. If, by contrast, the shock were permanent then the difference between the regions would persist and the interregional transfers, if they were not time limited, would become interregional redistribution.

Euro area fiscal policy

The EU budget under its current restrictions is unable to provide stabilization for EMU, either as a whole or for its regions. Aggregate stabilization is made impossible by the small size of the EU budget and the requirement for it to balance every year. Interregional insurance is ruled out by the way in which the structural policies operate to determine expenditure in particular regions. The situation in the EU to an extent inverts that in national monetary unions: most tax revenue and expenditure remains the responsibility of national governments, which for EMU is the regional rather than the federal level.

The norm in fiscal federations is for the federal government to determine the overall fiscal stance with the budgets of lower tiers regulated. With the EU budget balanced, the overall fiscal stance in EMU is the sum of the national fiscal stances but subject to EU regulation. This regulation is via the Stability and Growth Pact (SGP), which is a classic EU mix of legal regulation and intergovernmental co-operation (see Chapter 9, section on fiscal policy). The SGP consists of two regulations, first, for surveillance (Council of the EU 1997a) and second, for excessive deficits (Council of the EU 1997b). Surveillance seeks to ensure that member states' budgetary plans are such that they will avoid excessive deficits, with compliance achieved by peer pressure and the possibility of adverse publicity,[30] because the only sanction is a recommendation to a member state to modify policy. The UK is subject to these surveillance requirements despite its non-participation in EMU.

Fiscal policy is more tightly controlled by the Excessive Deficit Procedure. When a country's deficit exceeds 3 per cent of GDP the Economic and Finance Council of the EU can decide by a qualified majority that an excessive deficit exists, make recommendations for its correction, and impose penalties if the member state fails to remedy the situation. Excessive deficits are those exceeding 3 per cent of GDP except where the excess is not exceptional and temporary. Penalties include non-interest-bearing deposits and, ultimately, fines. The excessive deficit procedure does not apply to the UK or to Denmark as these countries have exercised their right under the Treaty to opt out of EMU.

> # The norm in fiscal federations is for the federal government to determine the overall fiscal stance with the budgets of lower tiers regulated

These procedures are geared to the achievement of medium-term budgetary positions close to balance or in surplus. If this is achieved then the overall fiscal stance for EMU should correspond to one appropriate to the cyclical economic situation as a result of the operation of automatic stabilizers. Thus, below-average growth for the eurozone will lead to an automatic counter-cycle expansion of the aggregate public-sector deficit, caused by falling tax revenues and rising expenditure. If, in the medium term, national budgets are close to balance, this will give sufficient headroom for the automatic stabilizing response to a recession. Given the continuance of a small EU budget and large national budgets, discretionary fiscal policy at the eurozone level would mean requiring individual governments to adjust their budgetary policies to achieve the overall EU stance. This is not politically feasible as member states are not prepared to change taxation or public expenditure to achieve some overall EU target. Thus, it is not surprising that the EU has opted for the fiscal stance of the eurozone to be determined by automatic stabilizers within a framework of responsible budgetary policies.

With the EU budget balanced and national budgets balanced over the medium term, the overall fiscal stance for EMU is one of balance. Although such fiscal rectitude seems desirable it could be questioned. One problem is that governments need to be debtors in order to provide the necessary depth and liquidity to financial markets. To an extent corporate debt can fulfil this function but would not offer the security and portfolio possibilities of government's debt (Gordon 1997). The need for balance also rules out the possibility of the government borrowing to cover investment, the 'golden rule' policy that Chancellor Gordon Brown is currently following in the UK. Thus, the UK's current expenditure and revenue plans do not meet EU medium-term requirements (ECOFIN 2001). Given the current importance ascribed to public investment in education and infrastructure as necessary for competitiveness, reductions in public investment to ensure budgetary balance could adversely affect rates of economic growth.

The continuance of large national budgets means that intertemporal stabilization is still possible via changes in these national budgets.[31] The fact that intertemporal stabilization is possible at the national level does not mean that it is optimal at the national level. There may be gains from operating fiscal policy over the larger federal area, for example liquidity effects on public debt may mean that debt is cheaper and thus the costs of intertemporal stabilization lower (Martin 1998, p. 197). A fiscal federation will also have a higher potential to stabilize against shocks unless the national component in income variation is negligible.[32]

Interregional stabilization, insurance and redistribution

Interregional stabilization is not however possible using either national or EU budgets. So how important is this stabilization and how much of a problem is its absence? The large transfers between regions in monetary unions in developed countries were estimated for the MacDougall Report (MacDougall 1977), which indicated that interregional flows of public finance reduced long-run per capita income differences between regions by between 25 per cent and 53 per cent. This conflated the redistribution and stabilization elements of the flows. The first attempt to separate these elements was carried out by Sala-i-Martin and Sachs (1992), whose results suggested that tax and transfers offset 35–44 per cent of variations in US regional income. Thus, despite the flexibility of private interregional adjustment in the USA[33] there is still a heavy reliance on fiscal transfers.

The high estimate of stabilization by Sala-i-Martin and Sachs prompted criticism that their method confused stabilization with redistribution. Thus, von Hagen (1992) assessed the effect of regional taxes and transfers on changes rather than levels of regional income and found that the reduction in the size of fluctuations in regional income was only 10 per cent. Unfortunately, the results of these two studies are not directly comparable because they use different variables. Goodhart and Smith (1993), using von Hagen's method but similar variables to Sala-i-Martin and Sachs, estimate the stabilizing effect at 20 per cent. This result is equivalent to that obtained by Pisani-Ferry *et al.* (1993) who used a simulation model. Bayoumi and Masson (1996), using another model specification, estimate stabilization at 30 per cent.

Mélitz and Zumer (1998) attempt a reconciliation of these competing results, estimating stabilization at 20 per cent and redistribution of 17 per cent for the USA. They demonstrate that the higher estimates of stabilization obtained by Sala-i-Martin and Sachs (1992) and Bayoumi and Masson (1996) are the result of the use of state personal income rather than gross state product, together with the inclusion of grants to lower tiers of government. With the exceptions noted, there seems to be fairly general agreement among these studies that in the USA around 20 per cent of the fluctuations in gross state product are offset by fluctuations in federal taxes and transfers. There are, however, four recent studies that come to a much lower figure of around 10 per cent (Asdrubali *et al.* 1996; Fatás 1998; Mélitz and Zumer 1999; Obstfeld and Peri 1998). The lower estimates by Obstfeld and Peri are due to a different specification and estimation technique (a bivarate VAR) but the other authors have more profound critiques of previous methodology.

Fatás (1998) argues that estimated stabilization effects include both intertemporal stabilization and interregional insurance. He estimates interregional stabilization separately as the reduction in the volatility of regional permanent income[34] relative to pre-tax income, giving an average value of 11 per cent. There are, however, some questions over his methodology (Andersen 1998). The relatively low stabilization in the USA is not just the result of low levels of transfers. It is also due to the high correlation and low persistence of shocks across states. Europe suffers from much more persistent shocks so Fatás's argument that stabilization should concentrate on short-term shocks has been questioned: 'A fiscal federation by acting through cross-sectional transfers can in principle reduce both short and long run variance' (Forni and Reichlin 2001, p. 124). The role of private capital markets is crucial in cushioning regional specific shocks in the US (Atkeson and Bayoumi 1993; Sorensen and Yosha 1998). Using accounting identities to decompose regional income into its components and then analyzing their fluctuations provides another route to estimate stabilization. Asdrubali *et al.* (1996) find that only 13 per cent of shocks are offset by the federal government, but the role of financial markets is crucial: 39 per cent of shocks are offset by cross-regional ownership claims to output and 23 per cent by the extension of credit on an interregional basis. Using a corrected specification and estimation procedure Mélitz and Zumer (1999) have a similar estimate of 13 per cent of the effect of federal stabilization, but the role of financial markets and credit is equally important, offsetting 24 per cent of the shock each.[35]

These estimates of stabilization are for the USA, a monetary union comparable in size to EMU. Whether it is a good basis for comparison with EMU could be questioned because of its much higher level of interregional labour mobility and lower level of unemployment persistence (Obstfeld and Peri 1998). Another fundamental difference between EMU and the USA is the much lower level of interregional ownership of assets and of credit markets. EMU may be vulnerable to shocks while ownership of assets changes and credit markets develop. The lower ability of the EU economies to absorb interregional shocks is perhaps reflected in the higher degrees of interregional stabilization estimated for EU countries. Estimates for the UK (Goodhart and Smith 1993), Germany and France (Pisani-Ferry *et al.* 1993) and Italy (Decressin 1999) suggest that national stabilization offsets somewhere between 20 and 40 per cent of changes in regional incomes. Melitz and Zumer's (1998) estimates are towards the bottom of this range with around 20 per cent for the UK and France.

EMU, of course, lacks any significant interregional stabilization between its regions. Is its absence a significant problem? This depends upon how significant asymmetric shocks[36] will be and on the efficacy of other adjustment mechanisms. The ERM (see Chapter 3, section 'The EMS') and the convergence process of monetary integration seemed to enhance the synchronization of European business cycles (Artis and Zhang 1999) and it seems likely that EMU will further intensify this process. The national economies[37] of EMU remain diversified, so their vulnerability to asymmetric shocks and, consequently, the need for interregional stabilization are less. But will the intensification of integration implied by EMU lead to greater specialization are hence vulnerability? By stimulating restructuring and promoting the mobility of factors of production, EMU enhances both economic integration and competitive pressures. It can be argued that this will tend to encourage the concentration of economic activity. This is because, as trade costs fall, agglomeration economies and supply-side linkages become more important and factor inflows limit the cost disadvantages of concentration (Krugman 1991; Krugman and Venables 1990, 1995, 1996). These effects may be reinforced by a dynamic interaction between agglomeration and R&D. Working in the opposite direction are cost differentials that remain in the EU, together with congestion costs and differences in the costs of non-tradeable services, which will encourage dispersion. Thus, the impact of the single currency on specialization is an empirical question, but the evidence is ambiguous. While providing some support for the variables important to the 'new geography' models, there is no very great evidence of significant agglomeration (Braunerhjelm *et al.* 2000). Thus, by comparison with the USA, European national economies are perhaps less vulnerable to asymmetric shocks than US states but Europe at present lacks adjustment mechanisms such as labour mobility and cross-border capital holdings and flows.

The absence of significant international transfers in the EU means that EMU lacks interregional redistribution as well as stabilization. Justification for redistribution may be political (the need for some equity in living standards to maintain the solidarity of the nation state) or economic (that efficiency will be enhanced). In EMU it could be argued that the political argument for redistribution is relatively weak. The eurozone is far from a homogeneous area in terms of citizenship, culture and language. The differences in income levels are such that it could be counterproductive to encourage the idea that

> # European national economies are perhaps less vulnerable to asymmetric shocks than US states

they should be similar across the area. At the moment there is only limited attachment to a European identity among the citizens of Europe. Within nation states such as Belgium, Italy and Canada it is proving increasingly difficult to maintain existing regional transfers. The failure to agree on even small increases in the EU budget to finance enlargement indicates an unwillingness among governments to finance large transfers. The economic case for interregional redistribution is also relatively weak and there are a number of problems with such redistribution. Transfers in the short term would boost income and economic activity in the region but this might lead to higher factor prices blunting productivity gains and innovation necessary for competitiveness. Continuing grants could create a situation of dependency, with moral hazard[38] and simply inefficient projects.

Conclusion

As Prime Minister Blair made clear on 7 February 2001, the UK could be taking decisions over membership of EMU in the near future. At present, as this chapter has made clear, EMU has surprisingly few implications for the EU budget. The real challenges to the current budgetary arrangements are coming from enlargement, renewed WTO negotiations over agriculture (Ferrer and Emerson 2000) and the current crisis in agriculture. So a more profound reform of policy and the budget seems likely in the future. This would again lead to a questioning of the British correction mechanism. The rebate is defensible with current policies but the UK should be prepared to forgo the rebate if there is a radical reform of the CAP.

EMU, as at present constituted, operates under very different budgetary arrangements from other monetary unions. The central budget is very small and is incapable of fulfilling a stabilization role at the EU level. There is no provision for interregional insurance or stabilization and that for redistribution is limited. National budgets remain very large and governments retain at least some flexibility to operate stabilization at a national level. There has been very little support in the EU to develop a fiscal federation, a position reinforced by the increasingly ambivalent economic evidence on its benefits. The unique fiscal arrangements of EMU may be sustainable while the eurozone continues to consist of distinct national economies. With higher levels of integration and greater comparability of the different national situations, there will no doubt be pressure to expand the EU budget. This could be the result of a perception of the need to fulfil the stabilization functions at the EU level or of the desire to limit differences in income levels to ensure the sustainability of EMU. In the benign economic environment the eurozone has enjoyed since its launch there is little pressure in these directions. If and when, however, the system is tested in recessionary circumstances and serious differentials in national income conditions emerge, pressure to develop an EU budget capable of significant interregional stabilization and redistribution could become intense. The differences between national government expenditure and revenue patterns and their complexity would, however, make it extremely difficult to develop a federal tax and expenditure system for the EU. Thus, in the medium term the EU seems destined to be a test bed for its current unique combination of a monetary union without a fiscal federation.

Notes

1 Research arising out of ESRC 'One Europe or Several?' programme award no. L213252034.

2 The only exception is monetary unions involving a micro-state, e.g. Belgium and Luxembourg.

3 The term region is used in this chapter to refer to sub-national units of federal states, e.g. Länder in Germany, but to individual nation states within EMU.

4 It is not true of agriculture and structural policies but even here significant national policies and expenditure persist.

5 The withholding tax.

6 Small deficits and surpluses do emerge but these are not allowed to cumulate.

7 Agricultural levies were variable taxes on agricultural imports. Sugar levies are a charge on sugar producers for production in excess of a defined output quota.

8 The maximum rate was increased to 1.4 per cent of EU GNP in 1984 and reduced back to 1 per cent in 1992, down to 0.75 per cent in 2002 and to 0.50 per cent in 2004.

9 Planned expenditure has to be kept below this level to allow a margin for expenditure overruns.

10 Even though they are far from complete they ignore the benefits of many policies that are likely to be much more significant, e.g. the single market.

11 Net contributions are the difference between payments to and receipts from the EU budget.

12 Regressing contributions per capita on GNP per capita yields an R^2 of 0.8.

13 Rotterdam imports products for re-export to other EU countries so tariffs are paid in the Netherlands but the burden of the taxes falls on citizens of other countries. Belgium is in a similar position with the port of Antwerp.

14 Regressing total expenditure per capita on GNP, per capita yields a positive coefficient on GNP, indicating that expenditure increases as GNP increases, but the coefficient is not significant and the R^2 is only 0.2.

15 Or if structural expenditure is really additional, i.e. on projects that would not be undertaken in its absence, then at least the member state obtains useful infrastructure or training for its population partly at EU expense.

16 This is not to deny the multiplier benefits of such expenditure. But employees of the EU are mostly from other member states and in the case of Luxembourg may even reside in other member states.

17 This is confirmed by a regression of expenditure less administrative per capita as a function of GNP per capita, which yields a negative but non-significant coefficient on GNP but an R^2 of only 0.2.

18 Excluding administrative expenditure.

19 As a result of the strong relationship between contributions and GNP per capita net contributions are a negative function of GNP per capita, but the relationship is weak, with an R^2 of only 0.3.

20 The fit of the equation improves, as shown by an R^2 of only 0.5.

21 The Luxembourg and Belgium situation is very sensitive to assumptions about administrative expenditures.

22 The suggestion that discretionary fiscal policy does not succeed in stabilizing the economy is, however, controversial. Noord (2000) presents evidence that for the OECD as a whole and the USA in particular there was a significant stabilizing effect from discretionary policy.

23 For example, the timing of discretionary policy.

24 Countries with large deficits and debt would find these rising to unsustainable levels in a recession and may, therefore, have to act counter-cyclically, tightening policy by increasing taxes and/or reducing government expenditure. Thus in the early 1990s even without the Maastricht convergence requirements EU countries would have been forced into fiscal consolidation despite the recessionary conditions. This meant that for the euro area as opposed to the OECD a neutral discretionary fiscal policy would have been less volatile than the discretionary policy actually employed (Noord 2000).

25 Governments, for example, reducing taxes before elections.

26 Automatic stabilizers are changes in budget deficits, which tend to offset variations in economic activity. Thus, if growth slows, the public-sector deficit increases as tax revenue falls and expenditure rises. This adds to demand in the economy, reducing the extent of the fall in economic growth.

27 This requires either that policy acts without lags or that government forecasting of economic activity is accurate. Another potential benefit of automatic stabilizers is the potential absence of a recognition and implementation lag in their operation.

28 By utilizing unemployed factors or by spreading economic activity more evenly, allowing a higher overall level of output without inflation.

29 These restrictions can take various forms such as limitations on local taxation or expenditure, or balanced budget rules.

30 Adverse publicity could exact a price, undermining confidence in the government and its debt, leading to an interest rate premium. Paradoxically, when Ireland in February 2001 was the first country to have a recommendation against it, the Irish government sought to use this to its electoral advantage by sticking to its policy in the face of what it claimed was EU intimidation.

31 Provided again that in the medium term national budgets are in balance or close to surplus, so that the excessive deficit limit of 3 per cent of GDP is not binding.

32 Although it is not negligible, Forni and Reichlin (2001) suggest that it is relatively small: 75 per cent of output variance is explained by global or local factors.

33 Via migration and integrated capital markets: see following section.

34 Regional permanent income is defined as regional income less future taxes on the region necessary to finance the current public-sector deficit.

35 The model does not yield significant results when estimated for the UK and Italy.

36 As well as differences in the impact and adjustment to symmetric shocks.

37 It is national economies that are important here because the persistence of large national budgets means that interregional transfers can continue within nation states, albeit constrained by the requirement of the Stability and Growth Pact.

38 The adoption of policy actions aimed to continue receipt of transfers rather than facilitate development.

References

Alesina A. and Perotti, Roberto (1995) 'Fiscal expansions and adjustments in OECD countries', *Economic Policy*, 21, pp. 205–40.

Andersen, T. M. (1998) 'Discussion: Does EMU need a fiscal federation?', *Economic Policy*, 26, pp. 193–95.

Ardy, B. (1988) 'The national incidence of the European Community budget', *Journal of Common Market Studies*, XXVI, 4, pp. 401–29.

Ardy, B. (2001) 'The EU budget and EU citizens' in S. Hatt and F. Gardner, *Economics, Policies and People: A European Perspective*. Basingstoke: Palgrave.

Artis, M. J. and Zhang, W. (1999) 'Further evidence on the

international business cycle and the ERM: is there a European business cycle?', *Oxford Economic Papers*, 51, pp. 120–32.

Asdrubali, P., Sorensen, B. and Yosha, O. (1996) 'Channels of interstate risk sharing: United States 1963–1990', *Quarterly Journal of Economics*, 111, pp. 1081–110.

Atkeson, A. and Bayoumi, T. (1993) 'Do private markets insure regional risk? – evidence from the United States and Europe', *Open Economies Review*, 4, pp. 303–24.

Bayoumi, T. and Masson, P. R. (1996) 'Fiscal flows in the United States and Canada: lessons for monetary union in Europe', *European Economic Review*, 39.2, pp. 253–74.

Begg, I. (2000) 'Reshaping the EU budget: yet another missed opportunity', *European Urban and Regional Studies*, 7, 1, pp. 51–62.

Begg, I. and Grimwade, N. (1998) *Paying for Europe*. Sheffield: Sheffield Academic Press.

Blake, A. P. and Weale, M. (1998) 'Costs of separating budgetary policy from control of inflation: a neglected aspect of central bank independence', *Oxford Economic Papers*. 50.3, pp. 449–67.

Bordo, M. and Jonung, L. (2000) *Lessons for EMU from the History of Monetary Unions*. London: IEA.

Braunerhjelm, P., Faini, R., Norman, V, Ruane, F. and Seabright, P. (2000) *Integration and the Regions of Europe: How the Right Policies Can Prevent Polarization*. London: Centre for Economic Policy Research.

Buti, M. and Sapir, A. (1998) *Economic Policy in EMU: A Study by the European Commission Services*. Oxford: Clarendon Press.

Buti, M., Franco, D. and Ongena, H. (1997) 'Budgetary policies in severe recessions – lessons from the post-war period for the Stability Pact', European Commission Directorate-General for Economic and Financial Affairs, Economic Paper 121.

Council of the EC (1985) '7 May 1985 on the Communities' system of own resources', *Official Journal L* 128, 4 May.

Council of the EU (1997a) 'Council Regulation (EC) No. 1466/97 of 7 July 1997 on the strengthening of surveillance of budgetary positions', *Official Journal L* 209, 2 August.

Council of the EU (1997b) 'Council Regulation (EC) No. 1467/97 of 7 July 1997 on speeding up and clarifying the implementation of the excessive deficit procedure', *Official Journal L* 209, 2 August.

Decressin, J. (1999) 'Regional income redistribution and risk sharing: how does Italy compare in Europe?', IMF Working Paper, WP/99/123.

ECA, European Court of Auditors (1998) 'Court of Auditors – Annual Report concerning the financial year 1997', *Official Journal C*, 349.

ECA, European Court of Auditors (1999) 'Court of Auditors – Annual

Report concerning the financial year 1998', *Official Journal C*, 349.

ECA, European Court of Auditors (2000) 'Court of Auditors – Annual Report concerning the financial year 1999', *Official Journal C*, 342.

ECOFIN (2001) 2329. Council meeting – ECOFIN, Press Release. Brussels Press: 35 – Nr: 5696/01.

El-Agraa, A. M. (2000) 'The general budget' in A. M. El-Agraa, *The European Union*, sixth edition. London: Prentice Hall.

European Commission (1998) 'Financing the European Union – Commission report on the operation of the own resources system', COM(98)560 final.

European Commission (1999) 'Budgetary surveillance in EMU', *European Economy, Supplement A: Economic Trends*, 3, March.

European Council (1999) Presidency Conclusion, Berlin European Council, 24 and 25 March, *Bulletin of the EU*, 3, I.2–43.

European Union (1997) *Consolidated Treaties*. Luxembourg: OOPEC.

Fatás, A. (1998) 'Does EMU need a fiscal federation?', *Economic Policy*, 26, pp. 163–203.

Ferrer, J. N. and Emerson, M. (2000) 'Goodbye Agenda 2000, hello, Agenda 2003: effects of the Berlin Summit on own resources, expenditures and EU net balances', CEPS Working Document 140.

Forni, M. and Reichlin, L. (2001) 'Federal policies and local economies in Europe and the US', *European Economic Review*, 45 pp. 109–34.

Goodhart, C. and Smith, S. (1993) 'Stabilisation', *European Economy: Reports and Studies*, 5.

Gordon, J. S. (1997) *Hamilton's Blessing. The Extraordinary Life and Times of our National Debt*. New York: Walker and Company.

Hall, S., Henry, B. and Nixon, M. (1999) 'Inflation targeting: revisiting the delegation and co-ordination of monetary policy', Centre of Economic Forecasting, London Business School, Discussion Paper DP 04–99.

IMF (1999a) 'Germany: selected issues and statistical appendix', IMF Staff Country Report 99/130, **www.imf.org**

IMF (1999b) *Government Financial Statistics Yearbook 1999*.

Krugman, P. (1991) 'Increasing returns and economic geography', *Journal of Political Economy*, 99, pp. 484–99.

Krugman, P. and Venables, A. (1990) 'Integration and the competitiveness of peripheral industry' in C. Bliss and J. Braga de Macedo (eds) *Unity with Diversity in the European Community*. Cambridge: Cambridge University Press.

Krugman, P. and Venables, A. (1995) 'Globalisation and the inequality of nations', *Quarterly Journal of Economics*, 110, pp. 857–80.

Krugman, P. and Venables, A. J. (1996) 'Integration, specialisation, adjustment', *European Economic Review*, 3, 5, pp. 959–68.

MacDougall, D. (1977) *Report of the Study Group on the Role of Public Finance in European Integration*. Luxembourg: OOPEC.

Martin, P. (1998) 'Discussion: does EMU need a fiscal federation?', *Economic Policy*, 26, pp. 195–97.

Mélitz, J. and Zumer, F. (1998) 'Regional redistribution and stabilization by the center in Canada, France, the United Kingdom and the United States: new estimates based on panel data econometrices', CEPR Discussion Paper 1829.

Mélitz, J. and Zumer, F. (1999) 'Interregional and international risk-sharing and lessons for EMU', Carnegie-Rochester Conference Series on Public Policy, 51, pp. 149–88.

Noord, P. van den (2000) 'The size and role of automatic stabilisers in the 1990s and beyond', IMF Economics Department Working Paper 230.

Obstfeld, M. and Peri, G. (1998) 'Regional non-adjustment and fiscal policy', *Economic Policy*, 26, pp. 205–59.

Pisani-Ferry, J., Italianer, A. and Lescure, R. (1993) 'Stabilization properties of budgetary systems: a simulation analysis', *European Economy: Reports and Studies*, 5.

Sala-i-Martin, X. and Sachs, J. (1992) 'Fiscal federalism and optimum currency areas: evidence from Europe and the United States' in M. Canzoneri, V. Grilli and P. Masson (eds.) (1992) *Establishing a Central Bank: Issues in Europe and Lessons from the US*. Cambridge: Cambridge University Press.

Sorensen, B. and Yosha, O. (1998) 'International risk sharing and European monetary unification', *Journal of International Economics*, 45, pp. 211–38.

Von Hagen, J. (1992) 'Fiscal arrangements in monetary union: evidence from the US' in D. Fair and C. de Boisseaux (eds) *Fiscal Policy, Taxes, and the Financial System in an Increasingly Integrated Europe*. London: Kluwer.

12

UK trade concerns

Nigel Grimwade and David Mayes

The consequences of the UK's (non-)participation in stage 3 of EMU for trade have been little studied. There are four main concerns: first that the exchange rate at which the UK enters could be misaligned (see Chapters 9 and 13); second that fixing the exchange rate with respect to some trading partners but not others may affect the composition of trade through a change in the volatility of relative prices; third that some of the remaining gains expected from the 'completion' of the Single European Market (SEM) may be realized in terms of reduced costs; and last, and most important, that there will be dynamic benefits from both the increased pressures of competition and lower real interest rates.

While there were some extensive calculations undertaken at the time of the launch of the SEM (see Emerson *et al.* 1988), these were not repeated when the prospects for EMU were discussed by the European Commission in 1990 (see Mayes and Burridge 1993a for some estimates). In part, this was a response to the criticisms of the original estimates, but in the main it was a reflection of the tentative nature of any calculations that could be undertaken. Estimates of static gains from reductions in costs tend to come up with trivial numbers amounting to less than 1 per cent of GDP. Given that the costs of the physical changeover to the euro may be larger than this in the first year or two (Mayes and Burridge 1993b) this would not make the calculations seem attractive – particularly if one were to add some adjustment costs from having a less flexible exchange rate.

Assessing any dynamic gain is even more speculative as there has not been much in the way of satisfactory modelling of the link between the underlying determinants of the growth process and the removal of barriers between countries (or other regulatory changes for that matter). The presumption is simply that such barriers must be acting as some sort of restraint, so their removal will have a positive effect.

As a means of assessing some of these concerns, we take a backwards look in this chapter at the sorts of assessments that have been made of the impact of the previous steps in European integration on trade and consider how they might be extrapolated to current circumstances. In any such assessment we are, of course, hampered by the usual constraint that there is a single path for history. In assessing the impact of integration it is necessary to hypothesize what would have happened otherwise. These hypotheses in themselves are the major determinant of the resulting estimates (Mayes 1997). Growth rates vary over time for a variety of reasons. While one may be able to identify the proximate causes of productivity shifts in the sense of increases in factor intensity or total factor productivity (Mayes 1996), it is much more difficult to assign them to more fundamental causes, such as integration. It is not possible to isolate a single determinant convincingly without running over the whole range of determinants (Gordon 2000, for example). Moore (1999) offers a comprehensive review of the UK's trade structure over the last 50 years on a sector-by-sector basis including both goods and services, focusing in particular on the impact of membership of the EU. Her detailed research reveals how trade has changed and the factors that have impacted on it. Unfortunately it does not include either backward- or forward-looking quantitative assessments of the impact of specific aspects of European integration as such.

Prior view

At the time of the UK's entry to the European Community (EC), forecasters were ambivalent about the likely effects of membership on the UK's balance of trade in manufactures. Although all were agreed that the effect on the UK's current account would be adverse, because of the need to make contributions to the EU budget and the higher cost of food imports under the Common Agricultural Policy (CAP), views differed concerning the effect on trade in manufactures. The official view (HMSO 1970) was that the UK would experience a deterioration in the trade balance for two reasons. First, as the UK's tariffs on EC imports were slightly higher than EC tariffs on UK exports, UK imports from the EC could be expected to increase by more than UK exports to the EC. Second, the UK would experience some reduction in her exports to members of EFTA and the Commonwealth due to her loss of preferences in these markets. However, some outside forecasts predicted a small increase in the UK's trade surplus in

> # At the time of the UK's entry to the EC, forecasters were ambivalent about the likely effects of membership on the UK's balance of trade in manufactures

manufactures (Kreinin 1974; Resnick and Truman 1975). Few considered the role of exchange rate adjustment.

Much of the ambivalence was the result of uncertainty about the dynamic effects on British industry of EC entry. If entry resulted in large cost savings from economies of scale and reduced X-inefficiency, British manufacturing would enjoy increased competitiveness vis-à-vis continental manufacturing. Moreover, if a large influx of foreign investment followed UK entry, British exports to the EC might enjoy a further stimulus. Opponents of entry, however, argued that the long-run effects of membership could be adverse for UK manufacturing, if higher food prices resulted in higher wage costs and if deflationary measures were imposed because of the need to achieve balance of payments equilibrium. Moreover, the exposure of British industry to increased competition could just as easily be adverse if British firms were unable to match the costs and prices of EC competitors.

Performance of the UK trade balance after entry

On first appearances, the predictions of the pessimists appear to have been closer to the truth. The UK's merchandise trade balance with the members of the EC changed from a surplus of some £120 million in 1970 to a deficit of more than £3 billion in 1979. The latter accounted for most of the UK's deficit on visible trade with the world as a whole (see Table 12.1). By 1989, the deficit with an enlarged EC had reached £17.5 billion (3.4 per cent of GDP), compared with a deficit of only £7.3 billion with non-EC countries. Thereafter, the deficit fell both in absolute terms and as a proportion of the UK's overall imbalance.

Table 12.1 | UK trade balance with the EU £million (%GDP)

Year	Balance with EU countries	Balance with non-EU countries	Overall balance
1970	120 (0.2)	−138 (−0.3)	−18 (−0.0)
1971	−217 (−0.4)	422 (0.7)	205 (0.4)
1972	−768 (−1.2)	32 (0.0)	−736 (−1.1)
1973	−1718 (−2.3)	−855 (−1.2)	−2573 (−3.5)
1974	−2623 (−3.1)	−2618 (−3.1)	−5241 (−6.3)
1975	−2667 (−2.5)	−578 (−0.5)	−3245 (−3.1)
1976	−2550 (−2.0)	−1380 (−1.1)	−3930 (−3.1)
1977	−2140 (−1.5)	−131 (−0.1)	−2271 (−1.6)
1978	−2835 (−1.7)	1301 (0.8)	1534 (0.9)
1979	−3048 (−1.5)	−278 (−0.1)	−3326 (−1.7)
1980	925 (0.4)	404 (0.2)	1329 (0.6)
1981	−205 (−0.1)	3443 (1.4)	3238 (1.3)
1982	−1468 (−0.5)	3347 (1.2)	1879 (0.7)
1983	−2978 (−1.0)	1360 (0.4)	−1618 (−0.5)
1984	−3710 (−1.1)	−1699 (−0.5)	−5409 (−1.7)
1985	−2775 (−0.8)	−641 (−0.2)	−3416 (−1.0)
1986	−10102 (−2.6)	485 (0.1)	−9617 (−2.5)
1987	−11214 (−2.7)	−484 (−0.1)	−11698 (−2.7)
1988	−15730 (−3.4)	−5823 (−1.2)	−21553 (−4.6)
1989	−17472 (−3.4)	−7252 (−1.4)	−24724 (−4.8)
1990	−11670 (−2.1)	−7037 (−1.3)	−18707 (−3.4)
1991	−2345 (−0.4)	−7878 (−1.3)	−10223 (−1.7)
1992	−4934 (−0.8)	−8116 (−1.3)	−13050 (−2.1)
1993	−5285 (−0.8)	−8034 (−1.3)	−13319 (−2.1)
1994	−5537 (−0.8)	−5554 (−0.8)	−11091 (−1.6)
1995	−4224 (−0.6)	−7500 (−1.1)	−11724 (−1.6)
1996	−4234 (−0.6)	−8852 (−1.2)	−13086 (−1.7)
1997	−4036 (−0.5)	−7874 (−1.0)	−11910 (−1.5)
1998	−5295 (−0.6)	−15242 (−1.8)	−20537 (−2.4)
1999	−6436 (−0.7)	−20331 (−2.3)	−26767 (−3.0)

Source: Office for National Statistics

Figures in parenthesis show balances as a percentage of current price GDP

Clearly, however, we cannot deduce from this evidence alon the effects of entry have been negative, as we have no way of kn what would have happened to UK trade with the EC had the L. joined. Before any assessment can be made of the effects of entry, we need to know how factors unconnected with EC membership, such as changes in aggregate demand or relative competitiveness, have affected UK trade. Only if the effects of these other changes can be separated can the effects of entry be estimated. Neither can we compare the performance of the UK's trade balance with the EU with that with non-EU countries, since the latter may itself have been affected by entry.

Even assuming that we can make some moderately intelligent guess at the probable impact of entry on UK trade, it is clear that this alone tells us nothing about whether the impact was a favourable or unfavourable one. To begin with, the fact that the trade deficit widened following entry need not constitute a major problem, providing that the real exchange rate is free to adjust downwards in response. Clearly, this was the case for the entire period in question. Of course, a decline in the real exchange rate is not without a cost to the UK, as import prices will rise and hence real incomes will fall. However, we need also to ask what benefits the rise in imports brought to the UK economy. This will depend on whether the rise in imports was the result of trade creation (lower-cost imports from the EC displacing higher-cost domestic production) or trade diversion (higher-cost imports from the EC displacing lower-cost imports from the rest of the world). If the net effect is a trade-creating one, real incomes in the UK will be accordingly higher and this must be deducted from the real income loss due to a worsening of the terms of trade. Clearly, we cannot answer this question without further information about trade creation and trade diversion following entry.

Estimating the entry effects

Various approaches have been employed to isolate the impact of EC entry on UK trade from that of other factors. The simplest approach is to assume that the *share* of UK imports coming from the EC and the share of UK exports going to the EC would not have changed had the UK not joined the EC. Then, any increase or decrease in the share might be attributed to EC membership. Clearly, however, this takes no account of any changes in the share that had taken place before entry. For example, if UK exports to the EC were increasing as a share of total UK exports before entry, it would be patently wrong to ascribe all the increase after entry to joining the EC. It might be better to assume that the pre-entry trend would have continued had the UK not joined and to count only the difference between this and what actually happened as the entry effect.

In one of the earliest attempts to estimate the impact of entry, Daly (1978) used a shares approach of this kind to make a qualitative assessment of the effects of entry. However, rather than looking at the share of UK imports coming from the EC in total imports, she used the import penetration ratio or the ratio of imports to apparent consumption. Likewise, for exports, she used the export sales ratio, which measures the ratio of exports to total sales. In both cases, she distinguished between total imports/exports, imports/exports from the Six and imports/exports from Ireland and Denmark, which joined the EC at the same time as the UK. As only three years of entry were covered, the results were of limited value. These appeared to show a sharp increase in import penetration caused by increased imports from the Six, especially for agricultural products and manufactured food, drink and tobacco. In terms of individual product groups, an integration effect was apparent for all product groups, except transport equipment where the Six's share of UK imports fell after UK entry. No attempt was made, however, to make a quantitative assessment of the overall effect on UK trade or to distinguish between trade creation and trade diversion.

Using a similar approach, Morgan (1980) went a step further and sought to estimate the entry effect. On the export side, she compared the actual growth of UK exports of manufactures to the EC after entry with the growth of exports that would have taken place on the assumption that the UK maintained market share. This exercise was performed for six markets including the EC. Before entry, UK exports of manufactures were losing ground in several major markets (including both the EC and its preferential markets such as EFTA and the Commonwealth). However, after entry, although they continued to lose ground elsewhere, they succeeded in increasing their share of EC markets. Moreover, the biggest losses in market share after entry occurred in 'neutral' markets and not in its former preferential markets, suggesting that much of the increase in its share of the EC market represented genuine trade creation rather than trade diversion. She estimated the total export gain at between £1075 and £1125 million between 1972 and 1977.

In estimating the effect of entry on UK imports, Morgan adopted a different approach. She argued that it was only reasonable to adopt the shares approach if it could be safely assumed that total UK imports were unaffected by UK entry. If, as a result of entry, the total UK imports increased by more than they would otherwise have done, not all of the increase in the EC share could be attributed to the UK's joining. In the case of exports, she argued, it was reasonable to assume that total EC imports were unaffected by enlargement because the reduction in the EC's average tariff on imports of manufactures was very small. However, this was not the case with UK imports, with the UK tariff falling on imports from the rest of the world by a relatively large amount. Therefore, Morgan used price elasticities estimated from previous studies to estimate the probable effect of the reduction in the UK tariff on imports from the EC to estimate the entry effect. She found that imports of finished manufactures increased by £500 million and of semi-manufactures by between £250 and £300 million between 1972 and 1977 as a result of entry. Putting these figures against the estimates for imports, the total effect was a net improvement in Britain's balance of trade in manufactures of between £300 and £375 million. In relation to the UK's total trade in manufactures and when set against the other costs of entry, however, the gain was fairly trivial.

The major problem with a shares approach is that it treats any change in market shares as being due entirely to the effects of integration. No attempt is made to estimate the effects of other factors, such as demand changes or changes in relative competitiveness, on exports and imports. For this reason, some studies have sought to isolate the integration effect by estimating how much of the change in exports and imports can be explained by these factors. The approach used by Featherstone et al. (1979) was to adjust the data for UK exports and import shares to and from the Six following entry for the effects of changes in aggregate demand and of unit labour costs relative to competitors. To do this, they used a range of estimates of assumed elasticities taken from other empirical studies: Winters (1987) criticized this procedure on the grounds that the range was too large for comfort. The adjusted data for UK exports and import shares following entry to the EC were then compared with the trend extrapolated from the period before entry. They found that, while there was a steady improvement in exports, this was dwarfed by a deterioration in imports, leaving a negative overall effect. They estimated that, by 1977, net exports were almost £2 billion lower than might have been expected on previous trends. They assumed that the resultant deficit implied a sacrifice of economic growth and hence a loss of real income, which was estimated at 6 per cent over the period 1973–77. However, this took no account of any welfare gain from net trade creation and so leaves open the question as to whether UK real incomes rose or fell as a result of entry.

Mayes (1983) made a later estimate of the impact of EC entry on UK trade using a shares approach and distinguishing between eight different product groups (see Chapter 1). The *anti monde* was the linear trend in the share of UK exports going to the EC in total UK exports and the share of UK imports coming from the EC in total UK imports in the period 1960 to 1972. For imports, the actual value of imports exceeded the trend value by $15 billion in 1980, with the difference being statistically significant in all cases except transport equipment. For exports, a similar trend was apparent with export shares rising above trend value in all cases except crude materials (where relative prices were not much affected by entry). In the case of machinery and transport equipment, however, the increases were neither substantial nor statistically significant. A similar exercise was also performed for the share of UK exports in EC imports. For all categories except crude materials, the share of UK exports in total EC imports increased above trend, although the result was statistically insignificant in the case of other manufactures. In total, the effect on UK exports was of the order of £5–7 billion. With EC tariffs of 5 per cent on finished manufactures, this translated into a welfare gain of £1.5 billion. However, as there is no breakdown of how much trade creation and trade diversion resulted, an overall assessment of the welfare gain is not possible.

> ## Only a formal model of macroeconomic behaviour for the period following entry could provide accurate estimates of the effects of entry

The attempts of early studies to estimate the entry effect by identifying an underlying trend in UK trade with the EC were criticized by Mayes (1983) on the grounds that the period before entry was too different from the period after. At best, the extrapolation of pre-entry trends, even when adjusted for changes in 'non-EC' factors, could provide an indication of what might have been the effects of entry. No more should, therefore, be claimed for the results than this. Only a formal model of macroeconomic behaviour for the period following entry could provide accurate estimates of the effects of entry. The first attempt to develop such a model capable of explaining most of the determinants of UK exports and imports following entry was made by Winters (1987). Using what is called the almost ideal demand system (AIDS), he sought to estimate the share of imports in total expenditure on manufactures coming from a particular source as a function of several variables. These were real expenditure (money expenditure divided by the price index) and the prices of goods from other sources, plus a series of dummy variables to represent the effect of preferential tariff reductions. The function was estimated for imports from 10 suppliers – the five EC partner countries and five other major industrial countries. The estimated figures were then compared with the actual values for exports and imports to derive the entry effect. Winter's results are summarized in Table 12.2.

The first column shows that, for imports from all of the EC countries, actual imports considerably exceeded the amount predicted by the

Table 12.2 Winters' estimates of the entry effects on UK manufacturing trade

| Trade with | Change in trade due to accession, 1979 | | | |
| | Imports | | Exports | |
	£ million	As % of actual	£ million	As % of actual
France	1,934	62	540	25
Belgium-Luxembourg	1,745	89	N/C	
Netherlands	1,315	70	N/C	
W. Germany	3,748	69	1,611	57
Italy	1,332	66	663	55
Sweden	−120	−9	N/C	
Switzerland	542	21	N/C	
Japan	722	49	−259	−48
Canada	−232	−44	N/C	
USA	1,186	32	−1,249	−44
UK (change in home sales)	−12,171	−17	N/A	

Note: N/C not calculated; N/A not applicable
Source: Winters (1987)

model. Of the non-EC countries, only imports from Sweden and Canada suffered any adverse effect. This suggests that external trade creation occurred in a number of supplier countries, not surprising given that UK tariffs on third-country imports fell following entry. However, the most dramatic effect was that actual sales of domestically produced manufactures were well below the level predicted by the model. The possibility exists, however, that some of the increase in imports from non-EC countries may have reflected secular trends in UK trade rather than the effects of accession. Winters suggested that a figure of £8 billion might be a more plausible estimate of the trade creation effect. The calculations on the export side were derived by estimating the same import function for five major markets – France, Germany, Italy, Japan and the USA – for manufactures coming from the UK. Although not quite as high as for imports, the results show that UK exports to the Six were higher than that predicted by the model. To some extent, however, these were offset by reduced exports to other markets, including Japan and the USA. Overall, Winters estimated that the net effect on UK exports was £2.8 billion, giving a net trade effect of minus £5.2 billion. On more conservative assumptions, Winters estimated that the effect of entry on UK manufacturing was the equivalent of 1.5 per cent of GNP.

Contrariwise, this says nothing about the positive effects on UK real income of any trade creation resulting from entry. As the figures appear to show that there was little if any trade diversion in manufactures, it is reasonable to conclude that all or most of the increase in imports was due to trade creation. Using Mayes' estimates for 1981, Winters estimated the resultant gain at £250 million or approximately £5 per capita. This must be offset against the effect on the UK terms of trade of the deterioration in the trade balance. The overall result, however, appears to have been substantially negative, even without the other costs arising from the adoption of the Common Agricultural Policy and the net transfers to the Community Budget (see Chapter 11).

Estimating the dynamic effects of entry

A drawback of the very early studies of the effects of EC entry on UK trade is that they may have been too soon to capture the impact of any dynamic effects on UK manufacturing fully. UK entry was expected to have a salutary effect on manufacturing through fuller exploitation of economies of scale and the exposure of companies to increased competition from the Six. However, these effects may take several years to work fully through into improved trade performance. Work by Owen (1983) had suggested that the formation of the EC had brought about a much more substantial boost to real GDP than estimates of the static effects alone had suggested. Based on estimates from other empirical studies about the relationship between market size and efficiency, he argued that the true increase in GDP was of the order of 3–4 per cent. Building on Owen's study, Shepherd (1983) provided a qualitative assessment of the effects of entry on UK manufacturing that incorporated these dynamic effects. The enlargement of the market in which UK firms could now sell could be expected to result in large cost reductions in those industries in which scale economies occur only at a very high level of output. However, in addition to these economies resulting from increased plant size, there were potentially greater gains to be reaped from increased plant specialization. These occur when producers reduce the number of products manufactured within a single plant, thereby achieving longer production runs. The latter types of cost saving are often the result of increased intra-industry trade, with different countries specializing in different products within any given industry. Shepherd pointed to the available evidence to show that much of the increase in UK trade with the EC in manufactured goods following entry was of the intra-industry type. This is indirect evidence that there were substantial gains to UK manufacturing following entry that were due to an enlargement of the size of the market.

A rather different approach was adopted towards the measurement of long-run dynamic benefits by Marques-Mendes (1986) using a balance of payments constrained growth model based on the work of Thirlwall (1979, 1982). This sought to measure the effects of integration by estimating the impact on economic growth of individual member states of changes in their external balance of payments, using a model that incorporated a foreign trade multiplier showing how growth in one member state spilled over into faster growth in others. In this model, the main limit to the growth of demand was set by the need to achieve external balance in the current account. Part of the study covered the period 1974–81 following UK entry, during which the UK experienced the lowest growth rate of any member state. Although the UK economy enjoyed sluggish growth during this period, the net effect of entry was positive. Of the 1.24 per cent growth rate, 0.37 percentage points could be attributed to entry to the EC. The effects of adopting the CAP (including the budgetary effect) had a negative effect by raising food prices and taxation and reducing real incomes. Likewise, the decline in the terms of trade caused by the worsening of the trade balance further reduced real incomes. However, the effects of the change in manufacturing trade balance, which incorporated the multiplier effects of growth in other member states on UK exports, was positive, as was the entry-induced impact of direct foreign investment. Although the effect of integration on growth was lower than in five other member states, it was higher than for Ireland, while being negative for Denmark.

Impact of membership on inward direct investment

One of the dynamic effects of entry that was anticipated at the time of British entry to the EC was an increase in inward investment in the UK by foreign firms seeking access to the EC market. It was argued that the attraction of more foreign investment to the UK following entry would have beneficial effects on both the competitiveness of UK manufacturing and long-run economic growth. Much the same difficulties are involved in assessing the impact of membership on direct investment to the UK from abroad as are involved in measuring the impact on trade. As we do not know what inward investment would have occurred if the UK had not joined, we cannot say how much investment was the result of membership. Moreover, we do not know whether such inward investment as did occur merely displaced domestic investment that would otherwise have taken place or whether it was additional to investment undertaken by existing UK and foreign firms. Clearly, it is only if investment adds to existing investment that long-run growth is enhanced.

Such evidence as is available does suggest that the formation of the EC did result in an increase in inward investment to the member state economies. Hence, investment by US multinationals in Western Europe in the 1960s appears to have shifted from countries that were not members of the EC to those that were (United Nations 1993). Thus, the UK's share of US foreign direct investment (FDI) in manufacturing (measured in stock terms) fell sharply from 58 per cent in 1961 to 36 per cent in 1973, the time of UK entry to the EC. At the same time, the share going to the Six rose. Although the UK share fell further in the years immediately after entry, it bottomed out in 1978 before beginning a slow recovery (Fleet 1982). By the mid-1980s, her share had risen to 41 per cent. In a similar manner, the UK has been the major recipient of inward investment by Japanese firms anxious to gain access to the enlarged European markets and overcome barriers on Japanese exports. At the time of British entry to the EC, Japanese investment in the EC was relatively low but rising. The UK succeeded in attracting about one-half of all direct investment by Japan in the 1970s (Fleet 1982). Between 1981 and 1986, the UK accounted for roughly 32 per cent of all Japanese FDI to the EC in manufacturing. The figure was 55 per cent for transport equipment, the sector in which Japanese FDI was greatest (Heitger and Stehn 1990). By 1987, the UK share of Japanese FDI in Europe stood at 31.3 per cent, down from 44.9 per cent in 1980 (Dunning and Cantwell 1992).

In the automobile industry, the UK was the main recipient of investment by Japanese firms, much of it in the form of transplants designed to circumvent quotas imposed on Japanese exports or negotiated under a series of voluntary export restraint agreements. While UK car production plummeted following UK entry, by the early 1980s production had

> **By the early 1980s production had begun to increase and the UK trade balance improved largely as a result of investment by Japanese firms**

begun to increase and the UK trade balance improved largely as a result of investment by Japanese firms. Likewise, much investment by Japanese and South Korean firms in the electronics sector went to the UK. It seems likely that most of this investment would not have occurred had the UK not been a member of the EC. The resultant output should, therefore, be seen as an addition to UK GDP over and above the increase in real incomes resulting from improved resource allocation.

Effect of the single market programme on UK trade

Since the UK joined the EC, the two most important integration events have been enlargement of the Community and the Internal or Single Market Programme (SMP). With regard to the former, there were two phases – the southern Mediterranean enlargement in the 1980s (leading to the accession of Greece, Spain and Portugal) and the EFTA enlargement in the 1990s (resulting in Austria, Sweden and Finland 's joining the EU). Both of these enlargements have had an impact on UK manufacturing exports and imports that would need to be included in any estimate of EC membership on the UK. No studies, however, appear to have been carried out that permit any quantification of these results. With regard to the SMP, however, some estimates can be obtained by drawing on the results of a series of studies carried out by consultants on behalf of the European Commission and published in a series of volumes collectively entitled *The Single Market Review*.

Two of these studies are of particular relevance for any assessment of the impact of the single market on the UK. One of the studies used a computable general equilibrium (CGE) model to examine the effects of the SMP on trade patterns in manufactured goods (European Commission 1997a). CGE models are widely used in studies of the effects of trade liberalization (Francois *et al.* 1996; Stoeckel *et al.* 1990). In essence, they are models covering a large number of countries and sectors within each country that set out in the form of a series of equations the conditions that must be met for equilibrium to pertain in the system as a whole. In their most sophisticated form, such models incorporate elements of both perfect and imperfect competition in product markets and increasing as well as constant returns to scale. The model was calibrated using 1991 data and then used to perform various simulations designed to capture the effects of the single market programme. The first of these simulations was an *ex ante* exercise, in which estimates of the likely effects of the SMP on intra-EU trade were imposed and the effects on equilibrium re-computed. Our interest is purely in the results for the UK. These showed an increase in the share of the UK market accounted for by imports of manufactures from the EU of 2.88 per cent, 2.55 per cent of which was accounted for by reduced domestic production, i.e. took the form of trade creation rather than trade diversion.

A second exercise was of an *ex post* type, in which the reduction in trade costs needed to bring about the increase in intra-EU trade shares that actually took place is determined. These are, then, compared with the estimated reductions in trade costs known to have taken place to determine the integration effect. Again, focusing just on the impact on UK trade, the share of imports coming from the EU rose by 1.87 per cent while the share of home production fell by 1.4 per cent. The latter measures the trade-creating effect with the difference constituting trade diversion. A further simulation was carried out in which there was a reduction in extra-EU as well as intra-EU trade costs. In this case, external trade creation also resulted, with the UK's extra-EU trade share rising by 1.87 percentage points. Translating these gains into welfare terms, the study estimated that UK real GDP rose by between 2.4 and 3 per cent, slightly more than for the other large member states (France, Germany and Italy) but less than for the small member states (Portugal, Spain, Greece and Eire).

The second of the Commission studies looked at the impact of the single market on the structure of intra-European trade (European Commission 1997b). This found that a growing proportion of the increased trade between the member states of the EC that took place over the period from 1980 to 1994 was of the intra-industry type. Whereas one-way trade in essentially different products accounted for over 45 per cent of intra-EC trade at the start of this period, this fell to 39 per cent by 1994. Thus, intra-industry trade predominated with vertical intra-industry trade (two-way trade in vertically differentiated commodities), as opposed to horizontal (two-way trade in similar commodities), accounting for most of the increase. The UK's trade with the rest of the EC roughly conformed to this pattern. Intra-industry trade rose from 32 per cent of UK trade in 1980 to 37 per cent in 1994, slightly below that of France and Germany, but a higher share than in the Netherlands and Italy. As in the other large member states, vertical intra-industry trade was more important than interindustry trade and accounted for most of the increase. As we observed earlier, dynamic gains from increased integration are likely to be quantitatively more important under intra- than interindustry specialization. Therefore, the fact that the UK, along with other countries, enjoyed increased intra-industry specialization in the 1980s would suggest that the deepening and widening of the Community brought further dynamic gains to the UK economy.

Withdrawal from the EU?

Given that nearly 30 years have passed since the UK joined the EC and the EC has undergone many changes, an alternative way of viewing the effects of membership is to ask what would be the impact of the UK's withdrawing from the EC. Pain and Young (2000) have sought to estimate the likely macroeconomic impact of a British withdrawal using a simulated model for the UK economy. Because of the increased share of UK exports now going to the EU, an estimated 14.4 per cent of output (equivalent to 3.9 million jobs) depend directly on access to the EU market. If allowance is made for the import content of exports (the imported inputs required to produce these goods), a more accurate figure would be 13.6 per cent of output (or approximately 3.7 million jobs). Because the sectors of the economy that export to the EU have a lower employment content than for the economy as a whole, however, Pain and Young estimate the number of jobs involved at closer to 2.5 million. Taking further account of the number of jobs indirectly dependent on exports to the EU pushes the figure closer to 2.7 million or roughly 10 per cent of total employment. The decline in demand that would follow withdrawal would cause some loss of these jobs, which would depress demand in other sectors of the economy. However, provided that wages and prices were free to adjust downwards in response to the fall in demand and monetary policy was eased to counter the deflationary shock to the economy, unemployment should not increase substantially in the long run.

Advocates of withdrawal have argued that there would be no adverse effect on UK exports because the UK could join the European Economic Area or negotiate a free trade agreement with the EU. By the same token, there could still be an initial dampening effect if a time interval lapsed between withdrawal and the negotiation of such an agreement. Neither is it reasonable to assume that the UK could raise output by imposing high tariffs on imports from the rest of the world, as to do so would breach agreements reached as a member of the World Trade Organization. If there were a dampening effect on UK trade, this could be offset by the rise in real incomes that would result from the UK's withdrawing from the Common Agricultural Policy. Although taxes would be unlikely to fall as farm subsidies would have to be paid for directly out of UK taxes instead of via the EU budget, some reduction in food prices might result if lower tariffs were imposed on agricultural imports. The fact, too, that the UK would no longer need to pay a large contribution to the EU budget would enable the government either to cut UK taxes or increase public spending. These considerations have led some critics of UK membership to argue that the effects of withdrawal on the UK economy could well be positive, at least in the short run. For example, Minford (1996) puts the combined costs of the CAP and the budget at £10 billion or 1.5 per cent of GDP. However, this ignores the effects of withdrawal on inward investment.

No one can be sure about the precise effect of a withdrawal on investment from abroad. However, there is sufficient evidence to show that membership of the EC has attracted investment from abroad in the case of all the member states. While this would not all be reversed following a withdrawal, some negative effect is likely, even if the UK were to retain membership of the European Economic Area. The results of a variety of econometric studies lead Pain and Young (2000) to conclude that the stock of manufacturing investment would be about one-third lower than would otherwise be the case if the UK were to

> ## Advocates of withdrawal have argued that there would be no adverse effect on UK exports

withdraw from the EU. Advocates of UK exit have argued that there will be offsetting gains from lower business costs as UK-based firms would not be subject to EU laws (e.g. the need to apply the Social Chapter) (Jamieson and Minford 1999). It seems unlikely, however, that this latter effect would be large, as there is no evidence that foreign firms have yet been deterred from investing in the single market by any legal encumbrances created by EU legislation. Even advocates of withdrawal are agreed that there would be some loss of inward investment if the UK left the EC, although there is no consensus on how much lower GDP would be as a result. Pain and Young (2000) argue that the effects go beyond the fall in output consequent upon a diminution in the size of the country's capital stock. Because inward investment appears to have important positive effects on technical efficiency, long-run productivity growth could also be lower.

Simulating the effects of a UK withdrawal on the assumption that tariffs are imposed on UK exports and direct investment is reduced, Pain and Young (2000) estimated that UK GDP would be 2 per cent lower than otherwise. The main reason for this was the adverse effect that reduced inward investment has on UK productivity. Manufacturing was especially badly affected with exports falling by 8 per cent over the long run. Employment fell in the short run, but in the long real wages were assumed to adjust sufficiently to permit a reduction in unemployment. Although the loss was not a massive one, it was equivalent to the gain that the single market was estimated to have brought for the member states as a whole. Advocates of withdrawal agree that the adverse effects on inward investment would offset any gains from abandoning the CAP and reduced budgetary contributions. However, they argue that the burden of economic and monetary union and the need to comply with EU social policy will impose costs on UK business that will result in lower output and employment in the long run (Minford 1996). As we have seen, the latter argument is far from being proven, while the case for or against entry to EMU can be argued either way.

Conclusion

After nearly 30 years of UK membership of the EC, the precise effects of membership on UK trade are difficult to ascertain. Although the UK trade balance in manufactures with the rest of the EC has deteriorated following membership, this in itself says nothing about the aggregate effect of membership on real GDP. Whereas the resource allocation effect has almost certainly been a positive one (with trade creation outweighing trade diversion), the deterioration in the UK terms of trade as a result of the deficit in the balance of trade may have been sufficient to cancel this out. The biggest imponderable, nevertheless, remains the size of the dynamic gain. The fact that entry was followed by increased intra-industry specialization suggests that the dynamic benefits of having access to an enlarged market were not inconsequential. To the extent that these fed through into lower prices, consumers enjoyed higher real incomes as a result, and lower production costs enhanced the competitiveness of British industry. Increased inward investment by US and Japanese companies also added to these gains.

Empirical work carried out to estimate the effects of the single market on UK manufacturing suggests further positive integration effects. The share of UK consumption of manufactures accounted for by imports from other member states is evidence that the lowering of non-tariff barriers resulted in net trade creation and even external trade creation in particular sectors. It appears, also, that, along with other member states, much of the increased trade resulting from the creation of the single market took the form of intra-industry specialization. If so, this is further evidence of additional dynamic gains in the form of increased investment and lower prices. The single market may also have brought a further stimulus to direct investment from abroad.

The fact that UK trade has now shifted more towards the EC means that the potential impact of any withdrawal from the EC on UK output and employment is much greater than was true a decade or so ago. However, it does not follow that withdrawal would lead to a large fall in output and employment, provided that monetary policy was eased to alleviate the impact on output and real wages were allowed to adjust to permit job creation. It is also possible to argue that, because withdrawal would reduce the burden of the CAP and of contributions to the EU budget, the short-run impact might be beneficial. However, that ignores the effect that a withdrawal could have on inward investment from abroad. Some foreign firms operating in the UK would almost certainly scale down those operations, if not close down altogether. Manufacturing output and exports could suffer and long-run productivity growth be damaged. Although this would be less likely if the UK were to negotiate a free trade agreement with the EU after withdrawal, some negative effects on inward investment would result. Such an agreement might not be concluded immediately. Moreover, it is likely that the attractiveness of the UK as a location base for foreign firms seeking access to the EC market would be reduced if the UK were no longer a full member of the EU. The imponderable is the balance between the UK's being able to apply more flexible or lower-cost operating conditions outside the EU compared to any loss of access.

Participation in stage 3 of EMU therefore has to be seen in this context. It is also a mixture of pluses and minuses, in the sense that there is a trade-off between a reduction in some possible opportunities for flexibility and some possible gains from lower costs, increased growth and perhaps increased foreign direct investment. It seems difficult

> **Because withdrawal would reduce the burden of the CAP and of contributions to the EU budget, the short-run impact might be beneficial**

to apply large numbers to this although a growth rate effect of even half a percent of GDP a year soon mounts up. The stabilization of trade shares in recent years suggests that the degree to which there would be a further increase in the EU share, other than through enlargement of the EU, may be relatively limited. It is thus not surprising that the political case is so contentious if the economic case is relatively balanced and ill defined. The rather hypothetical nature of the growth and other longer-run effects tends to focus attention on somewhat more measurable immediate concerns, such as the costs and benefits of entering at the 'wrong' exchange rate.

References

Commission of the European Communities (1990) 'One market, one money', *European Economy*. Special Edition.

Daly, A. E. (1978) 'UK visible trade and the Common Market', *National Institute Economic Review*, November.

Dunning, J. H. and Cantwell J. A. (1992) 'Japanese direct investment in Europe' in B. Burgenmeir and B. Muchielli, *Multinationals and 1992*. London: Routledge.

Emerson, M., Aujean, M., Catinat, M., Goybet, P. and Jacquemin, A. (1988) 'The economics of 1992', *European Economy*, 35.

European Commission/Centre for Economic Policy Research (1997a) 'Trade patterns inside the Single Market', Vol. 2, Subseries IV, *The Impact on Trade and Investment, The Single Market Review*. Luxembourg: Office for Official Publications of the European Communities; London: Kogan Page, Earthscan.

European Commission/Centre for Economic Policy Research (1997b) 'Trade-creation and trade-diversion', Vol. 3, Subseries IV, *The Impact on Trade and Investment, The Single Market Review*. Luxembourg: Office for Official Publications of the European Communities; London: Kogan Page, Earthscan.

Featherstone, M., Moore, B. and Rhodes, J. (1979) 'EEC membership and UK trade in manufactures', *Cambridge Journal of Economics*, 3.

Fleet, K. (1982) 'Investment into the United Kingdom by third countries'. European League for Economic Co-operation.

Francois, J. F., McDonald, B. J. and Nordstron, H. (1996) 'Liberalization and capital accumulation in the GTAP model', GTAP Technical Paper 7.

Gordon, R. (2000) 'Does the new economy match up to the great inventions of the past?' *Journal of Economic Perspectives*, 14, 4, pp. 49–74.

Heitger, B. and Stehn, J. (1990) 'Japanese direct investments in the EC: responses to the internal market 1993?' *Journal of Common Market Studies*, 29, 1.

HMSO (1990) *Britain and the European Communities: An Economic Assessment*, Cmnd 4289. London: HMSO.

Jamieson, B. and Minford, P. (1999) *Britain and Europe: Choices for Change*. Politeia and Global Britain.

Kreinin, M. (1974) *Trade Relations of the EEC*. New York: Praeger.

Marques-Mendes, A. J. (1986) 'The contribution of the European Community to economic growth: an assessment of the first twenty-five years', *Journal of Common Market Studies*, 24, 4.

Mayes, D. G. (1978) 'The effects of economic integration on trade', *Journal of Common Market Studies*, 17, 1, pp. 1–25.

Mayes, D. G. (1983) 'EC trade effects and factor mobility' in A. El-Agraa (ed.) *Britain within the European Community: The Way Forward*. London: Macmillan.

Mayes, D. G. (1996) *Sources of Productivity Growth*. Cambridge: Cambridge University Press.

Mayes, D. G. (1997) 'The problem of quantitative estimation of integration effects' in Ali M. El-Agraa, *Economic Integration Worldwide*. Basingstoke: Macmillan.

Mayes, D. G. and Burridge, M. (1993a) 'The impact of the internal market programme on European structure and performance', European Parliament Working Paper E–2.

Mayes, D. G. and Burridge, M. (1993b) 'A single currency for Europe by the year 2000?', National Institute Briefing Note 4.

Minford, P. (1996) 'Britain and Europe: the balance sheet', *European Business Review*.

Moore, L. (1999) *Britain's Trade and Economic Structure: The Impact of the European Union*. London and New York: Routledge.

Morgan, A. D. (1980) 'The balance of payments and British membership of the European Community' in W. Wallace (ed.) *Britain in Europe*. London: Heinemann.

Owen, N. (1983) *Economies of Scale, Competitiveness and Trade Patterns within the European Community*. Oxford: Oxford University Press.

Pain, N. and Young, G. (2000) 'Continent cut off? The macroeconomic impact of British withdrawal from the EU'. Report prepared for 'Britain in Europe'. National Institute of Economic and Social Research.

Resnick, S. A. and Truman, E. M. (1975) 'An empirical examination of bilateral trade in Western Europe' in Bela Balassa (ed.) *European Economic Integration*. Amsterdam: North-Holland.

Shepherd, G. (1983) 'British manufacturing industry and the EC' in C. D. Cohen (ed.) *The Common Market: Ten Years After*. Deddington: Philip Allan.

Stoeckel, A., Pearce, D. and Banks, G. (1990) *Western Trade Blocs: Game, Set or Match for Asia-Pacific and the World Economy?* Canberra: Centre for International Economics.

Thirlwall, A. P. (1979) 'The balance of payments constraint as an explanation of international growth rate differences', *Banca Nazionale del Lavoro Quarterly Review*, March.

Thirlwall, A. P. (1982) *Balance of Payments Theory and the United Kingdom Experience*, second edition. London and Basingstoke: Macmillan.

United Nations (1993) 'From the Common Market to EC92: regional economic integration in the European Community and transnational corporations', Transnational Corporations and Management Division of the United Nations Department of Economic and Social Development, New York.

Winters, L. Alan (1987) 'Britain in Europe: a survey of quantitative trade studies', *Journal of Common Market Studies*, 25, 4.

13

Will Britain adopt the euro?

Ali M. El-Agraa

Introduction

Now that the euro is a reality as an official money, and will begin to circulate as everyday currency by the beginning of the year 2002, and the number of participants has increased to 12 with Greece joining on 1 January 2001, let me reiterate what I stated in Chapters 1 and 3. The decision to introduce the euro is regarded as one of the most, if not *the* most, significant events of the 20th century. This is because most people equate currencies with national sovereignties and deem both sacrosanct; hence they cannot comprehend why EU member nations wanted to sacrifice them. Indeed, many would argue that that is precisely the reason why Britain (as well as Denmark) insisted on the inclusion of her 'opt-out' clause in the Protocol in the Treaty on European Union (hereafter, the popular term 'Maastricht Treaty') and why she exercised that option then and still continues to do so. They would add that although the British decision to exercise the option may be attributed to the disastrous experience with the Exchange Rate Mechanism (ERM) of the European Monetary System (EMS) in 1991, leading to withdrawal in 1992 (see Chapters 3 and 9), it can easily be substantiated that the real rationale lies deeper, given the long history of British insularity from serious matters European (see Chapter 3; El-Agraa 1983, 2000; and Young 1998).

In this final chapter, I wish to concentrate on the British attitude towards the euro two years after its inauguration to find out whether UK adoption of the euro is within the realms of possibility and in the process point out some general conclusions from the various chapters of the book. I shall not consider why the EU nations wanted the euro, describe how it came about, or prognosticate on its significance since these issues have been tackled in Chapter 3 (also see El-Agraa 1980, 1998 and 2000).

The decision to introduce the euro is regarded as one of the most significant events of the 20th century

The British attitude

What is the British attitude towards the euro? By 'British', obviously I do not just mean the official British government position, but also that of the major opposition party as well as of the general British public.

With regard to the official government position, as mentioned in Chapter 1, returned (with a majority only 12 short of the landslide victory of the 1994 election) British Prime Minister Tony Blair has stuck to his pre-election pledge to commit his government to taking a decision on the adoption of the euro within the first two years of his new term, i.e. by about 2003. He further pledged that if he opted for recommending adoption, then he will ask UK citizens, through a referendum, to decide on the issue. However, according to the official government position, a positive recommendation, hence the referendum, will not be forthcoming until Britain has met the five economic tests imposed by British Chancellor Gordon Brown in October 1997 (see UK Treasury 1997 and later). Thus, the official government position is clear: to recommend to the British people the adoption of the euro, *provided the economic conditions are right*. And, if the conditions proved right, Blair says that he will 'of course' be able to persuade the recalcitrant voters to support his recommendation, 'provided we are setting out why it is economically and politically in Britain's interest' (*Financial Times*, 25 May 2001).

Contrariwise, the official British opposition, the Conservative Party, seems to occupy the opposite end of the spectrum. This may sound surprising, given that its pre-election leader William Hague has quickly returned to the back benches after his party's humiliating defeat, but there is no evidence to suggest that his successor will espouse a *major* deviation in the Conservatives' overall policy towards the euro. This is because even a previous frontrunner for succession, the pro-euro Dennis Clarke, indicated that being at the helm means reflecting the sentiments of the grassroots of the party. Hence, Hague's election manifesto, although it needs slight toning down, has great relevance here. Under his leadership, the Conservatives seemed utterly opposed to British adoption of the euro. Indeed, as mentioned in Chapter 1, the policy towards the euro has recently gone beyond the single currency issue. In March 2001, Hague clearly demonstrated that his long-established antagonism to Britain's adopting the euro has culminated into an onslaught on all matters European: he also demanded a renegotiation of the Nice Treaty (signed in December 2000) on enlargement; asked for a major transformation of the Common Agricultural and Fisheries Policies (CAP and CFP) in such a manner that only narrow UK interests are better catered for; and insisted on Westminster's having the prerogative completely to ignore those rulings of the EU Court of Justice that it may find not to its taste. To put it differently, he was in effect demanding that Britain must be allowed to set its own rules for participation in the EU, a demand which would most certainly be dismissed by the other 14 members and which cannot be realized while Britain remained a member of the club (see El-Agraa 2000).

As to the British public, it has become increasingly antagonistic towards euro adoption. As mentioned in Chapter 1 and detailed in Chapter 8, in December 2000, opinion polls indicated that 73 per cent of the population was opposed to adoption, an increase from 60 per cent in 1998. What is even more revealing is that the percentage opposed among business people (in the Employers' Federation, Confederation of British Industries – CBI – and similar associations) was 62 per cent against, a reversal of their enthusiastically positive position of 1998 when only 30 per cent were opposed and a more than doubling of that percentage. Moreover, these percentages have essentially remained intact since then, becoming manifestly clear during the election campaign. This position may seem to be contradicted by the results of a Gallup poll carried out during the first week of June 2001, which reported that only 40 per cent indicated that Britain should never, or not for many years, adopt the euro, 11 per cent were in favour of joining now and 46 per cent were for adoption, although not yet. However, it was only a single poll (so it cannot be taken seriously until corroborated by further results and polling organizations) and the 'positive' responses are vague in terms of time horizons.

Hence both the official opposition party and the general British public are singing the same tune. However, before one jumps to the conclusion that this is tantamount to stating that the issue is as good as dead, one needs a detailed consideration of the Brown tests, the Maastricht criteria for euro membership and the motives behind the Conservative opposition, as well as what influences the general British public in this respect. Indeed, opinion polls carried out during the election campaign indicated that 70 per cent of the British public believe that Britain will eventually adopt the euro!

A closer examination

The official government position

As already mentioned, the second-term British Labour government, with Blair back at the helm, is expected to honour its pledge on the euro. As committed, Blair will recommend the adoption of the euro provided the Brown tests are met, but of course these tests must come on top of the Maastricht criteria if Britain is to lodge a successful application with its EU partners. Hence, one has to consider both.

At this juncture, let us simply recall the Maastricht criteria for euro membership, detailed in Chapter 3 (see also Chapters 8–10), then consider them where most appropriate. They are. *price stability* (an average rate of inflation – measured by means of the consumer price index on a comparable basis; the Harmonized Indices of Consumer Prices, HICP – not exceeding by more than 1.5 percentage points the average of the three lowest rates); *interest rates* (an average nominal long-term interest rate that does not exceed by more than 2 percentage points that of, at most, the three best-performing member states); *budget deficits* (should not exceed 3 per cent of GDP); *public debt* (should not exceed 60 per cent of GDP); and *currency stability* (a member country should respect the normal fluctuation margin provided for by the ERM without severe tensions for at least two years before the examination, in particular, it should not have devalued its currency's bilateral central rate against any other member state's currency on its own initiative for the same period).

As a digression, also recall that the only rationale for these criteria is that 3 per cent of GDP happened to be the average level of public investment at that time and, considering it acceptable, it has to be financed by a budget deficit of that amount; calculating this at the steady state of equilibrium and a compound rate of interest of 5 per cent per annum results in a public borrowing of 60 per cent of GDP (see Chapter 4). Also, these criteria were consistent with Germany's, hence adopting them implied that the European Central Bank (ECB) would be as solid as the Bundesbank in controlling inflation, which is the sole role presently attributed to the ECB (i.e. the ECB cannot offer credit or make bail-outs and the exchange rate will be the responsibility of the Council of Ministers – see Chapters 3, 5, 8 and 9), although there are developments suggesting an expanded role for the ECB (see Chapters 5 and 9). The important point is that the performance of the member countries must not diverge so much as to make it difficult for the Economic and Monetary Union (EMU) to operate and for the euro to be stable, and the members, in their wisdom, decided that the convergence criteria agreed upon are the ones that will ensure against such an outcome.

What are the five Brown economic tests? The first is about business cycles' and economic structures' being compatible 'so that we and others could live comfortably with euro interest rates on a permanent basis'. The second relates to whether there would be 'sufficient flexibility to deal with' any problems if they emerge. The third concerns whether the adoption of the euro would 'create better conditions for firms making long-term decisions to invest in Britain'. The fourth is about what the impact of euro adoption would be 'on the competitive position of the UK's financial services industry, particularly the City's wholesale markets'. The final test sums up the other four since it is about whether the adoption of the euro would 'promote higher growth, stability and a lasting increase in jobs'. The Treasury report tries to knit the tests together:

> Sustainable and durable convergence is the touchstone and without it we cannot reap the benefits of a successful EMU. It means that the British economy:
>
> ● Has converged with Europe;
> ● Can demonstrably be shown to have converged;
> ● That this convergence is capable of being sustained; and
> ● That there is sufficient flexibility to adapt to change and unexpected economic events (op. cit., p. 2)

However, when announcing these tests in October 1997, Brown added that the Treasury must decide that there is a 'clear and unambiguous' economic case for recommending British adoption of the euro.

What would be the assessment of the Brown tests if they had to be conducted today? With regard to the first, which is obviously the most important, the answer would be inconclusive. As Wolf (*Financial Times*, 21 February 2001) argues, on the presumption of equal competence, the Bank of England's Monetary Policy Committee (MPC) would, over the longer term, be virtually certain to do a better job of stabilizing the British economy than would the European Central Bank (ECB), since Britain would be only one-sixth of the eurozone area and hence easier to manage. By the same token, one would expect the ECB to perform better in today's conditions relative to those of October 1997 when the tests were announced, since at that time, short-term interest rates were 4 percentage points higher in the UK than in Germany, but today the difference between them is only 1 percentage point (see

In November 2000 eurozone unemployment was still 3.4 percentage points higher than in Britain

Figure 13.1). Also, according to OECD estimates, the output gaps (the deviation of actual from potential output as a percentage of potential output) are today much closer than they were three years ago. Moreover, in November 2000 eurozone unemployment was still 3.4 percentage points higher than in Britain. One should hasten to add, however, that the OECD has concluded that the remaining differences are mostly structural. Nonetheless, one must agree with Wolf that, overall, one can safely state that cyclical convergence is at least greater than in 1997, so why the inconclusiveness? The answer is that convergence remains incomplete even in monetary policy. The MPC still deems it necessary to impose higher short-term interest rates relative

Figure 13.1 | Performing to some of the Brown tests

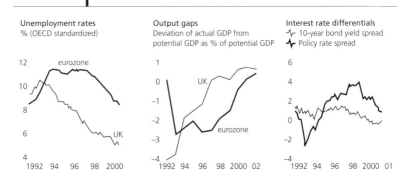

Source: *Financial Times*, 21 February 2001

to those of the eurozone, even though a strong pound sterling (hereafter, simply sterling) would exert persistent disinflationary pressure (see later). In addition, the high structural unemployment of the eurozone suggests that radical reform could give the ECB room for lower interest rates than those in the UK for some time to come.

As to the second test, the British labour market does not, on the whole, seem to be more flexible than in 1997, while the eurozone market may be marginally so. Thus, as long as country-specific shocks are modest, one should not expect great difficulties. Most economists, however, would go along with the proposition that when normal nominal wage and price rigidity prevail, floating exchange rates would always tend to provide greater flexibility to relative prices when responding to shocks than would fixed exchange rates.

With regard to the third test, the adoption of the euro would most certainly provide greater exchange rate stability for the sixth of the British economy subject to trade with the EU partners. However, this might be questioned since the major rationale for this statement is that exchange rate instability could be a bigger barrier to efficient specialization, which if true would mean that 'the world's bigger currency areas would normally be richer than its smaller ones. Yet some of the world's richest countries [for example, Switzerland and Singapore] are very small currency areas indeed. This suggests that exchange rate uncertainty is not that big an obstacle to economic efficiency' (Wolf. FT, 21 February 2001). Also, at the time, there was no evidence to suggest that investment in the UK was being adversely affected by the non-adoption of the euro: in 1999, business investment in Britain recorded a higher percentage of GDP than in Germany and France. Moreover, Britain continued to be the largest recipient of foreign direct investment (FDI) in the EU, absorbing 39 per cent of the total (more on this later).

As to the fourth test, 'the City remains the thriving home to the biggest and most sophisticated financial markets in the [eurozone]. As other economies deregulate, their financial markets are likely to grow, as is evidently happening to Frankfurt. But it is far from evident that the failure to [adopt the euro] has proved a decisive disadvantage to the City, at least so far' (Wolf, Ibid.). This argument is supported by Begg and Horrell in Chapter 10 of the current volume:

> The UK financial services industry is the best developed, most
> diversified and, arguably, most competitive in the EU. It has the
> manifest advantages of the City of London in its role as Europe's
> number one global financial centre and of having a regulatory

environment that has encouraged innovation and helped to sustain competitive advantage. Although there have, inevitably, been challenges to this ascendancy that have seen some segments of financial services lured away to other centres, the gravitational pull of agglomeration has easily offset these losses. Moreover, the capacity that the City has exhibited to reinvent itself has seen it accommodate far-reaching changes in the structure and ownership of financial and business services. As McRae and Cairncross (1991) note, 'to write a book about the City is to shoot at a moving target' (p.1).

This background suggests that whether the UK is 'in' or 'out' of the euro, its financial services sector will continue to be competitive and should maintain its leading role in the EU. This, however, is not a foregone conclusion.

With regard to the fifth test, which sums up these four, obviously one could not be certain since the answers to the four do not provide a decisively positive answer. Thus, a 'clear and unambiguous' economic case for euro adoption would be difficult to substantiate; hence, the recent analysis by Deutsche Bank (June 2001), which reaches the conclusion that 'a case can be made that the Chancellor's five tests are now met', may not register with Brown.

However, several authorities have argued that it is also vital to include an economic test omitted by Brown. It is the testing of a factor which, according to some of these authorities, would determine the economic performance of the UK for years to come: the value at which sterling would enter the euro. Contrary to popular perception, this need not be the present market exchange rate. This is clearly recognized by the President of the ECB, Wim Duisenberg, who in his quarterly testimony to the European parliament's Economic and Monetary Affairs Committee (on 20 June 2000) stated that Britain had met the conditions for entry into the euro, *but that sterling was at a high level*. Moreover, when the eurozone ministers of finance have consistently been of the opinion that the euro has been undervalued, they have been implicitly suggesting that other currencies, including sterling, have been overvalued relative to the euro.

This raises the question regarding how much lower sterling should be relative to the euro at the appropriate time. The Liberal Democrats, Group of Experts' Report (2000) provides an excellent summary of the state of the art. They select estimates (see Table 13.1) which broadly represent three different approaches to the exchange rate: purchasing power parity (PPP), equilibrium exchange rates and long-run averages of observed data.

The PPP approach is the traditional one. By comparing prices across different economies and presuming that in the long term markets must arbitrage the prices of traded commodities so as to equalize them, the approach would enable one to choose the exchange rate which would bring this about. For this purpose, the group opts for the PPP exchange rates estimated by the OECD but is quick to point out that the OECD itself would not go along with them, since for the OECD their rate for sterling is for GDP, not for just tradable goods and services. Although the group accepts this limitation and is aware of the waning popularity of this approach (due to disagreements on whether markets have exhibited a tendency to converge on PPP estimates over time), it nevertheless feels that it 'may still provide a guide to policy' (p. 20).

The group's preferred approach is that of the fundamental equilibrium exchange rate (FEER), pioneered by one of their own members, John Williamson. The approach seeks to find the exchange rate which would lead to equilibrium in the balance of payments such that the current account position matches the long-term flow of capital. Simultaneously, the approach seeks the rate that must generate domestic equilibrium with unemployment at its lowest possible level without accelerating inflation (see NAIRU earlier).

Table 13.1	Recent estimates of fundamental exchange rates between sterling and euro (euros and Deutschmarks – DEMs – per pound sterling)

Source	Euro rate	DEM rate
IMF (Alberola et al.[a])	1.23	2.41
Goldman Sachs[b]	1.30	2.54
OECD[c]	1.42	2.78
IIE (Wren-Lewis/Driver[d])	1.18	2.32
NIESR's Church[e]	1.16	2.30

Notes: [a] Bilateral time-varying equilibrium exchange rate; study date December 1999; estimate date end 1998; [b] time-varying equilibrium exchange rate; study date February 2000; estimate date 1999; [c] GDP purchasing power parity; study date 1999; estimate date 1999; [d] FEERs; study date 2000; estimate date mid-1998; [e] FEERs derived from HM Treasury model; study date July 1999 February 2000; estimate date mid-1997.

Source: Adapted from Liberal Democrats' Group of Experts' Report (2000, p. 19)

Obviously, FEER estimates would be influenced by model specifications as well as by assumptions regarding long-term capital flows.

The group chooses three independent estimates based on the FEER approach. These were carried out by Simon Wren-Lewis and Rebecca Driver (1998) for the Institute for International Economics, a group of economists from the University of Warwick (Church 1999) and the economics team at Goldman Sachs (2000). Also, they considered an analysis carried out independently by IMF staff (Alberto *et al.* 2000) which employs developments eliminating some of the guesswork and assumptions from the FEER approach.

The group draws attention to the fact that such rates can be checked against the real long-term averages for sterling, after making adjustments in costs or prices in Britain relative to UK competing economies. What this means is that a percentage increase in only British prices, hence a fall in British competitiveness relative to trading partners, matched by an equal percentage devaluation in sterling would leave sterling's real rate unchanged. Table 13.2 provides information on the difference between the sterling exchange rate and the long-term average real rate in the fourth quarter of 1999; the information is partly based on published data and on additional data made available to the group by the EU Commission's Economics Directorate-General (DG Economics). The group is quick to draw attention to the sensitivity of this calculation to two different options:

> # A recent analysis conducted by HSBC argues that an entry rate of between 1.48 and 1.53 euros to sterling would be fine

- First, it is sensitive to three separate estimates of cost and price movements relative to our trading partners shown in the table (unit labour costs in manufacturing; unit labour costs in the whole economy; and the overall price index for the whole economy or GDP deflator).
- Secondly, it is sensitive to the base period of comparison. We cite the long-run average between 1987 and 1999 because that is the base period used by the EU Commission, on the grounds that it excludes the distortions introduced by the rapid appreciation of the US dollar in the early eighties to peak in 1985. However, we have also calculated the same

overvaluation, using the Commission's data, over a twenty-year and over a thirty-year period. We also show charts of the three measures of the UK real exchange rate over the period since 1970 (p. 21).

After adding a further proviso, the group settled for a range of 1.25 to 1.45 euros to sterling (the Deutschmark – DEM – equivalents being 2.45 to 2.84) with the possibility that this could move higher with improvements in relative UK productivity. This possibility is prompted by a commentary in the *National Institute Economic Review* (August 2000) suggesting that productivity growth rates near 3 per cent per annum (as against the traditional 2 per cent) over about five years would enable a comfortable entry into the euro at 1.55 to sterling

Table 13.2 | Exchange rates implied by long-run real exchange rates, estimate for fourth quarter 1999 and studied in June 2000 (euros and Deutschmarks – DEMs – per pound sterling)

Source	Euro rate	DEM rate	Methodology
For 1987–99 average real exchange rate			
DG Economics	1.20	2.35	UCL all economy
DG Economics	1.08	2.11	UCL manufacturing
DG Economics	1.27	2.48	GDP deflator
For 1980–99 average real exchange rate			
DG Economics	1.22	2.39	UCL all economy
DG Economics	1.14	2.23	UCL manufacturing
DG Economics	1.32	2.58	GDP deflator
For 1970–99 average real exchange rate			
DG Economics	1.15	2.25	UCL all economy
DG Economics	1.04	2.03	UCL manufacturing
DG Economics	1.25	2.45	GDP deflator

Source: Adapted from Liberal Democrats' Group of Experts' Report (2000, p. 19)

(DEM 3.03). One should add that a more recent analysis conducted by HSBC (May 2001) argues that an entry rate of between 1.48 and 1.53 euros to sterling (DEM 2.90 to 3.00) would be fine.

Although Arestis and Sawyer (see Chapter 9) share this concern, stressing that getting that exchange rate wrong, and 'in particular setting the exchange rate too high would promise years, if not decades of deflation', the mentioned group does not go that far since they stress that over 'the long run, of course, the choice of entry rate will not be a matter of immense importance – the country will settle down to using the new currency. But . . . the choice of rate could have considerable importance for the economy over the transition period, before and after membership' (p. 22). Arestis and Sawyer would counter by drawing attention to interesting and revealing examples from 20th-century experience of what might happen under these circumstances: the return to the Gold Standard in 1925 at the pre-World War I parity and in 1990 when the UK joined the ERM at around 15 per cent overvaluation. Both were associated with long periods of economic depression.

Arestis and Sawyer (Chapter 9) stress that following the launch of the euro in January 1999, its value fell almost substantially from 1.18 to the dollar to 0.90 (see Figure 13.2). The value of sterling relative to the euro has to some degree reflected this decline in the value of the euro, although the value of sterling had been relatively high (in terms of European currencies such as the DEM) prior to the launch of the euro. In early 2001 sterling exchanged at 1.60 euros or 3.12 DEM. The euro is significantly undervalued against the dollar and sterling (Fred Bergsten, as reported in the *Guardian* of 22 January 2001, estimates the fundamental exchange rate at $1.25 = 1 euro) at that time and sterling overvalued against the euro. Bubbles in exchange rates (for whatever cause) are well known and it can be expected that the present bubble involving high values for the dollar and sterling and low values for the euro will eventually burst and the exchange rates move to more reasonable levels. But given the nature of exchange rate markets it could be expected that there will be future bubbles and no doubt at some point in the future the talk will be of low value of the dollar and high value of the euro. The immediate concern though is with the effects of the current high value of sterling and the consequences of any decline in the value of sterling.

Thus, despite disagreement regarding duration and irrespective of the various provisos attached, there seems to be general consensus that sterling is presently overvalued. As stated earlier, the study by Church (1999), based on the Treasury model, showed sterling to be 18 per cent overvalued in 1997 and 23 per cent in the second quarter of 1999. Recent movements in the exchange rate will tend to leave sterling even further overvalued.

As already mentioned, one of the Maastricht Treaty's criteria for a country to join the euro – and the only one which, given the preceding arguments, the UK currently clearly does not satisfy – is that relating to at least a two-year membership of the ERM with no significant change in the central exchange rate. But Arestis and Sawyer (Chapter 9) believe that this may not be such a serious hurdle for British entry. They consider the experience of other countries in the case of the Maastricht criteria in May 1997. In the event, as with other criteria, there was a degree of accommodation (Arestis and Sawyer prefer to call it fudge[1]) when decisions were made in terms of country membership of the euro. Take, for example, the experience of Finland. This country had only been a member of the ERM for one year prior to being an initial member of the eurozone in January 1999, yet Finland was deemed to

Figure 13.2 | Euro versus leading currencies

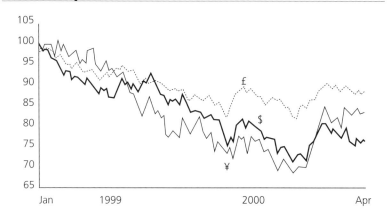

Euro exchange rates

Dollar	0.9012	Sterling	0.6252
Yen	110.56	Swedish krona	9.1007
Swiss franc	1.5303	Danish krone	7.4656

Rebased 1 January 1999 = 100

Source: Thomson Financial Datastream/*Financial Times*, 23 April 2001

have satisfied this particular criterion and thus became a full member of the EMU. They hastened to add, however, that it could be argued that Finland had satisfied the substantive part of this requirement, namely stability of the exchange rate of its currency against the ECU (the official EC money prior to the euro – the European Currency Unit). They conclude that it is clearly possible that the UK's entry into the euro would similarly not require formal membership of the ERM, but the stability of the exchange rate prior to entry should be seen as an important requirement.

As we saw in Chapter 9, Arestis and Sawyer consider the implications of meeting this criterion of a stable exchange rate for two years prior to entry for the UK's joining the euro in three years' time, by which they mean the date at which the value of sterling would be locked to the euro. This could then be followed by a period of transition of two to three years similar to that currently being undertaken by the original 11 eurozone members. Sterling might then disappear in five to six years' time.

It is helpful to consider the three possible scenarios suggested by Arestis and Sawyer, although they realize that actual events may well lie somewhere in between. The first is that sterling falls in value substantially over the next 12 months, followed by two years of exchange rate stability (vis-à-vis the euro) and, hence, in effect shadowing the euro. Whether or not sterling was in the ERM, it would satisfy the substantive requirement for entry into the euro and this could be seen as the dream scenario for such entry. It faces, however, the obvious but serious problems of how to engineer the reduction in the value of sterling and the implications of a rapid devaluation for inflation. The exact impact of a 20 per cent devaluation overall could be expected to have a direct impact on prices of the order of 6 to 7 per cent. This could be more if domestic prices respond, though it could be modified if the euro were to rise against the dollar, leading to devaluation in the effective exchange rate of less than 20 per cent.

The second scenario is that the value of sterling gradually declines in value over the next three years to reach a rate appropriate for entry. The interesting question would then be how this may be achieved. The obvious answer is through the rate of interest. But then this would contravene the objective of the Monetary Policy Committee (MPC) in view of their remit to achieve price stability and the 2.5 per cent target inflation rate. This is so since even if the MPC managed to lower sterling's, it may have such inflationary implications, which could very well imply an inflation rate above the target set by the Treasury. It would also require a bending of the Maastricht criteria to allow sterling to join. This would be the case in terms of both the inflation rate criterion (the UK would most certainly have under these conditions an inflation rate above the average of the three best-performing EMU countries in terms of their inflation rates) and the exchange rate criterion (two years of stable exchange rate without substantial devaluation, ruled out by definition).

The third scenario is that sterling remains overvalued, even if there is some decline in its value. The Maastricht Treaty requirement of a stable exchange rate vis-à-vis the euro would be satisfied, but entry occurs at an overvalued rate. This would be the nightmare scenario. Any benefits of lower transaction costs and reduced volatility of the value of the currency (zero, of course, against the rest of the eurozone) would be inconsequential against the cost of entry at an overvalued rate without any exit possibilities or indeed any other policy to account for it. The consequences of the entry of sterling into the eurozone at an overvalued rate are clear. The current position is that the UK is running a substantial trade deficit and the likelihood is that the UK would be entering the euro with a balance of trade deficit, a position that can only be sustained if others are prepared to lend to the UK. This can take the form of foreign direct investment, but then there is the obvious question of why all of a sudden and under these conditions multinationals would wish to invest in the UK. The alternative is that prices in the UK would have to fall by, say, 20 per cent, with an accompanying fall in money wages. Even if this fall is relative to prices elsewhere in the eurozone, and could be achieved by lower inflation in the UK compared with the rest of the eurozone, this would be far from painless. Years of deflationary policies to push down inflation (and into deflation) could well follow.

Arestis and Sawyer draw attention to the fact that during the 20th century the UK suffered two major episodes of joining a fixed exchange rate system at too high an exchange rate. The first was the return to the Gold Standard in 1925 at the pre-World War I parity, implying an overvaluation of around 10 per cent. The second was in 1990 when the UK joined the ERM at around 15 per cent overvaluation. Each was associated with a period of economic depression and both ended ignominiously, in 1931 and 1992 respectively. The obvious difference between those two experiences and adopting the euro at an overvalued exchange rate is that in the case of the first two it was possible to end the overvaluation. There were clearly costs involved in doing so and during the time of overvaluation there were always those warning of the disasters of leaving the Gold Standard and ERM respectively. In the present case of the UK's joining the eurozone, there would be severe legal and political constraints on reversing the decision and the only adjustment route would appear to be continuous deflation in the UK to reduce prices and wages.

Now that both the Maastricht criteria and the Brown tests have been covered, it is convenient to update them by reference to the Pricewater-houseCoopers (PwC) Convergence Index (2001), which is a combined indicator. It is based on a set of 10 main macroeconomic indicators on which comparable data are easily available from such reliable sources as the OECD and EU's Eurostat: the five Maastricht criteria and five real and/or cyclical variables on annual GDP growth, the estimated gap between actual and trend output, unemployment, the current account balance and short-term interest rates. The latest release of the index shows that the UK and eurozone economies are converging further – see Figures 13.3–13.8 and the Appendix to this chapter for an explanation of the Index.

The UK and eurozone economies are converging further

The general British public

As we have seen, all indicators suggest that Britain will have no major serious difficulties meeting both the Brown tests and the Maastricht

Figure 13.3 | PwC EMU Convergence Index for the UK

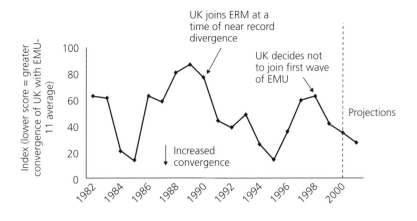

Source: PwC calculations using OECD, ONS and Eurostat data

Figure 13.4 | GDP growth cycle has begun to converge in recent years

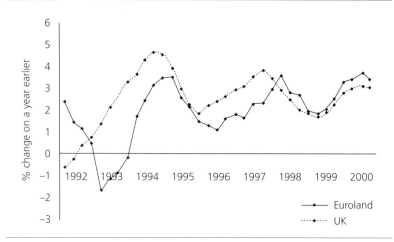

Note: UK and Euroland economic cycles were completely out of synch in the early 1990s, but have moved in parallel with each other since 1998. Euroland growth has been slightly higher, reflecting more unused capacity in early 1998

Source: Eurostat, ONS

Figure 13.5 | Long-term interest rates have converged to a large degree

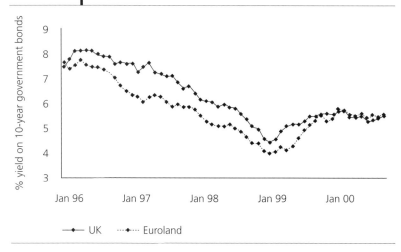

Notes: This suggests that long-term inflation expectations have also largely converged; * weighted average of major Euroland countries

Sources: Bank of England, Eurostat

criteria, *provided they are flexibly interpreted*. However, if Brown adheres strictly to a 'clear and unambiguous' economic case for euro adoption, then no referendum will be forthcoming unless Blair decides to go it alone. If either Blair decided to take unilateral action or Brown decided that his tests have been met so that both can recommend in unison, the likelihood of EU endorsement would be great even if the UK did not meet the exchange rate criterion. This would be due to the accommodation, or 'fudging', referred to earlier and clearly explained in Chapter 2 in terms of the general drive for European unification and in Chapter 3 in terms of the original decision to introduce the euro in 1999.

Yet, as we have seen, the British public remains very negative about euro adoption. What lies behind such negativity or downright antagonism?

One obvious answer is that the British people subscribe to what I stated in the first paragraph of this chapter and in Chapters 1 and 3: they equate the national currency, sterling, with national sovereignty. Although they supported EC membership through the Wilson government's referendum of 1975 by a margin of 2 to 1, the issue then

Figure 13.6 | Short-term interest rate gap has narrowed recently

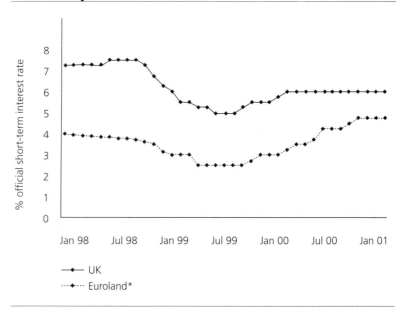

Note: * Germany before 1 Jan 1999
Sources: ECB, Bank of England

was purely economic. Burying sterling, however, is beyond economics since it touches British hearts; and when this comes on top of what is perceived to be complete loss of British sovereignty, it becomes a sensitive political issue. Yet because the government is avoiding the politics of the euro, presumably because it feels that British people will not buy it under such circumstances, it is relying on the economics of the situation. However, for the UK public, the economic issues involved are not those concerned with the meeting of the Brown and Maastricht criteria but concern rather the down-to-earth question of the net gains to be expected from the adoption of the euro, a question which assumes increasing importance when the public realizes the extra difficulties just mentioned about entering the euro at a rate appropriate for sterling. Telling the British public that this is in the order of 1–1.5 per cent of EU GDP (official EU Commission estimates: see Emerson *et al.* 1988) for the entire EU will seem very small indeed even when it is pressed on them that the euro is vital for securing the (minimum of) 5–7 per cent of EU GDP gains expected from the single market.

| **Figure 13.7** | Budget deficits are now comfortably within the Maastricht limit for UK and Euroland |

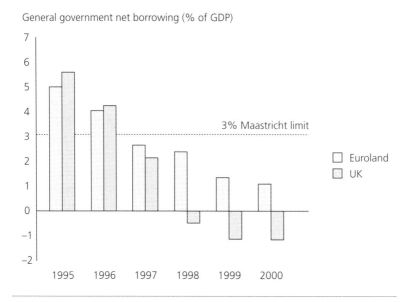

General government net borrowing (% of GDP)

Note: Estimates for 2000 exclude mobile phone auction receipts

Source: OECD

Furthermore, as Hughes Hallett clearly shows in Chapter 8, the situation is made worse by the realization that lack of euro adoption has *so far* not damaged the British economy when much of the pro-euro debate had argued that Britain could not afford to stay out. In December 2000 (see Figure 13.1), two years after the introduction of the euro, Britain's growth was 3.1 per cent, compared to between 2.7 and 2.9 per cent in the larger euro economies such as Germany and France. The UK annual inflation rate was 1.5 per cent or lower, compared with 2.75 per cent for the eurozone (6.8 per cent in Ireland and around 4–5 per cent for Spain, Portugal and the Netherlands). Unemployment had fallen to 5.5 per cent on the standardized measure, compared to 9–10 per cent in the eurozone, and the budget was showing a surplus of 2 per cent of GDP whereas France and Germany remain in deficit. Even trade with the eurozone had moved to a small surplus, despite the strength of sterling and weakness of the euro. People may therefore be asking themselves why they actually need the euro.

On the financial side too, the passage for Britain appears to have been easy. Foreign investment is up 50 per cent (of which 30 per cent has been from eurozone countries) and while interest rates are lower in Europe,

Figure 13.8 | Euroland unemployment remains above UK rate

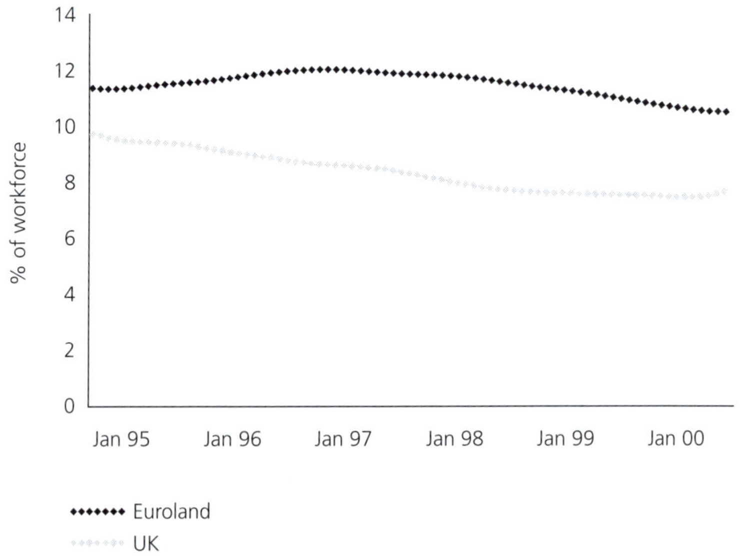

Note: There has been a slight narrowing of the gap since 1998
Sources: Eurostat, ONS (ILO measure)

they are only lower by a limited amount and then only at the short end of the market; at the long end, the sterling rates are typically about 100 basis points lower. Also, sterling has actually been more stable (in trade-weighted terms) than either of its main competitors: the euro had fallen from $1.18 to $0.88 by the end of March 2001 and from £0.74 to £0.61. That is a fall of 25 per cent against the dollar and 18 per cent against sterling. Sterling's fall against the dollar was 8 per cent during the same period. Using ECB figures for the trade weights, this implies a standard deviation of 6–7 per cent for the fluctuations of the euro against its trading partners, but only 2–3 per cent for sterling. That implies that there is a 30 per cent chance, on any day, that the euro will change its value by as much as 6 per cent, whereas the pound would change by only 2 per cent with the same 30 per cent probability. Sterling, therefore, has only one-third of the volatility of the euro, although a historical analysis might show that the volatility of both currencies was higher than normal. Hence, there seems to be some advantage in having a separate currency: one can steer a path between the fluctuations of the main competitor currencies, in order to minimize the (trade-weighted) volatility in one's own currency (all these points are discussed in detail by Hughes Hallett in Chapter 8).

British antagonism may also be attributed to a third factor. As Hughes Hallett argues, they may believe that international investment is vital and it therefore matters who the investment partners are, since they may be a different set of countries and require a different pattern of integration. Thus the 'optimum currency area' conditions need to include this dimension: the UK has to ensure that it links not only with its trading partners, but also with its investment partners. Although Britain trades predominantly with its EU partners, most investment flows are actually with the USA and Far East and are predominantly dollar based. If the two sets of partners move apart, as the USA and EU have done, then any currency links will imply extra costs. Hence, Britain has to decide which set of costs would be the smaller and whether staying with sterling and steering a course between the two currencies would not bring the lowest costs and the greatest stability.

The UK trades about 28 per cent of her GDP and roughly one-half of that goes to the EU partners while the other half does not (see Table 8.1). Thus, adjusting the trade figures for investment income, the percentage of foreign income derived by the UK from the EU partners drops to less than 41 per cent. As to foreign investments in the UK, a good three-quarters of such investment flows come from outside the EU area and only one-quarter from the EU partners (see Table 8.2). Hence, Britain falls into that category of 'in-between countries' that are linked to one set of partners for trade, but to another set for investment.

The Conservative Party

It may be claimed that because the Conservative Party was expected to lose the 2001 general election, if not by as wide a margin as in 1997 at least by enough to guarantee the Labour Party a very comfortable majority, their position against British euro adoption during the election campaign should not be taken seriously, especially when some Conservatives are not anti-euro. It should be seen as a pure election ploy, providing a good chance for attracting some votes from the anti-euro and anti-EU lobbies, by a party desperate to return to power. However, one can counter by arguing that it is precisely because of their expected defeat that their attitude to the euro represented the Conservative Party's general policy position: campaigning on the euro issue was expected to pave the way for a defeat for the government if its promised referendum on the euro materialized during Labour's second term in office. This would have the added advantage of improving the prospects for a Conservative government in about 2005. Further support for this argument comes from the fact that although several influential Conservatives have blamed their now ex-leader, William Hague, for his election campaign issues and style, practically none of them has come forward to advocate euro adoption, not even the pro-euro frontrunner for leadership of the party at that time. Moreover, Baroness Thatcher seems still able to exert great influence on the party and she has been categorical about Britain's never abandoning the pound. Therefore, as far as the adoption of the euro is concerned, we need say no more since obviously the Conservative Party can be seen in the same light as the general British public.

> As far as the adoption of the euro is concerned, the Conservative Party can be seen in the same light as the general British public

Conclusion

This chapter clearly shows that Britain will have no difficulties meeting the Maastricht criteria since she will continue to satisfy four of them, and the Treaty on European Union and its affirmation through the Amsterdam Treaty have built-in flexibility for accommodating any failure on the part of the pound sterling to demonstrate currency stability for two years prior to admission into the eurozone. Such accommodation is not just a theoretical possibility since it was indeed applied in the case of Finland in 1998 to enable her to join in the first wave on 1 January 1999. The chapter also shows that Britain is most likely to meet her own extra five tests, announced by Chancellor Gordon Brown in October 1997, unless he sticks literally to his 'clear and unambiguous' economic case for euro adoption.

The chapter also takes up a test which will have major effects on Britain during the transition period before and after the adoption of the euro: the rate at which sterling enters. This is on top of the five Brown tests and has to be carefully engineered to produce currency stability for two years prior to admission if Britain is not to rely on the accommodation factor just mentioned.

However, it is also argued that despite this extra test all indications seem to suggest that Britain will meet the conditions set by the British government as well as the Maastricht criteria. Hence the returned Prime Minister Tony Blair is in a position to honour his pledge to make a decision within the first two years in office on the euro and if positive to ask the British people, through a referendum, to choose between the adoption and rejection of the euro. Yet the chapter also suggests that the likely outcome of such a referendum would be a resounding rejection. This is because the British public continues to register an overwhelming 'no' vote and this has been on the rise. It is also due to the major employer associations' reversing their original 'yes' to a clear 'no' and, more importantly to the fact that the outcome of the referendum would not be tantamount to a rejection of a Labour government, otherwise Labour would not have been returned to power when the Conservative Party fought the general election on this very issue. Of course, a defeat would dent Blair's personal reputation and may force him to allow Brown to take over the leadership of the Labour Party, but then it may not, since this would depend on how the referendum campaign is conducted.

In the first draft of this chapter, written before the general election, I added that it was vital to bring the chapter to a final conclusion by considering what Blair needed to do in order to raise the possibilities for a 'yes' outcome for the referendum, if and when it came. He had to exploit the opportunity offered by the Conservative Party to fight the general election with the euro being a main item on the agenda and to do this within the context of EU integration in general. To confine the issue to just the economic benefits of euro adoption would be a great error of judgement since the British public would not likely appreciate the expected gains of

1.5 per cent of GDP even when augmented by the gains expected from the 'single market' of about 5–7 per cent. This was because the public would have to weigh these expected benefits against the sensitive issue of loss of sovereignty, the mentioned transition costs of achieving the right exchange rate for sterling and their being expected benefits for the whole of the EU that hence need not apply to every single member nation. Of course, this was a tall order, but it was about time that the British public was exposed to matters European rather than to the narrow economic costs and benefits. That 'ever closer union' should no longer be kept behind the scenes and there was not likely to be a better occasion to raise the subject than a general election which the Labour Party was expected to win with a comfortable majority. Blair did not oblige, probably due to the falling trend for Labour support during the election campaign, but at least he stressed the point that British citizens will get the chance if and when the referendum comes their way, and, as mentioned earlier, he has recently (June 2001) indicated that he can most certainly gain the voters' support for euro adoption if *both the economic and the political benefits* are put across to them.

> ## It was about time that the British public was exposed to matters European rather than to the narrow economic costs and benefits

Note

1 I use the term 'accommodation' in preference to 'fudging' simply because it was clear to me before the decision was taken on the euro that the member nations had allowed for accommodation (see pp. 78–83) for explanation).

Appendix

The Pricewaterhouse Convergence Index

The index is based on data for the 10 economic variables in the EU member countries (excluding Luxembourg) together with Norway, Switzerland, Hungary, Poland and the Czech Republic. Historic data come from the OECD and Eurostat sources, occasionally supplemented by those from Consensus Economics.

The value of the index for year t is defined as the sum of the normalized scores for each of the economic indicators in that year, as calculated by the formula:

$$Score = [D_j - D_A]/\acute{O}_D$$

where D_j is the absolute value of the difference between the value of the economic indicator for country i and the euroland average (weighted by GDP); D_A is the mean average of D_j across the sample countries and is the standard deviation of D_j across the sample countries. Note that for the exchange rate volatility factor, D_j in this formula is altered to be the standard deviation of the £/DM exchange rate over the three-year period $(t - 2)$ to t.

In the case study of UK convergence over time, the index is altered to measure the UK's convergence relative to its own average historic convergence. Hence, the value of the index for year t is defined as the sum of the normalized scores for each of the economic indicators in year t, as calculated by replacing by D_t in the above formula, where D_t is the absolute value of the difference between the UK and euroland indicator in year t; D_A is the average value of D_t over the sample period; and $\acute{o}_D$ is the standard deviation of D_t over the sample period. The exchange rate volatility factor D_t is defined to be the standard deviation of the monthly average £/DM exchange rate over the three-year period given here.

Further variations of both indices were then developed by altering the weights given to each variable's score when calculating the yearly index total.

References

Alberto, Enrique, Cervero, Susana G., Lopez, Humberto and Ubide, Angel (2000) 'Global equilibrium exchange rates: euro, dollar, "ins", "outs", and other major currencies in a panel co-integration framework', IMF Working Paper WO/99/175.

Arestis, Philip, Brown, A. and Sawyer, Malcolm (2001) The Euro: Evolution and Prospects. Aldershot: Edward Elgar.

Bergsten, Fred C. (1997) 'The dollar and the euro', Foreign Affairs, 76.

Church, Keith B. (1999) 'Properties of the fundamental equilibrium exchange rate in the Treasury model', National Institute Economic Review, July.

Commission of the European Communities (1970) *Report to the Council and Commission on the Realization by Stages of Economic and Monetary Union in the Community* (The Werner Report), *Bulletin of the European Communities*, Supplement 13.

Commission of the European Communities (1975) *Report of the Study Group 'Economic and Monetary Union 1980* (The Marjolin Report). Brussels: Commission of the European Communities.

Commission of the European Communities (1997) *Report of the Study Group on the Role of Public Finance in European Integration* (The MacDougall Report). Brussels: Commission of the European Communities.

Deutsche Bank (2001) *UK EMU Special*, June.

El-Agraa, Ali M. (ed.) (1983) *Britain Within the European Community: The Way Forward*. London: Macmillan; New York: Crane Russack.

El-Agraa, Ali M. (1980) *The Economics of the European Community*. Oxford: Philip Allan; New York: St. Martin's Press.

El-Agraa, Ali M. (1997) *Economic Integration Worldwide*. London: Macmillan; New York: St. Martin's Press.

Fl-Agraa, Ali M. (1998) 'The euro: why? how? significance?', *The World Economy*, 21, 5, pp. 639–57.

El-Agraa, Ali M. (1999) *Regional Integration: Experience, Theory and Measurement*. London: Macmillan; New York: Barnes & Noble.

El-Agraa, Ali M. (2000) *The European Union: Economics and Policies*. Hemel Hempstead: Pearson Education for Financial Times and Prentice Hall Europe.

Emerson, M., Aujean, M., Catinat, M., Goybet, P. and Jaquemin, A. (1988) *The Economics of 1992: The EC Commission's Assessment of the Economic Effects* of *Completing the Internal Market*. Oxford: Oxford University Press.

Feldstein, Martin (1997) 'The political economy of the European Economic and Monetary Union: political sources of an economic liability', *Journal of Economic Perspectives*, 11, pp. 23–42.

Goldman Sachs (2000) *The Weekly Analyst*, February.

Liberal Democrats' Group of Experts' Report (2000) *Britain's Adoption of the Euro*, September. **www.libdems.org.uk**

PricewaterhouseCoopers (2001) 'UK and Euroland economies continue to converge'. **www.pwcglobal.com**

UK Treasury (1997) *UK Membership of the Single Currency: An Assessment of the Five Economic Tests*. **www.hm-treasury.gov.uk**

Wren-Lewis, Simon and Driver, Rebecca L. (1998) *Real Exchange Rates for the Year 2000*. Washington, DC: Institute for International Economics.

Young, Hugo (1998) *This Blessed Plot: Britain and Europe from Churchill to Blair*. London: Macmillan.

Index